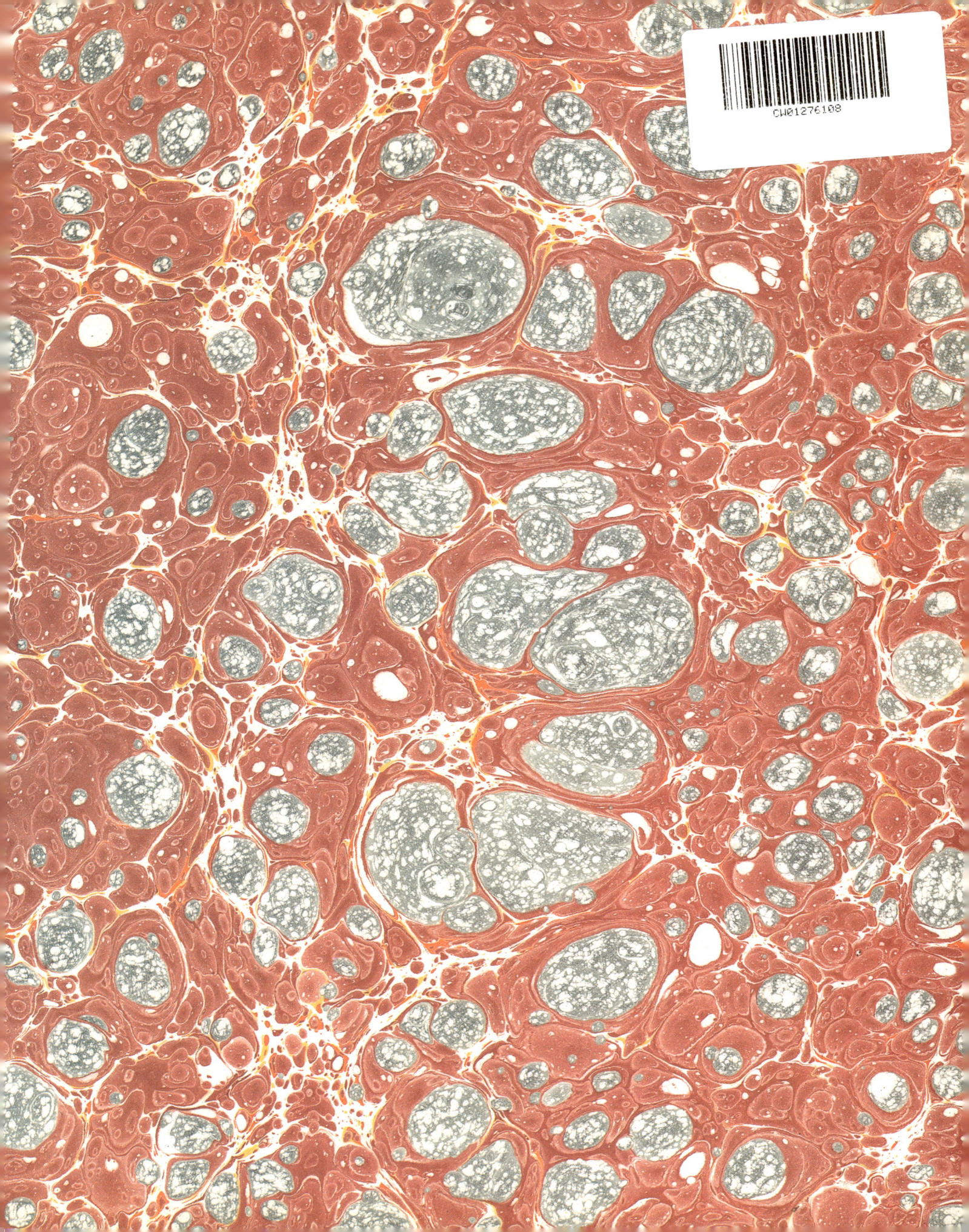

Arado
History of an Aircraft Company

Jörg Armin Kranzhoff

Translated from the German by Ray Theriault.
This book was originally published under the title,
Arado: Geschichte eines Flugzeugwerks,
by Aviatic Verlag, München.

Copyright © 1997 by Schiffer Publishing Ltd.
Library of Congress Catalog Number: 97-65441.

All rights reserved. No part of this work may be reproduced or used in any forms or by any means – graphic, electronic or mechanical, including photocopying or information storage and retrieval systems – without written permission from the copyright holder.

Printed in China.
ISBN: 0-7643-0293-0

We are interested in hearing from authors with book ideas on related topics.

Published by Schiffer Publishing Ltd.
77 Lower Valley Road
Atglen, PA 19310
Phone: (610) 593-1777
FAX: (610) 593-2002
E-mail: Schifferbk@aol.com.
Please write for a free catalog.
This book may be purchased from the publisher.
Please include $2.95 postage.
Try your bookstore first.

Arado

History of an Aircraft Company

Jörg Armin Kranzhoff

Schiffer Military History
Atglen, PA

Contents

Introduction　7

Part I — The Creative Years

Chapter 1
Beginnings of the Warnemünde Naval Facility and the Flugzeugbau Friedrichshafen　8

Chapter 2
Establishment of the Arado Handelsgesellschaft　8

Ar 65, D-IXYP.

Chapter 3
The First "In-House" Designs　15
Trainers for Land and Sea: the S I, SIII and SC I-II Biplanes　15
Fighters for Land and Sea: The SD I-III and SSD I Biplanes　25
The J 1 Torpedo Bomber　29

Arado W II over the Breitling.

Chapter 4
New Concepts　30
The Pioneering Spirit: The Luft Hansa-Postexpressflugzeug VI　30
The L I and L II Sportplanes　38

Chapter 5
Weapons and Alternative Production — Signs of the Economic Depression　43

Arado L II, D 1771.

Chapter 6
First Production Runs for the "Risky Air Armada"　46
The Ar 64 Fighter　46
The Ar 65 Fighter　47

Chapter 7
Redesignation as the Arado Flugzeugwerke: Personnel Changes and Expansion of Production　49

Chapter 8
Foundation of the New Luftwaffe
The Ar 66, 69, 76 and 77 Trainers　54
The Ar 67 and 68 Fighters　58

Chapter 9
The New Generation of Aircraft　62
The Jump to an All-Metal Monoplane: The Ar 80 Fighter　62
Competing for a New Weapons System: The Ar 81 Dive Bomber　65

Part II — New Role as a Reich-Owned Company

Chapter 10
The End of Independence　69
Forced Nationalization　69
Legal and Organizational Restructuring　72

Arado 231 being loaded.

Chapter 11
Structured Economic Dirigisme
74

License Building for Heinkel, Junkers
and Focke-Wulf   74
Restricted Developmental Activity:
Seaplanes and Reconnaissance Aircraft   75

Chapter 12
Mass Production: The Ar 96 Trainer   90

Ar 96 V 2.

Chapter 13
Experimenting with "Air Tourism": World Records with the Ar 79 Sport and Touring Airplane   94

Chapter 14
The National Socialist Model Operation   100

Chapter 15
**The Dream of a "High-Speed Two-Seater":
The Ar 240/440 Attack Airplane**   105

Chapter 16
Victim of the Red Pencil: The Ar 232 Combat Transport   122

Part III — Bearers of Hope in the War's Last Phase

Chapter 17
Total Commitment and Decentralization   130

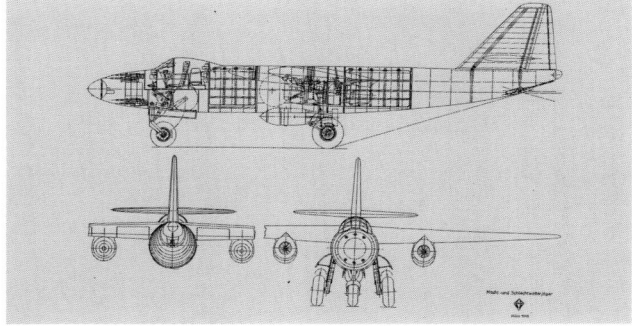

Ar 234 V 1.

Chapter 18
The Leap To Jet Engine Power   135
Entering into the Technology of the Future:
Projekt E 370   135
First Combat Missions: The Ar 234 A and B-1
Reconnaissance Planes   139
Series Production: The Ar 234 B-2 High-Speed
Bomber   141
The First With Four: The Ar 234 C
High-Speed Bomber   146
Emergency Measure: The Ar 234 "Nachtigall"
Night Fighter   148

Ar 234 V 13.

Chapter 19
Unrealized Projects   151

Chapter 20
Collapse And Liquidation   156

Notes   159

Ar E 583. Project design for a twin-jet night and all-weather fighter (March 1945).

Appendices

Technical Data   163
Arado Projects   164
Personnel of the Arado Werke   164
Table of Surviving Arado Aircraft   165
Bibliography   166
Photo Credits   166
The Author   167

5

Ar 66 C, D-IROZ.

Ar 77.

Ar 196 in front of the manufacturing plant in Warnemünde.

Ar 96 V 1, second version.

Ar 234 V 9 with bomb mounts under the engine nacelles.

Ar 232 B.

Ar 234 B-2 of 8/KG 76 in Burg.

The E 583 night and all-weather fighter project design.

Introduction

Over 60 years ago, on the 2nd of August 1944, an Arado jet succeeded in doing what was increasingly becoming impossible for German reconnaissance units to do: reconnoitering the actual scale of the Allied landing in Normandy. This reconnaissance flight — by a twin-jet Ar 234 A — together with the introduction of the Me 262 in July of 1944, marked the beginning of a new era in aviation. Even before this mission Arado had already completed the first flight of a four-engine jet aircraft, a prototype Ar 234 V 8, on 4 February 1944.

Although technical journals acknowledged these historical accomplishments, they limited themselves to general type descriptions or passing references made in articles on the company's history. For today's general public, the term "Arado" is almost as unfamiliar as it was then, since the company's existence didn't continue past 1945 and its name wasn't based on that of a famous designer. The firm's story, affected as it was by extraordinary armament-political confusion, remained partially shrouded in the mists of history. This was in no small part due to the Third Reich's falsification campaign waged on the pages of aviation literature.

This chronicle is the first attempt to bring to light that which has up to now remained silent and hidden from view. It spotlights the significance of the Arado Handels Gesellschaft, established in 1925 as a privately-run company, with regard to its pioneering efforts in aircraft design and its contribution to the armament programs of the Weimar Republic and the Third Reich. It provides a detailed account as to why Walter Rethel was forcibly expelled as the company's technical director in 1932, why four years later senior partner Heinrich Lübbe was eliminated as an obstacle on the path to the forced nationalization of the company, why matters eventually led to a forced, economically-planned license production operation by the Reich-owned company, and why, after the Technisches Amt had rejected future developments, an invigorated Arado was able to re-enter the field with the development of jet-powered aircraft.

The search for authentic material was, at times, difficult. Much knowledge has been lost, and much was destroyed or carted off to unknown locations in the confusion of the war's end. Therefore, no guarantee can be made in every case for the accuracy of performance figures, serial numbers and codes; these may have been provided after comparison with company records or official documents from the RLM, or based on discussions with eyewitnesses and technical experts. Information regarding events in the company's history was primarily derived from rediscovered material compiled by Heinrich Lübbe.

The author owes a particular debt of gratitude to Oberingenieur Hans Rebeski, former director of the design bureau, and the aviation historian Hanfried Schliephake, for their assistance in researching the material. Pilots Rudolf Jenett, Eduard Neumann, Gunther Eheim, Kurt Stark, Horst Götz, Richard Perlia and Adolf Galland, among others, offered helpful advice as eyewitnesses. Additional assistance was provided by Joaquim Ahlers, Gilberto Aleman, Gerhard Beer, Graham Boak, Frank Brekow, Peter W. Cohausz, Eddie Creek, Hans J. Ebert, Hubert Greim, Olaf Groehler, Manfred Griehl, Manfred Heber, Thomas Hitchcock, Edward L. Homze, Manfred Jurleit, Karl-Heinz Kens, Hannsjürgen Klemm, Rüdiger Kosin, Mike Norton, Stephen Ransom, Christoph Regel, Alfred Rethel, Egon Scheibe, Walter Schick, Franz Selinger, Kurt Schnittge, Ingeborg von Schoenebeck, Hans Sander and Günther Sengfelder. The author is also indebted to the following institutions for their support: Amt Falkenberg, Deutsches Museum Munich, Museum für Verkehr und Technik Berlin, Bundesarchiv Freiburg, Coblenz and Potsdam, Lufthansa Archiv Cologne, Brandenbürgisches Landeshauptarchiv, Rheinmetall-Archiv Düsseldorf, Maxwell Air Force Base Alabama, Rheinisch-Westfälisches Wirtschaftsarchiv Cologne, Fokker-Archiv Amsterdam, Dasa-Archiv Bremen and Hoover Institution on War, Revolution and Peace.

Dr. Jörg Armin Kranzhoff
Autumn 1995

Part I — The Creative Years

Chapter 1
Beginnings of the Warnemünde Naval Facility and the Flugzeugbau Friedrichshafen

Warnemünde was already a well-known location for naval flight activity long before the founding of the Arado Handels Gesellschaft in 1925. The site was occupied by the Gothaer Waggonfabrik, the Automobil- und Aviatic AG and the Flugzeugbau Friedrichshafen in the years following the construction in 1913 of an airfield on the east bank of the Breitling, an arm of the Baltic Sea at the mouth of the Warnow.

In the summer of 1914 Warnemünde was to have been the starting point for the "Ostseeflug Warnemünde." The war, however, prevented the planned flying competition, and the facilities were utilized as a base for naval aviators and for testing flight equipment by the Seeflugversuchskommando.

In conjunction with an expansion of the facilities in 1917, a branch of the Flugzeugbau Friedrichshafen was built on the west bank of the Breitling following the signing of an agreement with the city of Rostock. The city allowed the site to be flooded with assembly hangars which, up until the war's end, saw the production of floats and wings and even the final assembly of approximately 50 FF 49 C seaplanes. These aircraft, tested at Warnemünde before being handed over to the Reich, proved to be excellent reconnaissance platforms due to their seaworthiness and long-range capability.

The war's outcome brought a halt to aircraft construction in Warnemünde. After it was decided not to use the site as a location for an airborne police unit or a branch of the Deutsche Versuchsanstalt für Luftfahrt (DVL), Warnemünde initially served as a stopover point for the Deutsche Luftreederei and Lloyd Sablatnig routes and, later, a Junkers flight route. Beginning in 1924 the Aero-Sport GmbH began training naval pilots in Warnemünde, as did the Seeflug GmbH a year later.

Since the former Flugzeugbau Friedrichshafen had no sales and marketing organization — its products being delivered exclusively to the Reich during the war — a changeover in production was naturally unavoidable. Therefore, in close cooperation with the commissioner for Reichsfischerei, production was focused on fishing cutters, motorboats and ice sailing boats.

In October of 1920 the Dinos-Automobilwerke, a subsidiary of the Stinnes Konzern in Berlin-Charlottenburg, took over the facilities of the Flugzeugbau Friedrichshafen. Ship construction continued along with the newly implemented production of two-stroke engines. Yet the Stinnes Konzern pursued far-reaching plans for aircraft construction, initially in conjunction with the Fokker Werke, which had moved from Schwerin to Holland after 1918. Major a.d. Erich Serno, an advisor to the Turkish Air Force during the war, became the director of the Stinnes affiliate Aquila Verkehrs GmbH and began dealing in Fokker military aircraft on an international scale.[1] New Fokker works, along with Stinnes facilities for aircraft production based on standardized guidelines were to be established in the Balkans, the Far East and in North and South America. Accordingly, Stinnes acquired the Ikarus production facilities in Novi Sad in 1923. The business leadership of the Aquila Verkehrs GmbH signed up Ernst Heinkel as a designer; he had formerly designed aircraft in Warnemünde for Hansa-Brandenburg during the war. Under a secret contract with the Reichswehr, the Dinos docks license-built 15 Heinkel HD 21 biplanes (Wk.Nr. 001-015) and four HD 32 biplanes (Wk.Nr. 016-019) as well as armament. The HD 17 was also planned, but this type was never put into full-scale production.

Chapter 2
Establishment of the Arado Handelsgesellschaft

The year of 1925 saw significant changes with regards to the Warnemünde Dinos docks. When H. Stinnes' business collapsed following his death in 1924, bank pressure forced its sale under the direction of two colleagues in the Stinnes company, Walter Hormel and Felix Wagenführ. During the war, Kapitänleutnant a.D. Hormel, a pilot since 1911 and famous as the co-publisher of the "Taschenbuch der Luftflotten" aviation manual, was the director of the Warnemünder Seeflug-Abnahmekommission (Seaplane Acceptance Commission) and later was director of the Flugzeugbau Friedrichshafen docks. Wagenführ, from 1911 the director of the Lehr- und Versuchsanstalt für das Militärflugwesen (Instructional and Testing Institute for Military Aviation) in Döberitz, was heavily involved in the expansion of the Deutsche Fliegertruppe and, as Inspector of Aviation, from 1916 was responsible for matters of acquisition. As the director of the Luftfahrt-Friedenskommission (Aviation Peace Commission) after the war he was involved matters dealing with the usage of the Warnemünde dock facilities.

In February of 1925 the Dinos-Automobilwerke was subordinated to the Stinnes AG in Hamburg. On April 7th, 1925 Walter Hormel and businessman Dr. Werner Haensel filed a writ with the Hamburg notary Dr. Cadmus for the establishment of a successor company with the designation of "Arado Handels Gesellschaft GmbH." Address was listed as "Hamburger Hof", Jungfernstieg 30. Initial investment capital was 50,000 Marks, of which Hormel contributed 45,000 and Haensel 5,000 Marks. Walter Hormel and Felix Wagenführ were the managing directors. In order to hide the planned construction of aircraft from the Allied Inspection Commission, the purpose for the establishment of the company was listed as "the manufacture, sales and operation of vehicles of all types." The Arado Handels Gesellschaft was officially registered as the owner of the Warnemünde docks on 10 August. The company name of Arado, which means "plow" in Spanish, had previously been used by the Stinnes company as a cover term for ship deliveries to South America, and implied their ships plowing through the seas.

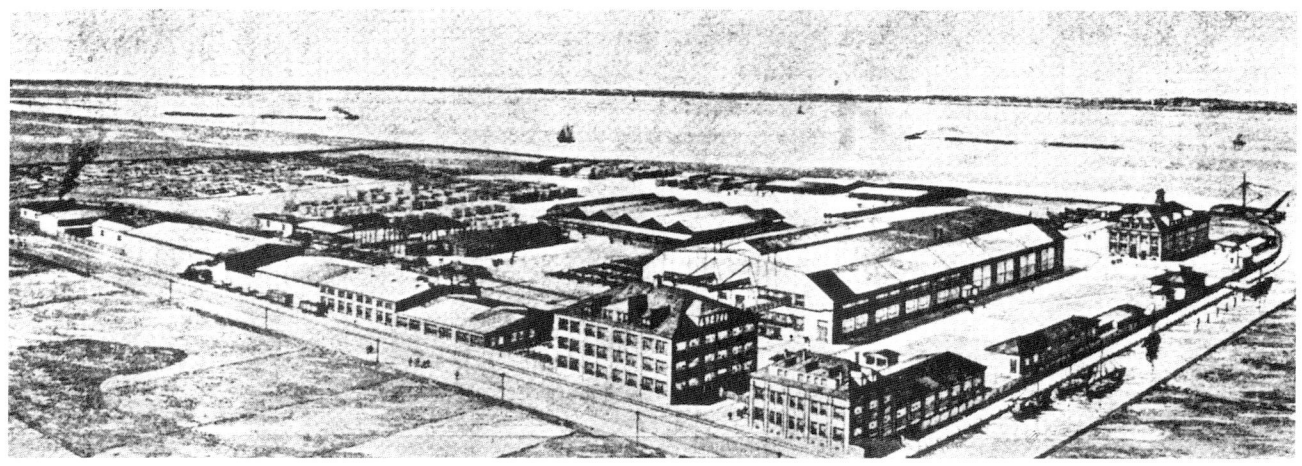

Friedrichshafen Flugzeugbau's shipyards at Warnemünde in 1917.

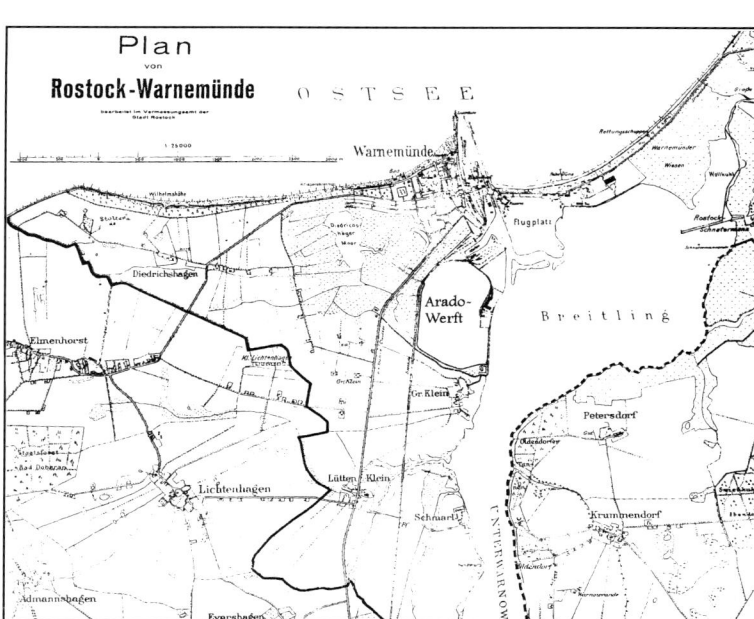

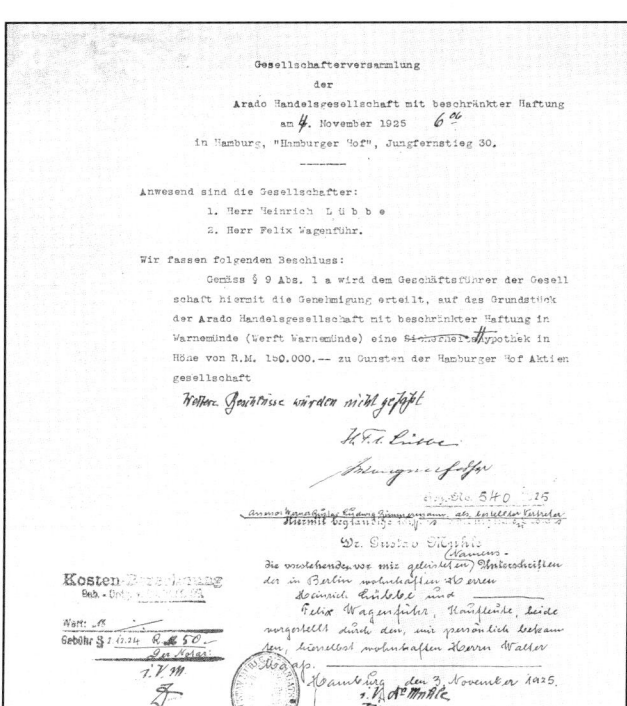

The Warnemünde shipyards of the Friedrichshafen Flugzeugbau after being acquired by the Arado Handels Gesellschaft. Plan dates from circa 1935. (above)

H. Lübbe, senior partner of the Arado Handels Gesellschaft in 1928. (above left)

Minutes of the business conference of the Arado Handels Gesellschaft dated 4 November 1925 following the buy-out of the Warnemünde shipyards by Heinrich Lübbe and Felix Wagenführ. (left)

However, before production of its own aircraft was achieved, the control of the Arado Handels Gesellschaft changed hands in the same year. On 4 November 1925, it was decided at a business meeting in the "Hamburger Hof" that the majority shares of Walter Hormel would be transferred to Heinrich Lübbe. Wagenführ remained manager and was made junior partner as a result of his acquisition of the initial investment capital of Werner Haensel. Remaining purchase funds were covered by a 150,000 RM security mortgage on the company's property in Warnemünde, taken out by Lübbe and provided by Hamburger Hof Aktiengesellschaft. At this same time the Dinos-Automobil

AG was dissolved. On 16 April Lübbe made private capital available to the company in the amount of 120,000 Goldmarks. This sum resulted in an agreement canceling the previously mentioned mortgage taken out at the Hamburg bank. On January 21st the company was entered into the trade registry of the court in Berlin-Mitte with its new business office address at Potsdamerstrasse 75 in Berlin. On the 22nd of December 1926 Felix Wagenführ and Heinrich Lübbe officially increased the investment capital from 50,000 Marks to 150,000 Marks. As the senior business partner, Lübbe assumed 90,000 Marks of the capital, with Wagenführ assuming 10,000 Mark.

Heinrich Friedrich August Lübbe, who unlike his partner Wagenführ, was an experienced pilot, designer and business manager, did not initially take an active role following the takeover of the Arado Handels Gesellschaft. Born in

F. Wagenführ, junior partner of the Arado Handels Gesellschaft, seen as a flying officer in the First World War. (right)

Minutes from the negotiations for increasing the authorized capital of the Arado Handels Gesellschaft, dated 22 December 1926. (below)

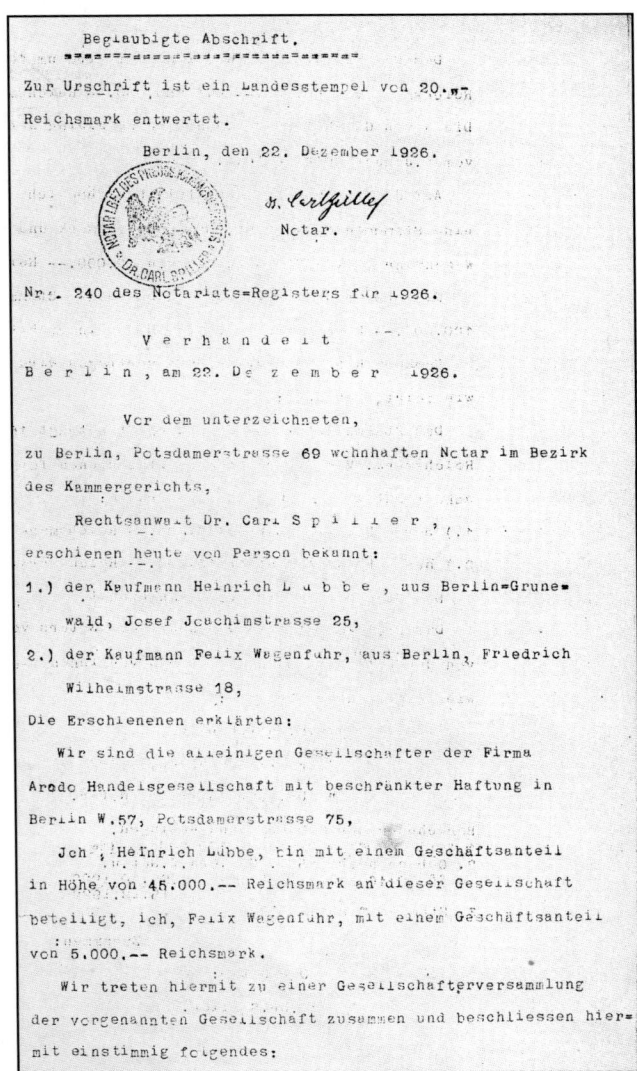

H. Lübbe as a naval recruit. (left)

Below (from left): The Johannisthaler "Icarians" —Fremery, Lübbe and Rosenstein posing for the camera on an Etrich Rumpler Taube (1911).

1884 in Nienburg an der Weser as the third of nine children to an innkeeper and cabinetmaker, he served a cabinetmaker apprenticeship under his uncle and then completed training as a clockmaker. After the family moved to Bremerhaven, Lübbe entered the merchant marine, where he received training in machinery. During his service, he made an early trip to the United States — where eventually all eight of his siblings emigrated — and there most likely became acquainted with the flight program of the Wright brothers. After a work accident he initially became financially independent with the opening of the first cinema theater in Utrecht in 1908, and kept himself occupied with precision instrument and optical experiments. Lübbe's interest in cinematography was apparently kindled while still in his youth with the discovery of film projector in the attic of his parents' home.

In 1909, with renewed interest in flying sparked by rapid developments in neighboring France, Lübbe made a number of trips to Paris — then the metropolitan center of aviation — where he became acquainted with the pilots Edmond Audemars, Louis Blériot and Roland Garros. He was probably an eyewitness as Blériot became the first flyer in the world to cross the English Channel on 25 July 1909. At the subsequent Utrecht Flying Week, he made contact with the Belgian Blériot pilot Jan Olieslaegers before deciding to become an "aviateur" himself. In July of 1911 he signed a training contract with Edmund Rumpler in Berlin-Johannisthal. "Was at Lunapark today. Enjoyed myself immensely", he reported on July 31st and added: "Flew twice yesterday. Would like to stay here." Two weeks later he moved to Berlin-Johannisthal, where he lived with his new friend Anthony Fokker in a house at Parkstrasse No. 18. Following his first solo flight on the 16th of September, he became the tenth pilot to certify on the Etrich-Rumpler Taube and was assigned the German pilot's license No. 134

on November 17th. In the spring of 1912 he supported himself with his own Taube as a flying instructor with the Schlesisches Aero-Club in Breslau.

With the goal of establishing the first practical use of an aircraft, Lübbe set up the first official German air post service between Mannheim and Heidelberg on the 19th of May 1912. A short time later he further promoted the rapidly expanding developments in aviation when he made his Rumpler Taube available to the British queen for courier services. His victory at the Wanner Pentecost Week festival at the end of May, 1912 — for which he was congratulated by the Kaiser's sister — made him into a famous Rumpler pilot.

The Rumpler pilot Lübbe:

While Lübbe endeared himself to the general public from the first day with his two flights, he has now completely won their hearts. Lübbe, who has only been flying since August of last year and has already survived three crashes, has become the darling of the public's eye.[2]

Accompanied by his bride, in the late autumn of 1912 he set out by ship for Buenos Aires with two Rumpler aircraft. In several flying competitions he bested the Blériot-designed airplanes (already being sold in South America) and opened up a new market for Rumpler's designs. After setting an overwater record with passengers on 6 January 1913, which later earned him the title "The La Plata Flyer", Lübbe undertook a flying expedition into the interior of Argentina which lasted several weeks.

The "aviateur" H. Lübbe (1912).

H. Lübbe in Argentina following his world record flight (January 1913).

H. Lübbe in the pilot's seat of a Rumpler Taube in Johannisthal prior to setting out on his South American expedition (December 1912).

A new flight record: recently the Swiss-Argentinean Teodoro Fels set a new record by flying his aeroplane over the Rio de la Plata from Buenos Aires to Montevideo. This event has already been surpassed, however, by a flyer of German blood. This time it was the German pilot Heinrich Lübbe, who only just arrived from Germany a short while ago to demonstrate his Rumpler Taube at crowded airfields. His feat even went beyond that of Fels, in that he carried a passenger on his journey to the capital city of the neighboring country. This journey was not only a triumph for the German pilot, but also for the German industry: the Rumpler Taube is a completely German product, even down to the engine. Germany has long been at a disadvantage in the aviation world due to its inability to produce small, powerful engines — something to which France owes its progress in aeronautics. Now, however, such engines are to be had in Germany; according to technical experts, the engine in the Rumpler Taube is even better than the French Gnome engine. In any case, yesterday's flight will certainly result in more attention being paid to German-produced flying machines.[3]

As the most experienced pilot in the Rumpler Taube, Lübbe was able to place in the German National Flying Sponsorship competition at the end of 1913 flying a Rumpler military monoplane — this despite two potentially fatal crashes.

Flight Attempt Berlin-Paris. It was reported to us by telegraph that the pilot Lübbe, who took off yesterday morning at 6:37 a.m. from Johannisthal without passengers on a Berlin-Paris flight, was forced to set down near Rheine i. W. due to an engine failure. He wasn't able to continue his flight yesterday, but will attempt to reach Paris early this morning. With a favorable westerly wind, Lübbe will then attempt to fly from Paris clear across Germany to Warsaw in a bid to win the grand prize in the National Flying Sponsorship.[4]

Flying Accident In Johannisthal. The Rumpler pilot Lübbe suffered an accident early today in Johannisthal during a landing in fog; he had taken off at 11:55 p.m. from Wanne in a Rumpler Taube on a long distance flight for the prize in the National Flying Sponsorship. In heavy fog, Lübbe arrived over the Johannisthal airfield at 4:30 early this morning, but had completely lost his bearings. He fired off alarm shots at various intervals, but these echoed through the morning unheeded. After flying around in the sea of fog for nearly an hour, Lübbe eventually decided to land. He misjudged the altitude, however, set the machine on the ground too hard and was thrown out of the cockpit. He survived with non-life threatening injuries to his head and feet and was taken at his request to the district hospital in Britz. The Rumpler Taube was completely wrecked in the landing.[5]

By the end of 1913 a lung ailment had forced Lübbe to give up active flying. Even as early as 1912, Heinrich Lübbe displayed business initiative in the form of a cooperative effort with the Rumpler Werke in Johannisthal, the Düsseldorfer Aeroplan Werke, the Flugplatzgesellschaft in Wanne-Herten and the Wanne aircraft designer Schumacher. On 23 January 1914 he offered to set up a joint-venture business with the chief designer of the Essen-based Kondor-Flugzeugwerke, Joseph Suwelak — who had also been his

H. Lübbe (left) in the cockpit next to A. Fokker during the first test of Lübbe's interrupter mechanism developed for aircraft machine guns. Standing beside the Fokker M 5K monoplane is Lübbe's colleague Curt Heber (May 1915).

flying instructor — in Düsseldorf for building and operating airplanes. After Hauptmann Felix Wagenführ of the Generalinspektion der Fliegertruppen in Döberitz declined to make any further purchases of Kondor aircraft on 5 February 1914, which in his view had become obsolete (he favored "fast monoplanes with rotary engines"), Lübbe submitted recommendations to the Kondor company for "an entirely new design in aircraft" which would set itself apart with its "high speed and load-carrying capability." He proposed a new type of bracing and special floats "for a short run on water" and ensured that: "if the first machine is built under my direct supervision, I guarantee that it will immediately have all my proposed qualities." He demanded royalties for deliveries made to German and foreign customers as well as an airplane and mechanic be provided free of charge for "competition and publicity flying." Negotiations, however, were unsuccessful on his part.

In 1914 Lübbe decided on a cooperative venture with his flying partner Anthony Fokker. Although he was officially employed as a flying instructor, Fokker's real interest was in Lübbe's many years of experience in the area of aircraft armament. By designing a machine gun mechanism which, for the first time, made it possible to fire through the propeller arc, Lübbe became heavily involved in the development of the first single seat fighter in the world — the Fokker E I monoplane.[6] At the end of 1916 Lübbe became the director of the newly-established Fokker-Waffenfabrik in Berlin. Realizing substantial profits from the production of approximately 42,000 firing mechanisms, in 1919 he was able to set up a "Test Institute for Weapons and Machinery Design" in Berlin, Potsdamerstrasse 27b.[7] In acquiring one of the country houses designed by the Berliner architect Muthesius in Berlin-Grunewald in 1921, he became a neighbor of the AEG industrialist and later foreign minister Walter Rathenau, belonging to those "simple, difficult capitalists", as the writer Alfred Kerr —

who lived in the immediate vicinity — mockingly referred to those living in the Grunewald district.

In 1923 Lübbe once again became affected by a bleeding condition in his lungs. "He caused me so much grief, such a clever man and so industrious", commented his wife with concern. For this and other reasons Lübbe set up a private laboratory in his house, which he eventually fitted out with a darkroom, a blueprint machine, welding equipment, a special oven for sintering light metals and a 20 meter long tunnel for firing tests. In addition to secret weapons patents, between 1919 and 1922 he acquired a series of public, civilian copyrights for current collectors, cranes, ship screws and optical sights, many of which found application in the Warnemünde Dinos dockyards. His diverse, often hidden business relations were hinted at in a note from 16 March 1921, which read: "Herr Lübbe told me that he now employed 3000 workers in three factories, had a lot of work to do and sees a rosy future ahead, although the forecast for business here in general is quite dark."

Even though aircraft production was once again permitted in Germany from 1922 onward and airspace authority was formally restored the following year, the Allies' construction restrictions still remained in force with regard to military designs. Yet despite these limitations Lübbe was able to continue his secret weapons developments under the protection of the German authorities. He was supported in this by Felix Wagenführ, whom he knew from the war years in his capacity as former director of the Fokker-Waffenfabrik and was a secret contact man for the Reichswehrministerium with the Stinnes corporation.

Anticipating foreign interference, in 1922 the Reich government made secret preparations for building up its air forces. But before contracts could be drawn up, Major Hellmuth Wilberg, who ran the Lusftschutztreferat in the Reichswehrministerium, secretly arranged the purchase of fighters from Fokker's stock which had escaped the Allies'

H. Lübbe (in hat) during an explanation of the machine gun interrupter. Next to him is flying officer Waldemar von Buttlar, while the man second from right is the pilot Oswald Boelcke (1916).

Twelve-barreled motor-driven aircraft machine gun of the Fokker Waffenfabrik, a branch of the Fokker company directed by Lübbe (1918).

H. Lübbe during firing trials with an LMG 08 on a pivot mount (1915).

grasp by being shipped to Holland under the protection of German authorities. Wilberg assigned the task to Hauptmann Kurt Student, who had flown Fokker's new single seat fighter back in 1915 and supervised comparison studies at Adlershof near the war's end. From 1923 he represented the "Flugtechnik" (Aviation Technology) department in the Heereswaffenamt, a department responsible for equipping and arming aircraft.

In order to ensure that the purchase went unnoticed, Student brought in the Stinnes corporation, which in turn used middlemen Wagenführ and Hormel to work out negotiations with Fokker's business manager Friedrich Wilhelm Seekatz for the delivery of 50 single-seat D XI and D XIII fighters fitted with British engines.[8] When Fokker learned that the aircraft were requested without armament, but with fittings for the installation of a German machine gun, he suspected that the actual contractor was the Reichwehrministerium — which in turn was probably utilizing the support of Lübbe in matters of weaponry. The supposed destination for the aircraft delivered to Stinnes was South America, but the actual destination was a Russian air force base in Lipetsk.[9] Lübbe, who in the interim had been trying to merge his weapons design bureau with an aviation company, obtained the financial backing for acquiring the Warnemünde docks in 1923 by selling a patent for a motor-powered machine gun to the Reichswehr for the sum of approximately 100,000 marks.

Chapter 3
The First "In-House" Designs

Trainers for Land and Sea: the S I, SIII and SC I-II Biplanes

From early on, Lübbe had a keen interest on expanding the Warnemünde naval station. When he tried to reenter the airplane manufacturing business in Warnemünde after the First World War, Heinkel, who had established his own company in Warnemünde in 1922, expressed no interest in a cooperative venture. Following this rejection, based on inside information provided by Stinnes — and probably due to old ties between Lübbe and Fokker — Lübbe obtained Fokker's designer Walter Rethel for managing his technical bureau, who resettled in Warnemünde with several of his colleagues. Born in 1892 in Wesel, Rethel had

Kurt Student, an official in the Heereswaffenamt after the First World War, seen as a flying captain in an E III Fokker single-seat fighter (1917).

attended a Dortmund engineering construction school from 1912 to 1914. With the exception of a year-long interruption from 1916 to 1917 when he was with LVG in Berlin, Rethel worked as an aircraft designer for the Kondor company in Gelsenkirchen, where he designed several single-seat fighters to include the cantilevered high-wing E-3 A. This airplane went on to achieve top marks in October 1918 at the third fly-off competition in Adlershof. After the war he worked at the Kondor offices in Hamburg and with the Dutch firm of NAVO before taking up a job with Fokker in the summer of 1920.

Chief designer Walter Rethel (right) in front of the E-3 A Kondor parasol fighter designed by him (1918).

W. Rethel (right) in the Fokker S II biplane designed by him (1922).

In 1925 the Warnemünde dockyards had an enclosed area of over 42,000 m². The facilities were situated on an area of 15,000 m². The individual buildings, made of brick or reinforced concrete, rested on foundations of wooden or reinforced concrete pillars. Surrounding the central assembly hangar and slipway to the Breitling were the administration building and design office, living and messing facilities, workshop with equipment for oxyacetylene welding and hot galvanization, as well as a weapons section on the second floor, a wood shop and space for storing and drying wood. The assembly area had approximately 60 modern machinery pieces, the majority of which were acquired from the Dinos Werke, and an electric 5-ton mobile crane. Power for the dockyards was supplied by the electrical power station in Rostock. With two transformers at the facility, the 6,000-volt current was stepped down to 380 volts for machinery operations and 220 volts for lighting. In addition to the slipway, the docks were also connected to Warnemünde by a rail line and a road. Initially no factory airfield was available, necessitating the ferrying of airplanes for testing and flight trials to the opposite bank of the Breitling, where a DVS airfield was available to be shared with the Heinkel and Bachmann companies. The number of employees was initially 68, but quickly grew to 150 and by 1932 had reached 475.

Until 1932 the technical director was Fridolin Keidel, who, like Lübbe, had also been employed by Rumpler. From 1931 to 1932 Otto Affeldt stood at his side, providing organizational assistance to chief administrator Siecke and dealing with matters such as accounting, work planning, material preparations and equipment building. As the company director in Berlin, Felix Wagenführ was supported by Erich Serno, formerly a notary with the now-dissolved Aquila Verkehrs GmbH. Even though the young company produced at least one new aircraft type each year, it suffered from a

Aerial photo of the Warnemünde shipyards after the takeover by the Arado Handels Gesellschaft. —middle: assembly hall. right: slipway to the Breitling and the administration/design offices. foreground: warehouses, pier for cabin cruisers on the Laak Canal. left: porterhouse with mess hall, behind this are the metal shop/weapons department, wood shop and warehouses.

The Arado S I trainer, the first indigenous design of the Arado Handels Gesellschaft, with H. Lübbe and his wife posing (1926).

shortage of customers and was only able to sell little more than 10 to 12 airplanes per year.[10] In order to ensure the survival of the Arado docks, other types of contracts had to constantly be solicited. Even pure trade operations, which Arado still conducted internationally, brought in some profits.

Few details were written down when planning new types; instead, the company built according to the oral instructions of the designers. The first indigenous design was the two-seat S I trainer.[11] It was a biplane with a cantilever upper wing supported by V-braces and a two-part lower wing braced to the fuselage. The wings were a twin box spar design made of spruce and having wooden ribbing. They were covered on the underside by birch plywood. The fabric covering the upper wing surfaces could be removed without being damaged thanks to a special process developed by the company. The fuselage, also covered in fabric, was made of welded steel tubing. The front part of the fuselage was covered with metal. The fuselage's upper decking was fitted with a removable shell, designed primarily to ensure that the controls were operating properly. The landing gear consisted of four struts and a cross brace, with a carry-through axle and rubber springs on the rear struts. The first aircraft of this type (Wk.Nr. 20, so numbered because of previous license productions) was fitted out with a Bristol Lucifer three-cylinder radial engine, which had an advertised output of 100 hp and a maximum output of 120 hp. The airplane was registered with the DVS in Adlershof in February 1928 under the registration D-817 and served in the training role until 1930. It was re-fitted with the Siemens Sh 12 engine, built from 1925 onwards, which had a sustained output of 112 hp and a maximum output of 125 hp. The second type (Wk.Nr. 21) was fitted with this engine from the beginning, and under the registration code D-994 successfully competed in the BZ-Flight with Hauptmann Lorenz at the controls. No suitable engine was found for the third airplane (Wk.Nr. 22). An old 100 hp Mercedes engine dating from the war proved to be inadequate, since it negatively influenced the aircraft's center of gravity. Eventually, after five years the finished airplane was sold to the company of Bachmann in Warnemünde.

The aerobatic design met all requirements of a training aircraft for its time: outstanding handling characteristics, good stability and maneuverability, forgiving of heavy-handedness and overcorrection, short takeoff and landing runs, and easy to repair. All components were easily accessible and replaceable. The engine could be swung down and forward, enabling two men to remove it without the need for a pulley and tackle. Rethel placed particular emphasis on safety measures for the aircraft's occupants and designed student controls which could be switched off, a reliable fuel gauge, a firewall between the engine and seats,

Arado S I (Wk. Nr. 20 D-817) fitted with a Siemens Sh 12 engine, seen at the DVL in Adlershof (February 1928).

Arado S I powered by the Bristol Lucifer engine.

Arado S I with Lucifer engine being loaded onto a ferry for transport to the testing field.

a fire extinguisher, parachute packs and quick-release shoulder harnesses. The two copper fuel tanks, installed in the upper wing, permitted a flight endurance of four hours and were suspended from strapping, enabling them to remain tension-free in any flying attitude. Tank leakage was prevented through the use of a special design. In 1927 the simple, yet well-planned and useful airplane was shown at the Milan Prototype Exhibition, where the German aviation industry was represented for the first time in a collective showing by the companies of Arado, Albatros, Caspar, Dornier, Focke-Wulf, Junkers, Messerschmitt, Rohrbach and a handful of engine and accessories manufacturers. The two-seat cantilever S III biplane was also completed in 1926, with Turkey as the customer for this primary trainer. The delivery date was cut particularly close, forcing the airplane to be built in the shortest possible time — without design drawings — before being transported overland to its destination. It was similar in dimensions to the S I, but was fitted with a 95 hp Siemens Sh 11 radial engine which gave the airplane a top speed of 128 km/h.

The Arado S III trainer (1928).

After its positive experiences with the first aircraft types, in 1926 the Arado Werke also produced a more developed, heavy trainer, designated the SC 1, which bore a remarkable resemblance to Fokker's C IV being delivered to Russia at the same time.[12] The cantilevered, two-seat biplane of composite design was fitted with a 230 hp BMW IV inline engine, giving the airplane a rather impressive top speed for the day of 180 km/h. Endurance was up to six hours. The upper wing was flexible and attached to a removable cabane, which was in turn affixed to the upper fuselage by a V-brace and to the lower fuselage by two additional single struts. The shorter-span lower wing was attached to the bottom of the fuselage. The wings were sharply staggered, but notably absent of dihedral. N-shaped braces were fitted to the ends of each wing. Fuselage, control surfaces, engine block and all welded seams were coated with aluminum fire-bronze, which would chip off when high-stress key points became deformed. Wing attachments and

Arado SC I with the director of the technical office Rüter (second from left), in front of the assembly hall in Warnemünde.

Arado SC I V 1, D-965 (Wk. Nr. 23) in the Warnemünde assembly hall.

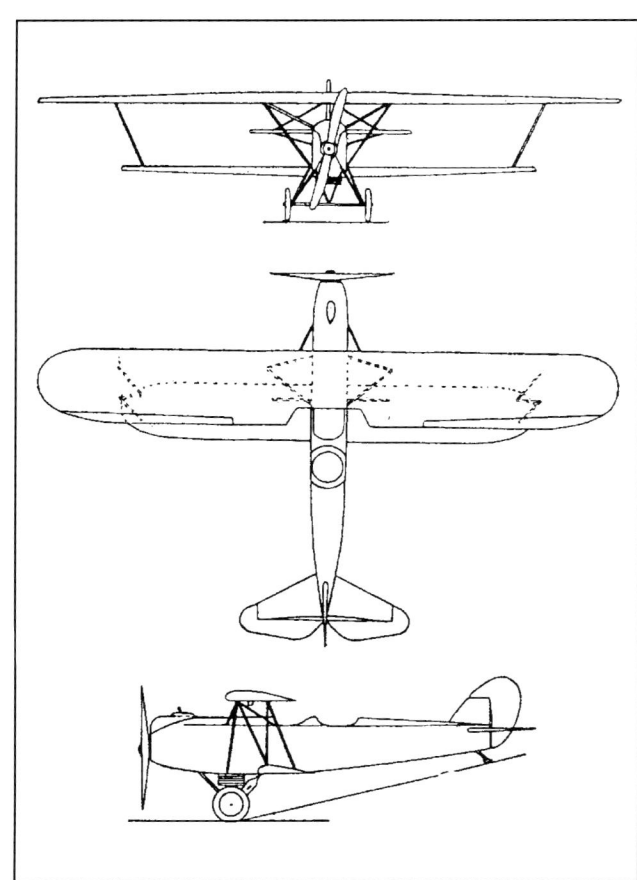

Sketch of the Arado SC I trainer. (1926).

Arado SC I, D-1311 (Wk. Nr. 37), at the airfield in front of the Heinkel plant.

strut end fittings were made of Duraluminum with flush rivets. 14 aircraft (Wk.Nr. 23 to 30 and 32 to 37) — a relatively large number — of this type were constructed. Officially they were declared as being contracted to Turkey. In reality, however, the airplanes were destined for the DVS flight schools, including Schleissheim and Staaken, where the first example entered service as registration number D-965.

This aircraft type was nearly involved in a fateful accident over the center of Berlin. Just as the Rechlin pilot Stephan von Prondzynski and his partner Georg Wolle found themselves approaching their destination at Adlershof, the engine gave out and it was only with difficulty that a suitable clear flat area was found for an emergency landing.

The SC II, a follow-on with a more powerful 320 hp engine and slightly larger dimensions, came into being in the years 1928 to 1930 and was designed with advanced flying students in mind. The prototype, a modified Arado SC I (Wk.Nr. 37) that was the only aircraft of this type on the aircraft register in 1928, was completely wrecked when its engine failed and it crashed during an acceptance flight in front of DVL representatives on 24 April 1928 in Warnemünde.

Nearly all of the ten aircraft produced in quantity went to the DVS. Among other places, they were assigned to the Verkehrsfliegerschule Warnemünde and Berlin-Adlershof, where at least one plane, registration number D-1984 (Wk.Nr. 62), remained in service for a considerable length of time. One aircraft is reputed to have been delivered to China. Although the aircraft displayed functionality and was shown at the International Aviation Exhibition in Berlin and the Paris Aero-Salon, no further types were built; the weak landing gear structure and short, fixed tailskid were faulted, undesirable features which gave the aircraft a tendency to tip over on its wings and veer during landings.

As early as the summer of 1926 Arado took up the old tradition of the dockyards by producing seaplanes — in direct competition with Heinkel — and assumed construction of the three-engine Gerbrecht W 3 floatplane for the seaplane contest in Warnemünde. Unfortunately, the aircraft could not be completed in time to meet the required deadline. In 1927 Arado began work for the Deutsche Verkehrsfliegerschule in Warnemünde on its own seaplane design, of which two were delivered in 1928 under the designation W II. The goal was to develop a trainer with the minimum possible performance surplus for retraining budding pilots on large, multi-engine seaplanes. In order to keep procurement, maintenance and operational costs down the engine performance was to be low, the materials used were to be inexpensive and the flying qualities tailored to training operations. Additionally, it was required that the aircraft be seaworthy in swell conditions up to three. These requirements were solved using the simplest methods. Since the airplane was not to be built with Duraluminum (for cost-cutting reasons), but with composites and wooden floats, it was expected that the airplane would have a large gross weight. In view of the high power loading, efforts were made to keep the wing loading low, which nevertheless increased the all-up weight even more. In order to keep takeoff and flight characteristics favorable, the following points

Arado SC I V 1.

Fridolin Keidel (front), a technical director at the Arado Handels Gesellschaft, in Johannisthal (1909)

The Gerbrecht W 3 seaplane (in background) and fuselage frameworks of the SC I (foreground) in front of Arado's assembly hall (1926).

Arado SC I being ferried to the testing field.

Arado SC Is in front of the Warnemünde assembly hangar, with D-1015 in the foreground. (above)

Arado SC Is, D-1035 (Wk.Nr. 27) and D-1241 (Wk.Nr. 35), both operated by DVS Schleissheim, seen here over the "Wild Kaiser" (left).

Arado SC II, D-130 (Wk.Nr. 46, above).

Arado SC II three-view (1927 — below).

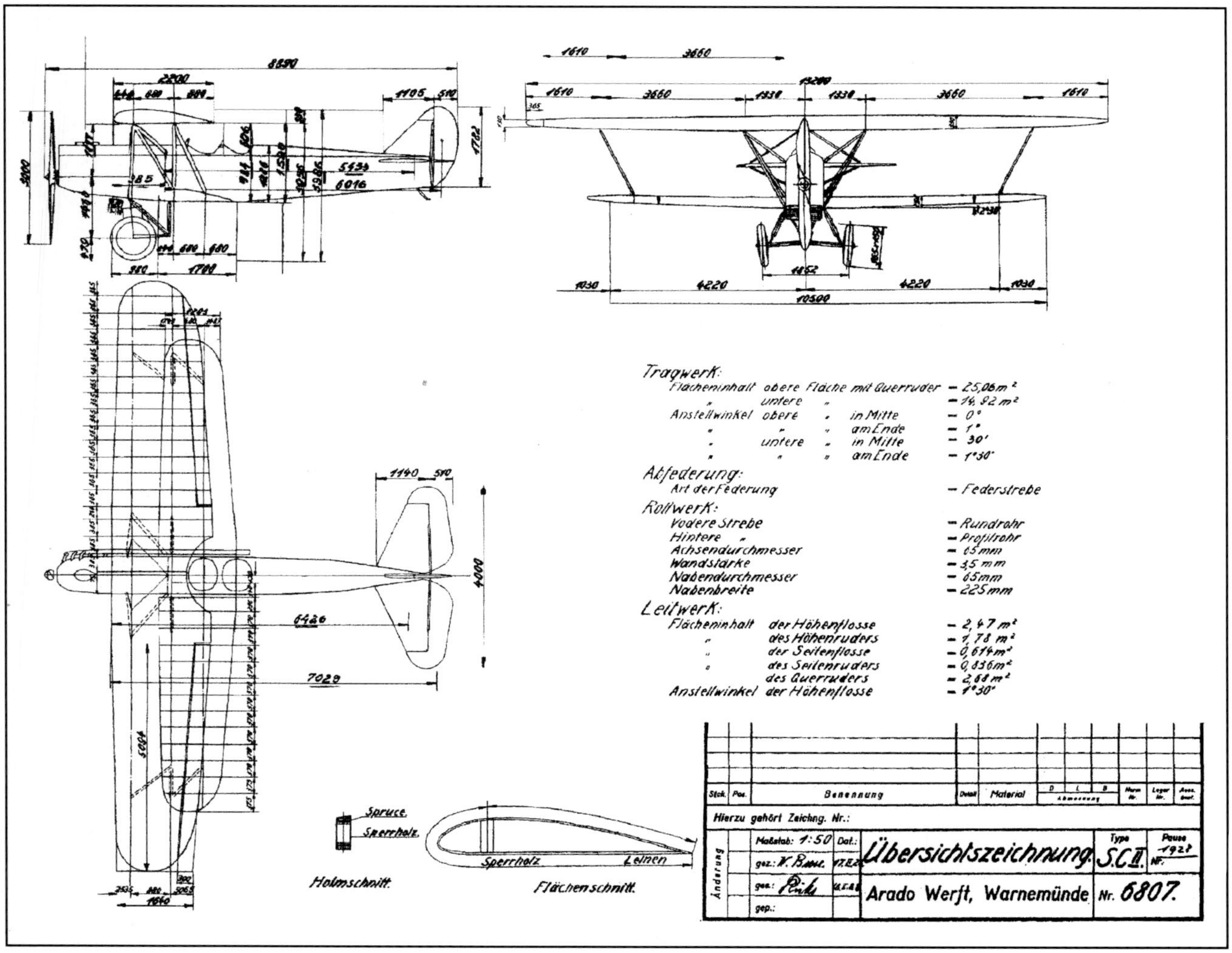

were critical: the wings should be free of airflow interference, meaning a cantilever monoplane design. This design, with the large interval between the spars, provided a large area for attaching the floats and correspondingly low forces being placed on the struts. The low-wing profile allowed the struts to remain short, keeping the center of gravity low over the water. Propeller efficiency was kept high by moving the engines well forward of the wing leading edges, keeping the engine nacelle cross section low and ensuring the area behind the propeller was free of supports. The semi-circular floats had a relatively small cross-section while retaining adequate surface area and volume. The wings, made entirely of wood, consisted of two continuous spars made of laminated strips, plywood webs and spacers. The webs had air vent openings in each spacer section. The ribs were of lattice-work design with reinforcing strips on either side. A tubular steel support framework was designed to take the weight of the engine nacelle, which also served as a compartment for the fuel tanks located behind a firewall. As a precaution against warping, the wings were covered with plywood sheeting from their leading edge to the rear spar; from that point to the trailing edges they were covered in fabric. The fuselage was built of steel tubing and rods. The two seats, arranged in tandem, were equipped with dual controls. The rudder was operated using suspended

Three-view of the Arado W II seaplane (8 March 1928 — below)

Arado SC II, D-1330 (Wk.Nr. 46 — above).

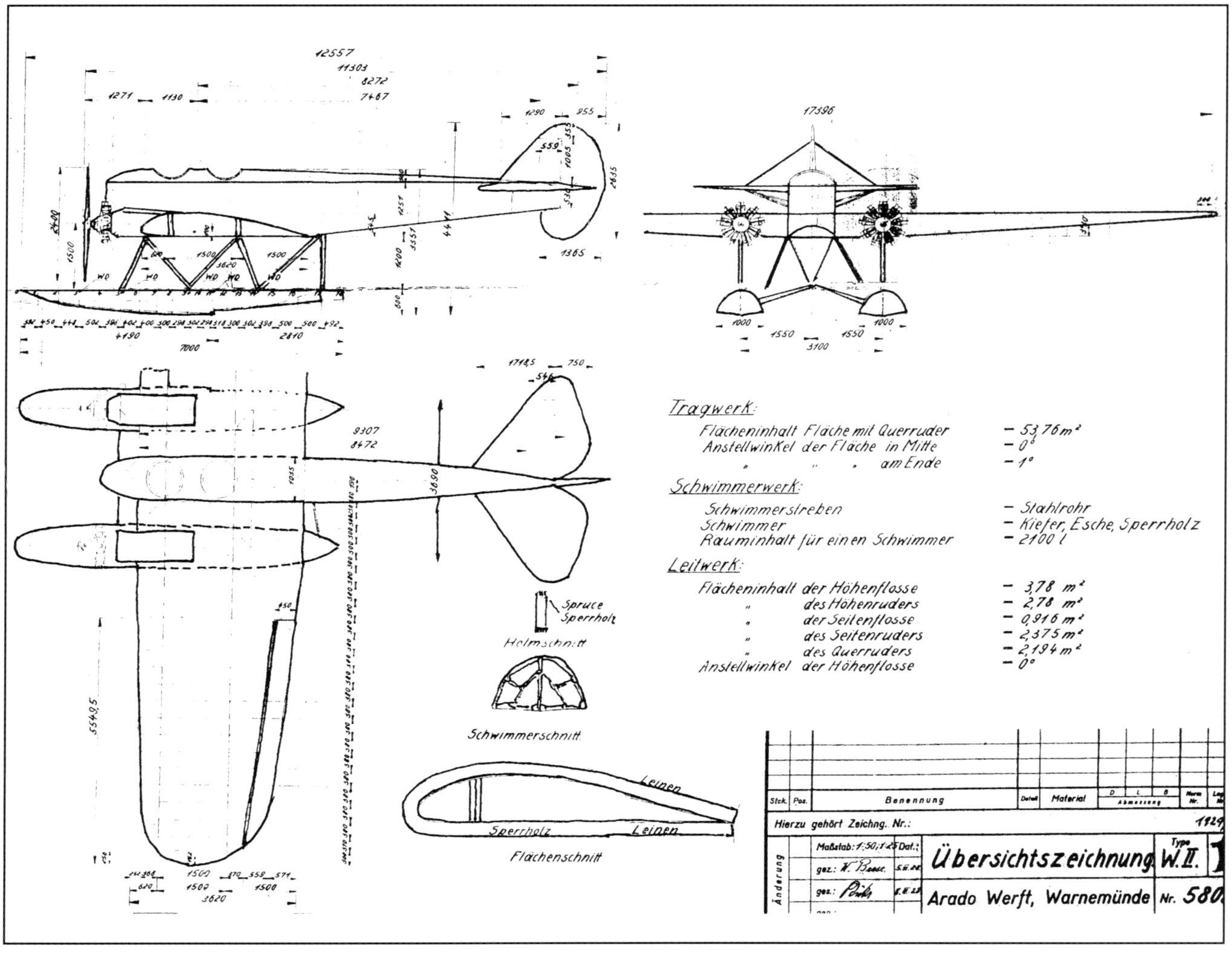

Arado SC II, D-1562 (Wk.Nr. 51 — above) *Arado W II, D-1412 (Wk.Nr. 38 — below)*

foot pedals, while lateral control was maintained by a hand wheel. Control of the horizontal stabilizers was accomplished by a joystick. Since an electric starter was out of the question due to its weight, a type of kickstarter was developed. Using a crank and coupling rod, each engine could be turned over individually. The twin-engine twin-float cantilever monoplane was powered by two Siemens Sh 12 radials, each with an output of 108 hp. Despite its high performance weight, takeoff time was just nine seconds, and the top speed amounted to 145 km/h. Two models were produced in 1928, registration numbers D-1544 and D-1412. In spite of the practical solutions and satisfactory performance figures, the airplane was regarded less favorably for training purposes than the competing design from Focke-Wulf, chiefly due to the glued-on wing covering made of wood veneer and the limited seaworthiness caused by a weak float design. The two aircraft were taken on charge by the DVS in List on Sylt and in Warnemünde and were flown primarily in the immediate airfield areas. D-1412 was written off following a crash in 1935, while its sister ship remained in service until 1937.

Arado W II, front view showing the two Siemens Sh 12 engines.

Arado W II, D-1412 (above).

Arado SD I (Wk.Nr. 31 — below).

Fighters for Land and Sea: The SD I-III And SSD I Biplanes

The exclusive production of trainers in and of itself wasn't enough to keep the Arado Handels Gesellschaft alive. However, since the Bayerische Flugzeugwerke was not yet playing a significant role in fighter design and the Reich government was not cooperating with Junkers in the area of armament, Arado was given an early chance to gain a leading position (along with Heinkel) in the manufacture of fighter aircraft. For Arado, the conditions appeared favorable, since Lübbe (like Fokker during the war) had plans for his company to produce both airplanes and aircraft weapons.

Once the Paris Accords, signed on 28 May 1926, loosened the manufacturing restrictions by revising its definitions it became possible to construct airplanes with acceptable performance characteristics for fighters. The Reichswehr therefore began secret plans in 1927 for four of the first military types. These were projects for a fighter plane with the covername "Heitag"[13], a reconnaissance aircraft for the divisional reconnaissance squadrons, a night fighter and reconnaissance airplane and a multi-role aircraft for long-range patrol and bombing missions. The agency responsible for issuing these contracts was the Aeronautical Development Branch in the Heereswaffenamt. Kurt Student and its director (operating under the covername Seebach) Hauptmann Hellmuth Wilberg carried out secret talks — in civilian attire — with Albatros, Heinkel and Dornier and placed one of the first development contracts for a fighter with Arado.

Arado conceived the SD I prototype, which was developed in the style of the D VII and D XIII Fokker fighters from the First World War era, and like the previous SC I model was reputed to have been tested in Lipetsk. Officially the aircraft was declared as a "single seat mailplane."[14] The type, apparently only one of which was constructed, was a cantilever sesquiplane of composite construction (Wk.Nr. 31), fitted with a 425 hp Bristol radial engine. It

The prototype Arado SD I fighter (1928).

25

had a wingspan of 8.4 m and with a weight of 1,230 kg was able to reach a speed of 345 km/h at low altitude and 275 km/h at 5,000 m. The wings were braced at their ends by V-struts and were attached to the fuselage with two supports each side. Armament was to have been one or two MG 08/15 machine guns.

A flying demonstration took place before an observation commission on 18 June 1927 in Warnemünde under the direction of Kurt Student. The airplane wasn't able to be shipped to Lipetsk, however, because on 11 October it was lost in a crash at the test center in Rechlin. Dr. Theodor Bienen, an experienced pilot from the war and a member of the DVL at Müritzsee, had previously trained on the plane, which up to that point had chalked up 20 test flights but was not yet certified.

Unlike those found in Germany, the British aircraft engine rotated in the opposite direction to that of the propeller, and after one takeoff the aircraft began veering sharply to the right. With considerable effort Bienen was able to regain control and pull the aircraft up just before running into a tree-lined avenue. On another flight, as he attempted an aerobatic maneuver with low-altitude rolls, the airplane slipped over onto its right wing. It impacted with the ground and burned. The incident was initially kept a secret. It wasn't until the following year that the Berliner "Illustrierte Flugwoche" reported the crash. Publisher A.R.

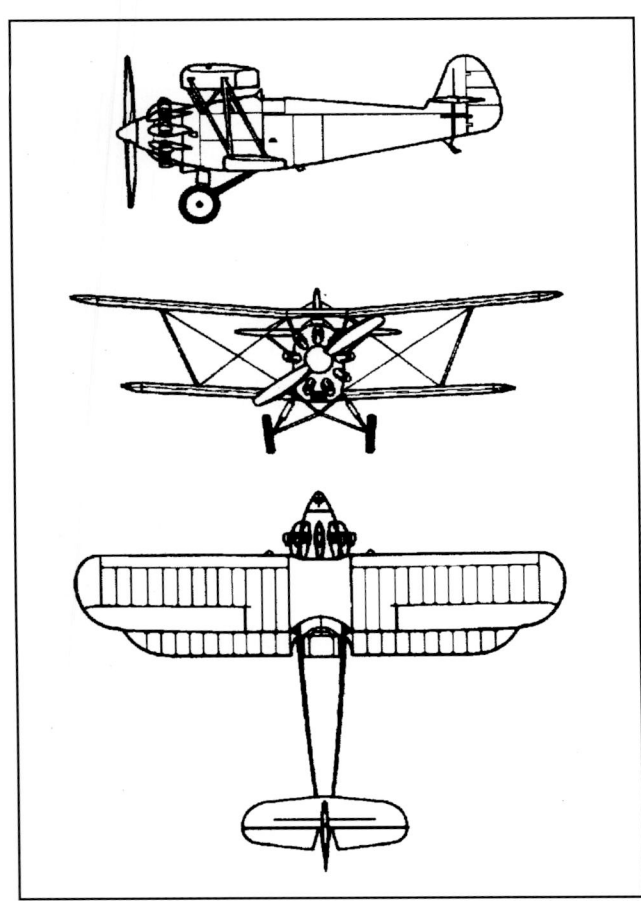

Sketch of the Arado SD III with shortened landing gear (1929 — above).

Arado SD II (Wk.Nr. 49) with three-bladed propeller, geared engine and lengthened nose (right).

Weyl had to keep its military purpose hidden, however, and wrote of an accident involving an "Arado sportplane."[15] As described in the "Rechlin Letters" Lübbe rushed to the scene of the crash as soon as he learned of it. The Arado company had cultivated good relations with Rechlin. In view of the modest equipment at the test center, Lübbe had provided the technicians there with one of his private automobiles. The vehicle was powered by a 100 hp aircraft engine and Lübbe enjoyed using it for driving in virtually impassable hunting terrain. However, it proved too expensive from a tax standpoint and in Rechlin was not used for traveling on public roads, but simply for driving around the airfield. Most of the young technicians enjoyed driving it immensely: "Who can say to himself that his school car had a six-cylin-

Arado SD III, D-1973 (Wk.Nr. 54).

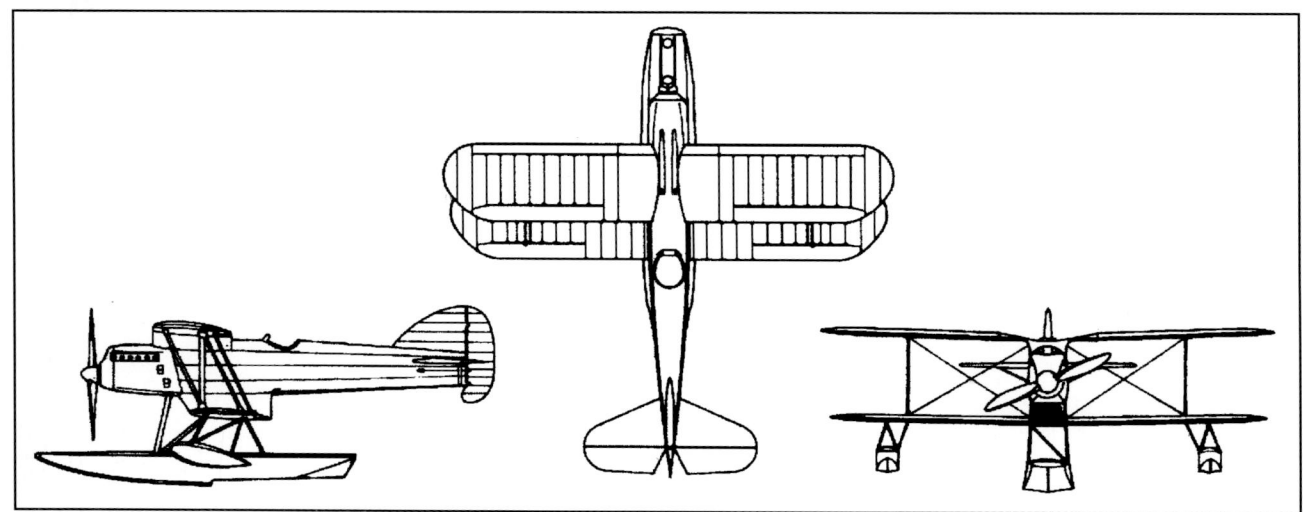

The Arado SSD I seaplane fighter. Sketch from 1929 (above).

Arado SSD I, D-1905, just before the catapult launch (left).

der engine with such great power?" later reminisced Georg Wolle, one of the Rechlin group.[16]

Since the SD I fighter had proven to be too unstable in the turn with its high wing loading, there followed the SD II prototype at the end of 1928; only one example of this was built as well and, like its predecessor, was never certified. The airplane had somewhat larger dimensions and was powered by a Bristol Jupiter geared engine of 530 hp driving a three-bladed wooden propeller, giving it a longer nose. The previous strut supports to the fuselage were absent. Instead, the wings were diagonally braced and fitted with N-struts at their outer ends. Unusual, too, was the three-bladed propeller. The airplane easily improved the time-to-climb rates, while the data for maximum speed was lower than that of its lighter predecessors.

Due to secrecy measures, there are few known company documents regarding a third variant, the SD III prototype (Wk.Nr. 53). The wing bracing of the airplane, which was not logged in the official type listing of 1942, corresponded to that of the SD II. The fuselage was different in

Arado SSD I on the Breitling.

Arado SSD I, D-1905, with wheeled landing gear, in front of the DVS headquarters building in Warnemünde (July 1930).

having a shorter nose due to the absence of the geared engine. Additionally, the landing gear was shortened, the fuselage lengthened by 35 cm and the rudder was more rounded at its tip. Like the SD II, the aircraft may have been tested in Lipetsk, but wasn't certified until October 1932 under the registration D-1973.

In accordance with a requirement issued for a catapult-launched naval multi-role fighter, the SSD I biplane strutter appeared in 1929 with the Werknummer 54. It was of composite construction and was camouflaged as a "single-seat maritime mailplane."[17] It was the first German plane to be designed with a central main float and wingtip support floats. It was able to be converted to a landplane with normal landing gear for the testing in Lipetsk. The BMW VI inline engine provided the aircraft with its power. Despite a relatively high weight of 2,030 kg the airplane reached a maximum speed of 280 km/h, had a time-to-climb rate of 1.5 minutes to 1000 m and a ceiling of 6,800 meters. Unusual was the fact that the upper wings were joined directly to the fuselage, over which the pilot had an unobstructed view. A tunnel radiator was installed between the upper and lower wings.

Since Heinkel's competing twin-float HD 38 demonstrated better performance, only one Arado prototype was constructed. In July 1930 it was entered in the German aircraft roster as D-1905, and was subsequently owned by Luftdienst GmbH and the DVS before it crashed in 1933 when attempting a landing on the Breitling.

The Arado J 1 prototype torpedo carrier (1929).

The J 1 Torpedo Bomber

Around 1929 Arado designed the prototype for a single-seat low-wing J 1 torpedo bomber, powered by a BMW engine. In order to be able to carry the load of two underwing torpedoes the wings were of a semi-cantilever design whereby the braces joined the wings at roughly the same point as the torpedo attachment points. Little is known about this aircraft, on which no further developments were made.

Chapter 4
New Concepts
The Pioneering Spirit: The Luft Hansa-Postexpressflugzeug VI

Previous successes gave Lübbe the impetus to develop larger commercial airplanes in 1927. As early as 1912, when Rumpler unveiled the first German "air limousine", Lübbe had already made the first official German airmail flight. He was sickened to learn that the Deutsche Reichspost (under suspicious circumstances) later recanted its recognition of this pioneering feat in favor of later postal flights with an Euler aircraft, and felt that it was time to renew efforts in the area of commercial airmail under more favorable conditions.[18]

In post-WWI Germany, commercial aircraft were at first nothing more than converted military planes. The "Rumpler-Luftverkehr" of Lübbe's former business partner logged over 82,000 flying kilometers between 1919 and 1920. In February 1919 the Deutsche Luft-Reederei, cofounded in 1917 with his Grunewald neighbor Walter Rathenau, established the first regular German flight route between Berlin and Weimar and, at the same time, carried air mail. With the Fokker F II and F III, which among other carriers were operated by Luft Hansa (founded in 1926), Lübbe's former partner Fokker became involved in the business. The FF 45 and FF 49, seaplanes built by the Warnemünde dockyards of the Flugzeugwerke Friedrichshafen (the company taken over by the Arado Handels Gesellschaft), also found service in the civilian aviation sector. An increasing number of German aircraft companies began taking part in the race to develop more capable commercial aircraft.

Even before the dawning of intercontinental flights was heralded with Charles Lindbergh's 1927 Atlantic crossing, Rumpler had already begun working on a transatlantic project involving a 10-engine floatplane. However, the project, begun in 1924, was ahead of its time and never came to fruition.[19] In 1927 a Dornier airplane reached South Africa from Switzerland. In April 1928 the crew of a Junkers W 33 succeeded in making the first crossing of the Atlantic in an east-west direction.

The modern commercial airplane:

With few exceptions, we are still far away from a true commercial airplane. The future commercial airliner necessitates a commercial aircraft engine, requires a low purchase price and operating cost, good performance and excellent handling qualities, comfort for the passengers and a long life.[20]

Walter Rethel had accumulated considerable experience after the war which he put to good use building multi-seat commercial planes. For the Kondor Werke he had designed the low-wing P-8 with a cabin for ten passengers, for the Dutch company NAVO a four-seat airliner and for Fokker a single-engine prototype for the legendary F-VII commercial plane — on 9 May 1925 the first plane to reach

H. Lübbe in an Etrich Rumpler Taube prior to taking off on the first official air mail delivery, in Heidelberg (19 May 1912). Handwritten cancellation: "Me overleaf as the carrier of the first German Imperial Air Mail."

A four-seat passenger plane designed by W. Rethel for the Dutch NAVO company. (1920).

the North Pole. Since it appeared necessary to incorporate both economy and safety in the fundamental design of an airliner, the Warnemünde Arado dockyards made use of an inexpensive composite design, rejecting the metal designs such as used by Junkers, Rohrbach and Dornier.

Company description of the Arado V I:

As a commercial aircraft, the spacious cabin has the following dimensions: length: 22.0 m, width: 1.35 m, height: 1.90 m. The four passenger seats face the direction of flight. The seats are removable and can be exchanged for reclining seats. A baggage compartment is located behind the cabin, with the following dimensions: length: 0.95 m, width: 1.30 m, height: 1.70 m. The baggage compartment is separated from the cabin by a plywood wall. A connecting door is in the wall, which joins the cabin and baggage compartment. A toilet can be installed in one-half the baggage compartment without difficulty. The cabin windows, made of Triplex, are clear and can be partially opened. A heater and ventilation are also planned for the cabin. If the aircraft is to be operated as a transport, the dividing wall can be removed. The entire cargo area then has a length of 3.15 m. Additionally, the aircraft may be utilized for other purposes, e.g. photography, since the flooring is removable and can be exchanged for other types.

The two pilot's seats are raised higher than the seats in the cabin. During flight the seats may be adjusted up or down as well as forward and backward. The raised seats ensure a good view forward over the engine. The pilot's cockpit is completely enclosed. The Triplex panes in front of the pilot can be opened halfway. In front of the pilot is a well organized instrument panel with all flight and monitor instruments as well as control levers. The cockpit is accessed from the cabin by a door in the forward cabin wall and by a hatch in the roof of the compartment. The fuselage with engine block is of steel-tubed lattice design. The rear fuselage decking is removable to permit a quick and thorough check of the fuselage interior. The landing gear has a wide track of 3.51 m. The axles are independent and attached to the fuselage underside. The vertical and horizontal stabilizers are made of steel-tube construction. The tailplane is adjustable in flight, enabling the aircraft to be balanced for various loads. This is a particularly desirable feature during long-distance flights since the pilot won't become overworked flying the aircraft. The wing comprises two sections and attached to the fuselage by hinged supports. A V-brace supports the wings from the fuselage. The wing is covered with plywood from the rear spar to the leading edge, and from rear spar to trailing edge is covered in cloth. When disassembling the wing the V-braces can easily be folded up under the wing. The fuel tanks are contained in the wings to the right and left of the cabin. The oil tank is designed to fit in the leading edge and is located to the right of the pilot's compartment. The 500 hp Pratt and Whitney Hornet engine is fitted to the fuselage nose. The engine is started by means of an Eclipse hand starter. The hand crank is easy to operate from the ground.

The Arado V I (Wk.Nr. 47) was a semi-cantilever high-wing commercial aircraft with applications as a passenger airliner or transport, as well as for diverse special roles. At the time, Germany was lacking in the design of powerful air-cooled engines, meaning that initial provisions were made for the V I passenger airliner to use the American Pratt & Whitney 500 hp engine in addition to a Junkers-built engine. The less-powerful Junkers engine, with only 300 hp, was lighter by 150 kg and required 40 kg less fuel to be carried, so that with a cargo of 485 kg the total weight of 2,350 kg was 200 kg less. The Junkers engine, with 7.83 kg/hp, would have given a higher wing loading, so that the speed would have been 25 to 30 km/h less. While the long-term plans called for a BMW engine then in development, only the foreign engine was planned for the aircraft in the role of a transport. The clockwise-rotating engine burned fuel at the rate of 90 liters per hour, was fitted with a Standard Steel three-blade propeller and provided the airplane with an impressive 210 km/h maximum speed and 185 km/h cruising speed.

The cargo plane, designed with economy and robustness in mind, proved to have good natural stability and re-

The Pratt & Whitney Hornet radial engine which powered the Arado V I1.

sistance to weather during trials conducted beginning in February 1928 and was generally praised at the ILA in Berlin.

The trade press's assessment of the Arado V I commercial airplane:

It is welcome to know that, with the Arado V I, a second high-quality postal carrier has arrived on the public scene, one which has been designed with a view to addi-

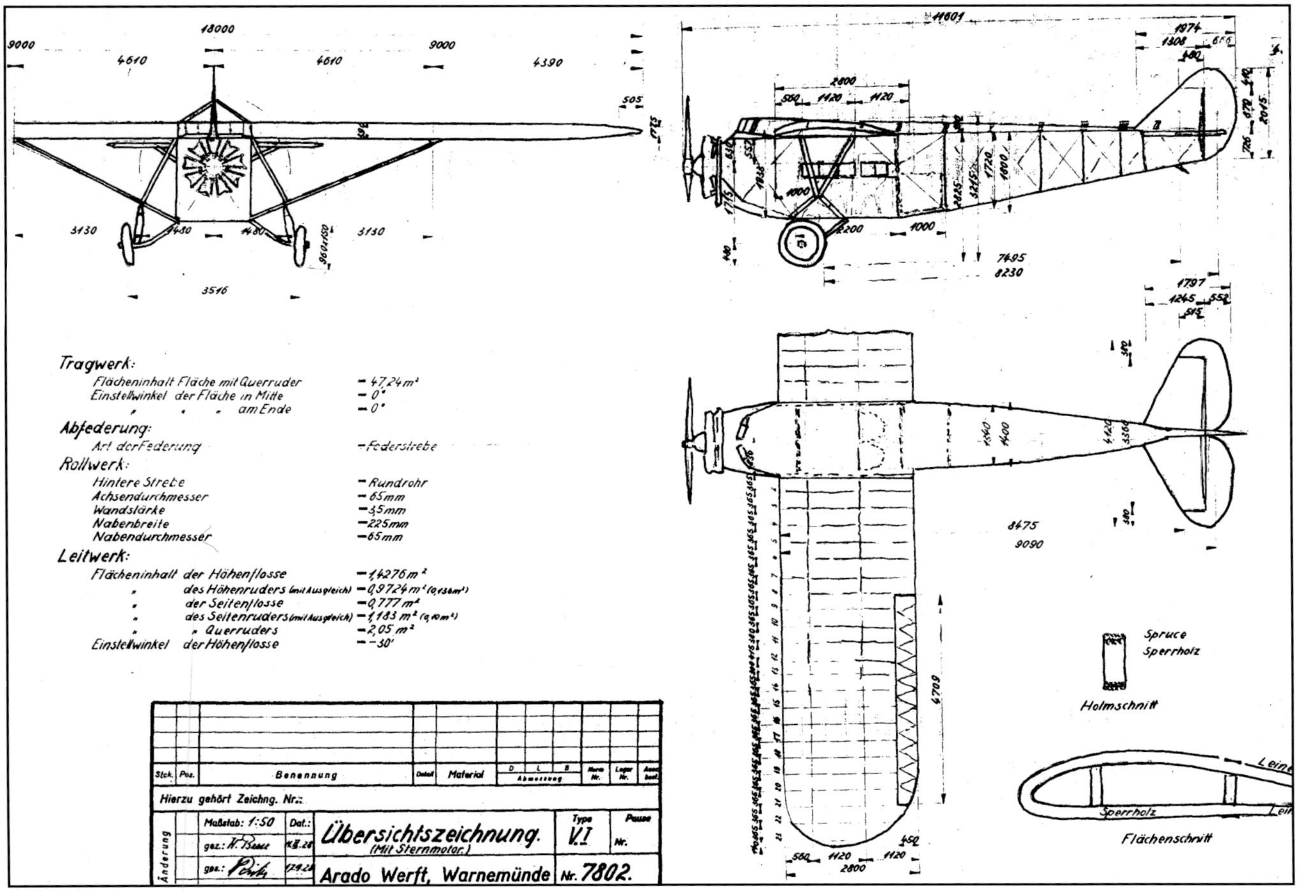

Three-view of the Arado V I postal express aircraft (1928).

32

Arado V I, D-1594 (wk. Nr. 47) with Lufthansa markings, posing in front of the Warnemünde assembly hangar.

The Arado V 1 at the ILA in Berlin (1928).

tional roles and which can be utilized in these roles ... The Arado Werke, Warnemünde, have hitherto done little to promote themselves as designers of commercial aircraft. However, they enjoy a solid reputation from their well-known and excellent quality workmanship in the construction of sport and training airplanes, an area where they number among the leading producers.[21]

The aircraft attracted the attention of Luft Hansa representatives, such as Carl August von Gablenz and Joachim von Schröder, as an airplane which could be utilized for purposes of charting the most favorable air routes, as well as determining the economic and technical requirements for establishing new mail routes on the South Atlantic runs. These two individuals had been involved in the establishment of a Junkers-operated night route from Berlin via Warnemünde to Stockholm. Mail transport, because of its better utilization of cargo capacity and time advantages, seemed to be particularly sensible from an economic standpoint. The powerplant in the Arado plane ensured a high safety factor on non-stop flights, due to the fact that it could be throttled back to 60% of its output. The large fuel reserves permitted a range of 2,000 km and ensured the aircraft would have enough fuel to deviate to an alternate airport in the case of poor visibility. In contrast to other mail carriers operated by Luft Hansa, the superior power reserves of the engine permitted adequate climbing performance with a full load when flying over bad weather areas. The airplane was capable of rapidly breaking through the cloud ceiling and continuing on its course at high altitudes, unhampered by weather problems. It was hoped that in this

The crew of the Arado V 1 after landing in Tenerife. From left: Eichentopf, von Schröder, Albrecht.

manner the larger mountain ranges could safely be crossed while flying blind and without navigational aids, plus night flights could be carried out without the need for extensive illumination of the route on the ground.

The conversion to a postal express carrier included lowering the roof above the pilot's compartment, fitting the strut attachment points with aerodynamic coverings and swapping the cabin accoutrements for fuel tanks. The plane was fitted with an Askania navigational compass, a "Gyrorector"-type attitude indicator which displayed the bank angle of the aircraft, dual controls, a remote thermometer for measuring the temperatures at high altitudes, formation lights and a specialized carburetor fire extinguisher. The speed was measured by a normal speedometer, but more often by simply 'eyeballing' the speed at which the ground slipped by underneath the airplane. Course calculations were made through the use of maps showing the terrain being overflown. During blind flying in fog and poor weather conditions, which in the best of scenarios could easily cause a deviation of 50 km from the intended destination, the crew made use of the compass, taking into account the flight time and the anticipated speed — and then factoring in any drift caused by the occasional crosswind as indicated by a wind triangle.

The shortcomings of such methods were already known. Electrical and acoustic means for determining altitude were at the time just being developed, as was wireless equipment for determining an airplane's bearings. Although flying in fog had been put to the practical test, landing in such conditions was another matter altogether, as a confession by Erhard Milch — at the time a member of Luft Hansa's board of directors — bears out. He stated: "Nowadays there is no interruption in air operations when the destination point is shrouded in fog. Work is being undertaken on instrumentation which will solve this, the final problem with all-weather flying."[22]

In the autumn of 1929 Luft Hansa decided to carry out test flights to Spain using the Arado aircraft. Two years previously, the national airlines known as Iberia was founded with the involvement of a German bank consortium. Iberia's initial airliner inventory included two three-engine, all-metal, high-wing Rohrbach Rolands, with which the Madrid-Barcelona passenger service was opened on 14 December 1927. On 7 and 24 September 1929 long-range flights were undertaken using the Arado V I mailplane between Berlin and Seville, where Delag had a relay station with a mooring mast for airships. The pilots were Erich Albrecht and Joachim von Schröder, who as Luft Hansa's authorized signatory had assumed directorship of the project. Eichentopf was the on-board engineer and took care of technical maintenance and repairs at the stopover airfields. Earlier, the same crew had carried out express mail runs to Irkutsk in a Junkers W 33. The nearly 2,500 km route to Seville was accomplished in just under 27 hours with a short layover in Marseilles.

One month later the aircraft was made ready for a nonstop flight to Constantinople.[23] On the 25th of October 1929, pilot Albrecht began warming the engine up shortly after 3 o'clock in the morning, before lifting off from Berlin-Tempelhof's illuminated airfield at 3:25 with 16 hours' worth of fuel on board. After only a short time, the plane was on course toward its first checkpoint at Brünn. The destination point, some 1,820 km away, was reached after 10 hours and 35 minutes of flying. After a circuit over Constantinople with a Turkish pilot on board, the return flight to Berlin began four days later on a moonless night with a cargo of mail and newspapers. Weather conditions were relayed to the crew from Berlin by telegraph. Hedges and uneven terrain at the provisional airfield posed a serious risk for the heavily-laden airplane taking off at night. The crew procured white, green and red storm lanterns, which the Turkish airfield personnel used to mark out the takeoff run. In view of the absence of expensive route markers for night flying (already being introduced on inner-German routes), the crew plotted the return course with the aid of the compass; orientation based on ground lighting would have been impossible given the sparsely-settled regions and a total cloud cover along the route. They were able to circumvent a weather front over the Balkans thanks to the large power and fuel reserves, which enabled the plane to climb to an altitude of 3,500 m. They then dropped to low altitude to fly beneath the low-hanging clouds and localized fog in the Danube valley. The situation became critical just before reaching the Hungarian plains, for stratus clouds

The "first air express letter" delivered by the Arado V 1 mail plane on 29 October 1929 to the company's senior clerk Erich Serno.

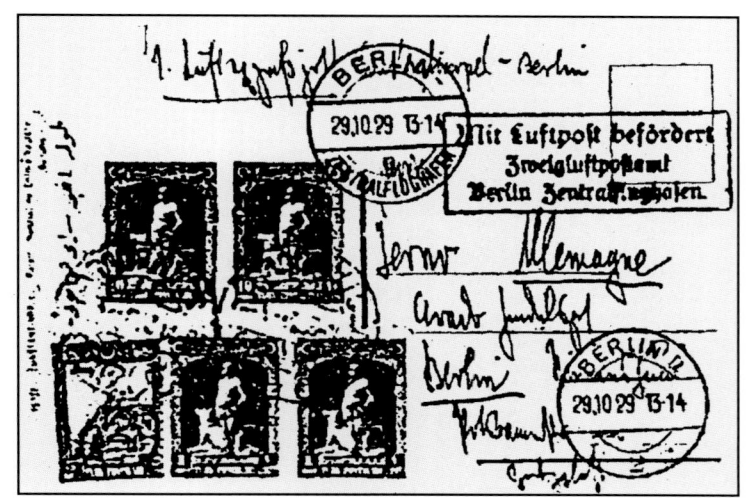

Postlangstreckenflüge der Arado V I

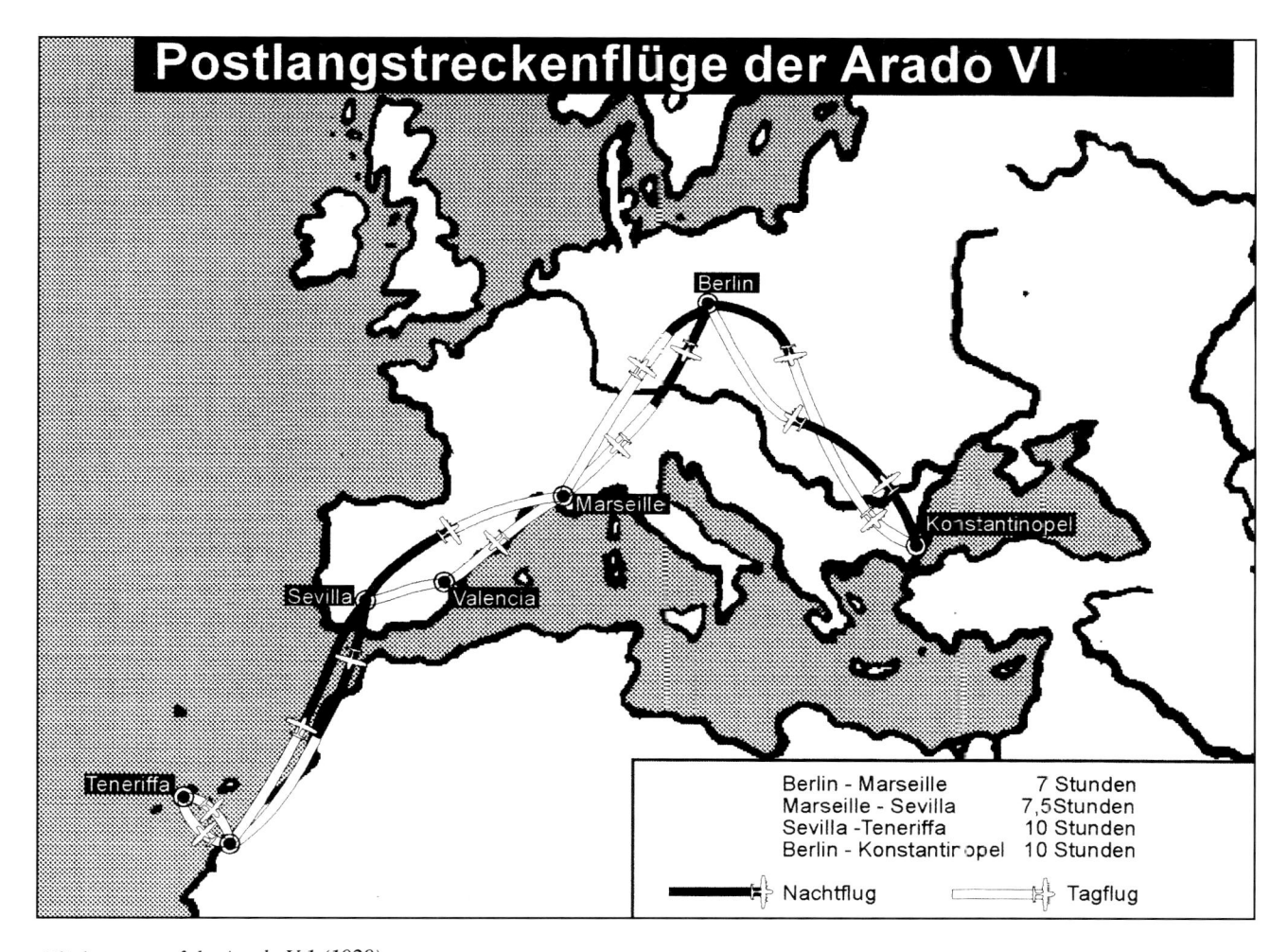

Berlin - Marseille	7 Stunden
Marseille - Sevilla	7,5 Stunden
Sevilla - Teneriffa	10 Stunden
Berlin - Konstantinopel	10 Stunden

Nachtflug / Tagflug

Flight routes of the Arado V 1 (1929).

reached down to touch the highest peaks of the mountains at the point where the Danube breaks through on the Serbian border.

Vienna was reached at 11:15 under sunny skies. A pre-arranged circuit over the city was the signal for relaying an "aircraft warning service telegram" to the flight monitors in Berlin-Tempelhof via the Austrian Luftverkehrs AG. The "race with the telegram", as the Turkish newspaper 'Sonsaat' characterized the event, was won by the mailplane; the telegraph message arrived with the landing of the airplane in Berlin at 1:05. The actual flight time for the entire trip of over 3,670 km took 20 hours and 45 minutes. The mail brought back from Constantinople, which included a "first air express postcard" addressed to the Arado Handels Gesellschaft, was disseminated shortly after 1 o'clock, just after being delivered to the "branch post office" at Berlin's central airport. Representatives of Arado, the Reichsverkehrsministerium, the airport administration and Luft Hansa, with Erhard Milch at their head, had an enthusiastic reception waiting for the returning crew.

On 16 November 1929 the postal express aircraft took off on a closely monitored flight to the Canary Islands, with stopovers in Marseille, Valencia and Seville. The total distance from Berlin to Tenerife and back was over 8,000 km. Following on the efforts of Luft Hansa in the north Atlantic routes, the flight to the Canaries was a further step in the establishment of regular south Atlantic mail routes. It was to "document in the most effective way the significance and great possibilities, and at the same time demonstrate to the authorities, the economic circles and the general public that with the current state of aviation it is entirely possible to carry out regular mail service."[24]

Upon landing at the provisional airfield of Los Rodeos near La Laguna (Tenerife) the crew was greeted by repre-

Arado V I at the Los Rodeos airfield in Tenerife (13 December 1929).

35

sentatives of the Spanish authorities, various aeronautical organizations and the German legation. After numerous interviews and reception parties the crew undertook several flight to reconnoiter seaplane and landplane airports in the region. On the 13th of December the local bishop christened the aircraft with the name "Tenerife." Nearly 15,000 spectators witnessed the solemn ceremony, conducted under tight security. Following this, the airplane took off to the sounds of the Deutschlandlied and the Spanish national anthem, made a circuit of the island, and then headed in the direction of the Gando airstrip at Las Palmas on the neighboring island of Gran Canaria. During takeoff, von Schröder radioed: "Just so that nothing goes bad on Friday the 13th!"

On the 14th the route continued from Las Palmas to Cape Judy, where the crew met with the French pilot Challe; he had interrupted a transoceanic flight to South America there. The return flight to Berlin took place under what turned out to be a fateful time pressure. "We wanted to be home in time for Christmas, and therefore decided to fly straight to Berlin without a layover", remembered the engineer Eichentopf later, and added: "The Berlin-Tenerife-Berlin mail run was to be the highlight of our successful year of 1929 ... and then we wanted to make new preparations for long distance flights to China and Japan and India."

After the takeoff in Marseille on the 19th of December at 8:30, it was expected that the final stretch of 985 km would mean an arrival in Berlin at around 17:15. Shortly before reaching their destination, the adventure was brought to an abrupt end when the plane crashed in foggy weather. The accident was the result of inadequate navigational aids, coupled with carelessness on the part of the crew, who chose to fly visually in the fog. Around 19:20 the main administration office at Luft Hansa received a telephone call from engineer Eichentopf, who reported that both pilots had been killed. Eichentopf himself had been thrown from the airplane and survived with minor injuries.[25] An hour after the crash he gave Luft Hansa representatives at the crash site an initial report on the events of the catastrophe.

The crew ruled out an alternate airfield landing after entering the fog, then made an error and flew well past Berlin to the area of Neuruppin. As darkness fell, they found their way by following ground landmarks at low altitude. Near Wustrau, at around 18:15, the aircraft's right wing struck the ground while turning, crashed and caught fire.

Erhard Milch, who had been waiting in vain at the Tempelhof airfield for the return of his friend von Schröder, immediately set out for the crash site with Director von Gablenz and several investigative experts, where they arrived at around 21:30. Even while sitting in his Nuremberg prison cell, the later RLM chief thought of the fateful accident and wrote: "Jochen von Schröder's death 18 years ago ... all that has happened since then, and yet how painful is the memory of that night as I drove to Wustrau!"[26]

Balance sheet for the Arado Handels Gesellschaft for 1929. The crash of the V I was entered as 154,440.02 Marks under "aircraft construction loss."

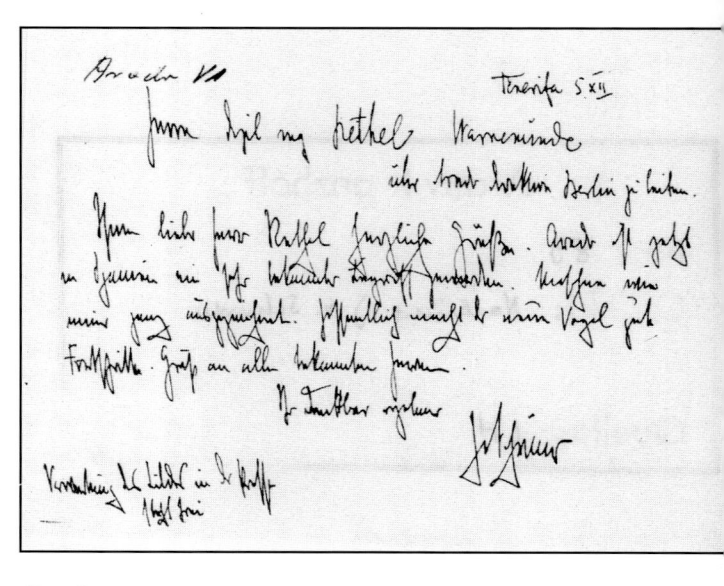

Note from pilot J. von Schröder from Tenerife (5 December 1929): Greetings to our dear Herr Rethel. Arado has now become a household word. We always do quite well."

The news of the accident, which was heard in Tenerife via radio and shortly thereafter confirmed by Baron von Winterfeld, a Luft Hansa representative who just happened to be there, was cause for much mourning. The local German consul was given a film of the christening ceremony, which was then sent to Berlin.

Since Luft Hansa was not contractually involved in the cost of the venture, the loss of the airplane was a serious financial blow to the Arado Handels Gesellschaft and was entered into the year's books as 154,440 marks for "loss of aircraft." The company, which did not realize a profit that year, was unable to continue the project with its own means. Since Luft Hansa's limited investment capital left room for few additional projects, Arado was forced to temporarily cease development of larger commercial aircraft.

The second prototype V Ia (Wk.Nr. 55) then under construction had to be scrapped, although before his death von Schröder had made improvement suggestions which led to an extended operational radius of 4,000 km, an increase in speed from 220 to 230 km/h and an increase in cargo capacity to 500 kg.

The effectiveness of Arado's purpose-built V I mailplane design was made manifest in a 1932 Luft Hansa requirement for a future mailplane. The aircraft was to be a two-seater, capable of 230 km/h, have a range of 1,000 km and a capacity of 500 kg. These requirements resulted in Messerschmitt producing his all-metal M 28, powered by BMW's license-built Hornet radial engine. The aircraft was operated by Luft Hansa in 1932 and 1933.

Arado L I, D-1707. Front view showing the marking "Ostseebad Warnemünde" (Baltic Sea Resort Warnemünde) and the competition number C 9 (above).

Three-view of the Arado L II sportplane designed by W. Rethel (1929).

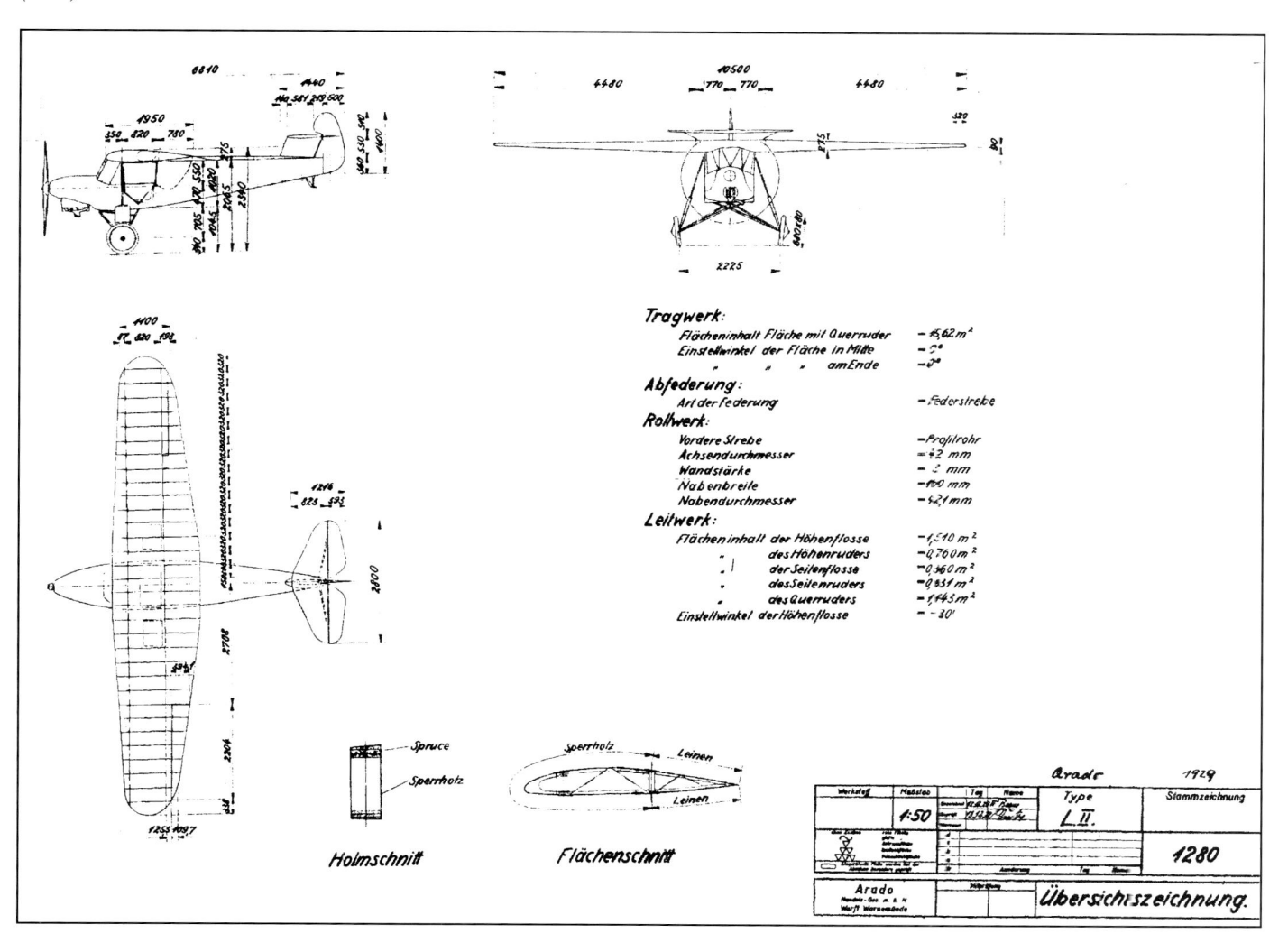

The designer Hofmann with a pilot of the MAC in the Arado L I sportplane, D-1707 (Wk. Nr. 56) during preparations for the Trans-Europa circuit (1929).

The first scheduled daily airmail service was undertaken on the Vienna-Constantinople route from 5 May to 31 October 1930, using a Junkers W 33. Mail was shipped to Vienna from Berlin by rail.

In 1932 a Do X flying boat overflew the Canary Islands on a trip from Lisbon to the Cape Verde Islands to open up Atlantic routes to Natal in Brazil and New York. The first scheduled south Atlantic mail run took place in February 1934, with the Berlin-Seville portion of the route being flown by Heinkel's commercial He 70. The remaining stretches via Las Palmas to West African Bathurst utilized Ju 52 aircraft and Dornier Wal flying boats making the transoceanic journey to Brazil.

The L I and L II Sportplanes

At approximately the same time as the development of commercial aircraft was being undertaken, Arado hoped to pick up business with the construction of light sport and pleasure aircraft. But even this undertaking was hampered in its initial phases by an accident, before collapsing altogether from the fallout of the general economic Depression.

After the Seeflug GmbH was disbanded in 1927, Arado committed to the support of setting up a Verkehrsfliegerschule (DVS) and the establishment of the Mecklenburgischer Aero-Club (MAC) in Warnemünde. The latter wanted to take part in an international Trans-Europa circuit, scheduled from 2-20 August 1929, for which the Aero-Club of France had donated a prize. MAC contracted with Arado for a light, two-seat aircraft and recommended that Ingenieur Hofmann at Akaflieg Darmstadt be brought in for the development. Hofmann had developed the "Westpreussen" sailplane, made famous through the flights of Ferdinand Schulz, and the GMG lightplanes of the Griesheim-based company of Gebrüder Müller. Construction of the Arado L I sportplane (Wk.Nr. 56) was accepted on the condition that the designer assumed sole responsibility for the construction and cost. At the expense of aerobatic handling, Hofmann developed a high-wing cantilever monoplane with a wingspan of 10 m. With good aerodynamic form and a weight of only 500 kg, he hoped to achieve a relatively high cruising speed using a Salmson Ad-9 radial engine having just 40 hp. The classy airplane, with two open seats in tandem, was given the name "Ostseebad Warnemünde" and registered in July 1929 as D-1707. Flight testing, which was carried out by Hofmann, revealed a maximum speed of 150 km/h, satisfactory flight handling characteristics and an advantageous all-round view. It's only negative quality was a certain instability along its pitch axis, which was deemed insignificant. The ferry flight to Paris, during which Hofmann was accompanied by a MAC pilot, occurred without incident despite bad weather. After a technical inspection the airplane took off on 5 August for a fuel consumption test flight. The airplane was forced to set down 30 km south of Paris when the engine overheated. After changing the carburetor Hofmann began the return flight to Paris alone and, while he was performing aerobatic trials, the aircraft went into a spin while upside down. It is thought that the unusual, suspended-type control stick led to an operator error of pushing on it, a task which the wing design wasn't up to. It came loose and broke in the center. Hofmann was critically injured in the plunge from 400 m and subsequent crash.

Following this the Arado Handels Gesellschaft assigned Walter Rethel with the design of a follow-on model, the L II, which was planned as a touring and commuter plane as well as a display, mail and photography airplane. Testing began in November 1929 and the first machine (Wk.Nr. 57) was registered in February 1930 as D-1771.

The design was based on the principles of economy, reliability and safety. The cantilever high-wing monoplane weighed 670 kg and had wooden wings set directly above

Arado L II (Wk. Nr. 57) with special "Ace of Clubs" markings.

Arado L II, D 1771 with rubber ring suspension.

Sketch showing the landing gear suspension of the Arado L II. —Left: Rhombus-shaped spatted type with rubber rings. Right: Rectangular spatted type with rubber discs. (below right)

Arado L II. Front view showing well the Argus As 8a engine (inverted cylinder). (below)

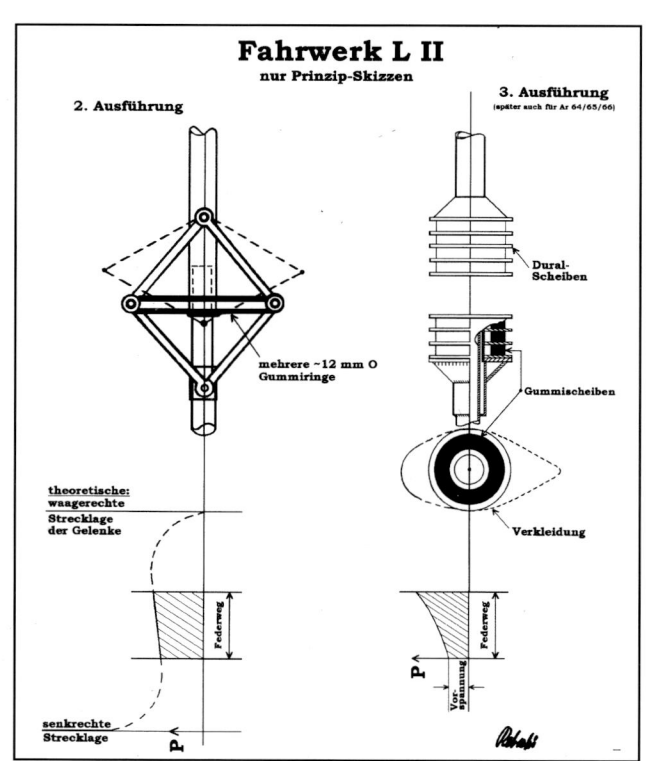

the cabin which, including the ailerons, were completely covered with plywood sheeting all the way back to the rear spar. The fuselage was made of fabric-covered steel tubing. In order to achieve a good horizontal stabilizer position with regard to the width of the fuselage and the high-wing design, the tailplane was attached high onto the vertical fin, which in turn was welded solid with the fuselage. It was braced on either side by means of a strut leading to the fuselage's upper former. This design gave the airplane's fuselage end considerable ground clearance. The rudder overhung the fin and had a counterbalance on the topside. The engine was an air-cooled Argus inverted-cylinder inline AS 8 which had an output of 85 hp at 1400 rpm. A firewall was fitted behind the engine which kept the interior compartment free of spraying oil. Two 65 liter fuel tanks were fitted into the wings, giving them protection in case of crash landing. Fuel was gravity-fed to the engine. The engine nacelle was made of aluminum. The landing gear was of an independent axle design, so that the risk of nose-overs during emergency landings on uneven terrain was kept to a minimum. The landing gear suspension, originally fixed with rings welded onto the sides, was replaced by a type consisting of stacked layers of rubber rings which could expand within a rhombus-shaped housing. The cushioning effect could be altered by adding or removing individual rings. A reduction in wind drag was achieved with a further improved model which saw the rubber discs housed within a smaller, rectangular housing. However, the suspension was stiffer with this design. The tail skid, located at the rear tip of the fuselage, was similar in shape to one-half of the landing gear and also had a shock-absorbing brace. A small caster, which could be extended from the pilot's seat, easily permitted taxiing on cement runways without scraping off the tailskid. For better communication between instructor and student, the seats were located side-by-side for the first time. The interior was protected against the force of the wind from the front by large cellulose acetate clear panels and non-fragmenting Triplex glass. Two side doors reached to elbow-height, above which was open to allow for unrestricted visibility in rainy weather or damage to the windscreen. Two side-mounted adjustable deflectors protected the interior from the wind, enabling the 'gentleman pilot' and 'independent lady flyer' to travel unencumbered by protective clothing or goggles. Behind the seats was a baggage compartment extending the breadth of the fuselage, which was accessed via a zipper. Two nets were located above the seats and served as a storage area for maps or gloves.

The airplane, nicknamed "Ace of Clubs" and given an appropriate paint scheme, was used exclusively as a touring plane by the Lübbe family who, like the Hugo Junkers family, occasionally spent their vacation time in Warnemünde. Lübbe's daughters always looked forward to the arrival of their busy father, who was looked upon as a 'dashing' automobile driver. Erika, the older one, noted in her diary during a holiday on Borkum: "Hurrah! Today is a happy day ... Daddy's coming! ... We went with a bouquet of roses to the outer harbor, the steamer arrived, and lots of people got off, but not Daddy! Why? Because he had driven from Berlin to Emden in the car."

The design of the Arado L II, the only prototype of which was destroyed in 1936, soon led to the follow-on development known as the L IIa. Since the aircraft had been planned for the Trans-Europa circuit, the requirements of which called for folding wings, the continuous-spar wing was dropped and it became necessary to brace the outer wing area to the fuselage. The forward strut could be unlocked and folded up to the wing. Then the aileron pushrods were freed by quick release catches, and after releasing the forward spar connection the wings were folded back and secured to the tips of the tailplane by connecting cords; this method meant that it wasn't necessary to uncouple the metal tubing of the fuel lines. With folded wings, the aircraft occupied an area of 2.75 x 3.26 x 7.52 m. Slightly longer and with a larger wingspan, four of these aircraft were produced and registered as D-1873 to D-1876 (Wk.Nr. 58 to 61).

Arado L IIa with folded wings.

On the 15th of April 1930 all machines were signed on for the International Trans-Europa Circuit, including three from the Arado Handels Gesellschaft and one from the DVS Braunschweig. Arado's pilots included Peschke (D-1875) and Dr. Pasewald (D-1876).

During initial testing at the end of June it was discovered that the air-cooled Argus As 8 inline engine was not adequately cooled. The oil temperature rapidly climbed to over 90 degrees Celsius. Overheating of the cylinder heads led to two emergency landings caused by 'eaten up' heads. A practical solution to the oil cooling problem was eventually found by running an oil line outside the fuselage. The engine nacelle was no longer aligned laterally with the fuselage, but now had a gap of several centimeters along its sides, allowing the free flow of air around the motor housing. The compass mounting was also unsatisfactory. Fitting it onto a pedestal support led to unfavorable oscillations, leading to a makeshift solution by suspending it from rubber cords and temporarily securing it to a side brace.

The rules for the 1930 Europa Circuit were set up by the Deutscher Aero-Club. Of the original 101 participants which had signed up, 60 arrived to begin the 7,560 km contest. Two of the Arado planes dropped out, including the one flown by the DVS pilot instructor Stutz, number D-1873. Stutz flew the 818 km Berlin-Braunschweig-Frankfurt/Main-Rheims stretch on 20 July with an actual air time of 7 hrs, 15 mins in good weather. On 21 July the 865 km route took 9 hrs, 22 mins and led from Rheims via Bristol and London and back to St. Ingelvert. After a temporary takeoff delay in Rheims due to bad weather, the flight was seriously hampered by rain and poor visibility. The clouds dispersed somewhat over the Channel, and there was a powerful headwind of 60 km/h with force 4-5 seas. After reaching the English coast, rain showers and thick clouds forced the airplane down to altitudes of 50 to 100 m. On the return leg, visibility conditions improved slightly over the Channel. Takeoff on the third portion, from St. Inglevert via Paris to Poitiers was delayed by a defect in the landing gear. On the 23rd of July the fourth stage ended after 350 km with

Arado L IIa with strut-braced folding wings. Three-view drawing (1930 — below).

Arado L IIa, D-1874 (C 8) with rubber ring suspension (above).

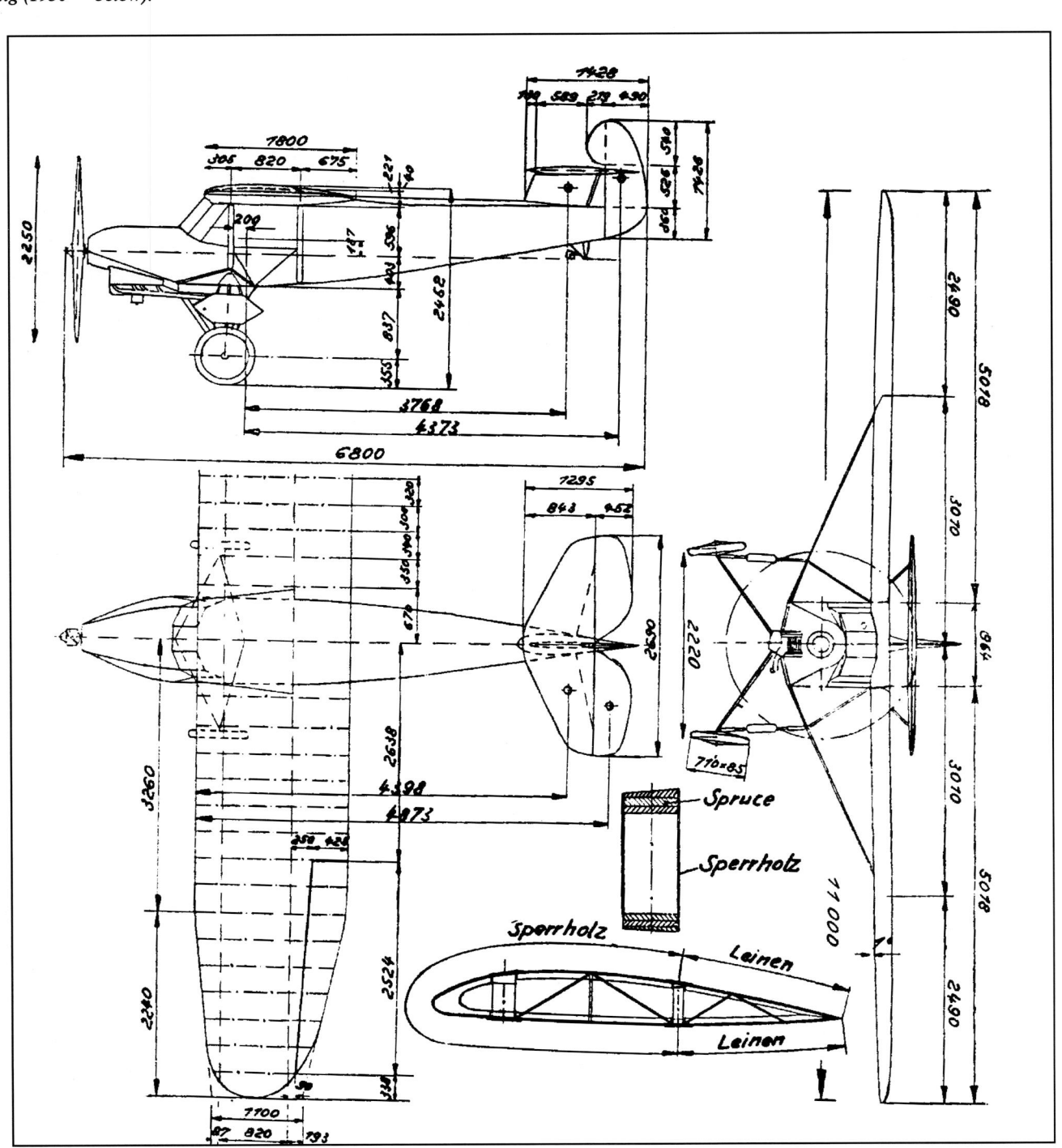

This shows two of the four Arado L IIa aircraft which were built, being readied for the Trans-Europa circuit of 1930 in the Warnemünde assembly hangar: D-1874 (later given competition designation C 8) is in the center. To the right is either D-1873 or D-1876, later designated B 4 or C 7 for the competition. The man in the overcoat is Flugbaumeister Kürth, responsible for the final assembly and test flight program.

an emergency landing near Pau. The reason for this was the inattentiveness of the passenger, who lost the map when opening the forward wind deflector. The pilot continued on for nearly 150 km without map orientation before deciding on an improvised landing in order to get a new map. The landing site, only 150 m long, was surrounded by a hedge two meters high. As Stutz attempted to 'drop' the plane down from a height of two meters the landing gear and the propeller broke, removing the machine from the remainder of the contest.

Two of the participating Arado aircraft, along with 33 other participants, were awarded scores after completing the long-distance routes. They took 18th and 22nd place and attained three-quarters of the points of the first place contestant.

A pilot's view of the Arado L IIa sportplane:

From a purely aeronautical standpoint the Arado L IIa possesses all the good qualities of a small touring plane. The two side-by-side seats are comfortable and well protected against the rain. Aside from the good flight handling, it should be particularly mentioned that it oscillates of its own accord in storm gusts, something I experienced in the gusty weather over England.[27]

At least one example of the L IIa was flown by the Akademische Flieger-Gruppe Berlin in 1932 and 1933. Despite the positive experiences with the 'wedding coach' (as the airplane was nicknamed) Arado was unable to continue with the production of sport and touring aircraft due to the poor sales situation brought on by the economic crisis. It can be deduced from a January 1931 advertisement that Arado, like Junkers and the Bayerische Flugzeugwerke, was forced to offer its small aircraft for sale with a rebate of 4,000 marks.[28]

Chapter 5
Weapons and Alternative Production — Signs of the Economic Depression

From 1926 to 1929 the Arado Handels Gesellschaft produced approximately 60 aircraft of the most varied types. After this relatively successful start and modest profits the company found itself on the brink of financial collapse with the onset of the worldwide economic depression, as shown by losses on the balance sheets for the years 1930 and 1931. This occurred despite aid provided by the Reich government in the amount of 250,000 Reichsmark.

Effects of the Depression:

Here, particularly in the city, unemployment is quite widespread, and no one seems to know what to do; one sees and hears only worries. I feel that nobody could have anticipated such consequences from the war. And each country, unusually, is affected by it. It means a bleak Christmas for everyone. Our factory is one of the few aircraft factories that still has any work left to do.[29]

In order to pay workers' wages, in October 1930 Lübbe felt compelled to give up part of his profits and convert a 120,000 RM loan offered to the business into a non-interest bearing encumbrance. It was only thanks to this personal involvement that Arado was spared the wage strikes which affected the likes of Heinkel. Despite this, Arado was forced to lay off workers and seek other manufacturing ventures. Boat repairs were undertaken, 10,000 rudders were delivered to Argentina and furniture was produced for the Rostock hospital. Nevertheless, in order to ensure long-term survival it was necessary for the company to undertake additional, clandestine weapons manufacture. Gun breeches for the Heer, carts for the W 300 bomb and bomb release mechanisms for the C 50 50-lb bombs were delivered. Construction of the release mechanism was based on the design of Curt Heber, Lübbe's former co-worker at Fokker, in a cooperative effort with Siemens. Heber maintained a design bureau in Berlin-Britz and occasionally carried out secret discussions with the technical dockyard manager Otto

Affeldt in the upper story of the metalworking shop, to which only a few people had access. Affeldt was initially quite surprised when, under tight security, bombs were delivered to the dockyard in 1930.

Another matter under tight security in 1930 in Warnemünde was the production of 200 machine gun mechanisms, designed by Lübbe. On occasion, Lübbe discussed details with production supervisor Hans Rebeski, who had not been told that his small and outwardly reserved partner was actually the owner of the company. At that time, pains were taken for security purposes to ensure that co-workers were not given access to the inner operations outside their immediate scope of responsibility.

To mask the rearmament efforts, in February 1930 a test installation of the mechanisms was undertaken using a Junkers W 33. This was conducted under the scrutiny of the Reichsverband of the Deutsche Luftfahrtindustrie inside a covered hangar at the Staaken aerodrome, prior to the system being disassembled and individually sent to Lipetsk for military testing. After an agreement was reached with the management in Berlin Rebeski, who for six months in both 1930 and 1931 had supervised the testing on behalf of the Heereswaffenamt, was officially released from Arado and given a covername.

Lübbe's activities as a weapons designer was, for the reasons mentioned above, known only to a select group of individuals. Otto Affeldt never saw him in Warnemünde in 1931 and 1932. But together with Curt Heber, he found him in Grunewald to discuss the purchase of an industrial

Article in the German newspaper "Weltbühne", revealing that secret armament subsidies were being paid to Arado — news which led to the imprisonment of the publisher Ossietzki (1929 — right).

German aircraft industrialists in 1931, with Arado general manager F. Wagenführ (front, third from right), Arado senior clerk E. Serno (back, eighth from left) and Walter Hormel, who in 1925 was briefly the senior partner of the Arado Handels Gesellschaft (left, behind Wagenführ — below).

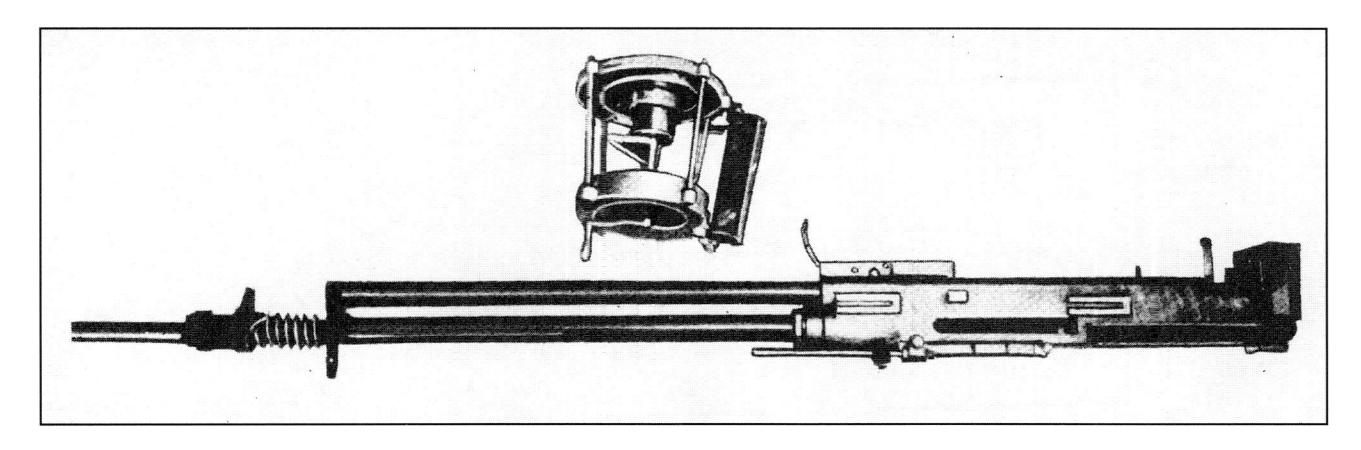

2-cm aircraft cannon designed by H. Lübbe (1931).

lathe. The visitors were struck by Lübbe's attractive and pleasant wife Ottilie. She appeared to "have matters quite under control" when it came to business, and Heber felt that they could work with her. On the other hand Lübbe, who seemed quiet and reserved, appeared to have no interest in expensive equipment for the dockyard and, to the disappointment of Affeldt, only approved a simple machine.

Affeldt had learned through Heber of Lübbe's suspicious dealings with the Reichswehr. Lübbe, despite his health problems, paid more interest to these weapons projects than the running of his own aviation company, which apparently was nearly exclusively represented by Felix Wagenführ and Erich Serno. "He works almost too much", complained his wife at the time, "and he sometimes gets these pains again... In addition to his business, Heinz keeps on working on these new projects and has just been awarded another patent. A nice Christmas present and something for the future."[30]

20 mm Aircraft Cannon (H. Lübbe 1931):

In 1929 the well-known engineer H.F.A. Lübbe demonstrated a working model of an automatic weapon, which he considered the non plus ultra in the area of aircraft weapons. This gun had a pressurized gas drive and a caliber of 20 mm and was able to fire 360 rounds per minute. It was air cooled, had a drum magazine and without the feed mechanism weighed only 107 lbs (48.5 kg). These features are proof of the careful planning which went into this design. The individual components were constructed in such a way that they could be mass produced, and the pleasant simplicity of the design can be recognized in the fact that the entire weapon consisted of just 50 parts. Rheinmetall, Germany's largest weapons manufacturer, expressed an interest in the cannon, and in 1931 was given an excellent appraisal by leading experts in the company. The German Waffenprüfungsamt supposedly took three examples for testing at their range. The results of these tests were said to have been unsatisfactory, and after one final attempt to bring the weapon into quantity production, no further such efforts were made either by the inventor or by the German Beschaffungsamt.[31]

Lübbe's patent, which is not described in further detail due to security reasons, was for a 20 mm aircraft cannon, the first prototype of which was produced as early as 1929. Despite a successful test at Rheinmetall, it did not enter production, although there was an urgent need for such weapons; well into the 1930's only WWI's MG 08/15 was available.[32] The gun which Lübbe developed was certainly of a relatively simple design, but in the initial stages of German rearmament there was little interest in introducing the technically more demanding pressurized gas mechanism in place of the standard recoil device — for cost reasons and also due to an initial failure to recognize its significance.

Aside from technical and economic risks, issuance of armament contracts was also dependent upon whether or not the company appeared cooperative in the eyes of the Reichswehr — which now was working closely with the NSDAP. The failure to accept Lübbe's patent in Germany and urgings by economically influential relations in the USA prompted Lübbe to offer the weapon for sale to the United States. On December 8th, 1931 the American military attaché in Berlin sent out a secret file which contained a description of the gun and seven photos, along with the comment that the inventor is prepared to sell the weapon.[33] It is possible that, because of this offer (the result of which remains unknown), Lübbe became suspect.[34] In this context it is significant to note that the only description of this gun in existence today is from the Americans — despite Rechlin sources indicating that Lübbe's development of heavy caliber weapons was known to the Waffenprüfanstalt: "Building upon the state of development at the end of the First World War, Wa Prüf 6F undertook renewed development of several weapons systems, e.g. the continued development of the 2 cm Lübke-MG, the 7.8 cm Gebauer-Motor MG and the Siemens Motor-MG."[35]

Furniture products by the Arado Handels Gesellschaft.

Chapter 6
First Production Runs for the "Risky Air Armada"
The Ar 64 Fighter

Arado's eventual entry into the military arena began in conjunction with the Reichswehr's provisional armament phase from 1926 to 1929, where concerted efforts were made to develop available military prototypes for quantity production. As chief-of-staff of the Inspektion der Waffenschulen, Oberstleutnant Felmy pushed for the separation of the aviation units from the Heer up until the establishment of the Reichsluftfahrtministerium in 1933 and laid the foundation for a so-called "risky air force", whose "A-Plan" called for the establishment of 22 aviation squadrons — including six fighter squadrons. The first call-up orders for the 'display squadrons' (as they were disguised) was dated 1 October 1930. On 20 January 1931 they were made available for the state of emergency. On 1 February 1932 Felmy authorized an increase in the number of airplanes to 960, including 162 fighters.

Due to the economic crisis the Reichsverkehrministerium's ability to support aviation was limited. According to the Douhet theory (much debated at the time) a defensive structure without a bomber force held little promise, to be sure; the Truppenamt was initially reluctant to institute an energetic build-up in this sector — not only for financial reasons, but also because of the fear that foreign governments would see it as an aggressive act. Efforts were therefore secretly put into building up the fighter force and developing better performing engines.

A 'report on the current state of the aviation industry' from 4 April 1932 came to the conclusion that, with the exception of Junkers, only a handful of aircraft manufacturers were capable of quantity production. Even Junkers, despite generous support from the Reichsverkehrsministerium, was on the brink of bankruptcy, and the company's director, Sachsenberg, was suffering from bad relations with the ministry. He placed little significance on the fighter in an air war and stood by the concept that the only truly sensible defense was a counterattack using bomber aircraft. An all-metal fighter developed by Junkers proved to be too costly to be considered for the armament program at the time. Dornier, along with the dissolved Albatros Werke (absorbed into the Focke-Wulf Werke) and the Bayerische Flugzeugwerke, had little experience in the construction of fighter aircraft or were for the time being relatively insignificant because of their economic state.

Although Heinkel was considered as a possible source for developing fighters, the Arado Handels Gesellschaft was the first to be awarded a production contract. An improved version of the SD II, the composite-designed Ar 64 open biplane, had been produced in 1930. It differed from its predecessor by a somewhat longer fuselage and a larger rudder unit with a slightly smaller fin for improving handling characteristics. The aircraft had a normal wing stagger arrangement with N-struts and was fitted with a Siemens Jupiter VI geared engine of 530 hp, giving the plane a top speed of 250 km/h. Characteristic features were the streamlined deflector shroud around the radial engine's cylinders for reducing wind drag and the four-bladed wooden Schwarz propeller. Because of the gearing the motor was set far back, and the propeller was attached to something resembling a torpedo nose. It was the first Arado aircraft to be fitted with hydraulic brakes. Its weapons consisted of the standard twin fixed 08/15 synchronized machine guns.

The final production version, the Ar 64 D with improved airframe, followed the Ar 64 A to C models built in 1931. The Ar 64 E was given a spatted landing gear and a two-bladed propeller.

The Lipetsk aircraft inventory listing for 1 October 1929 carried no Arado airplanes, and all Ar 64 A to C series were shipped to Rechlin for testing. Only a few versions of the Ar 64 D and Ar 64 E were registered with the DVS, as D-1039, D-2075, D-2277 through D-2082, D-2338 and D-2470. In 1934 and 1935 the Jagdfliegerschule Schleissheim had a squadron of Ar 64s, including D-1039, D-2280, D-2470 and D-2275.

Although the Russians were extremely interested in the Ar 64, changes in the political situation in Germany threatened to bring an end to the Lipetsk cooperative effort. On 26 March 1932 the chief of the Russian air force, Alksnis, requested from Hauptmann Hans Jeschonnek a demonstra-

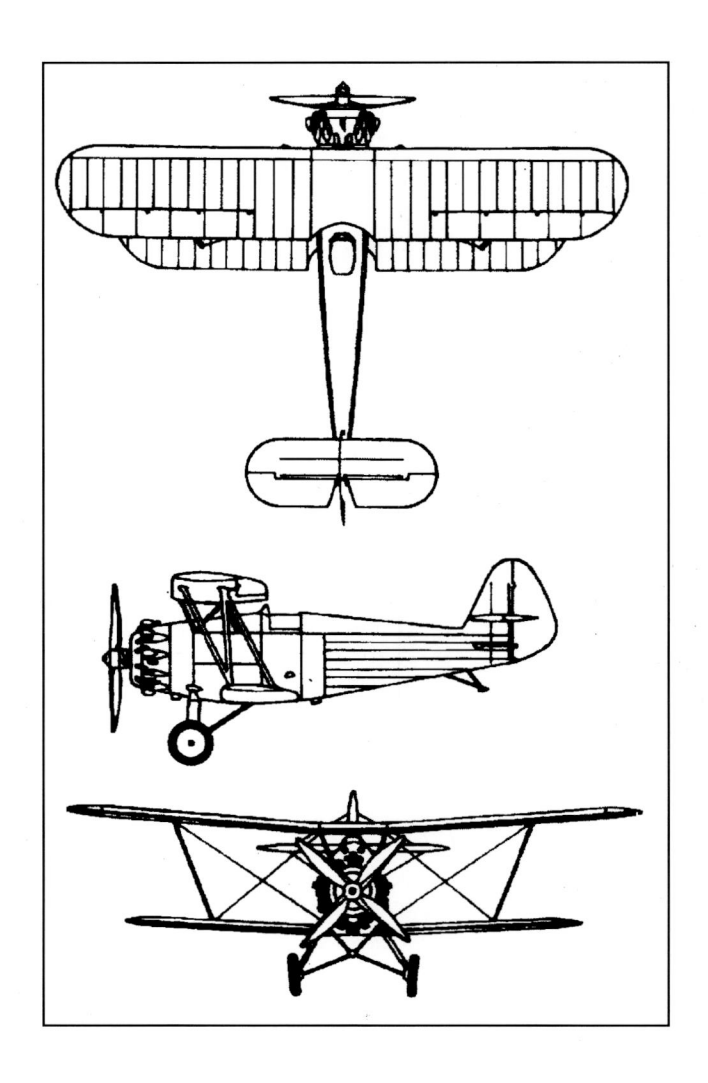

Three-view of the Ar 64 A single-seat fighter (1930).

Ar 64 C (below). Prototype Ar 64 (above). Three-view of the Ar 65 single-seat fighter (1932 — below right).

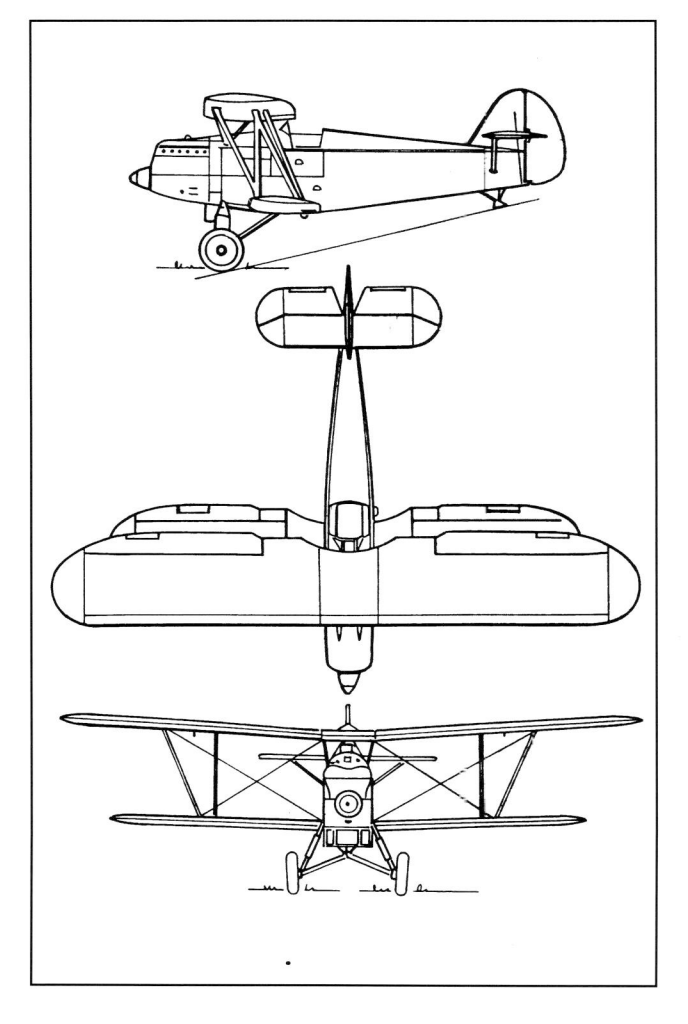

tion with a Rolls-Royce engine. He implied that he had information from the press claiming that the airplane could reach a speed of 430 km/h and climb to 5,000 meters in five minutes. The Germans responded evasively, calling the reports unsubstantiated. Nevertheless, according to minutes from 21 December of that same year, there was a demonstration of an Ar 64 with the British engine.[36]

Altogether, a monthly production of 27 Ar 64s was to have begun in 1932. This target was never attained, since its successor proved to be faster than expected. 25 airplanes were said to have been produced in quantity. According to company records, the total planned production goal of 19 machines was reached on 30 April 1936. Despite the fact that the aircraft had a tendency to break up and had rather unpleasant takeoff and landing characteristics, overall it proved to be a successful design and easily outshone its competitor, Heinkel's HD 43, which was never put into production.

The Ar 65 Fighter

Developed in 1931, the Ar 65 fighter bore little difference in construction from its predecessor. The staggerwing biplane had a somewhat longer fuselage and, for the first time, ailerons both in the upper and lower wings joined by a connecting rod. An unusually good-natured, easy-to-fly airplane was born through a concentrated attention to detail. The decision to fit the aircraft with the newly-developed BMW VI inline engine, tested in a few models of the Ar 64, was a decisive step forward. The engine had an output of 750 hp and gave the plane an unusually high top speed of 282 km/h.

Six different series were produced, the Ar 65 A through F, which other than minor changes to the airframe, differed

The prototype Ar 65 A in Warnemünde.

Ar 65 F.

little. Weaponry consisted of two synchronized MG 08/15. Due to the bomber shortage the aircraft was also fitted with a vertical rack for dropping six 10-kg bombs.

Two Ar 65s were under construction in April of 1932. A further ten were planned for the following year. Since Arado did not have sufficient construction capacity, twelve examples were license-built in Erla.[37] According to company records, a total production run of 157 units was planned to 30 April 1936. In actuality, by this time 171 aircraft had been delivered. By 1 October 1936 the total production of Ar 64s and Ar 65s had reached 189. Production ceased after this date.

This was the last Arado aircraft type to be tested in Lipetsk and, along with the He 51, was assigned in large numbers as the original equipment of the "Mitteldeutschland" display squadron in Döberitz and to squadrons at DVS Schleissheim. As the flight log of the Arado test pilot Richard Perlia shows, he carried out his first test flight in this aircraft, an Ar 65 F (D-IHOO) on 8 June 1935 and his last in December 1937. The type was still in use during the war and in 1943 was listed in official maintenance plans.

The British considered the Ar 65 to be the 'top performer' of the German industry and having a 'superior attack capability'

Ar 65 F, D-IROV, at the Warnemünde airfield.

Foreign Opinion:

It's significant to note that the Richthofen Kampfgeschwader, the first officially named aircraft organization since Göring's announcement of military aviation in Hitler-Germany and an elite unit, is equipped with Arado 65 aircraft. Arado 65 airplanes took part in the mass-formation flyover of Berlin on the occasion of the large-scale air exercise held in March 1935. Also, according to the 'Berliner Börsenzeitung" from 10 April 1935, nine squadrons from the Richthofen-Geschwader took part in the flying display in honor of Göring's wedding.[38]

Truman Smith, the American military attaché in Berlin beginning in August 1935, sent an internal memo to the USA in which he assessed the Ar 65 fighter (which he erroneously noted as Ar 55) to be inferior to American fighters. Two years later, when he warned of the potential threat posed by the German air armament, he was unjustifiably accused of being a victim of exaggerated German propaganda.

Chapter 7
Redesignation as the Arado Flugzeugwerke:
Personnel Changes and Expansion of Production

In an effort to economically stimulate the aviation industry through armament production, in 1931 the Reichsverkehrsministerium decided to offer increased subsidies and begin exerting influence on the management of aviation companies. Attached to the armament contracts with the Arado Handels Gesellschaft were 'advance and interim payments for contracted acquisition and development agreements' amounting to 200,000 RM, for which an encumbrance in favor of the German Reich was placed on the Warnemünde dockyards. Although the company depended on such influx of capital for its economic survival, internal differences cropped up because of the attached conditions. Heinrich Lübbe, whose refined financial politics had rescued the company during the economically difficult times, feared that he would lose control of the company. When he withdrew a substantial amount of private capital on 2 November 1932 as a preventative measure, just when increased investment was expected, the ministry became suspicious of the company's willingness to cooperate. It attempted to put pressure on the company's owners by arranging for a surprise audit of the balance sheets for the Arado Handels Gesellschaft on 29 December 1932. The results, released on 18 January 1933, revealed apparent discrepancies.[39]

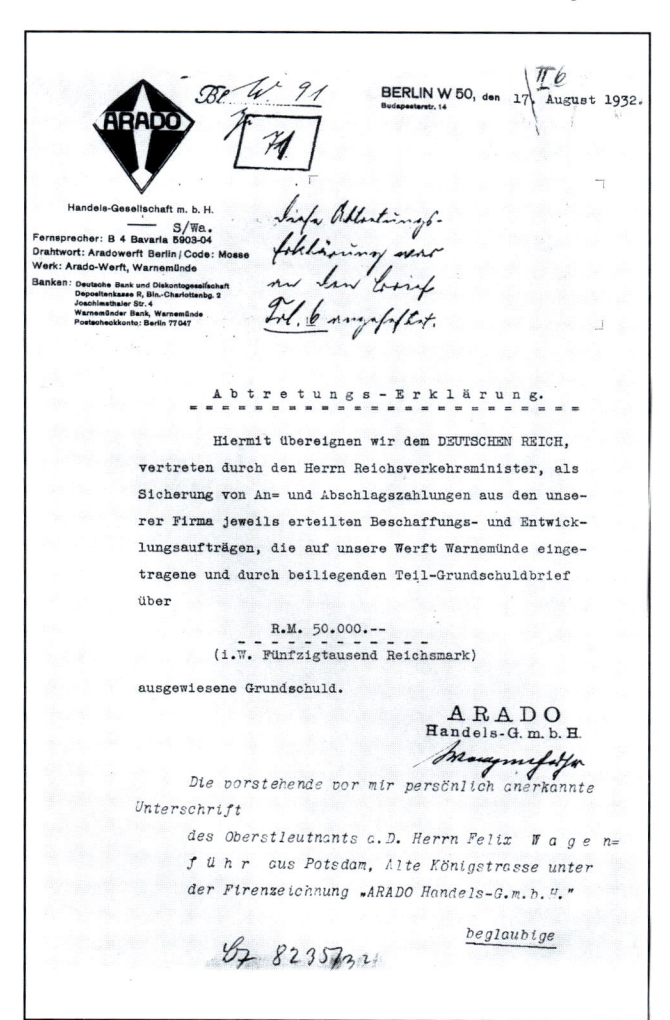

When the Albatroswerke went into receivership in 1931 the time appeared ripe for immediate controlling action to be taken on the part of the state, which orchestrated the merger of Focke-Wulf and Albatros under the direction of Kurt Tank. In January 1932 it appointed Walter Blume, the former technical director at Albatros, to be the new technical director of the Arado Handels Gesellschaft in place of Walter Rethel. At the same time Arado was forced to accept seven of Blume's former colleagues, including Wilhelm Blass, Oskar Liebing, Franz Meyer and Walter Reinhardt. Long-time company managers felt cast aside. The exclusion of company director Otto Affeldt, chief of administra-

H. Lübbe's withdrawal of a loan to the Arado Handels Gesellschaft (2 November 1932 -above).

Transfer document of the Arado Handels Gesellschaft for advance and interim payments on behalf of the Reichsverkehrsmininisterium (17 August 1932 — left).

49

tion Sieke and technical operations manager Fridolin Keidel, a friend of Lübbe's who was forced to leave the company because of sketchy demands made by radical members the works committee, further weakened the position of the company's owners. Sieke went to the Bachmann company in Ribnitz, Affeldt to Curt Heber in Berlin-Britz, and Keidel was employed as a flight engineer at the Warnemünde seaplane station.

Walter Blume was borne on 10 January 1896 in Hirschberg, Silesia. Following his graduation and a short stint as an engineer's apprentice, he volunteered for military service at the outbreak of the First World War. He was awarded his pilot's license on 30 March 1916 and in 1917 was assigned as fighter pilot to Staffel 25, led by Bruno Loerzer and Hermann Göring. In 1918 he became commander of Jagdstaffel 9. Blume scored 28 victories during the war and was presented the 'Pour le Mérite'. In 1919 he began studying at the Technische Hochschule Hannover with his former squadron mate and later sailplane record holder Fritz Heinrich Hentzen, but these studies were interrupted several times. In the summer of 1919 he served as a pilot with the mobile Reichswehr airbase in Döberitz and in the spring of 1920 was a temporary volunteer flyer with the courier squadron of Reichswehrbrigade 10. He worked for a brief period with the 'Rumpler-Ozeanflug GmbH' in Berlin during 1922 and played a role in that company's project for transatlantic aircraft. Working with the Akademische Fliegergruppe Hannover, Blume was also involved in the design of the 'Vampyr' sailplane conceived by Professor Madelung.

After eventually receiving his engineering degree, in 1924 he developed two lightplanes in a trial workshop operated jointly with Hentzen in Berlin-Adlershof. From 1924 to 1926 he was active as a consulting engineer with the Inspektion für Waffen und Gerät, before becoming chief engineer at Albatros in the autumn of 1926. At Albatros, he was involved in the design of various lightplanes developed for sport and training, most of which were produced as biplanes of conventional composite design and built in small numbers. His appointment was not unanimously welcomed within the firm, since many of the managing directors felt that, in contrast to Rethel, Blume was not automatically qualified for the technical administration of a company which was already producing well-recognized fighter types. Although the decision involuntarily pushed the long-time and experienced chief designer Walter Rethel into the background, Arado was forced to accept the appointment of Blume, an appointment which had been driven by influential circles within the Reichwehr and which was in all likelihood a prerequisite for a large contract being issued for the Ar 66 trainer.

From early on the future Reichsluftfahrtminister, Hermann Göring, had taken great pains to maneuver his flying comrades from the First World War into leadership positions. This was how, according to his own words, Carl-August von Schoenebeck became chief pilot of the Arado Handels Gesellschaft in 1931 after six years in Lipetsk "since Berlin placed great faith in my ability to advise the German industry in developing fighter planes based on my experience with single-seaters."[40] He described further developments as follows: "There began for me a quite active period of flying, since all companies such as Arado, Heinkel, Junkers and Dornier now began developing specific types, trainers as well as military aircraft, which demanded a lot

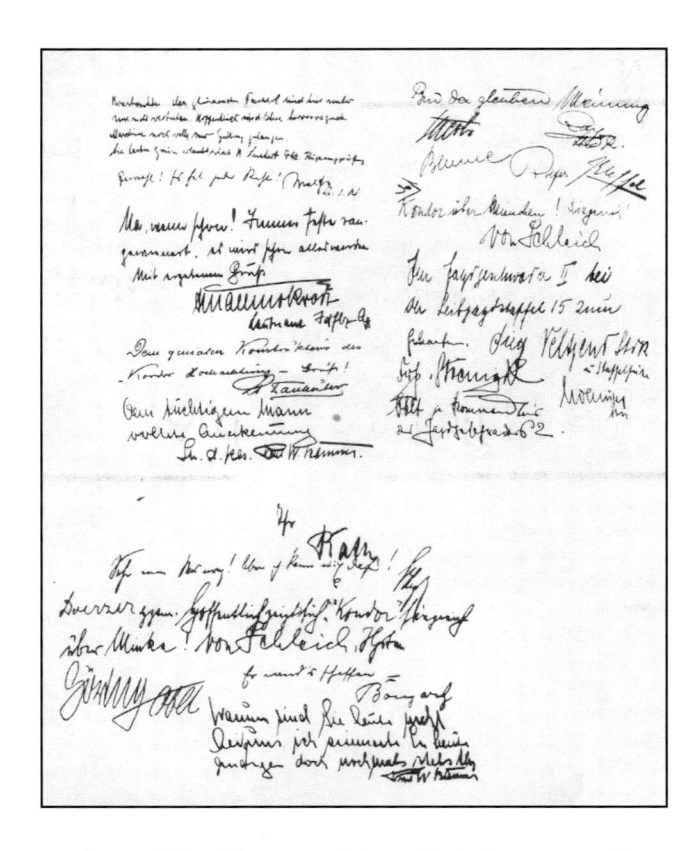

Above: Walter Blume as a fighter pilot in the First World War.
Below: Congratulations to W. Rethel with the signatures of the pilots W. Blume (above right) and H. Göring (below left).

of work. An entire decade for development had been lost through the Treaty of Versailles. The Arado 65 (developed specially by me) was the fighter which later became the standard weapon of fighter pilots." Von Schoenebeck, who familiarized the DVS fighter pilots with the latest Arado designs, had a 'good and independent position' at Arado.[41] He described his role in the appointment of Walter Blume as follows: "My employment at Arado often brought me in contact with the future RLM in Berlin, with my friend Ernst Udet and General Milch. Göring was in Berlin as well, and in earlier days I had often helped him sell his parachutes. In addition to Arado there was also the naval aviator's school, with which we had close contact. Among other things, we regularly visited the home of the aircraft designer Heinkel ... Oberst a.D. Wagenführ and Major a.D. Serno could also be included among the managing directors, they also sat in Berlin. In Warnemünde the company was directed by chief designer Rethel, later by Walter Blume, a Pour le Mérite fighter pilot form the First World War. He had earlier worked at Albatros and I then brought him to Arado."

After the National Socialists came to power, on 26 February 1933 a proclamation was issued for the creation of an independent Reichsluftwaffe with Hermann Göring as the Reichsluftfahrtminister. His state secretary, Erhard Milch, had previously worked for Junkers and had been on the board of directors at Luft Hansa. In addition to the formation of a strict and ideologically regimented command structure, the ministry was interested in the rapid expansion of the aviation industry's production capacity. In a secret memorandum from 20 May 1933 it reads: "our current state in the air leaves us virtually defenseless if war were to break out now ... ways and means must therefore be found to improve and overcome this condition."[42] In April 1933 Göring introduced his cabinet at a conference of German aviation industrialists and announced that it is now a matter of German equality in the air. He would carry on this

Carl-August v. Schoenebeck, who in 1930 became the first military test pilot at Arado, seen here as a fighter pilot in World War I.

W. Blume wearing the Pour le Mérite in the uniform of the Standartenführer of the Nationalsozialistisches Fliegerkorps (NSFK — left).

battle with the passion and aggressiveness which had been said of the old National Socialists until he knew that the safety of the German nation had been achieved. He gave assurances that the government would make generous credit available to the aircraft industry beginning immediately. Göring used the same rhetoric at an industrial conference on 20 October, where he was greeted by the assembly with outstretched arms in solemn silence. He told the group that he'd received instructions from the Führer to "within a year bring about the change to Germany's position in the realm of aviation."

The promised financial backing for air armament had already been approved by the cabinet on 2 February 1933. After an initial emergency measure of 40 million RM had been approved, within the first six months of 1933 over 53 million RM in armament contracts had been divided among the six most important firms.[43] Arado was included in this program, receiving 5,849,000 RM worth of contracts.

On the 10th of June 1933 Milch signed an "order for secret contracts within the Reichsluftfahrtministerium", wherein all agreements were to be handled exclusively through an internal "Cashier's Office L.'" "The fact that brisk activity in the realm of aircraft construction and training is being implemented won't be hidden from the eyes of foreign governments" stated an internal RLM statement from 25 July 1933. "Nevertheless, it is necessary to conduct our affairs so that it will be impossible for these foreign governments to have proof of violations against the current foreign political restraints."

Plans were made to have 225 front-line aircraft by 1 April 1934, to include the creation of six fighter squadrons of nine airplanes each. One year later it was decided to increase the number of front-line aircraft to 450 and the individual fighter squadrons to twelve.

An effort to bring Arado into line was made manifest in a modified board of director's agreement dated 4 March 1933. Erich Serno, the company's former authorized signatory, was appointed alongside Felix Wagenführ as the second senior partner.[44] The company name was changed to the Arado Flugzeugwerke. The entry in the Berlin court records to this effect occurred on 7 April, with the entry in the Warnemünde land register following on 19 May.

Beginning with the Ar 64 model, future designation of aircraft was to be 'Ar'. The Arado company logo disappeared from the fin with the Ar 65 and was replaced by the swastika.

The increased flow of the state's financial support corresponded to an expansion of the Arado Flugzeugwerke's production capacity.

By exercising an existing right-of-purchase option the Arado Flugzeugwerke in Warnemünde obtained additional space north of the existing facilities for the purpose of in-

Advertisement of the Arado Flugzeugwerke (Arado Bote).

The company's registry application, dated 7 April 1933, following changes made to the deed of association on 4 and 29 March 1933; notice the initial use of the title "Arado Flugzeugwerke."

Above: Arado Flugzeugwerke. Main offices in Berlin, Budapester Str. 45 (circa 1934). Below: Arado Flugzeugwerke. Brandenburg facilities (1939).

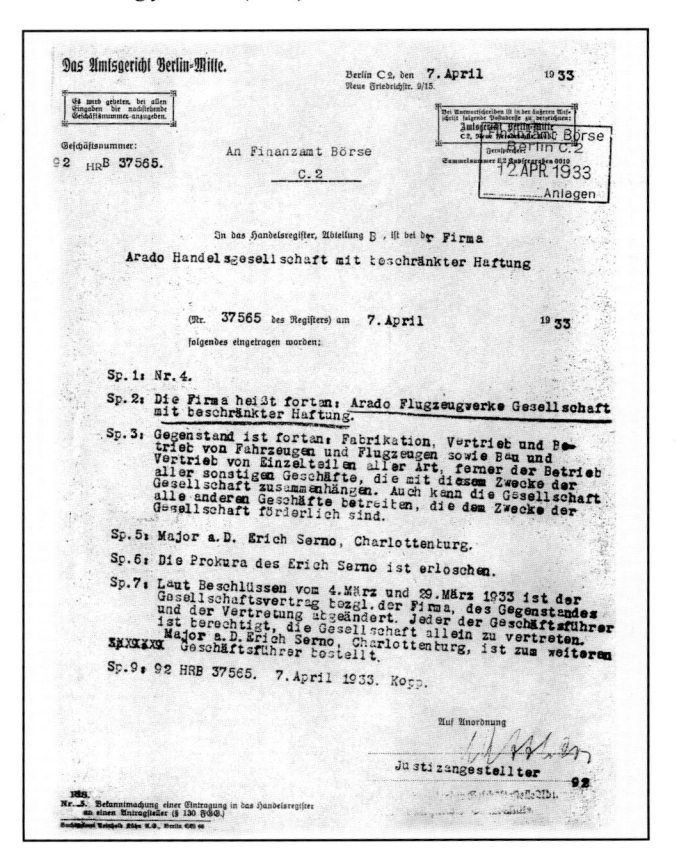

The design bureau after its move to the Wilhelm-Bahms-Strasse in Brandenburg (1936).

creasing its production capacity. As a 13 September 1934 document concerning the applicable boundary negotiations shows, by this time significant expansion of the company facilities had already taken place. In 1936 the Chemische und Teerproduktenfabrik Warnemünde GmbH, located on the south side of the Laak Canal, was acquired. A company airfield was built on land which had been drained from around the Laak Inlet.

On 6 September 1934, the first of six branches was founded with the purchase of the company buildings of the former Hartungsche Eisengiesserei in Brandenburg. Initially, the design bureau was moved from Warnemünde to Brandenburg, before modest production began in February 1935 and, on 11 April 1935 the first airplane (an Ar 66) was test flown. At the insistence of the RLM the Arado Handels Gesellschaft had purchased a shut-down factory in Potsdam-Babelsberg at the end of 1933. It was into the administration building of this factory that the main administration center (formerly in Berlin) was moved on 25 June 1936.[45] Later, the remaining Babelsberg facilities served to relieve the Brandenburg factory of its production of turned pieces. The Anklam branch began operations in the spring of 1937, followed by Wittenberg and Rathenow that summer and Brandenburg-Neuendorf in 1938. In October 1941 the facilities of the Märkisches Metallbau were taken over. By 1942 18 and licensed construction repair facilities had been established both at home and abroad.

Confidentially classified HSK statistics show a rapid expansion of the corporation from 1932 to 1942. The site's built-up area increased from an initial 48,000 square meters in 1934 to 79,000 square meters in 1935.[46] The number of personnel on 31 December 1932 was 287 in Warnemünde, climbed to 753 by the end of 1933 before reaching a total of 2,485 employees at Warnemünde and Brandenburg at the end of 1934. According to the HSK statistics, in October 1935 Arado's number of employed personnel at Warnemünde and Brandenburg came to a total of 3,749, but reaching 6,785 by year's end. After a relative slow down to 8,875 by the end of 1936, the number of employees rose to 10,428 at the end of 1937 and by the end of 1938 had reached 14,577. While Arado had jumped from fifth to fourth place among the German aviation companies from 1935 to 1938, it took the forefront in 1940 with 22,000 and

in 1942 with 27,000 employees. According to data from the Reichsverband der Deutschen Luftfahrtindustrie, in 1943 the organization was in third place, just behind Heinkel, with 26,800 workers. In 1944 Arado dropped to fourth place behind Messerschmitt. The corporation reached its highest employee number on 30 June 1944 with 30,670 workers.

Employment Figures for	July 1935	(October 1938)
Junkers	9,483	(25,855)
Heinkel	7,611	(18,297)
Dornier	7,080	(15,344)
ATG	3,902	(6,356)
Arado	3,749	(14,090)
Henschel	3,672	(8,851)
Focke-Wulf	3,174	(8,428)
Bayerische Flugzeugwerke	2,344	(9,257)

Arado		Werk Warnemünde				Seite 3	

"Verzeichnis der Bauwerke".

Lf. Nr.	Art	Zweck	Im Werk übliche Bezeichnung	+	++	bebaute Fläche qm	umbaut Raum cbm
1	Geschoßbau	Wirtschafts-gebäude	Gebäude K	N	1/2	2890	15 882
2	Baracken	Unterkünfte	Wohnbaracken	N	1	1220	3 410
3	Geschoßbau	Wohlfahrts-räume u. Bloxalbad	Halle M (a und b)	E	1	--	--
4	Geschoßbau	Fahrzeuggeb.	Gebäude W	N	1	770	3 475
5	" "	Trafogebäude	Gebäude X	N	1	320	1 770
6	" "	Pumpenhaus	" Y	N	1	45	135
7	Tankanlage	-	Tankanlage	A	-	--	--
8	Abbrems-platte	-	Abbremsplatte	A	-	--	--
9	Kohlenbun-ker	-	Kohlenbunker	A	-	--	--
10	Halle	Montage	Halle K	Ab	-	--	--
11	Geschoßbau	Pumpenraum	Heizhaus Q	U	1	--	--
12	" "	Abortanlage	Block D 3	U	1	108	408
13	" "	" "	Heizhaus F	U	1	143	543
14	Halle	" "	Halle G	U	1	285	1 710
15	Geschoßbau	Abortanlage	Block E 1	U	1	59	240
16	" "	Prüfabteilg.	MP	U	1	550	2 750
17	Geschoßbau	Schmiede u. Bloxalbad	Block E 2	U	1	364	1 457
18	Kläranlage	--	Schlammtrocken-beete	A	-	--	--
19	Schutzräu-me	Luftschutz	Luftschutzräume	A	-	--	--

Bemerkung:

+ N = Neubau   ++ Anzahl der Geschosse.
  E = Erweiterungsbau
  A = Außenanlagen
  Ab= Abbruch
  U = Umbau

Bearbeiter:

Invoice showing expansion of the facilities in Warnemünde (10 September 1939).

Chapter 8
Foundation of the New Luftwaffe
The Ar 66, 69, 76 and 77 Trainers
The Ar 66 trainer

After Walter Rethel's Ar 65 fighter proved itself to be a great design, it was only a matter of time before Arado would be awarded contracts for the development of military training aircraft. Accordingly, project designs began appearing in 1930. However, at that time the Deutsche Verkehrsflieger Schule(DVS) did not have sufficient funds available, and no contract awards were immediately forthcoming. Nevertheless, the Arado Handels Gesellschaft continued developmental work at its own expense. When the first prototype of the Ar 66 A trainer (Wk.Nr. 78) was given civil registration D-2335 in September 1932 and two competing designs proved unsatisfactory, the test center of the Reichsverband der Deutschen Luftfahrtindustrie(RDL) in Staaken began flight testing the Arado design.

It was a stagger-wing biplane of composite construction. An Argus As 10 engine with 200 hp was sufficient to power the light twin-seat aircraft, but limited it to a maximum speed of 200 km/h. Its main unique feature was the fact that the tailplane, set unusually high, was attached well forward of the tailfin. The Ar 66 C and Ar 66 D versions,

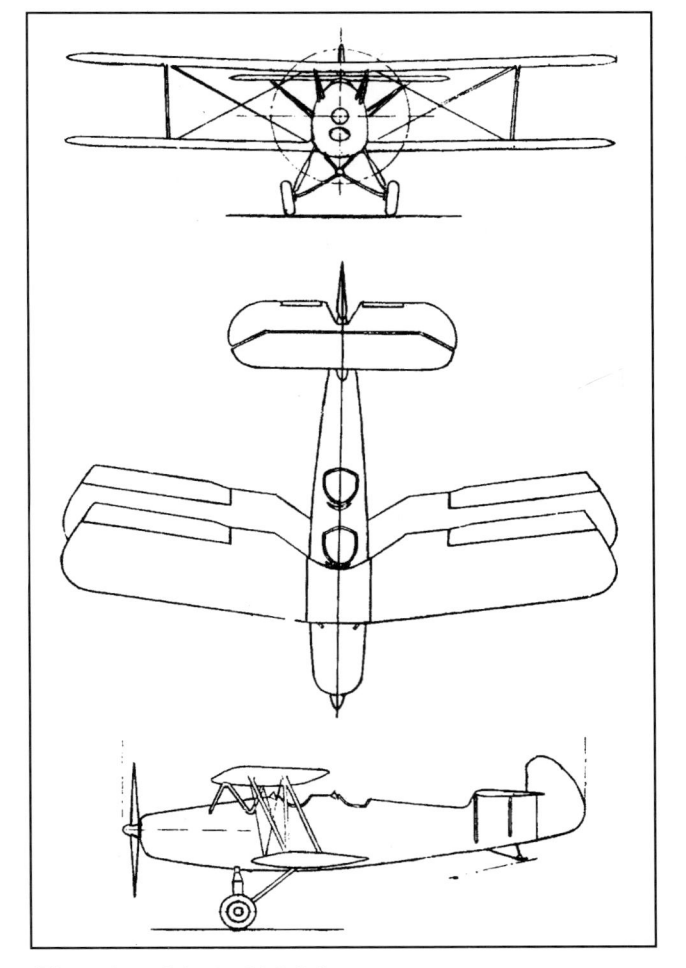

produced in quantity beginning in 1933, had an improved undercarriage with oil-cushioned spring struts, wheel brakes and low-pressure tires, counterbalanced ailerons on both upper and lower wings as well as vertical and horizontal stabilizers with horn balances. It was powered by an Argus As 10C-2 engine having an output of 240 hp. The aircraft, of which ten examples of the Ar 66 B floatplane were also built, could be used as a primary trainer and a single seat fighter-trainer, for training machine gun operators, radio operators, bombardiers and aerial photographers, as well as for aerobatic, blind- and night-flying.

For many years, virtually all pilots came in contact with the Ar 66 trainer at some point during their training period. The first contract was for 320 machines. With the sudden increase in production, it became necessary to adjust to new planning and production methods. By 1932 the total yearly production of the Arado Handels Gesellschaft was at just 19 aircraft, with a minimum of four machines produced in 1930. Arado was in ninth place among the aircraft companies at the time with a total output of 82 aircraft by 1932. Because of an initial lack of production capacity for large-scale production at Arado, license building of the Ar 66 took place at Miag, BFW and the Gothaer Waggonfabrik. In 1936, the Bayerische Flugzeugwerke was assigned the

Ar 66 C, D-IDEZ (above). Ar 66 C, D-IRNY (below).

production of 88 license-built models. According to company records a total run of 1315 aircraft was planned. The quota of 712 machines to be built by 30 April 1936 was exceeded by 20 aircraft. In 1936 270 machines were delivered, 109 in the following year.

The type found considerable favor due to its general 'goodnaturedness'. Despite being used on a wide scale, there

Three-view of the Ar 66 C fighter-trainer (1932).

54

Ar 66 squadron of the Deutscher Luftfahrt Verein (DLV) in Hamburg (above). Ar 66 B/See (below).

Ar 66 Cs, D-ISEQ and D-IUHA, flying in formation (above).

Ar 66 C, D-IOVN, seen after a crash landing .

were relatively few serious accidents with the type, not counting the fateful collision of an Ar 66 with a Ju 52 over Hamburg on 9 May 1935. For the first time, Arado published eye-catching multi-language advertisements. A cameraman filmed spectacular air-to-air footage from an Ar 66 for the 1938 Ufa film 'Pour le Mérite'. In 1939 the type

performed aerial reconnaissance duties over the Danzig Corridor, and soldiered on to serve during the early stages of the war.[47] Even as late as 1943 the Ar 66 was used in Nachtschlachtgruppen to conduct harassment strikes behind the Eastern Front.

Remains of an Ar 66 C are located in the Keski-Suomen Ilmailumuseo in Tikkakoski, Finland. In the Deutsches Museum in Munich is the wreck of an Ar 66 D (Wk.Nr. 1198, delivered in 1936) which was recovered from the bottom of the Starnberger See on 13 November 1983. The airplane had taken off from a field airstrip near Zwickau on 9 April 1945. The date, the direction of the flight and the unusually long route to the crash site lead one to suspect that this was no 'training flight', as was claimed at the time.

The Ar 69 Trainer

Between 1934 and 1935 Arado produced further military trainers in smaller quantities, most of them to compete with Focke-Wulf. The Ar 69, a 'training, sport and touring airplane' was developed parallel to the Fw 44. It would serve as an interim design in the continued development of fighter aircraft. The sharply staggered wings were both long and swept back 10 degrees. A noticeable design feature was the typical layout of the empennage, first introduced by Walter Blume on the Ar 67. The fin was set forward of the tailplane, a feature which reduced the effects of a spin on the static and aerodynamically balanced rudder. The ability to control an aircraft during spins was considered critical for military operations, so testing this feature played a major role during flight testing of the prototype and production aircraft.

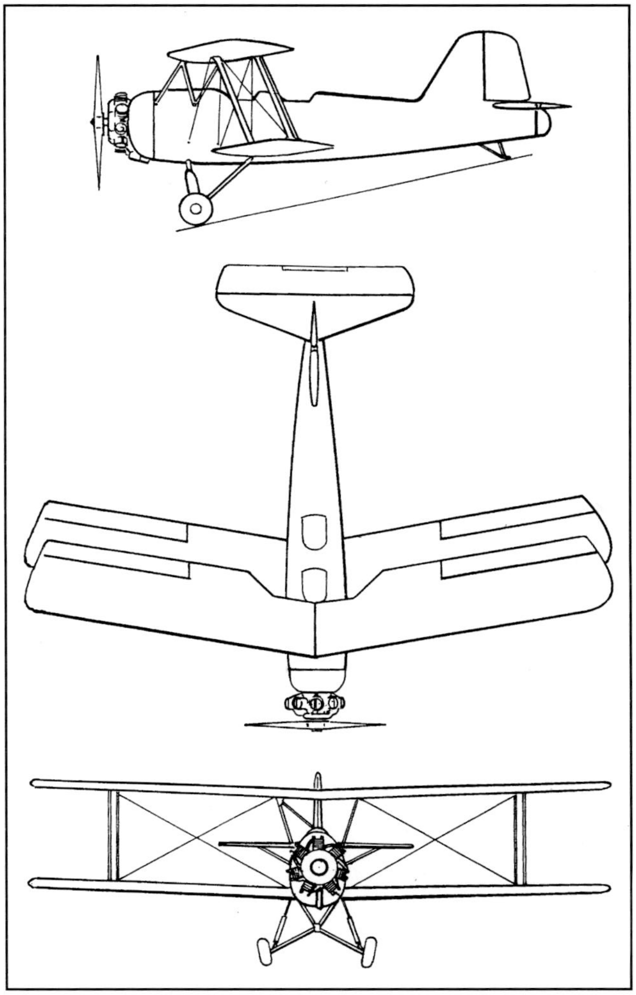

The A-model, shown at the XIV Paris Aero-Salon and weighing just 505 kg empty, was fitted with an Argus As 8 B engine of 135 hp. The B-model had a Siemens Sh 14 A engine of 150 hp, giving it a speed of 184 km/h. Company records show that the total production run of seven aircraft had been completed by 30 April 1936.

In 1936 a requirement was issued for an aerobatic, single-seat trainer for advanced pilot students, which despite low engine performance could also be used as a point defense fighter. Arado entered the competition with its high-wing Ar 76. This wing design had been recommended in the requirement, which also enticed Henschel, Focke-Wulf and Heinkel, due to its improved visibility. Arado's design once again made use of a forward rudder, with an Argus As 10C engine serving as a powerplant. In 1934 the first prototype began flight testing. The aircraft was fitted with one to two MG 17s and a bomb magazine. During a fly-off in Rechlin, the Arado design took second place behind the Focke-Wulf Fw 56 'Stösser'. Production contracts were placed with both companies. The aircraft, which was produced in larger numbers that originally projected, was also planned for export and was shown at the Stockholm 'ILIS' exhibition in 1936. Company records show that a planned output of 182 machines was expected. The quota of 158 aircraft to be produced by 30 April 1936 was exceeded by 18. With 105 aircraft delivered that year, the major portion of total production was achieved in 1936.

The Ar 77 Trainer

Among the trainers developed by Arado up to 1935 was the low-wing cantilevered Ar 77. This time, the tailplane was moved forward and set high on the fin, braced to the fuselage with N-struts. In the forward, open part of the cockpit there was room for an instructor and student; the rear portion was enclosed and designed for a radio operator and observer. For the first time Arado made use of wood-metal bonding methods. The outer wing joints were made of Nudu plates, made by bonding walnut and Duraluminum together.

Ar 66 C, D-IZOF. In 1939 this aircraft was used as the camera platform for outside filming in the Ufa film "Pour le Mérite."

Ar 66 B/See, D-2557 (above left).

The Ar 69 trainer. Three-view (1934).

Nose and underside were metal plated. The step from composite construction to an all-metal design had not yet been made, however, nor was a retractable landing gear incorporated into the design. The two Argus As 10C engines, each having 240 hp, gave the plane a top speed of 243 km/h. The aircraft was the largest plane built by Arado up to

Ar 69 A, D-2822, with the Argus As 8 B engine (135 hp. — above).

Ar 69 B, D-EPYT, with Siemens Sh 14 A engine (150 hp. — above right).

The Ar 76 single-seat fighter-trainer. Three-view (1934).

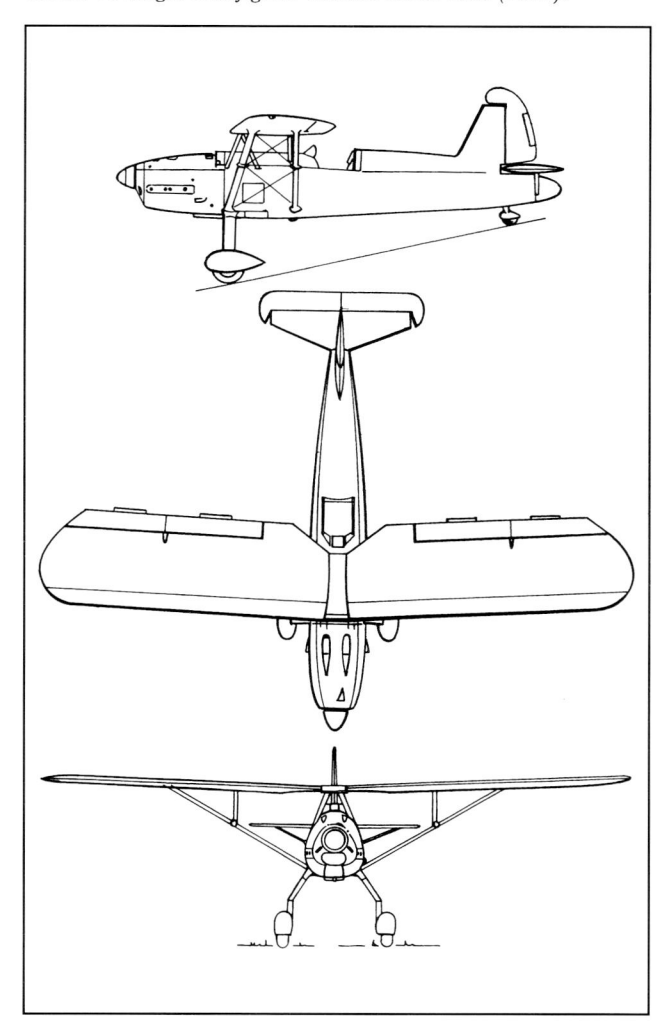

The prototype Ar 76 V 1 D-IRAS (Wk. Nr. 365), registered as a "sportplane", displaying the Arado company logo and the swastika on the tailfin.

Ar 76, D-IXUS.

Ar 76, D-IQUO.

that point, having a wingspan of 19.20 m and a weight of 2,940 kg. Although it was planned as a multi-purpose aircraft, especially in the role of a 'feeder airplane', its primary function (as with the competing Fw 58) was training pilots on twin-engine aircraft as well as radio operator and observer training. Equipment for blind flying, radio operation, navigation and night flying was also provided.

Ar 77.

Three-view of the Ar 77 twin-engine trainer (1935).

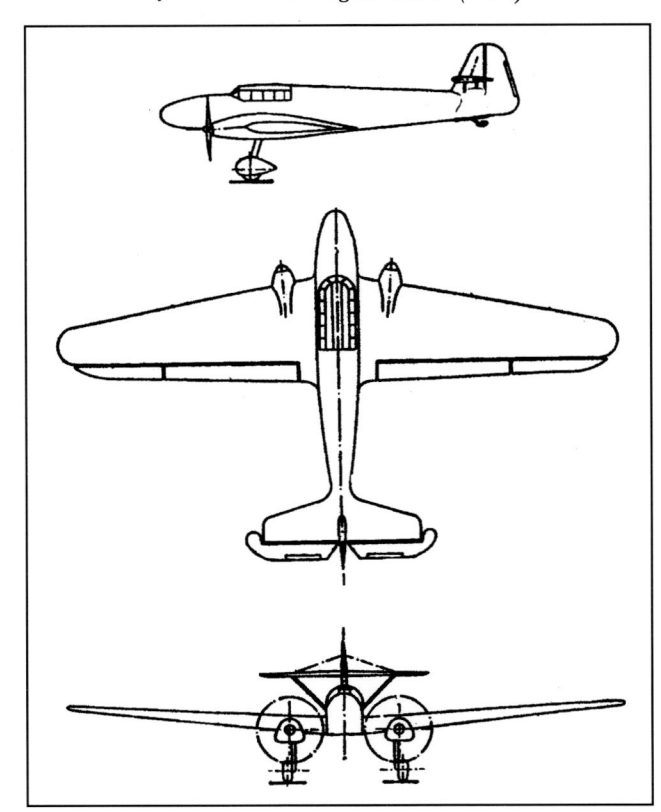

Despite a good evaluation in Rechlin, there was some reluctance to certify the aircraft because of a conflict regarding the sturdiness of the wing joints. Only a single prototype was built, registered as D-ABIM in 1934.

The Ar 67 and 68 Fighters

The Ar 67 prototype, conceived in 1932 as part of the continuing development of fighter design, was a biplane using the standard composite construction with forward-set tailfin. The lower wing was relatively large compared to the upper wing to provide enough area for the full-span landing flaps to work effectively. Even though the ailerons (located in the upper wing only) had been designed with quite generous dimensions, their effectiveness in achieving the desired roll rate was reduced by the damping caused by the large lower wing. The Rolls-Royce Kestrel engine, a highly-regarded British motor, provided less power than the BMW engine used in its predecessor, the Ar 65. It was hoped that the lower flying weight and aerodynamic improvements would give the aircraft a top speed of 340 km/h. But the drop in rpms due to the propeller, which had been designed for higher altitudes, led to a significant reduction in the engine's performance at ground level. Instead of the 640 hp which could be attained at 4,200 m altitude with a full weight, the performance at ground level was just 525 hp. Because of this lackluster takeoff and speed capability, and with a view to the Ar 68 follow-on design, only a single prototype was built in 1933.

The Ar 68 fighter continued with the biplane design favored by Rethel. The first prototype, D-IKIN (Wk.Nr. 99), was fitted with the BMW VI engine developed in 1929. The engine's main disadvantages were that it had a continuous rating of only 550 hp, ill-suited for higher altitudes, and the engine design itself, with the cylinders jutting upward from the fuselage, not only hindering the pilot's visibility but placing him unprotected in the exhaust path as well. For this reason Heinkel, which used the same engine in its competing He 51 design, installed the exhaust system facing downward, thereby reducing the aerodynamic qualities of the aircraft. Junkers began offering its new 12-cylinder Jumo 210 in 1935, which had an inverted V design of-

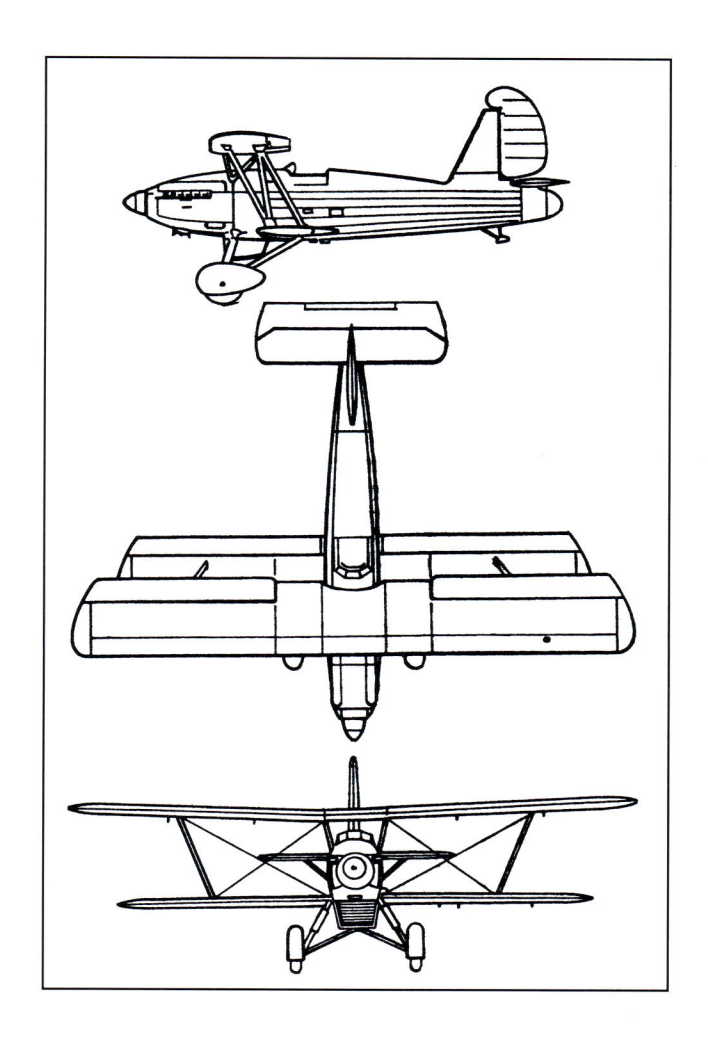

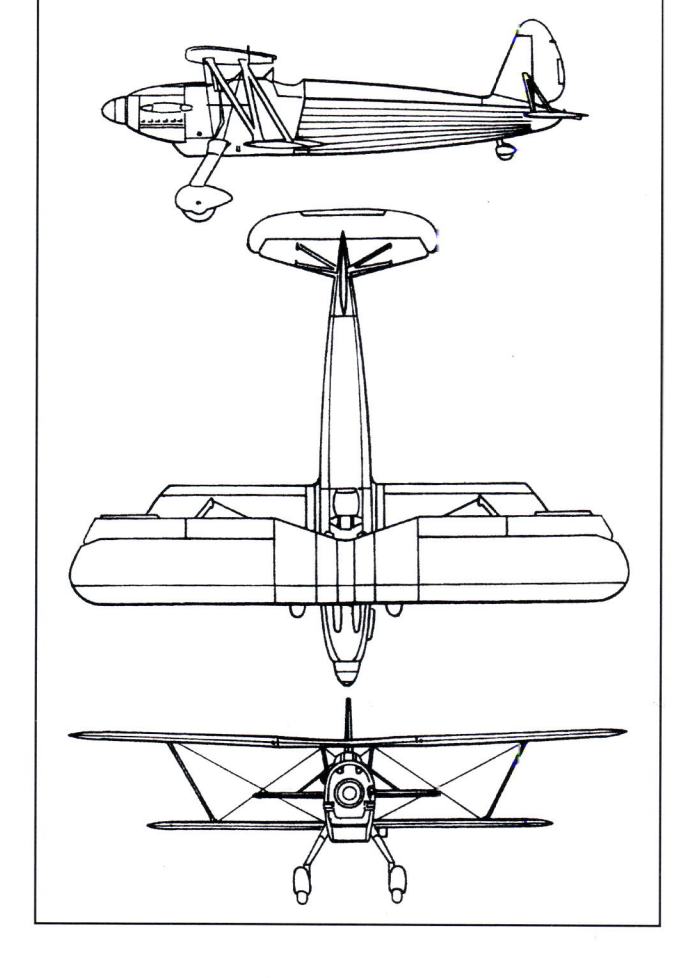

The Ar 67 single-seat fighter with a newly designed forward-set tailfin. Three-view (1933 — above left).

Three-view of the Ar 68 E single-seat fighter (1935).

Ar 68 V 1, D-IKIN (Wk. Nr. 99) with BMW VId (left).

Ar 68 B V 2, D-IVUS, with twelve-cylinder Jumo 210 engine (610 hp) flying over the Warnow (1935 — below)

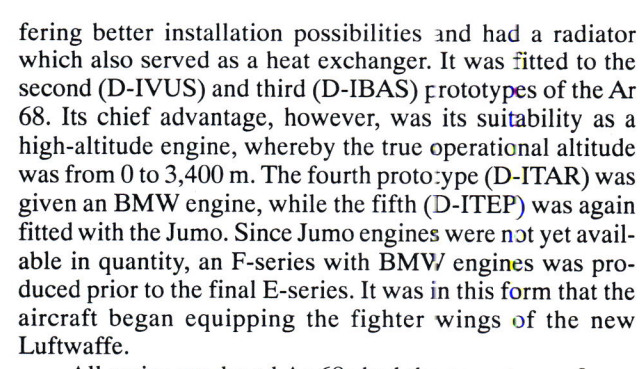

fering better installation possibilities and had a radiator which also served as a heat exchanger. It was fitted to the second (D-IVUS) and third (D-IBAS) prototypes of the Ar 68. Its chief advantage, however, was its suitability as a high-altitude engine, whereby the true operational altitude was from 0 to 3,400 m. The fourth prototype (D-ITAR) was given an BMW engine, while the fifth (D-ITEP) was again fitted with the Jumo. Since Jumo engines were not yet available in quantity, an F-series with BMW engines was produced prior to the final E-series. It was in this form that the aircraft began equipping the fighter wings of the new Luftwaffe.

All series-produced Ar 68s had the same type of construction. The fuselage of the sesquiplane was made of the standard steel tubing design and metal-plated from the cockpit forward and along the spine up to the empennage. Fuselage sides and underside were covered in cloth. The fixed, aerodynamically shrouded undercarriage had shock-absorbing struts with oil damping. The tailwheel was fitted with a compressed rubber shock absorber. The upper of the two wings, both of which were covered in plywood and cloth, had the ailerons and was attached to the fuselage in the center by a cabane using N-struts, while the lower wing was fixed directly to the lower part of the fuselage and had metal-covered landing flaps. The empennage was made of a metal skeleton, with the tailplane and fin covered in sheet metal and the control surfaces covered with cloth. The one-piece horizontal stabilizer was set far back and low and was fitted with trim tabs which could be adjusted in-flight. Both parts of the tail were braced to each other using V-struts to increase the sturdiness of the design. Two MG 17s, located in the upper engine cowling, served as the aircraft's armament. Some airplanes were also fitted with a bomb bay for six SC 10 bombs. By reducing the number of tension cables and stretching the fuselage slightly to the rear, Arado created a particularly elegant, maneuverable and non-spinning aircraft. Ernst Udet, at the time the Generalluftzeugmeister, personally took the controls during a fly-off with the He 51; in a mock dogfight he playfully flew circles around his 'enemy'. After the Ar 68 G project was canceled due to the absence of an adequate high-altitude engine, at the end of 1936 Arado produced the Ar 68 H prototype (D-ISIX), which had a cockpit enclosed beneath a sliding canopy and was the first German fighter to be fitted with the nine-cylinder BMW 132 Da, a license-produced Pratt & Whitney Hornet. The performance of the 850-hp radial engine gave the aircraft a maximum speed of around 400 km/h and a ceiling of over 9,000 m.

Ar 68 F of JG 134 "Horst Wessel" (1937 — right).

A squadron of Ar 68 F fighters (below).

Ar 68 V 3, D-IBAS, with Jumo 210, new radiator and two MG 17s. Prototype for the C-series (above).

Ar 68 F. Production version with BMW VId engine (right).

According to company files dated 20 April 1936, total production was to have been 324 units. A quota of 63 machines was to have been manufactured by this date, but only ten were actually delivered by then. In 1936 302 aircraft were delivered, with 73 the following year. By 31 March 1938 total production had risen to 514 aircraft.

The Ar 68, along with the He 51 (of which 506 examples had been built — some by Arado — by 31 March 1938), became the first standard aircraft to equip the Luftwaffe's seven fighter squadrons.[48] Two squadrons of these aircraft took part in the reoccupation of the Rhineland. Two E-series were combat-tested in the Spanish Civil War in 1938. When the Second World War broke out, 28 Ar 68 Es were still in service in one of the 17 fighter groups, employed as night fighters against British bombers.

1935-36 Production Figures for Fighter Aircraft:

Type	To 1 Oct 1936	To 31 Mar 1938	Total
He 51	504	2	506
Ar 64/65	189	0	189
Ar 68	242	272	514

Ar 68 E. Production model powered by the Jumo 210 engine (right).

Ar 68 H, V 1, D-ISIX, with BMW radial engine.

Ar 68 E.

Test Flights of Company Test Pilot Richard Perlia, 2/5/1936 — 3/16/1936:[49]

2/5	Ar 76 (1379)	D-IJMA	2/26	Ar 76 (1732)	D-IZVA
2/9	Ar 68 (1305)	D-IXUQ		Ar 68 (1607)	
2/10	Ar 76 (1399)	D-IDPA		Ar 76 (1734)	D-IXPO
	Ar 68 (99)	D-IKIN	2/27	Ar 68 (1610)	D-IRVO
2/11	Ar 76 (1388)	D-IDPA	2/28	Ar 76 (363)	
2/14	Ar 68 (99)	D-IKIN		Ar 68 (1608)	
2/15	Ar 68 (1305)	D-IXUQ	3/3	Ar 76 (1235)	D-ITRE
2/18	Ar 76 (1398)	D-IRTE		Ar 76 (1727)	D-IAMI
2/19	Ar 76 (1394)	D-ISBO	3/6	Ar 76 (1235)	D-ITRE
	Ar 76 (1396)	D-IXKO	3/7	Ar 76 (1735)	
2/20	Ar 76 (1398)	D-IRTE	3/9	Ar 76 (1738)	D-IJRJ
2/21	Ar 76 (1398)	D-IRTE	3/10	Ar 76 (1798)	
	Ar 76 (1728)	D-IBME	3/14	Ar 68 (1609)	
	Ar 68 (1604)	D-IFZA		Ar 66 (1111)	
2/22	Ar 76 (1722)	D-IAMI		Ar 68 (1112)	
	Ar 76 (1729)	D-IHGO	3/16	Ar 66 (1110)	

Chapter 9
The New Generation of Aircraft

The Jump to an All-Metal Monoplane: The Ar 80 Fighter

In early 1933 Arado and Heinkel submitted preliminary design studies to the Amt for a new-generation fighter. A requirement was issued that same year, which not only included Heinkel's He 112, but also permitted Focke-Wulf to submit its Fw 159. The Bayerische Flugzeugwerke also eventually took part with the Bf 109. It was expected that Arado or Heinkel would win the competition.

The C-Amt called for a cantilever low-wing all-metal design, paying particular attention to aerodynamic shape, good turning and roll capabilities, absolute robustness in a dive and flawless spin-handling characteristics.

The forward fuselage of the Ar 80 was made of the usual welded steel tubing. The frame was covered with removable panels made of aluminum, ensuring easy accessibility to all installed components during maintenance. The rear part of the fuselage was made of a light metal skinning using longitudinal panels. In order to achieve a double oval fuselage the smooth panels were stave cut, interchanged with bevel-edged grooved profile panels. Once the profile panels had been laid onto the formers and attached using tacking bolts, they were machine riveted together with the smooth panels. Then both half-panels were affixed by hand riveting.

In a lecture, Rethel described the 'Arado method for monocoque fuselage construction' which he developed as follows:

1. Producing a double oval skin by reducing as much cupellation as possible and keeping a smooth, clean aerodynamic profile,

2. Use of standard tooling machinery, dispensing with the need for specialized equipment,
3. Creation of standard semi-finished material, suitable for various fuselage types,
4. Option of machine riveting/electric spot welding,
5. Use of assembly-line materials, even for the skin.[50]

From a manufacturing standpoint, the slender longitudinally-running panels had an advantage over lateral panels — cutting them to shape was easier. However, this fundamentally sound and simple method of construction had the disadvantage of not permitting any variation in the sheet metal gauge, so that the fuselage was 16 percent heavier than proposed and the number of rivets was relatively high — not only increasing the weight but also manufacturing requirements.

The outer wings were fitted with landing flaps and were of all-metal construction. The steel-tube center sections, covered in formed sheet metal, were of the same inverted gull design introduced by Heinkel in 1932 on its He 70 high-speed airliner; this feature kept the length of the landing gear struts as short as possible. The cantilever control surfaces had trim tabs and balance horns.

The first Ar 80 prototype (D-IRLI) was given an open single-seat cockpit and the strongest foreign engine then available, the Rolls-Royce Kestrel V with 695 hp. The RLM had obtained four of these coveted engines from England and had made two of these available to the Bayerische Flugzeugwerke, with Arado and Heinkel receiving just one each.

Ar 80, V 2, D-ILOH, fitted with Rolls-Royce Kestrel V engine.

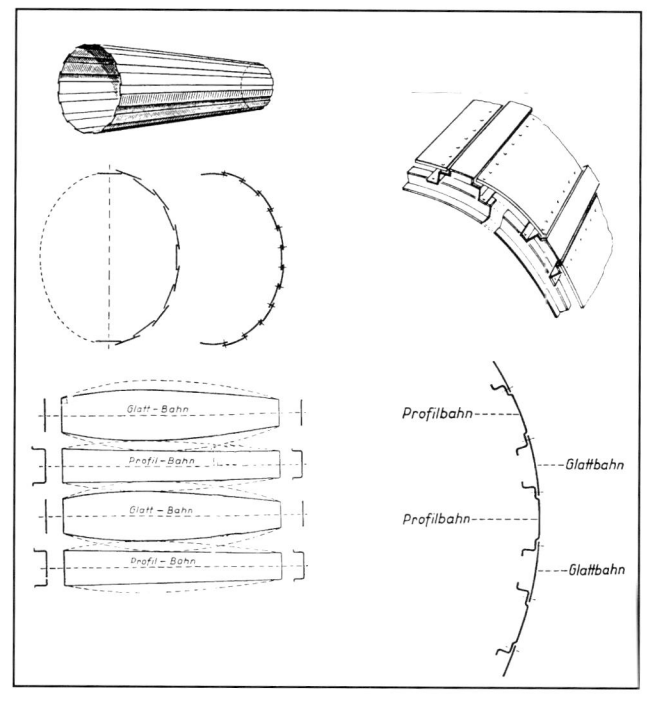

Ar 80. Schematic drawing showing the fuselage covering (W. Rethel). From above: Monocoque design with overlapping longitudinal panels. The finished fuselage skin. Alternating use of smooth and grooved profile panels.

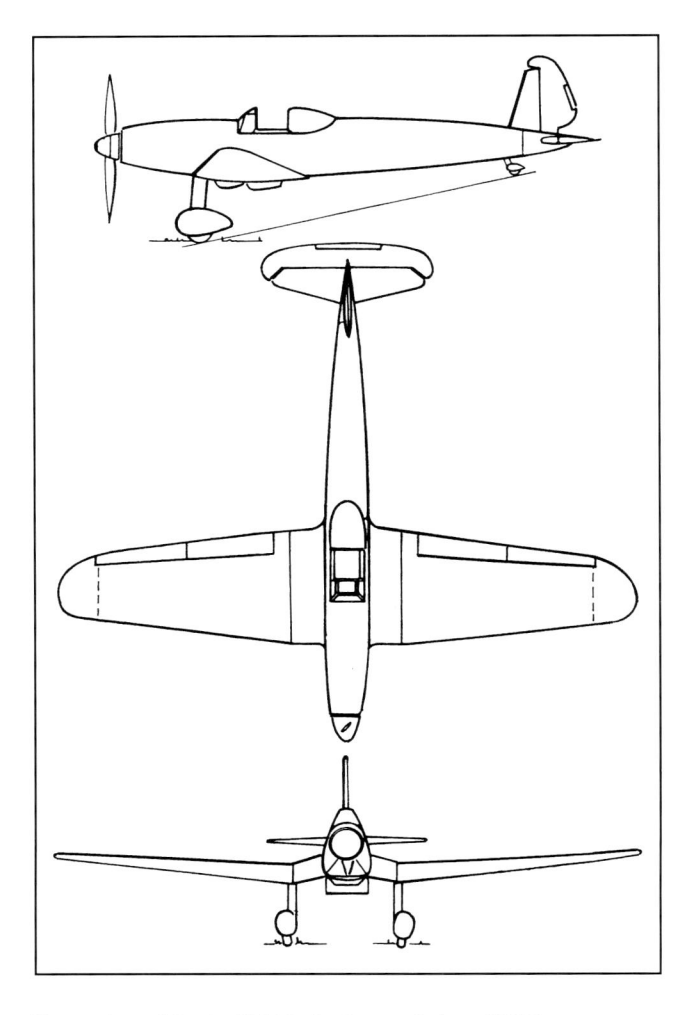

Three-view of the Ar 80 V 1 single-seat fighter (1935).

Ar 80 V 2, D-ILOH, with Jumo 210 engine.

Ar 80 V 3 with enclosed two-place cockpit.

After the first prototype was lost in an accident, a second prototype (D-ILOH) was built using the same engine. The other V-series prototypes were fitted with the 610 hp Jumo 210.[51] With few minor exceptions, the aircraft possessed pleasant flight handling characteristics. The retraction mechanism on the braced retractable undercarriage caused endless problems. Blume, who bore chief responsibility for all new designs, was initially reluctant to become involved in the proven construction methods employed by Rethel. Blume had originally been opposed to the retractable gear because he believed that the requisite mechanism would lead to an unfavorable weight increase and the wheel wells would negatively impact the aerodynamic qualities. Valuable time had been lost by the time he revised his opinion. In order to avoid cutting through the outer wing formers a landing gear strut was chosen which would have a pivot point in front of the front spar and retract to the rear. The wheel itself was attached to a vertical sleeve arm slipped over the gear strut. To keep it from jutting out into the airstream, the wheel would rotate through 90 degrees during retraction, lying flush with the wing behind the rear spar. This necessitated a complicated and weight-increasing mechanism for rotating the wheel in addition to the one for retracting the strut. Although the mechanism functioned flawlessly when the aircraft was blocked up on the ground, during flight, at a point where the wheel was halfway rotated, the sleeve's rubbing (caused by the dynamic pressure) became so great that the push rod running to the leading edge of the wing could not rotate — halting the retraction process. Reinhold Platz characterized his former Fokker colleague's work methods as follows: "Rethel ... was certainly quite good, but wasn't the man for the simplest approach to design which I consistently advocated."[52] Even though the airplane was flight-ready in the autumn of 1935, an additional three-month period of experimentation with the landing gear retraction mechanism was undertaken, with little success. The aircraft was built with a fixed, shrouded strut and wheel as a result. This design, coupled with a relatively high all-up weight, meant that the aircraft didn't stand a chance compared with its competitors in the postponed demonstrations held in 1935 at Travemünde. The Heinkel aircraft, which saw constant changes being made during

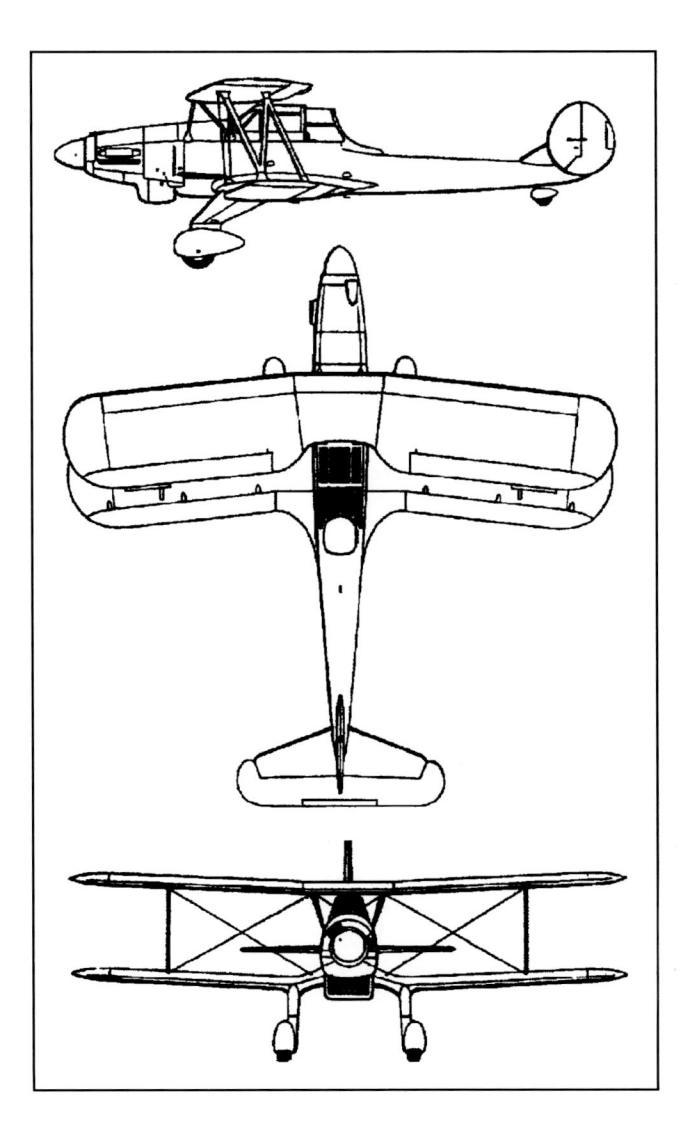

The Ar 81 dive bomber. Three-view (1935).

the developmental stages, was eliminated from the competition because it was ill-suited for aerobatics and proved to be too slow. Messerschmitt, the outsider, had fewer problems meeting the requirements of the Technisches Amt and emerged from the competition as the victor with a light, aerodynamic and well-conceived all-metal design. But Messerschmitt's design, too, had its weaknesses — the landing gear initially had a tendency to collapse and the narrow track of the undercarriage allowed the plane to easily tip over onto its left wing during takeoff. However, it was clearly superior due to its high speed. The speed advantage was nevertheless achieved, in part, at the expense of a design which was too light and therefore risky.

Despite its failure, Arado decided to continue developmental work on the design. The third prototype (D-IPBN) lost the inverted gull wings in a weight-saving measure. The airplane was fitted with a two-seat enclosed cockpit and a Jumo 210 engine with variable-pitch airscrew, which increased the maximum speed to over 410 km/h. Once it became apparent that the design would not be produced in quantity, prototypes V 2 to V 5 were converted into testbeds for 20 mm MG-FF cannons firing through the propeller, which was later installed into the Bf 109. The Ar 80 thereby became the first German cannon-armed fighter.

The Ar 80 also played a significant role in the further development of new types of landing aids for Arado's later high-performance aircraft designs. Once the previously-mentioned aerodynamic improvements had led to a reduction in resistance, efforts were undertaken to increase the range between maximum and minimum speeds by utilizing features which would provide maximum lift. In 1938 chief engineer Hans Rebeski began working on such a project, requested by the Aerodynamisches Büro, designing wings utilizing a type of Fowler flap and testing them on the Ar 80.

It was imperative to the design that an absolutely rigid landing flap be achieved, one which eliminated any type of vibration risk. The flaps were therefore fixed to three rails which fitted inside tracks firmly attached to the main wing. The inner and outer rails were each connected to a carriage situated between the spars and running along tracks. The carriage itself was vertically adjustable by means of a self-restraining spindle. The two spindles were connected to each other by chains in such a way that both spindles turned in different directions, thus achieving the trapeze-style extension of the Fowlers. The flaps were lowered by means of two push rods connected together by a lever, which in turn could rotate around the forward axis of the carriage and slide along a rail fixed to the wing rib.

A parallel version was also developed which permitted the simultaneous extension of the aileron, designed to rectify the unfavorable distribution of lift along the wingspan generated by the extended Fowler flap.

Measurements taken during test flights showed significant differences between the lift in the Fowler high-lift area and the normal aileron. These studies eventually led to improvements in the form of the 'Arado travelling aileron' and an 'Arado landing flap'.

Competing for a New Weapons System: The Ar 81 Dive Bomber

The dive bomber developed by Arado wasn't successful either, despite good handling qualities. The American Navy had used a comparable weapon for striking point targets in the '20s, but didn't intensively pursue the concept. In 1930 Curtiss designed the Hawk dive bomber, the aerobatic qualities of which fascinated Ernst Udet. Udet predicted that the handling characteristics of the Hawk opened up completely new military applications, convinced Göring to buy the aircraft using Reich funds and demonstrated it in December of 1933 in Rechlin. The anticipated official support of the concept wasn't forthcoming, however, since it was felt that the He 50 under development by Heinkel would have adequate dive-bombing capability.

Udet continued his efforts, carrying out demonstrations with the Fw 56 Stösser (developed by Focke-Wulf as a 'home defense fighter'), and the Amt decided to develop true dive bombers. It was recognized that, in view of bombing accuracy problems with horizontal release methods and the critical raw material situation, the dive bomber was a sensible alternative to a heavy bomber and was particularly suited to the role of supporting ground troops. In one of the first 'emergency programs' the choice fell on the Hs 123

Ar 81, V 1, D-UJOX, with twin vertical stabilizers.

sesquiplane from the Henschel Werke, which first officially demonstrated the design in May of 1935. Despite fateful crashes, which were caused by design flaws in the wing construction, the aircraft achieved series production and was used in the Spanish Civil War as well as in the Polish and Norwegian campaigns. The second phase of the emergency program actually ran parallel to the first, and included Junkers, Arado, Heinkel and the Hamburger Flugzeugbau. The development, however, was heavily influenced by Junkers, which had quietly submitted a preliminary mockup of a second-generation dive bomber in 1934. The RLM approved the construction of three prototypes and in January 1935 published a requirements listing which was tailor-made for the Junkers concept. Selection of an acceptable design, however, led to problems. Milch was strongly opposed to Messerschmitt, Udet initially favored Arado, then Heinkel, and there was resistance to Junkers from Oberst Wolfram von Richthofen of the Technisches Amt after a Junkers prototype had been completely destroyed during testing when parts of the outer skin had come off during a dive.

In 1935 the first dive bomber to enter flight testing was the Ar 81 V1 (D-UJOX) developed by Arado. It was a two-seat strutted biplane of all-metal construction with fixed, spatted landing gear and enclosed cockpit. Udet had apparently talked his friend Blume into using a biplane design.[53] The critical disadvantage of such a design was that, unlike that of a monoplane, the speed of a biplane could not be significantly increased by follow-on developmental work.

A 610 hp Jumo 210 C served as the powerplant and was fitted with a variable-pitch propeller. Maximum speed was 345 km/h at 4,000 meters altitude, maximum speed attainable in a dive was 600 km/h. Armament consisted of a fixed MG 17 for the pilot, a pivoting MG 15 for the rear gunner and a 500 kg bomb underneath the fuselage. Just as with the first two test versions from Junkers, both of the initial prototypes had twin rudders, ensuring a good field of fire for the rear gunner. Since it was discovered that this rudder arrangement led to fluttering, the third prototype was fitted with a single vertical stabilizer.

After the Hamburger Flugzeugwerke's design had been rejected early on, trials were conducted with the remaining competitors in Rechlin beginning at the end of 1936. Heinkel, Junkers and Arado took part, although Arado's third prototype wasn't quite finished at the time. The pilot of Heinkel's dive bomber conducted a tightly constrained flight profile, since the adjustment control for the airscrew was still giving problems. Udet had begun favoring Heinkel in the meantime and let the American military attaché, Truman Smith, on a tour of the modern manufacturing facilities at Henschel in October 1935. His guest subsequently reported to his superiors that the Heinkel dive bomber would be built there. This news was outdated, however. Udet himself crashed the airplane because of a failure in the pitch adjustment control, meaning that the prospects for Heinkel began looking even worse. According to the Arado pilot, Kurt Stark, the Junkers pilot, Hesselbach, also decided to limit his dive angle to 45 degrees during the demonstration. However, he reports that the Arado aircraft proved to be the best: "I was able to consistently push the Ar 81 into a vertical dive, without flaps,

reaching a final speed of approx. 600 km/h, without any problems. During the demonstration in front of the general staff, where the He 118, Ju 87 and Ar 81 were demon-

Ar 81 V 2, D-UPAR, with twin rudders.

Ar 81 V 3, D-UDEX, with single rudder.

strated, I was the only one able to drop a 500 kg bomb from a vertical dive. Udet, who had known me since 1931, clapped me approvingly on the shoulder as he took over the aircraft for a test flight ... The Ar 81 was, in my experience, the best-suited for the dive bomber role."[54]

W. Rethel (right) and W. Messerschmitt (fourth from right) during a visit to the Aeroplani Caproni company.

Congratulatory note from A. Fokker addressed to W. Rethel (1936).

The impression that Arado didn't stand a chance against Junkers was not felt by Stark, nor was this considered the case with Arado engineers Hans Rebeski and Rüdiger Kosin. The latter two felt that the deciding factor in being excluded was that Blume "was no businessman" and in dealing with the Technisches Amt was "easily moved to the back seat" by his competitors. On behalf of the Amt, Blume thanked his coworkers for the quality workmanship, but had to inform them that the Junkers design would be taken for "cost reasons"; a larger quantity of material had been apportioned, apparently with the prior approval of the Technisches Amt. This was felt to be "a poor excuse", and that Junkers had "a better hand at the Amt." Adolf Galland summed up the situation of the Arado Werke at the time in a similar manner: "I personally knew Prof. Blume quite well. He was a very capable man. I believe that both he and the company were lacking a strong lobby to counter Heinkel and Messerschmitt." Göring at least was clearly interested in a rapid expansion of the Bayerische Flugzeugwerke and, despite resistance from Milch, pushed for Messerschmitt to receive favored treatment when issuing developmental contracts. Even abroad, there were doubts that the issuance of contracts followed the rules of a fair contest. On 29 October 1942 the British journal "Flight" wrote: "Between 1934 and 1939 the Arado Flugzeugwerke developed a series of aircraft types, which were planned to equip numerous Luftwaffe units ... With one exception, none of these became operational with the Luftwaffe in any significant numbers. With regard to the quality of construction and the flight characteristics, the prototypes actually met the Luftwaffe's requirements better than other designs which have since become standard." The author of the article came to the conclusion that Arado was forced to dispense with its own developmental work from early on, that the Junkers Werke and Messerschmitt were "favorites of the Nazi party, which they had financially supported between 1933 and 1935", and had won the upper hand in the hushed dividing up of the spheres of interest, while Heinkel was compensated with contracts in the area of bomber development. The activities of the Arado Werke, whose "relationship" wasn't as good, was significantly restricted. From the American side there was even speculation that Arado was placed at a disadvantage in the fighter requirement by not being informed of the criteria for the retractable undercarriage until it was too late.[55]

When Blume subsequently put the sole blame on Rethel for the failure, the final rift between the two became unavoidable. Rethel left Arado in March of 1938 and went to Messerschmitt, where he was employed as a welding construction specialist and worked on the Bf 109 fighter design, among others. In an ironic twist, he also was involved in the development of the Bf 110 and Me 210 attack aircraft — direct competitors of Arado.

Der Generalluftzeugmeister

Berlin W 8, den 30. Juni 1939
Leipziger Straße 7
Fernsprecher: 12 00 47

Herrn
Oberingenieur Walter R e t h e l
i.Fa.Messerschmitt A.G.

A u g s b u r g.

Lieber Herr R e t h e l !

Am 1.Juli dieses Jahres blicken Sie auf eine 25-jährige ununter=
brochene Tätigkeit im Flugzeugbau zurück. Ich möchte hierbei
besonders anerkennend hervorheben, daß Sie als Flugzeugkonstruk=
teur vielseitige und hervorragende Erfolge errungen haben.
Auch auf anderen Gebieten der Luftfahrt außerhalb des Flug=
zeugbaues hatten Sie bedeutsame technische Erfolge zu verzeich=
nen. Ich darf Sie auch im Namen meiner Dienststelle zu Ihrem
bisher erfolgreichen Wirken beglückwünschen und hoffe, daß
Sie noch lange segensreich für die deutsche Luftfahrt und
Luftwaffe schaffen können.

Mit besten Grüßen und

Heil Hitler!
Ihr

Congratulations from E. Udet to W. Rethel on the latter's 25 years of exemplary service in the aviation design industry (1939).

Part II — New Role as a Reich-Owned Company

Chapter 10
The End of Independence

By 1935 the RLM was determined to break any resistance to the planned economic assimilation of Arado into the air rearmament program. State secretary Erhard Milch, accompanied by Oberst Wimmer and Major Loeb, representing the L-Amt für Beschaffungsfragen, undertook a three day business trip beginning on 2 July, the purpose of which was ostensibly an inspection of Arado's Brandenburg branch. In a show of decisiveness and in order to lay down the requirements for the company's future role, the first-ever mobilization exercise at a German aviation company took place in Brandenburg in October of that year. On a Sunday afternoon, the administration in Brandenburg was notified by an officer of the RLM to initiate the exercise starting at 7 A.M. the following morning. The work management was to be notified at precisely the same time. However, they were only to be told that it was a "sudden necessary increase in production." Production was to increase on a monthly basis and was expected to reach its peak after an 18-month period.

At the time the Brandenburg site was still being enlarged, with production just beginning at the facility. At the time of the mobilization exercise 20 aircraft were being produced monthly, the majority of these being the Ar 66 and Ar 68 models. License production of the Junkers W 34 was being set up in anticipation of large-scale production of additional all-metal designs from Junkers and Heinkel. After six weeks production had increased to 40, after another six weeks to 70 and eventually was to reach 120. Personnel at the branch site prior to the exercise numbered approximately 2,000. By the end of the mobilization this figure had been continuously strengthened to roughly 6,000, although the requisite minimum number of productive employees on the mobilization implementation date of 1 October 1935 was estimated to be just 3,125.[56] This took into account that skilled workers such as foremen, engineers and administration personnel, whose skills were being employed by the RLM throughout the entire Reich, were expected to report back to the company within three days. The new work force was, with the exception of a few specialists, entirely untrained in aircraft construction, and before they could be utilized were required to complete a company-designed training course lasting three to four weeks.

The expansion of production facilities ran in conjunction with the exercise. At the beginning of the mobilization approximately 10,000 square meters were available, with the expansion program due for completion in the autumn of 1936. On-going construction work was accelerated, so that within just four weeks nearly 21,000 square meters of space became available for use. Useable space for construction and material control, warehousing, an RLM construction supervision office, purchasing and accounting departments, the technical bureau and the test flight office could only be obtained by utilizing a temporary barracks. Significant effort, which initially could only be accomplished with outside help, was devoted to the installation of kitchen and sanitary facilities, plus areas for the medical and social needs of the new workers.

A key element resulting from the exercise was that material stock was to be maintained at a higher level than normal requirements dictated, guaranteeing an adequate supply of reserve materials for increased production in the event of war. The lessons learned at Arado in 1935 led to the establishment two years later of a "mobilization calendar", the directives of which were made applicable to all aviation companies through secret, written orders. These companies were in turn required to provide continuously updated detailed reports on all internal operations.

The full scope of German air rearmament was hidden from the world by taking strict censorship measures. Foreign publications drew attention to Schutzpolizei putting businesses under surveillance and workers being required to take oaths of silence, and warned of a "national socialist conqueror's morality."

Foreign Opinion:

> Yet despite how fantastic the lies of the Hitler Government have been: they alone have not been sufficient to deceive its neighbors ... the secret of Göring's military aviation remained hidden primarily because the German Lie was matched by the German Silence. Strict censorship measures have prevented opinions from appearing in German newspapers and magazines which would permit conclusions to be drawn as to the actual scale of Göring's aviation and the pace of its expansion ... In Germany, anyone who even innocently chats about matters of German rearmament, or who talks about his work at home or in the pub is threatened with prison and death.[57]

Forced Nationalization

On 19 March 1934 airplanes of unknown nationality supposedly appeared overhead in the skies above Berlin. This information promoted a fear among the public of foreign intervention, and prospects improved for a general endorsement of the air rearmament program which had hitherto been conducted in secret. On 3 March 1935 the German leadership felt that the time had come for lifting the veil of secrecy. In a 'decree regarding the Reichsluftwaffe' it stated: "The Reichsminister der Luftwaffe is empowered to gradually reveal the Luftwaffe at a pace and scale to be determined by him. Every appropriate means is to be implemented to prevent the public from being agitated. In particular, interviews with the press are to be refrained from as before."[58] On 20 April 1935 the Völkischer Beobachter reported the delivery of Arado fighters to the "Horst Wessel" Jagdgeschwader as a 'gift' from the SA to the Führer. In 1936 Arado fighters carried out a demonstration flight over the grounds of the "Reichsparteitag der Ehre" in Nuremberg. Its slogan was: "In its rise and very being the German Luftwaffe is borne aloft by the National Socialist will and National Socialist achievements. And therefore it can only embrace one ideal: the National Socialist ideal — a community sworn to National Socialism."

Prior to the government takeover by the Nazis, in addition to Arado the eight leading aviation manufacturers included Junkers, Heinkel, Dornier, Rohrbach, Focke-Wulf, Albatros and the Bayerische Flugzeugwerke. Albatros, Rohrbach and the Bayerische Flugzeugwerke had gone into receivership in the meantime and, aside from the Bayerische Flugzeugwerke, no longer played an independent role. The managers of the remaining firms reacted in various ways to the new political course. Heinkel and the Bayerische Flugzeugwerke under Willy Messerschmitt were prepared for unlimited cooperation with the Ministerium. Focke-Wulf's attitude was similar once Professor Focke stepped down and Kurt Tank took over management. Dornier discreetly remained in the background. There would be little opposition from those climbing the ladder in companies such as the Gothaer Waggonfabrik, Blohm & Voss, Fieseler, Siebel, MIAG, Ago, Erla and von Henschel, firms which hoped to be able to expand their interests at the expense of economically weak companies or businesses with bad credit.[59] Resistance was only encountered on the part of Arado and Junkers. Junkers, more of a researcher than a businessman, had for a long time been defending himself against intrusions into his company's independence. Eventually, however, control of his business was wrested away from Junkers by driving him into a corner through such methods as denying him credit, through Gestapo surveillance and by threatening to file charges of high treason against him.

As the senior partner of Arado, Heinrich Lübbe rejected every directorial attempt at economic planning from the radical parties.[60] From early on Lübbe was subjected to physical attacks from both leftist and rightist brute squads, who threw bottles at him in his open-topped car or forcibly accosted him, compelling Lübbe to defend himself with a revolver. Later Lübbe found listening devices in his house and had to fire his gardener, who turned out to be an informer.

His often stubborn attempts to fend off the increasing efforts of state influence were not successful in the long run and isolated him from sections of the business management and technical directorship. By 1935 the RLM had decided to rid itself of this unmanageable senior partner and the deliberate ongoing undermining of their plans caused by the Arado-Werke. When around lunchtime Lübbe's housemaid, her face chalk-white, reported that the police would like to speak to the 'Herr Direktor', Lübbe smashed his fist so hard against the table that a plate broke and his hand began to bleed. After the initial excitement had abated somewhat, he left the room without saying a word, later stating that his files had been searched and that he was being placed under arrest.

The Arrest of H. Lübbe:

I can clearly still remember that horrible day in 1935 when the doorbell rang during lunch and the Geheime Staatspolizei stood outside. My father had to go with them. The Nazis demanded that he should work with them, meaning join the Nazi Party and have the Reich become involved in the Arado-Flugzeugwerke. Daddy of course refused. Then he was forced to sell the company to the Reich. He only got a twelfth of what the Nazis assessed it to be worth, the rest was to have been paid later — which hasn't happened yet. Yes, those were bad times, and Daddy never fully recovered. We were thankful, though, that he wasn't sent to a concentration camp.[61] He lost both his aircraft factories because he wouldn't build for Hitler's war.[62]

During his confinement, Lübbe was forced to give up his share in the company. Once he was released from custody he was a broken man, both physically and spiritually, a man whose life's work and economic reason for being had been destroyed. Aside from the previously mentioned expropriation of the Junkers-Werke, this was the sole case of a direct forced nationalization of a larger aviation company during the Third Reich.

The expropriation occurred during a time when Germany's political leadership was attempting to show the world that Germany was indeed making great strides in aircraft construction, but was not pursuing aggressive intentions. In April 1936 the American military attaché, Truman Smith, was encouraged to invite Charles Lindbergh on a tour of German aviation companies. This took place in July 1936, when Berlin was experiencing the fever of the Olympic Games. Lindbergh was taken to Rostock's Heinkel Werke and the Junkers company in Dessau. Significantly, there was no visit to be made of the Arado Werke, which had only recently extracted itself from its above-mentioned troubles. It is safe to assume that Lindbergh, who may have had personal ties to Lübbe, had not been informed of the personnel changes taking place at the time. This despite the fact that the American military attaché had given instructions in March of 1936 to relay detailed secret reports regarding all developments in the realm of German aviation. It was only during his second visit to Germany in the winter of 1938/39 that he personally became aware of the RLM's forced nationalization measures, when a guest whom the military attaché in Berlin had invited on the occasion of his visit was arrested for anti-National Socialist opinions.

Senior partner H. Lübbe at the time of his company's expropriation (1936).

Der Reichsminister der Luftfahrt

LD I 1 E Nr. 2509/36, geh.

(Bitte in der Antwort vorstehendes Geschäftszeichen, das Datum und kurzen Inhalt anzugeben.)

Berlin W 8, den 14. Mai 1936.
Behrenstraße 68-70
Fernsprecher: A 2 Flora 0047
Tel.-Adr.: Reichsluft Berlin

Eing. 15 MAI 36
Reichsfinanzmin.

Geheim

An den
Herrn Reichsminister der Finanzen,
Berlin W 8,
Wilhelmplatz 1/2.

Am 25. April 1936 hat gemäß beiliegender Abschrift des notariellen Vertrages die zu meinem Geschäftsbereich gehörende Luftfahrtkontor G.m.b.H. von dem Kapital der Arado Flugzeugwerke G.m.b.H. von 150.000,-- RM die Anteile des Hauptgesellschafters, des Herrn L ü b b e , im Betrage von RM 135.000,-- übernommen. Eine Prüfung der allgemeinen und wirtschaftlichen Verhältnisse der Arado Flugzeugwerke G.m.b.H. hatte ergeben, daß Herr Lübbe als Hauptgesellschafter einen sehr schädlichen Einfluß auf das Werk ausübte. Die rüstungspolitischen Erfordernisse machten deshalb eine Übernahme der Anteile auf das Reich erforderlich. Um weiteren Schaden zu verhüten, war dringende Eile geboten, sodaß die Zustimmung des Herrn Reichsministers der Finanzen vorher nicht mehr eingeholt werden konnte. Ich bitte deshalb ergebenst nachträglich um Genehmigung zum Erwerb dieser Anteile.

Ferner bitte ich um Zustimmung zur Beteiligung an der Gummiwerke Ballenstedt G.m.b.H. Die Firma Franz Clouth, Rheinische Gummiwaren-Fabrik A.G., Köln-Nippes, errichtet auf meine Veranlassung ein neues Werk in Ballenstedt a.H. Von dem Kapital von RM 500.000,-- übernehmen je 200.000,-- RM die Firmen Franz Clouth, Rheinische Gummiwarenfabrik A.G. und die Land- und Seekabelwerke A.G., Köln, während sich das Reich mit 100.000 RM beteiligt. Das sonst noch benötigte Kapital wird durch Bankkredite bezw. durch einen Kredit der Mehrheitsaktionärin der Rheinischen Gummiwarenfabrik A.G., der Felten & Guilleaume A.G. in Köln, aufgebracht. Dieser Gesellschaft ist eine Option auf die Reichsbeteiligung eingeräumt worden, die sie innerhalb kürzester Frist, wahrscheinlich schon im Laufe des Jahres 1937 ausüben will.

Die Satzungen der Gesellschaften werden den sonstigen mit Beteiligung des Reiches gegründeten Gesellschaften angepaßt werden. Ferner werde ich für eine Vertretung des Reiches in den Beiräten Sorge tragen.

Jm Auftrag
gez. Dr. Hergesell

Für die Richtigkeit:
Amtsrat.

Private correspondence from the RLM to the RFM concerning the dispossession of the Arado Flugzeugwerke and investment in the Franz Clouth rubber goods factory (14 May 1936).

At the time, Lübbe's expropriation was kept under strict secrecy. A query by the Rostock court regarding the legal changes at the Warnemünde branch was untruthfully answered by the business management on 14 February 1936 with the statement "we currently do not have plans for any changes."

On 25 April 1936 the expropriation was mad official by a secret contract. In the presence of his partner Felix Wagenführ and notary public Dr. Karl Fritz Jonas, Lübbe stood across from Rudolf Heinemann and Carl Hennig, representatives of the Luftfahrtkontor GmbH and declared: "I hereby transfer my shares of the Arado Flugzeugwerke GmbH in Berlin in the nominal amount of RM 135,000 to the Luftfahrtkontor GmbH, effective immediately."[63] According to the contract, the "purchase price is to be determined by a commission, consisting of a mediator appointed by the Reichswirtschaftsminister and a negotiator appointed by each of the two parties" in the event that a suitable agreement on the purchase amount couldn't be reached within 14 days. The parties both agreed in advance to this condition.

The remarkable thing about this rather 'unassuming' agreement was the planned composition of the arbitration body. Given the relations at the time, the objectivity of the arbiter appointed by Reich officials was seriously questionable, meaning that Lübbe's representative could be outvoted at any time. Since there could obviously be no conjoint regulation of the purchase price, the arbitration body composition guaranteed that the price could be dictated by the Reich at all times.

Even more obvious were the intentions and the background behind the Ministerium's actions, revealed in a confidential message from Wilhelm Hergesell to the Reichsminister für Finanzen, dated 14 May 1936, in which Lübbe's surrender of his investment was announced after the fact, adding further that: "a review of the general and economic state of the Arado Flugzeugwerke GmbH has shown that Herr Lübbe had a profoundly damaging influence on the company. The rearmament policy requirements therefore necessitated a takeover of the shares by the Reich. The utmost urgency was required in order to prevent further damage, which is why approval from the Reichsminister der Finanzen could not be obtained in advance."

In the spirit of the government then in power, another reason was falsely given for the expropriation, in "that the owner of the firm was not actively involved in its administration; from and through him there was no possible financial support, instead there were financial burdens which he yearly placed upon the company and which could barely be compensated for with sales."[64]

In order to quickly meet those 'rearmament policy requirements' the way was paved for state financing, since the employment of private capital and utilization of credit institutions was not considered to be expedient. Business management considerations, specifically profit margins, were excluded along with regard for business law. This meant that the interests of private businessmen could no longer play a role and that resistance, if any, should be crushed with all means available.

State Dirigisme:

Despite the difficult task, the short time allotted and the tight budget, the technical expansion of the aviation industry has been accomplished. In doing so, the shape and potential consequences of the applied financing methods were not allowed to play a critical role. This type of thinking would only have been appropriate in situations where considerations for arms policy made it necessary. Subtle discussions on the legal ramifications associated with state intervention would have effectively stymied the technical expansion of the industry. The acceleration of work was, however, the primary duty of the responsible departments with regard to the general public, for whose protection the expansion served. Those firms in the aviation industry participating in the rearmament program were not considered by the Reichsluftfahrtministerium to be companies, but to be the executors of a national directive.[65]

Legal and Organizational Restructuring

Following the finance ministry's subsequent approval of the Arado Flugzeugwerke's takeover, the RLM informed the Reichsfinanzministerium on 11 June 1936 that the 150,000 marks of registered capital was inadequate for the current 12 million RM investment, and that it would be raised by 7.85 million RM to 8 million RM. This increase was officially agreed upon on 26 June 1936 with Wilhelm Hergesell and Carl Hennig representing the Luftfahrtkontor and businessman Felix Wagenführ representing Arado. In an ensuing business conference an alteration to the memorandum of association was approved, calling for a five-man advisory board to monitor the company's management. In addition to chairman Wilhelm Hergesell it would include the Fliegeroberstabingenieur Günther Tschersich, Emil Meyer representing the Dresdner Bank and two representatives from the Reichsfinanzministerium.[66] The Reichsfinanzministerium suggested "checking as to whether paragraph 8 could remain in force as it currently reads, with the current holdings ratio, particularly if the company shares of Oberstleutnant Wagenführ were assumed by the Reich."[67] Although management was required to submit all significant decisions to the advisory board, where Wagenführ's voice carried very little weight, there was apparently a lingering concern that Reich interests could be jeopardized.[68] On 22 December 1937 the Reichsfinanzministerium prepared an internal memorandum regarding Felix Wagenführ's holdings. The minister apparently did not wish to be involved in the affairs of the RLM any longer and accepted that these shares "for reasons unknown to me" would continue as they were. Wagenführ, whose holdings remained untouched until his death in 1947, stepped down on 30 June 1943 as business director and was selected as a member of the advisory board.

New postings and transfers occurred shortly following the reorganization of the company's management core. In 1936 businessman Rudolf Heinemann was appointed as an additional managing director. After 1935, when Blume had already become the technical director and manager of development and, in 1936, named as one of four authorized signatories, he also assumed Erich Serno's vacated position of managing director at the end of 1938. In 1938 Blume was called to the company's board of directors and functioned as the general director of the firm. In addition, he was a member of the Deutsche Akademie für Luftfahrtforschung, the Lilienthal Gesellschaft and Ava Göttingen. Later Blume was appointed Wehrwirt-

Correspondence from the RLM to the RFM recommending an increase in the registered capital and noting the planned investment costs (27 November 1937).

schaftsführer and in the spring of 1945, on the recommendation of Reichsminister Speer, given the title of Professor. Nevertheless, he was not privileged to designate those aircraft developed under his supervision with the letters "Bl", like the "Me" and "Ta" designations introduced with Messerschmitt and Focke-Wulf.[69]

Two of the officiating advisor board members from the Reichsfinanzministerium were given a leave of absence and took jobs in the private sector. Under the personal direction of Erhard Milch on 5 July 1938 the SS-Oberführer Fritz Kranefuss was assigned in Wilhelm Hergesell's place as the new chairman of the advisory council, which by 1940 had expanded to nine members and from time to time had a seat and vote in business meetings.

Advisory council of the Arado Flugzeugwerke (as of Sept. 1940):

Fritz Kranefuss. Chairman. Member of the board of directors of the Braunkohle-Benzin AG, Berlin.

Hellmuth Roehnert. Vice chairman. Chairman of the board of Rheinmetall-Borsig AG, Berlin.

Alois Cejka. Ministerialdirektor in the RLM.

Josef Mayer. Ministerialrat in the RFM.

Professor Dr. Dr. Emil Meyer. Board of directors of the Dresdner Bank, Berlin.

Dipl.-Ing. Gottfried Reidenbach. Oberstingenieur in the RLM.

Fritz Rudorf. Chairman of the board of the Bank der Deutschen Luftfahrt AG, Berlin.

Günther Tschersich. Generalingenieur in the RLM.

Dr. Heinrich Wiegand. Oberregierungsrat in the RLM.

The first increase in capital, amounting to 7,850,000 RM, was obtained by converting a portion of the previously authorized credit into equity capital in order to achieve a proper ratio between capital and credit. In doing so, the Reich became both the owner and the creditor. After another increase in the registered capital to 30 million RM in 1938, the final increase took place in 1943, amounting to 50 million RM.

Construction measures necessitated by the boost in work capacity required investments of 29.5 million RM in 1937, which were distributed among the individual branches as follows:

Babelsberg 4.6 million RM, Wittenberg 4.3 million RM, Rathenow 3.1 million RM, Neuendorf including Brandenburg 3.0 million RM, Warnemünde 2.3 million RM, Anklam 1.8 million RM. In addition, payments totaling 10.4 million RM were made on facilities then under construction.

In 1938 new investments of 16 million RM were made, primarily in Neuendorf (3.8 million RM), Warnemünde (3.0 million RM) and Babelsberg (3.8 million RM). In 1939 another 14 million RM in construction expenses was accrued, with this amount shrinking to 2 million RM in 1940.

Construction plans required investment which could not be met by the company using its own means. By 31 December 1935 the public's shares amounted to 4,555,000 RM. During the course of 1936 an additional 13,650,000 RM was made available. Further supplements were made by the Reich in 937 totaling 29,379,000 RM, of which 12,000,000 RM was diverted for the second increase in capital. When credit requirements climbed to 80 million RM in January 1938 yet another infusion of 15,950,000 RM was made, so that by the end of 1938 63,330,900 RM in credit had been approved. In July of 1939 the company's burden of debt was formally reduced through a one-time public subsidy program amounting to 26.5 million RM, which in turn was applied a portion the already approved credit. Arado was nevertheless obliged to take out a 7,180,900 RM bank credit to cover a portion of its credit debts to the Reich. Another prerequisite for the subsidy's approval was that in the future the company would renounce any input from the German Reich's Court of Audit, instead accepting that cost and economic monitoring would be conducted by the RLM directly. These conditions also applied to an additional public funding measure in 1941, which this time totaled 8.4 million RM.

Chapter 11
Structured Economic Dirigisme

License Building for Heinkel, Junkers and Focke-Wulf

From mid-1936 onward the RLM radically shifted production of the now quasi-Reich owned Arado company to license building of other companies' products. At that time only indigenous designs were rolling off the assembly lines, chief among these being the Ar 66 trainer. By 23 July 1938 Arado was shown in an RLM listing of current aircraft to no longer be producing any of its own designs.

Production Overview
Total Deliveries to 30 April 1936:

Design	Total #	Quota	Actual	(-)	(+)
Ar 64	19	19	19	-	-
Ar 65	157	157	171	-	14
Ar 68	324	63	10	53	-
He 51	470	292	301	-	9
Ar 69	7	7	7	-	-
Ar 66	1315	712	732	-	20
Ar 76	182	158	176	-	18

As a result of the consequential assimilation into this state-directed planning the size of the design bureau was reduced, in contrast to the general trend, and a new department for license construction was established under the direction of Ingenieur Holmig. The Technisches Amt made all decisions regarding quantity, deadlines, estimated and fixed prices as well as distribution of production among the branch sites. It organized the acquisition of blueprints for license models and the cooperation with other license-building companies. The Henschel Werke in particular, which had only been established in 1933, had experience in license-built Junkers designs and, at the request of the RLM, loaned personnel out to Arado.

By 1936 Arado was so heavily involved with the expansion of its production facilities that the output of delivered aircraft in 1936 (839) dropped to nearly half (440) in 1937. In contrast to 1936, the following year saw license production of the He 51 taper off considerably, while in 1936 and 1937, respectively, a total of 65 and 150 examples of the newly introduced He 59 and He 60 seaplanes were license-built. In 1937 138 examples of the Junkers W 34 were built.

Aircraft Delivered
(unit price/total value in millions of RM)

	1936	1937
Ar 66	270(26,900/ 7.3)	109(30,700/ 3.3)
Ar 68	302(49,500/ 14.9)	73(50,800/ 3.7)
Ar 76	105(- / 1.0)	-
Ju W34	-	138(93,200/ 12.9)
He 51	65(- / 0.7)	2(84,000/ 0.2)
He 59	16(211,000/ 3.4)	49 (209,000/ 10.3)
He 60	81(77,500/ 6.3)	69(82,000/ 5.9)

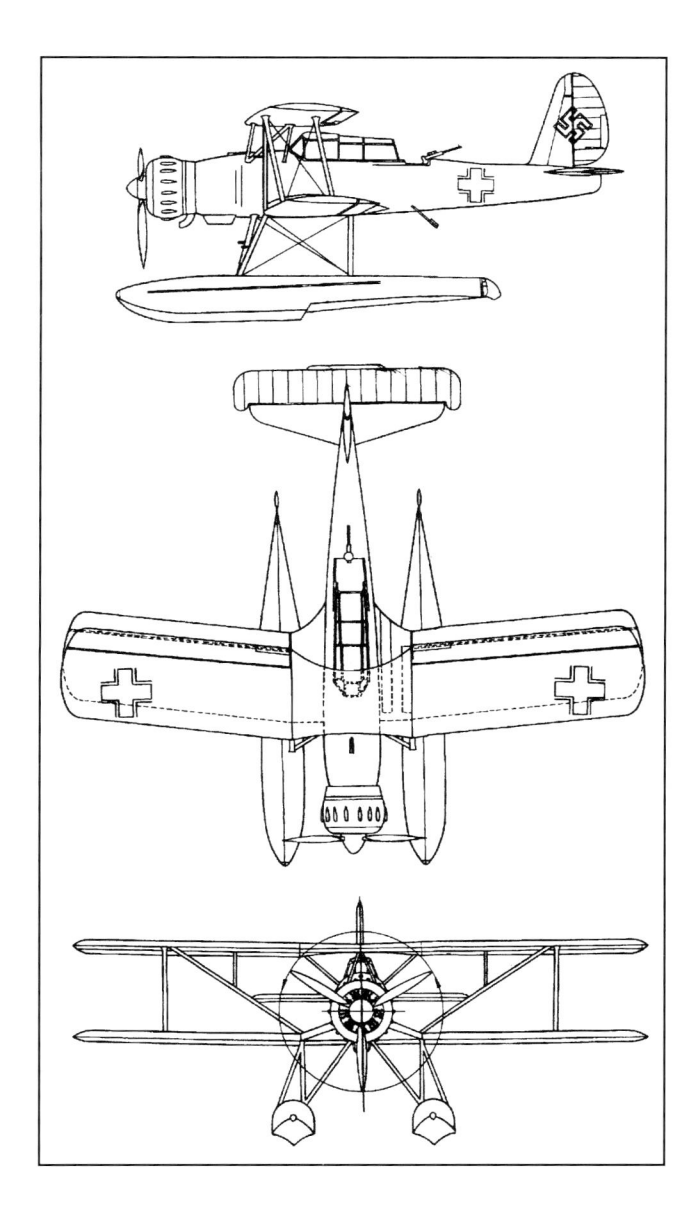

Three-view of the Ar 95 multi-role airplane (1936).

Despite intensive efforts on the part of company management to not be technologically overtaken by leading aviation companies such as Junkers, Heinkel and Messerschmitt with forward-looking projects, for years Arado was only awarded developmental contracts with the stipulation that license production would not be affected.

The RLM's long-term planned distribution of license production called for the Brandenburg branch to devote itself exclusively to airframe construction and final assembly of bombers. The newly established sites at Wittenberg and Rathenow were to undertake wing construction, while Babelsberg was designated for empennage and turned parts production. Warnemünde was primarily involved in the license building of fighter aircraft, the components of which were supplied by the Anklam branch. During fiscal year 1937/38 Warnemünde was planned as an assembly site for the Bf 109 fighter and the He 114, He 115, He 59 and He 60 seaplanes, before the Focke-Wulf Fw 190 was also eventually put into production there.

Arado had to content itself with finding developmental niches, for which generally only small numbers were built, and in developing training aircraft. With the exception of a large-scale contract for the Ar 96 military trainer and a smaller production run of the Ar 79 sport and commuter plane, the RLM limited its approval to the development of multi-role and reconnaissance aircraft. Only in the case of the Ar 196 naval plane would there be any type of long-lasting quantity production.

Restricted Developmental Activity: Seaplanes and Reconnaissance Aircraft

In order to provide the desired high lift, the RLM called for a traditional biplane design for its multi-role aircraft and limited production to the Warnemünde site, since it provided the ideal conditions for developing seaplanes. Unlike in the USA and Japan, shipborne aircraft had been given a low priority in Germany, since experience with such designs had been comparatively limited and the RLM's directives allowed for little freedom in planning. Disregarding these facts, Arado succeeded in maintaining its traditional role in seaplane building with solid and well-conceived designs. Future prospects seemed bleak, however, because virtually all construction had ceased on aircraft carriers even before the war had broken out. Following on the heels of its SSD and W II seaplanes, in the '30s Arado produced a reliable seaplane trainer in the form of a maritime version of its Ar 66. In addition, Heinkel in Warnemünde had produced improved seaplanes with their He 59 and He 60, not to mention the earlier seaplane version of the He 51. By the mid-'30s it became apparent that these aircraft, utilized chiefly in the training and air-sea rescue roles, would not meet future requirements. Better-performing, more seaworthy, catapult-launched and more effectively armed combat capable seaplanes were in demand. From a design standpoint, this meant replacing the biplanes of composite construction (some of which were still wire-braced) such as the He 59 and He 60 with modern all-metal aircraft.

The Ar 95 Multi-Role Airplane

The Ar 95 multi-role aircraft, developed in 1936, was the beginning of a series of similar looking airplane types produced at Warnemünde which, for reasons of rational planning, were to be utilized in various roles. Although it was soon found that a monoplane design was more applicable to the multi-role concept than a biplane, the all-metal Ar 95 indeed proved to be a technically sound design.

Arado Advertising:

The Ar 95 is a multi-purpose high performance aircraft having the primary functions of torpedo carrier and long-range patrol. In addition, the airplane may be employed in such diverse roles tactical reconnaissance, artillery spotting, bombing, laying smokescreens or towing targets. By trading the floats for landing gear and fitting a tail wheel the machine can be based on land and used in the same roles. The all-metal design is a match for the particular demands of maritime flying, weather conditions and life of the aircraft. Its small dimensions, catapult-launch capa-

75

Ar 95 See V 2, D-OLUO.

bility and folding wings are additional features of the design which, with regard to the concept of a multi-role aircraft, are quite beneficial — particularly when considering the use of the seaplane from ships and the landplane from aircraft carriers. The aircraft's long range, 2400 kilometers for the seaplane and 1610 kilometers for the landplane, permit it to undertake missions which would otherwise be the domain of specialized aircraft.

In view of the RLM requirements, Arado was forced to conform its proven biplane configuration to modern standards. The airplane's fuselage was of a Duraluminum monocoque design, consisting of formers which had the outer skin riveted to them. The wing center section was joined to the fuselage by means of its continuous spars. Located in the upper part of the fuselage in front of the pilot's cockpit was a space for marine gear, while below that was an area for equipment. Both compartments were accessible from the outside by hatches. Fuel tanks were installed beneath the cockpit. The observer's compartment located behind the cockpit comprised the entire height of the fuselage and allowed for a two-man crew. A sealable window was located in the floorboards.

The wings were of all-metal construction and consisted of folding upper and lower sections, an fixed upper wing section and the interwing struts. The outer wings included a leading and trailing edge spar and were of monocoque design. The ribs running between the spars were metal covered on their upper surfaces and fabric covered on their underside.

Ar 95 See V 1, D-OHEO.

Ar 95 See V 3, D-ODGY, with a modified tailfin in front of the Warnemünde yards.

Tailplane and fin were of lightweight metal and cantilever attached to the fuselage. The tailplane was adjustable in flight using a handwheel. Trim angle for the horizontal stabilizers was adjustable in flight, while that of the vertical stabilizer and ailerons was adjustable on the ground. All control surfaces were counter-balanced.

Four prototypes and 17 series aircraft were produced. The first prototype, D-OHEO, was a two-seat seaplane with two non-stepped floats which also contained fuel tanks. The floats, jutting out forward of the nose, reduced the chance of taking on spray when taxiing on the water. Retractable water rudders fitted beneath the float keels provided the necessary maneuverability in narrow waterways and when docking.

Since the first prototype only achieved a top speed of 280 km/h with its water-cooled Jumo 210 A engine, beginning with the second prototype (D-OLUO) the aircraft was fitted with an 800 hp air-cooled BMW 132 Dc radial engine and NACA nacelle. From the third prototype on a three-blade Junkers-Hamilton metal variable-pitch airscrew was fitted, having an automatic rpm controller. Raising the crew from its initial two to three men, it now consisted of a pilot, an observer/radioman and a gunner. The fourth prototype was an Ar 95 L landplane with fixed gear, carrying fuel tanks in its trouser-like spats. The fifth (D-OHGV) constituted the basis for the improved Ar 95 A-0 See series.

Depending on the mission, supplementing the armament were six 50 kg bombs attached to the lower wing, a fog generator weighing 375 kg on the lower fuselage, an 800 kg torpedo, radio equipment in the observer's compartment for transmitting and receiving HF and VHF signals, telephone and telegraph operations, photographic equipment for taking 300 pictures, a tow target apparatus for towing four targets and a lifeboat.[71]

Since its performance did not quite match up to the requirements of a carrier aircraft and the 'Graf Zeppelin' aircraft carrier was, in the event, never completed (due to cost), the RLM never issued a production contract for the landplane version. At the start of the war eight Ar 95 seaplane variants were assigned to the Luftwaffe (3/SAGr 125) and operated in the Baltic during the Russian campaign, later seeing service in Romania.

In view of the limited interest shown by the RLM at home, Arado sought out customers abroad. The type was on exhibit at the Belgrade Airshow in the summer of 1938, but the outbreak of the war stymied a potential delivery to Turkey. Only three each of landplane and seaplane versions were delivered to Chile, with an additional six of the seaplane types going to Spain. The latter operated with the Condor Legion in 1938 on Mallorca and soldiered on until 1948.

The aircraft's development was overshadowed by a tragic accident at the end of March 1938 during a demonstration before a Chilean commission at the Plauer See. The Arado test pilot Richard Perlia had first noticed a slight vibration in the airframe when testing a float model during a factory flight. This had occurred after he'd made a shallow dive followed by a pull-up into a turn-and-slip. He attributed this to the relatively heavy floats and reported to Walter Blume that any type of excessive demands on the aircraft were to be avoided. Test pilot Graf Rességuier, who was to continue the demonstration in front of the foreign guests, made a snap roll at 200 meters despite the restriction. In doing so, the tailplane mounts broke and the aircraft went out of control. Pressure from the defective stabilizer on the control stick jammed the pilot in the cockpit and prevented him from bailing out in time.

Ar 95 See, DK+UI.

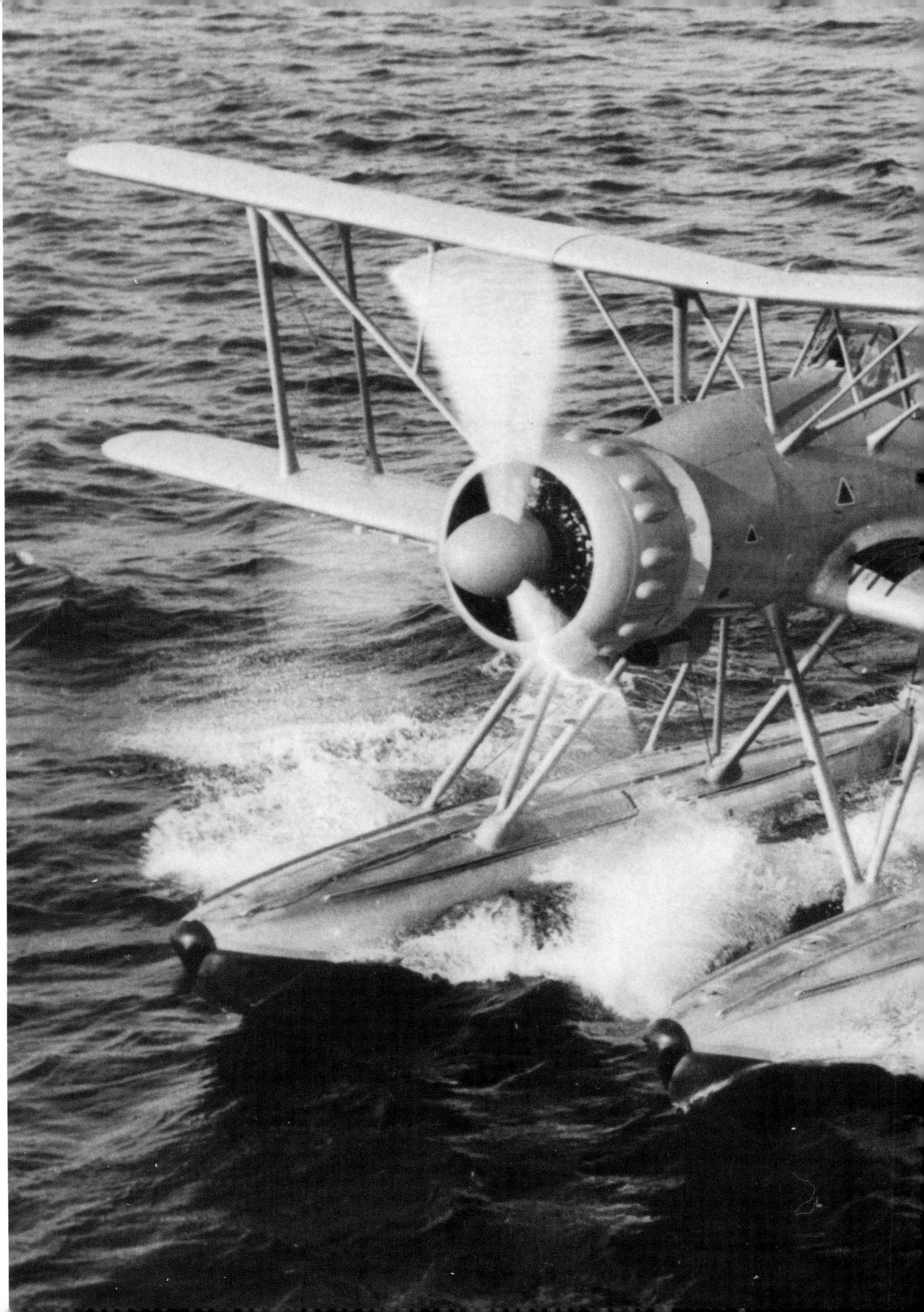

Ar 95 See V 5, D-OHGV.

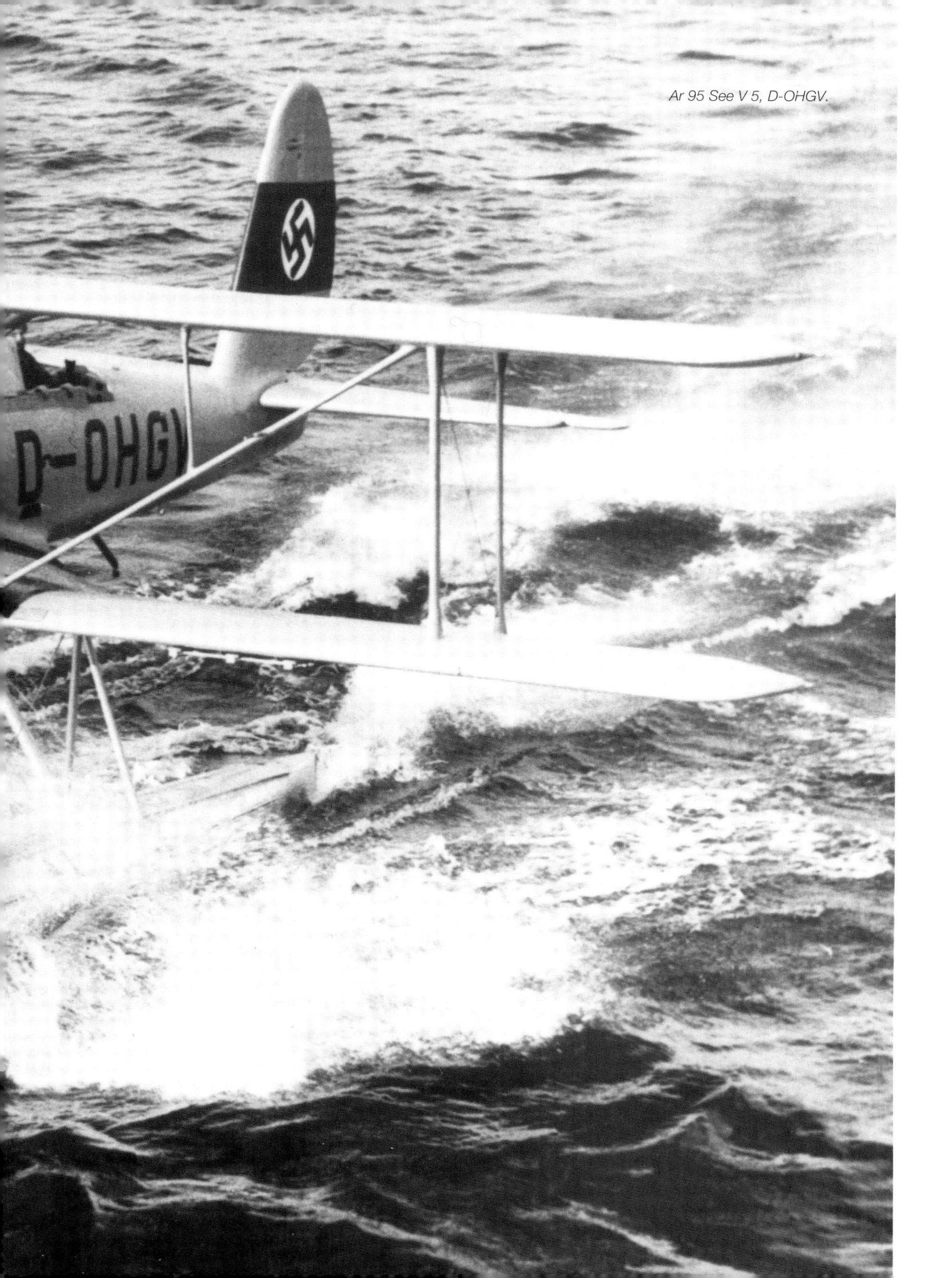

Dimensions, Weights and Performance of the Ar 95 (reconnaissance versions) with BMW 132 Dc:

	Seaplane	Landplane
wingspan:	12.5 m	12.5 m
width with wings folded:	5.8 m	5.8 m
length:	11.1 m	10.8 m
height:	5.2 m	5.1 m
wing area:	45.4 m²	45.4 m²
engine performance at maximum altitude:	880 hp	
fuel consumption@cruising speed:	255 g/hp	
empty weight:	2540 kg	2265 kg
total load:	1025 kg	1010 kg
gross weight:	3565 kg	3275 kg
wing loading:	78.5 kg/m²	72.1 kg/m²
max speed@3000 m:	310 km/h	328 km/h
time-to-climb 1000 m:	2.3 min	2.0 min
time-to-climb 4000 m:	9.0 min	7.6 min
time-to-climb 6000 m:	15.5 min	12.9 min
service ceiling:	7800 m	8300 m
takeoff time	17 sec	
takeoff rolling distance:	-	150 m
landing speed:	90 km/h	88 km/h

The Ar 195 Carrier Aircraft

The single-seat Ar 195 biplane, specially designed for the carrier role, met with just as little success as did the Ar 95 multi-role aircraft. Using the Ar 195 design, Arado participated in competition with Fieseler for a specification requirement in the spring of 1937. Similar in its design and fittings to the previous Ar 95 landplane, the new aircraft included features such as a forward, raised cockpit for optimum visibility during carrier landings, jettisonable undercarriage to prevent the aircraft from nosing over when ditching in the sea, the fitting of extra buoyancy materials for keeping the aircraft afloat until rescue and a hook in front of the tailwheel for catching deck wires. The airplane was also to have a minimum range of 1,000 km, external fuel tanks for increasing this range, a maximum speed of 300 km/h with a full combat load and a rated dive capability of 600 km/h.

Like Fieseler, Arado had completed its first prototype by the summer of 1937, but it was discovered that Arado's biplane — using the 960 hp BMW 132 K powerplant —

Ar 195 V 3, D-ODSG.

Ar 95 V 4 with wheeled undercarriage (1938).

Ar 95 Land.

Ar 95 See, export model for Chile. During the demonstration the Arado test pilot Graf Rességuier was killed.

achieved neither the performance of its Ar 95 predecessor nor the required minimum acceptable top speed and desired range. According to the 1944 edition of the Flugzeugtypenbuch (aircraft type handbook), with the use of the BMW 132 M engine (830 hp) the aircraft was only able to achieve a maximum speed of 250 km/h at an altitude of 2,000 meters. Gert Heumann notated it as having a maximum speed of 290 km/h (Flugrevue 12/1966). Eventually the Fieseler Werke was awarded the contract for building twelve of its Fi 167 carrier airplanes. It remains a mat-

Ar 197 V 2, D-IVLE (1937).

Ar 197 V 2, D-IVLE.

Ar 197 V 1, D-ITSE.

Ar 197 O-series.

ter of conjecture whether the Arado project was canceled after the third Ar 195 V-3 prototype, D-ODSH, because of problems fitting a different powerplant or because of difficulties in improving its aerodynamics.

The Ar 197 Carrier Aircraft

Arado introduced a third airplane into the carrier aircraft program with its Ar 197 model, a follow-on development to the Ar 68 H. The first prototype of the Ar 197 V 1, D-ITSE, was flown in the spring of 1937 in Warnemünde and was laid out as a pure fighter. The powerplant was a 12-cylinder DB 600 A having 900 hp. Because of the low priority given to this type of airplane the second (D-IVLE) and third prototypes were fitted out with the BMW 132 J radial engine, with an output of just 815 hp. From the second prototype onward the airplane was fitted with specialized equipment for carrier operations, to include a tailhook and racks for bombs and torpedoes. The third prototype was kitted out with full armament, having two fixed MG 17s in the fuselage and two 20-mm MG FF cannons in the upper wings. Although this, the last of the German biplanes to be produced, was the fastest of its kind with a top speed of 400 km/h, only a pre-production series resulted.

The Ar 196 Seaplane

Among the many projects for multi-role aircraft, only the Ar 196 proved to be successful in the marketplace. Heinkel's offer, the He 114 seaplane replacement for the obsolete He 60, was quickly found to be unsuitable for shipborne operations. It did not meet strength requirements for catapult launch, and pilots complained of its flight characteristics as well as its taxiing qualities on rolling seas.

In accordance with a 1936 specification Arado was awarded a contract for the development of four prototypes of a catapult-launched seaplane with features to include reliability in high seas, instrument flight controls and stressed for dive bombing. It was to have retractable wings and be tested in both a twin-float version and one having a centerline float. At the same time, a parallel contract was placed with Focke-Wulf for two biplane prototypes (designated as the Fw 62), each having the different floatplane configurations previously mentioned.

By the end of 1937 all prototypes had entered the flight testing stage. At the end of this evaluation period, which took place in Travemünde, Arado's monoplane came out the overall winner due to its higher loading, lighter handling qualities, more robust design and better flight characteristics.

The Ar 196 seaplane was a semi-cantilever low-wing design, whose airframe was strongly reminiscent of the Ar

95. The folding wings were metal-skinned, as was the fuselage up to the point just behind the two-place, glazed, rear-opening canopy. As with the Ar 197 the remainder of the fuselage and empennage — unlike the earlier Ar 95 and 195 models — made use of the standard fabric type of covering. The first two out of a total of five prototypes were fitted with twin floats, the remaining with centerline floats. The centerline-float design was more durable during landing on rolling seas, since the impact was absorbed directly by the fuselage, whereas with the standard twin-float version the wings were subjected to greater stress. On the other hand, the twin-float model was more stable when taxiing and taking off from water. The outer wing support floats required on the centerline-float design could easily lead to the aircraft tipping over if struck from the side by a wave. This became apparent during the testing in Travemünde in 1938, when the engine broke from its mount, the aircraft caught fire and burned up.

Ar 196 V 1 with twin floats, three-blade airscrew and a lower profile canopy used for attempts at the world's record.

Ar 196 V 2, D-IHQI (Wk. Nr. 2590) with twin floats. Prototype for the A-series.

By November of 1937 the design blueprints for the pre-production series had been drawn up. Final assembly of the first ten Ar 196 A-0 pre-production models began in November 1938. Testing with front-line units began in the first weeks of 1939. The aircraft were fitted with standard twin floats like prototypes Ar 196 V 1 and V 2, since no final decision had yet been made as to which of the two float configurations was assessed to be better. The two floats were interchangeable and could replaced by cushioned ice skis. Unlike the first prototype the horn counterbalance on the tailfin was dropped and the BMW 132k engine, which had an 80 hp advantage, was used in place of the BMW Dc. Additionally, full production versions were fitted with a three-blade propeller, which had already been tested on the V 1 prototype D-IEHK (Wk.Nr. 2589).

Ar 196 V 1, DIEHK (Wk. Nr. 2589) with two-blade propeller and twin floats. This was the prototype for the A-series.

By upgrading to a different engine, creating a flatter profile canopy enclosed at the rear and removing the military equipment, the first prototype was converted into a special version with improved performance characteristics which was to be used for record-setting flights. This version, however, was not approved by the RLM for security reasons.

In mid-1939 Arado had fallen behind in its delivery quota as dictated by to the general staff's program, but by the end of the year had made up for lost time.

Ar 196 — Procurement figures for 2nd half 1939

	August	September	November	December
quota:	12	18	22	26
actual:	7	15	28	34

From June 1939 to the end of the year an initial batch of 20 Ar 196 A-1 shipborne aircraft were delivered. This was followed by the production of the Ar 196 A-2 coastal patrol aircraft. Altogether, 96 aircraft of both versions were manufactured in 1940, the majority of which were the A-2. In 1941 there followed 140 aircraft, and in the following year a further 79 (Wk.Nr. 132-211) of the A-3 version were built, the latter having improved armament.

The question of armament was not addressed in the initial specification order. The first airplanes were fitted as pure reconnaissance aircraft and were primarily utilized in

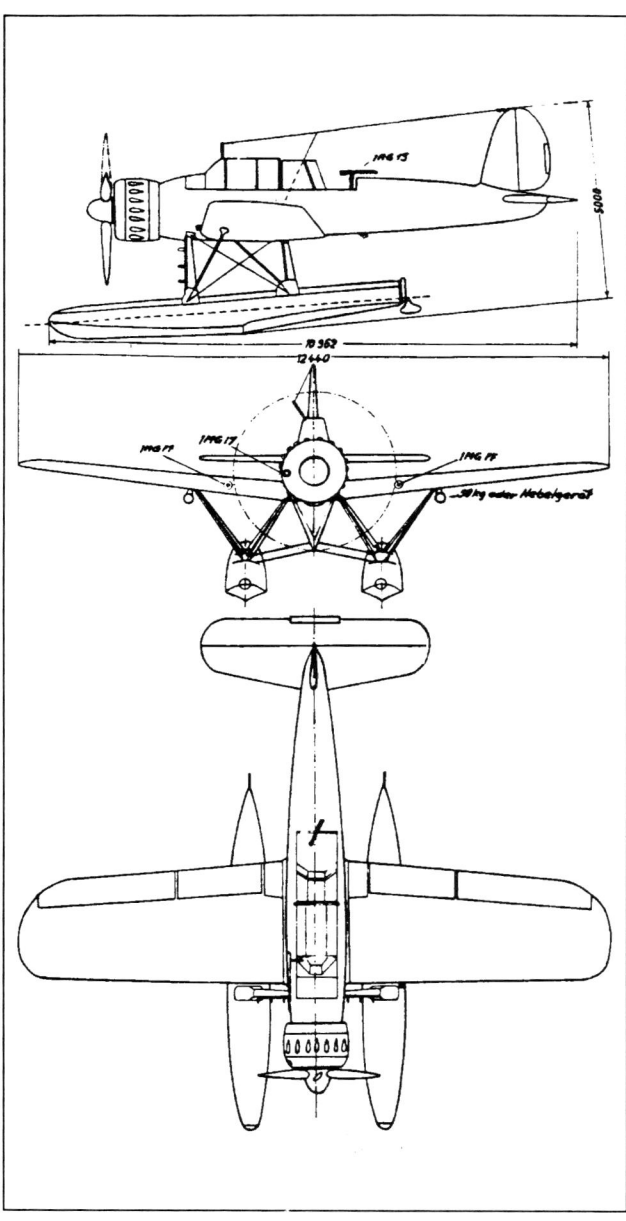

The Ar 196 A-3 maritime reconnaissance aircraft. Three-view (1942).

Ar 196 V 4, D-OVB (Wk. Nr. 2592) with two-blade airscrew and single centerline float (above).

Ar 196 V 3, D-ILRE (Wk. Nr. 2591) with centerline float and wing support floats. Prototype for the B-series.

the role of submarine hunting.[72] They were armed with a simple pivoting MG 15 on an Arado cranked mount for the observer and racks for two 50-kg bombs for attacking smaller ship targets. The absence of attack weaponry was sorely felt during encounters with the enemy. Accordingly, improved armament for fending off enemy fighters was tested with the V 4 prototype D-OVMB (Wk.Nr. 2592) and the A-4 series (Wk.Nr. 117-131), produced in small numbers. Additional armament in the shape of a fixed, forward-firing MG 17 and two 20-mm MG FF cannons in the wing was first introduced on the Ar 196 A-2. These were fitted with special protective sleeves over the muzzle to prevent water spray from damaging the guns.

Production of the Ar 196 A-4 began at the end of 1940. This version was designed exclusively for operating from cruisers. Manufacture of the final version, the Ar 196 A-5, was begun in the spring of 1943, with the majority of the 83 aircraft produced (Wk.Nr. 212 onward) being built by Fokker. The airframe was identical to that of the Ar 196 A-3 series. Radio equipment was improved. Provisions were made in the observer's compartment for twin MG 81 guns

Ar 196 A-3, GA+DX (Wk. Nr. 0124).

A captured Ar 196 A-5 from the "Prinz Eugen", seen at the Willow Grove Naval Air Station in Pennsylvania. Markings are probably T3+CH.

in place of the MG 15 fitted earlier, a feature which was also retro-fitted to the A-3 series. These aircraft were chiefly employed as submarine hunters in the Mediterranean, Aegean and Black Seas, as well as along the coast of western France.[73]

In 1942 approximately 30 license-built Ar 196 floatplanes were under construction at the French company of SNCASO (Societé Nationale de Constructions Aéronautiqes du Sud-Oest). Production of the type continued until the summer of 1944 and may have reached at total of 435.[74] This particularly robust and versatile design, which in September 1940 was the only Arado aircraft to be included in the 'special category' of the acquisition program, was the only German seaplane to serve throughout the war.

The Ar 196 B-series, which like prototypes V 3 to V 5 was fitted with a centerline float, was built in small numbers during 1940/41 as a pre-production batch. These were delivered to front-line units for testing and, for a time, were stationed with the Bordfliegerstaffel 1/196 in Wilhelmshaven. Larger dual floats were developed for the aerodynamically improved Ar 196 C-series due to its higher all-up weight. Testing was carried out in Hamburg by the Institut für Seeflugwesen of the DVL. The MG 151 gun was also tested on this project, although it didn't go into quantity production. Plans called for work to begin in 1942 on a follow-on development, designated Project E 380, which was to have had thicker armor protection and improved armament as well as a higher-performing engine. Construction of the aircraft, which was expected to achieve a maximum speed of 383 km/h, was prevented by the course of the war.

The Ar 196 in propaganda literature:

The young naval officer's adrenalin begins pumping, and he can't believe his eyes: a submarine! A Brit? Get the signal lamp! And then the dirty yellow light flashes forth from the glittering mirror: "What ship?" No answer. The Brit is silent. Prepare for attack! The order echoes through

Der Reichsminister der Luftfahrt
und Oberbefehlshaber der Luftwaffe
Technisches Amt
GL/C — TT

Kennziffer: II Ar 196, A 1, Nr. 2/43
Anforderzeichen: Lfd. Nr. 66/43

Nur für den Dienstgebrauch

Technische Anweisungen des Generalluftzeugmeisters

Betrifft: **Ar 196.** — Änderung der Baureihenbezeichnung Ar 196 A-3 in Ar 196 A-5.

Die Ar 196-Flugzeuge der Baureihe A-3, die mit FuG XVI ausgerüstet sind, erhalten ab Werk-Nr. 196 0212 die Baureihenbezeichnung A-5, sofern nachstehend aufgeführte Änderungsanweisungen und TAGL (Technische Anweisungen des GL) durchgeführt sind:

1. Änderungsanweisung Nr. 43 (Einbau MG 81 Z),
2. Änderungsanweisung Nr. 44 (Feststellbarer Horizont),
3. TAGL lfd. Nr. 718/42 (Mech. Kompensiereinrichtung),
4. Motoränderung, Einbau der UKW-Entstörung durch Fa. BMW (bedingt durch FuG XVI-Einbau).

Nach Durchführung dieser vier Punkte ist in der Datenkarte, dem Typenschild und in der Lebenslaufakte die Bezeichnung Ar 196 A-3 in Ar 196 A-5 zu ändern.

I. A.
gez. H ü b n e r

Ar 196 A-5 and technical specifications dictating the conversion from the A-3 (1943 — above and below).

Ar 196 A with BMW 132 K engine

Dimensions, weights and performance:

wingspan:	12.44 m
length:	10.96 m
height:	4.45 m
wing surface:	28.30 m²
propeller: three-blade all-metal variable-pitch	
engine performance:	920 hp
empty weight:	2335 kg
total weight:	3303 kg
max speed@1000 m:	315 km/h
service ceiling:	7000 m
range:	800 km
endurance:	4 hrs, max 5 hrs
can be operated in up to force 4 seas	

the radio helmet's throat microphone to the pilot. Unteroffizier B. readies himself for the attack run. The machine seems to fire straight down on the target, the airframe shudders. At the last moment the machine is pulled up, the bomb falls directly toward its target. It impacts 25 meters off the stern. The submarine rocks. This massive, stretching iron monster has been struck as if by a giant's fist smashing down into the water. A second dive: the second bomb hits the controls of the Brit and damages his rudder. This last strike has rendered it unmaneuverable. Now one thing is certain, the enemy can no longer escape. It is in the hands of this lone aircraft, suddenly appearing and striking as if from nowhere.[75]

The Ar 231 Submarine Reconnaissance Aircraft

Because of its many years' experience in the design of maritime aircraft Arado was given an exclusive limited-production contract in the summer of 1938 for the development of a submarine-based aircraft design. As early as 1915 the German navy had recognized that submarine-based airplanes would be an ideal way to increase the inadequate reconnaissance range of submarines. In 1917 there were plans for a floatplane which could be disassembled and stowed in a container on board a submarine. The project never materialized because the planned submarine design was not able to be completed before the end of the war. Once France and Japan began experimenting with the concept in the early '30s, in 1938 the Oberkommando der deutschen Kriegsmarine (High Command of the German Navy) began planning for the construction of larger submarines for long-range missions in the Atlantic. This was done in conjunction with the general fleet expansion program. Before radar became available for finding targets, it was expected that an aircraft which could be disassembled and carried onboard would serve in the reconnaissance role as a submarine's "eyes." The size of the new submarines permitted their stowage in pressure-proof containers. The airplane was to be removed from and inserted into its container by means of a boom crane, have small dimensions, be easily assembled, have communications and signals equipment, safety and rescue gear and be able to land and takeoff in short periods of time.

Beginning in mid-1938 Arado began preliminary work in Brandenburg on several design variants under the project number E 300. Factory flight testing was to have taken place on the Breitling in Warnemünde. On 1 December 1938 the naval high command held a meeting, during which the permissible dimensions of the aircraft, the arrangement of the aircraft chamber, desired flight characteristics, and the suitable radio equipment were discussed and clarified. The Institut für Seewesen of the DVL in Hamburg carried out all studies for the floatation system using an original float and a 1:3 scale model. The preliminary mockup's final requirements, determined by the naval high command and the Luftwaffeninspektion der Marineflieger, were submitted on 27 February 1939 to Generalluftzeugmeister Ernst Udet.

Tactical technical requirements for the development of a submarine-borne aircraft, dated 27 February 1939 (excerpts):

1. Role: Reconnaissance for submarines operating on the high seas (Atlantic).

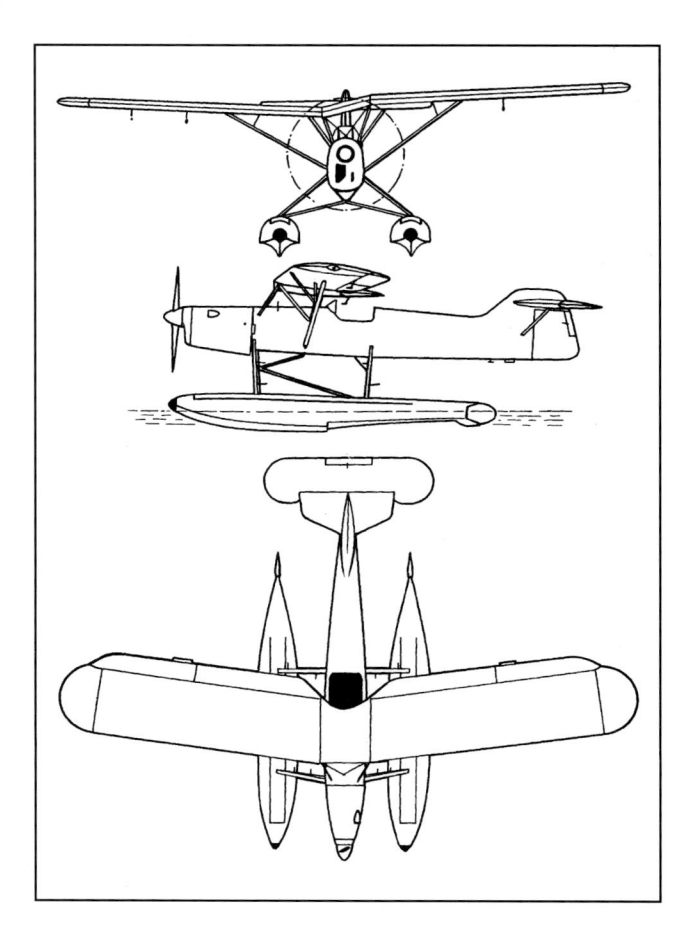

The Ar 231 anti-submarine patrol plane. Three-view (1940).

2. Dimensions: The largest possible space which can be provided for the storage of the aircraft on the submarine, based on safety and structural soundness, is a vertical shaft of having a maximum length of 7.5 m and width of 2.25 m. It is urgently requested that a length of 7 m be utilized, since the submarine's construction depth is just 7 m and a shaft rising 1/2 m above the deck would restrict the accessibility of the crew and storage of the aircraft.
3. Crew: 1
4. Engine: single
5. Airframe: When building the prototype, pay particular attention to the following: in order to prevent damage resulting from the submarine's limited stability in rough seas, the aircraft is to be folded up while in a horizontal position and clamped to a trough-shaped sled. This sled is to be mechanically operated both in the storage shaft and on deck, and be able to accept all strains incurred during pre-warming. Since there is no other way found to warm the aircraft on deck without damaging it, this sled must also be accommodated in the given space of the storage shaft.
6. Armament: none

A day after the final specifications were established, a contract was issued for the immediate commencement of preliminary developmental work of a "Kleinflugzeug See" (compact naval aircraft)[76] to begin. This designation, instead of a shipborne aircraft for submarines, was applied for security reasons. In internal correspondence between the Amt and the company, the purpose of the aircraft was referred to as 'whale-spotting'.

During the subsequent project development phase, particular attention was to be paid to the following details: the storage compartment was to be kept completely dry to prevent corrosion and fuel for 10-15 missions was to be stored outside the submarine's pressure hull in float chambers. A special crane and special sled were to be carried within the shaft of the submarine. The airplane was to be lowered into the shaft propeller-end first to prevent leaking engine oil from getting into the aircraft's cockpit.

Even though the final construction contract for four prototype models wasn't issued until 8 January 1940, on 9 October 1939 Arado began production, immediately following the completion of developmental work. A mockup unveiling took place on 6 December 1939, and deliveries began on 5 January 1940.

The high-wing braced monoplane was fitted with an air-cooled, inverted six-cylinder, four-stroke Hirth HM 501A engine (160 hp) and twin floats. Its monocoque fuselage was covered with hydronalium plating and had an oval cross-section, tapering back to the fixed tailfin. This in turn was raked backward and ended with the rudder attached to the lower part of the fin. The all-metal two-piece tailplane joined to the tailfin at three points. This was the first example of a tailplane mounted above the rudder. The fabric-covered horizontal stabilizer was counterbalanced and featured a trim tab for trimming the aircraft during flight, which could be adjusted from the pilot's seat. The two floats were single stepped, with a semicircular deck and keel-shaped base, and were fitted with counter-balanced non-retracting hollow body water rudders. The float framework was attached to the fuselage and floats by means of hinges. When stowing the aircraft, the floats could be folded up to the fuselage without removing bolts or strut supports. The wing was designed with a fixed center section and braced, folding outer sections to accommodate the storage of the airplane inside the submarine. Viewed from the direction of flight, the centerwing was angled 11.5 degrees upward to the left, thereby permitting the wings to rest snugly on top of each other when folded.

Following the first prototype's maiden flight on 25 July 1940, a demonstration flight took place at the E-Stelle Travemünde on 20 November 1940. Four prototypes had been delivered to Travemünde by May of the following year for the purpose of carrying out airframe and engine endurance testing, plus testing on the floats' impact resistance, flight characteristics and seaworthiness. The test program, lasting until September 1941, revealed numerous shortcomings which, with the exception of uncontrollable flight when the aircraft was stalled, were all corrected. Too late, it was recognized that the airplane could not be brought on board the sub in rough seas without the risk of collision. In addition, submarine commanders feared exposing themselves in daylight on the surface for the nearly ten minutes it took to haul the plane aboard and dismantle it. Before the sudden cancellation of the project, by August the first front-line units had been familiarized with the type, with the notable exception of sea landings. Its only operational role was the assignment of prototypes V 3 and V 4 to the convoy cruiser Stier in 1942. As a replacement, approximately 100 examples of the less expensive, engineless, collapsible Focke-Achgelis FA 330 gyro glider were employed on subs. Towed behind the submarine, they enabled a pilot to carry out airborne observation duties and, in an emergency, could be detached from the sub.

Although the aerodynamically sound machine fulfilled the requisite specifications and all in all was a successful design, its flight handling qualities were apparently unsatisfactory and only two prototypes were built.

The Ar 199 Seaplane Trainer

The Ar 199 seaplane trainer, conceived in 1938, was a modern all-metal low wing design with an Argus 410 A engine, fixed wings and large-area ailerons and flaps. Student and instructor sat side-by-side. Behind them was space for a radio operator. Five prototypes were built beginning in 1939. The first four prototypes had a VDM fixed-pitch propeller, whereas the last and the 26 production models had Argus variable-pitch airscrews. At the least, E-Stelle Travemünde reputedly conducted a thorough evaluation of prototypes V 1 (D-IRFB) and V 3 (D-ITLF), and these were possibly also fitted with ice floats for a short period during testing.

Ar 231 V 1, KK+BP.

Ar 231 V 2 with folded wings.

The failure of the Arado project, whose deficiencies could easily have been detected earlier, meant a loss of approximately 85,000 work hours during the preliminary design phase and 25,000 to 30,000 hours for producing the first four prototypes. Construction costs amounted to between 15,000 and 20,000 RM per unit.

The Ar 198 Tactical Reconnaissance Aircraft

In 1936, along with Blohm & Voss, Focke-Wulf and Henschel, Arado took part in a specification for a battlefield reconnaissance airplane. In addition to Henschel, in July of 1937 Arado was given a construction contract for a pre-production batch of tactical combat reconnaissance aircraft. Demonstrating a unique design approach, the Ar 198 was the answer.

Company description:

The type can be utilized for tactical and battlefield aerial reconnaissance. Either a small or medium size camera is fitted for this purpose and can be removed easily. Windscreen and both side windows made of non-fragmenting hardened glass, glass panels for the remaining parts of the canopy made of plexiglas. The left side window can be folded down to provide fresh air. The liberal glazing of the observer's compartment ensures a wide field of observation in all directions limited only by the horizon.

Of the two generously glazed compartments, the upper one was for the pilot and gunner, while the one beneath the wings was for the observer. This design gave the aircraft its nickname of 'Flying Aquarium'.

The airplane was a cantilever, shoulder-wing design with fixed gear. The forward part of the fuselage was made of a steel framework, into which the engine was integrated, and covered in alloy metal panels. Wings were in two parts, of all-metal construction and designed with twin spars. The slender rear fuselage was laid down for the sole purpose of supporting the empennage, with no provisions for internal equipment.

Its planned role as a battlefield reconnaissance platform necessitated optimum minimum-maximum speed characteristics in addition to good visibility. The high-performance BMW-Bramo 323 A rated at 900 hp was therefore selected. Maximum speed at 3,500 m was 360 km/h; loitering speed near the ground was 118 km/h. Adequate means of defense against attacks from both air and ground forces dictated the requirement for suitable weapons. Incorporated into the design, but not tested, were two fixed, forward-firing MG 17s in the wings, a traversable upward-firing MG 15 in an Arado cranked mount in the rear upper compartment and a downward-firing traversable MG 15 in a bulletproof glass mount in the lower canopy. Additionally, provisions were made for racks to carry a bomb load of four 50-kg bombs.

Ar 198 V 1, D-ODLG, prior to being handed over to the Luftwaffe Central Testing Facility in Rechlin.

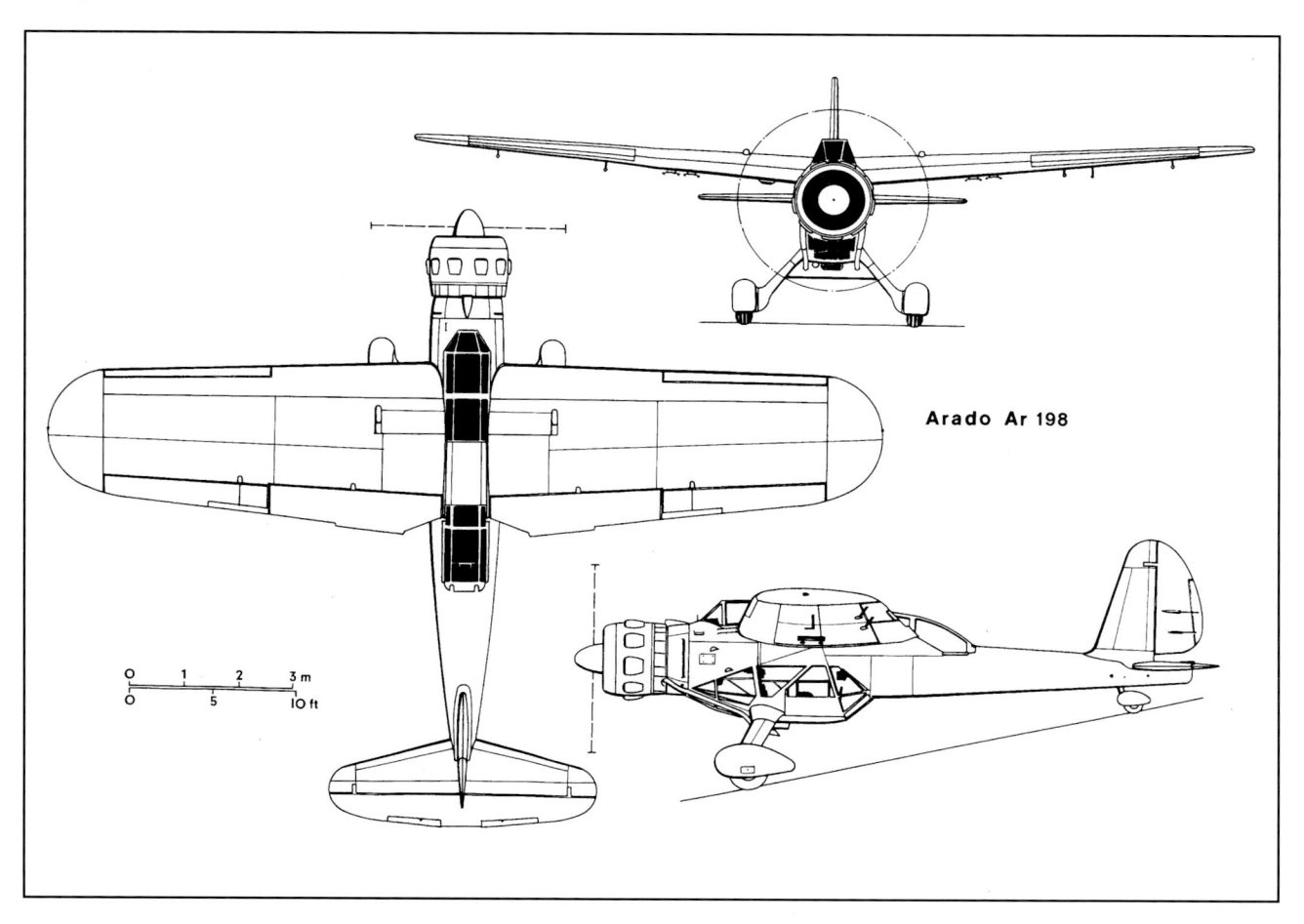

Three-view of the Ar 198 tactical reconnaissance plane (1938).

88

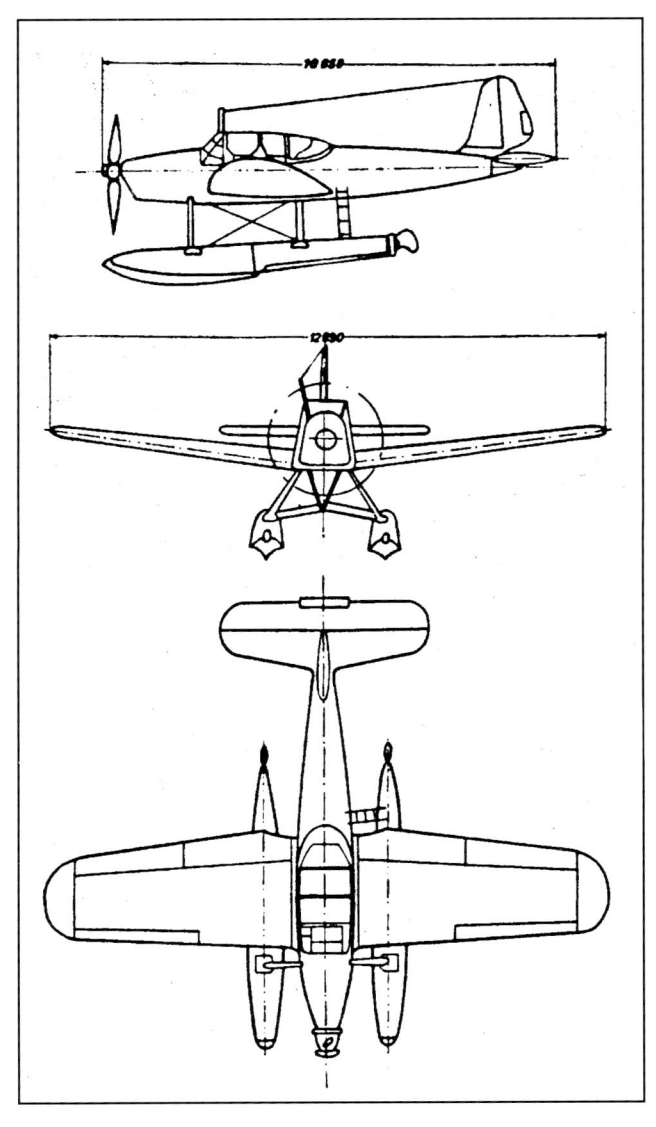

The Ar 199 maritime training aircraft. Three-view (1942).

Ar 199 V 2, D-ISBC (Wk. Nr. 3672).

Known Ar 199 Aircraft:

V 1 (Wk.Nr. 3671) D-IFRB, later NH+AM. Assigned to E-Stelle Travemünde in 1940; Kemi, Finland in 1943.

V 2 (Wk.Nr. 3672) D-ISBC, later probably BH+BM. Probable crash at E-Stelle Travemünde in 1940.

V 3 (Wk.Nr. 3673) D-ITLF, later TJ+HL. Eventually to Seenotkommando IX. Lost 14 August 1942. Recovered in 1993 from Lake Vernj, Lappland.

V 4 (Wk.Nr. 3674) Prototype for pre-production series. E-Stelle Travemünde summer 1940.

V 5 (Wk.Nr. 3676) RC+HR. Testbed for modified landing flaps. Assigned to E-Stelle Travemünde on 27 January 1941. Last documented there in November 1941.

A-0 (Wk.Nr. 0007) May 1940 designated for marsh rescue operations in Finland.

A-0 (Wk.Nr. 0011) May 1943 transferred to Pori, Finland.

A-0 (Wk.Nr. 0017) 28 May 1943 damaged in crash landing at Chartres, France. Handed over to LZA Travemünde.

A-0 (Wk.Nr. 0020) Marsh rescue operations with SNK IX.

A-0 (Wk.Nr. 0026) October 1943 with 10 Seenotstaffel Stavanger.

Ar 199 V 3, D-ITLF (Wk. Nr. 3673).

A-0 KK+BT. October 1942 E-Stelle Travemünde. May 1944 Seefliegerschule Bug on Rügen Island.

A-0 BH+AN. April 1940 in Bergen, Norway.

A-0 DM+ZE. 15 May 1943 crash landed w/o damage near Tournai.

A-0 KK+BX. January 1944 in Tromsö with 5./Sn.

A-0 BH+AM. Summer 1943 in Kemi, Finland.

Despite adequate flight handling characteristics, only a pre-production series was manufactured since it was felt that an adequate supply of obsolescent machines was on hand for training. The recently recovered wreck of an Ar 199, which had primarily been used for marsh rescue operations in Finland, is currently being restored in the USA.

Chapter 12
Mass Production: The Ar 96 Trainer

When the Fw 55 trainer proved unsatisfactory, Arado was assigned the development of a corresponding aircraft type. The cantilevered, all-metal low wing Ar 96, designed by Rethel, Meyer, Blass and Reinhardt, proved to be a successful concept with harmonious dimensions and the typical Arado forward-set tailfin, a feature designed to reduce the dangers of spinning. With around 12,000 examples produced, the Ar 96 is numbered among the most numerous aircraft of the German Luftwaffe. The airplane was initially envisaged for training, night flying, aerobatics, radio operator training, machine gun firing with automatic target camera, aerial reconnaissance using serial photogrammetric cameras and bombing; later it was used almost exclusively for fighter pilot training.

The first V 1 prototype, D-IRUU (Wk.Nr. 2067) was completed in the autumn of 1936 once developmental work had concluded earlier that year. The original tubular steel bridge linking wings, fuselage and landing gear was replaced with a continuous spar design on the Ar 96 V 1. The horn counterbalance on the rudder was dropped, the wings fitted with automatic slats and canopy glazing was increased. The original outward retracting landing gear was replaced by an retracting design having a wider track in order to meet training safety requirements.

The first batch of prototypes proved to be so versatile that in 1937 Ernst Udet, as chief of the Technisches Amt, traveled to the Arado Flugzeugwerke's facilities and personally flew the type.

The second prototype of the Ar 96, V 2, D-IFHD (Wk.Nr. 2068), embodied the changes incorporated from the flight testing of the first one. Performance of the Argus 10 C engine, with 240 hp, proved to be too low for the aircraft's weight of 1,400 kg, and the third prototype was therefore kitted out with the newly-developed 360 hp (later 465 hp) Argus As 410 having twelve suspended cylinders in V-form and a variable-pitch propeller. The Ar 96 V 3 was, together with the fourth prototype, turned over to the E-Stelle Rechlin in the summer of 1938 for follow-on testing.

Due to insufficient quantities of the As 410 engine, the A-series (designed on the basis of the Ar 96 V 6) was shipped beginning in 1939 with the weaker Argus As 10, small numbers of which had found their way to a number of flight training schools towards the end of 1939.

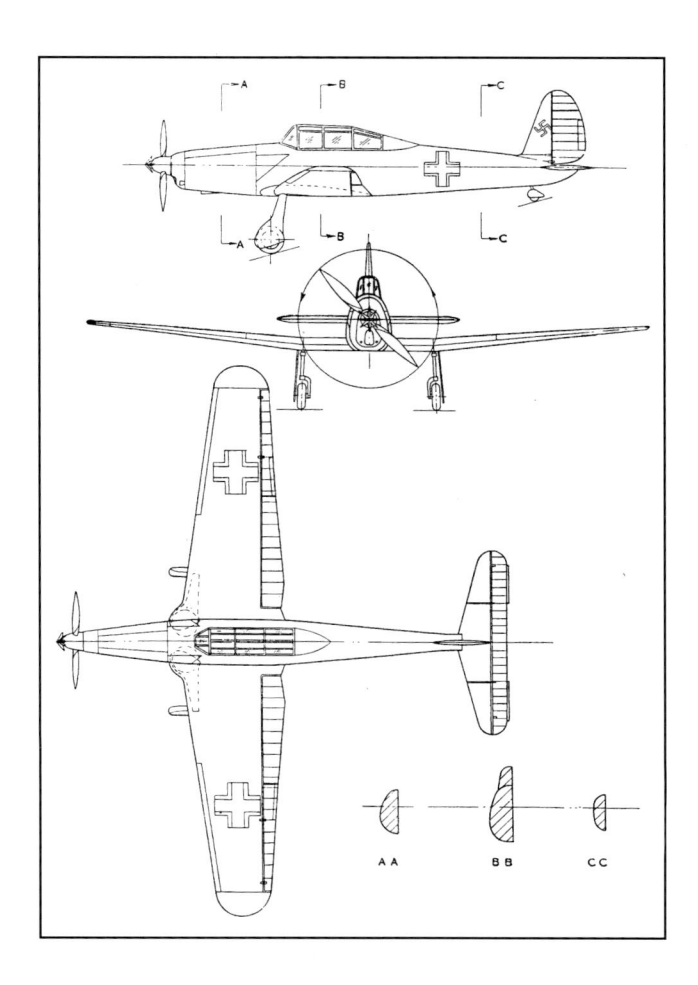

The Ar 96 B trainer. Three-view (1939).

Ar 96 V 1, D-IRUU (Wk. Nr. 2067). Model with Argus As 10 engine and outward retracting landing gear.

Ar 96 V 2, D-IFHD (Wk. Nr. 2068).

Ar 96 B, BH+AX, with Argus As 410 engine.

During the winter of 1939/40 the first Ar 96 B-1s, designed from the Ar 96 V 5, D-INDQ (Wk.Nr. 2071), were delivered. These were true training aircraft having the more powerful engine. Later these were supplanted by the Ar 96 B-2, an armed version destined for fighter training schools. All production airplanes were robust, having good flight handling characteristics, were easy to maintain and technologically up-to-date. They possessed a suite of safety features tailored to training operations. The automatic slats could be set by the pilot. All control surfaces were aerodynamically and statically balanced and could by adjusted in flight. Were the trainee to forget to retract the landing flaps, this would be done automatically once a certain airspeed had been attained. The main landing gear and brakes were activated hydraulically and in the event of hydraulic failure the student could operate them manually by means of a hand pump. The fuselage's all-metal monocoque design was an improvement over the Ar 80 fighter. In place of the initial standard interchange of smooth panels and narrow, grooved profile strips the designers made use of curved, wider longitudinal panels electrically spot welded to standardized, z-shaped longitudinal stringers. The formers were slid into the finished fuselage halves before being riveted together. The panels were spaced longitudinally so that for weight-saving purposes on several of the formers their strength tapered off toward the rear.

Once production was underway, the Arado test group TFo Weigmann studied the possibility of a more economical approach to manufacturing by using an hydraulic extrusion press and an electric roll welding process, with these methods being employed in the tailplane sub-assembly production.[77] The goal was a reduction in the number of individual parts and a shorter production time. The new press frame construction, which was a partial deviation from the previous semi-monocoque design, necessitated the use of large quantities of expensive Duraluminum sheeting. A reduction in cost was accomplished by using 450 to 500 mm wide panel material vice the 1x2 m standard size sheeting. Overall, the tests showed that the number of individual parts utilized in the Ar 96 tailplane could be reduced from nearly 67 in production models to just 26. It was hoped that total production time for an airplane would drop from 110 hours to 60 to 65 hours. During the course of later construction phases Arado conducted studies on accelerating the riveting process by utilizing snap riveting and improved automation, already being employed by Focke-Wulf and

Ar 96 B instrument panel.

Vertical stabilizer of the Ar 96 V 1.

Messerschmitt.[78] Comparison studies between riveting and the electric roll welding process on the tailplane's wingtip former and spar web revealed various advantages. The significant amount of work involved in preparing the sheeting and the risk of corrosion at the weld points spoke out against the welding process.

Utilization of modern production techniques:

Particularly good examples of this can be made of the Me 109 and the Fw 190 which, due to their open design, have virtually gone completely over to machine riveting in their production process. The rudder of the Fw 190, for example, utilizes 41% automated riveting, 38% snap riveting and 21% hand riveting. In a plant using production state I, meaning a factory not utilizing the advantages of automated riveting, rivet time is increased by 40 percent. In a factory not even employing snap riveting in any significant way, rivet time is increased by 120 percent over a plant with production state II.[79]

Whether or not there was ever an Ar 96 B-3 or B-4 series is open for speculation. The final variant, designated the B-5, had the same basic airframe as the B-2, but was fitted with the improved FuG ZY radio system. A C variant with equipment for ordnance-dropping was never put into production.

Our Ar 96 B Trainer.
Arado-Company release:

Training of the flying personnel of our proud Luftwaffe is carried out at specific schools with complete thoroughness. Above all, these aspiring fighter pilots are provided with a high amount of flying potential ... Our Arado Ar 96 has proven itself outstandingly as a trainer during the training process of these future combat pilots. A young fighter, leaving this school for the front-line, will — after only a few combat missions — become a fighter pilot to be feared by the enemy.

A large number of airplanes were built under license by the Ago Flugzeugwerke. The Klemm Werke took part in setting up production in 1940 and in 1941 was involved in replacement part production.[80] A production site was never established in Hungary, however, although previously a few examples of the Ar 96 had been exported there. It is unclear whether in 1938 an export version was built utilizing the 365 hp Wright Whirlwind R 975 E radial engine. The Ar 96 b V 9 formed the basis for a multi-role version, 24 of which were built for Bulgaria in 1939. The first of these was delivered in the autumn of 1940 and the last in early summer 1941. The airplane had an open rear cockpit with traversable defensive gun on an Arado mount and was also equipped for dropping bombs.

As the war progressed, an increasing shortage of materials forced Arado to produce the aircraft in a simplified composite construction design using lower grade steel and wood in areas where the use of metal wasn't a critical factor. An initial version, the Ar 296, proved unsatisfactory and was not pursued further. Beginning in 1943 a cooperative effort was undertaken with the French company of SIPA, which was awarded a contract for three prototypes of the follow-on Ar 396 plus a pre-production run of 25 aircraft. The Argus As 411 A-1 engine powering a two-blade autopitch Argus wooden airscrew served as the powerplant. This engine was a follow-on development of the As 410 with a performance of 440/580 hp at 3,250 rpm. Despite a 250-kg jump in the all-up weight this engine boosted the plane's top speed to roughly 354 km/h. In order to simplify production the individual components were built as straight as possible, dispensing with aerodynamic refinements. With regard to landing gear, the concept of a nose strut was toyed with initially. But the shift in the center of gravity with this potential arrangement would have negatively influenced the aircraft's taxi and takeoff handling. In addition, the side wheel position precluded an effective way to attach the compression strut and its direction of compression, making any type of shock absorption nearly impossible. This landing gear design was deemed "unfavorable" in a company memorandum, in that there were concerns that "all kinds of compromises would have to be made and that "an effective solution would have to be implemented by force."[81] Eventually a conventional main gear/tailwheel design was decided upon, which, by dispensing with a 90 degree rotation and gear covers the wheels retracted only halfway into the inner wing sections, enabling them to roll freely when making a belly landing.

Ar 96 V 9, D-IXWZ (Wk. Nr. 2075). Export model for Bulgaria, fitted out with variable-pitch propeller, radio, bomb mounts and traversable rear-firing armament resting on an Arado mount.

Ar 396 SIPA; this, the last surviving example of its kind, was written off after a crash in 1978.

Ar 396 V 5 SIPA S. 111 with variable-pitch propeller and wearing French markings (above).

The Ar 396 A-1 variant was planned for fighter pilot training and was to have been fitted with an MG 17 in the right wing center section, a gun camera, a gunsight and provisions for carrying two 50 kg bombs. The unarmed Ar 396 A-2 was to have served for instrument flight training.

Development was deliberately hampered by the French and the first prototype wasn't completed until after the Normandy invasion. Its maiden flight didn't take place until 29 December 1944 after France had been occupied by Allied forces. The subsequent 27 license-built aircraft were delivered to the newly established French air force under the designation SIPA S.10. Follow-on developments included the all-metal S.11 and S.12, powered by a SNECMA-produced Renault engine, of which 50 each were produced until 1956, and the S.111 and S.121 (production amounting to 53 and 50, respectively).

With the fear of a loss in production caused by the French company, before the end of 1944 plans were made for supplementary production to be undertaken by the Czech company of Letov, near Prague. Along with Avia, Letov had earlier been involved in the production of the Ar 96 B.

But only a few aircraft were ever delivered to the German Luftwaffe. After the war, the Czech air force was no longer interested in the Ar 396 version. Instead, until 1948 Avia and Letov produced the Ar 96 B under the designation of C.2B-1, using the original production facilities.

Ar 96 B1(Ar 396 A-1) Dimensions, weights and performance:

Ar 96 B1(Ar 396 A-1) Dimensions, weights and performance:

wingspan:	11.00 m(11.00)
length:	9.13 m(8.80)
height:	2.64 m(2.40)
wing surface:	17.10 m2(18.3)
wing loading:	99.50 kg/m2(116)
engine	As 410 A(As 411 MA)
takeoff performance:	460 hp(580)
empty weight:	2335 kg
total weight:	3303 kg
max speed:	340 km/h(348)
service ceiling:	7100 m(6800)
range:	990 km(790)
time-to-climb 1000 m:	2.2 min(2.6)
time-to-climb 2000 m:	4.3 min(5.2)
time-to-climb 3000 m:	6.8 min(-)
landing speed:	103 km/h(116)

Chapter 13
Experimenting with "Air Tourism": World Records with the Ar 79 Sport and Touring Airplane

In 1937, shortly before Walter Rethel was driven out of the company, Arado succeeded in developing the robust, reliable and economical Ar 79 sport and touring plane, based on the earlier L I/L II sportplane. This was the last civilian aircraft produced by this company and was conceived for the Class A 2/K 1 training, although following approval and promotion by the RLM, the option of military application was not completely ruled out. This fully aerobatic airplane possessed excellent features, particularly with regard to its maneuverability and the reliable Hirth engine, which could be flown for long distances at full throttle.

Advertising:

The Ar 79 is a purpose-built cantilever low-wing composite design, drawn up to meet the requirements of a training and touring aircraft.

The use of the most modern design concepts in the development of the lightplane has interestingly given the Ar 79 excellent flight characteristics and outstanding performance at a low price — and along with this, safety and economy.

The forward portion of the fuselage is made of steel tubing to a point just behind the twin seat cabin, then continues in monocoque form made of electron. The fully glazed cabin is aerodynamically and integrally part of the fuselage. The sliding glass upper portion ensures a rapid and easy entry and exit. The cabin has all the features (instrumentation, dual controls, good visibility) to be expected in a high-quality, light training and touring airplane.

The landing gear is of course retractable. It is operated by means of a collapsible hand crank. The 2 meter wide track, the hydraulic brakes and the free traversing tailwheel provide the machine with superior taxiing characteristics. The tailfin, firmly riveted to the fuselage, and the adjustable tailplane are of all metal construction. Both the ailerons and rudder are made of a light metal framework covered in fabric, as are the horizontal stabilizers (which can be trimmed in flight). The employment of split flaps passing underneath the fuselage provide the Ar 79 with unusually low minimum flying and landing speeds. The wooden wings — covered in plywood and fabric — are detachable from their centerpiece by just three bolts. The fixed portion consists of a spar with attached torsion head. The Hirth HM 504 A2, an air-cooled inline engine with 105 hp, was developed as the powerplant. A lighter engine, such as the 80 hp Hirth HM 60R can be utilized in its place. The two fuel tanks located beneath the luggage compartment each have a capacity of 60 liters, giving the Ar 79 a range of over 1000 km.[82]

A pilot's assessment of the Ar 79:

When cruising, the Ar 79 needed no more than nine liters for each 100 kilometers, so that it could be considered a prototype for the energy-conscious times of the '90s.

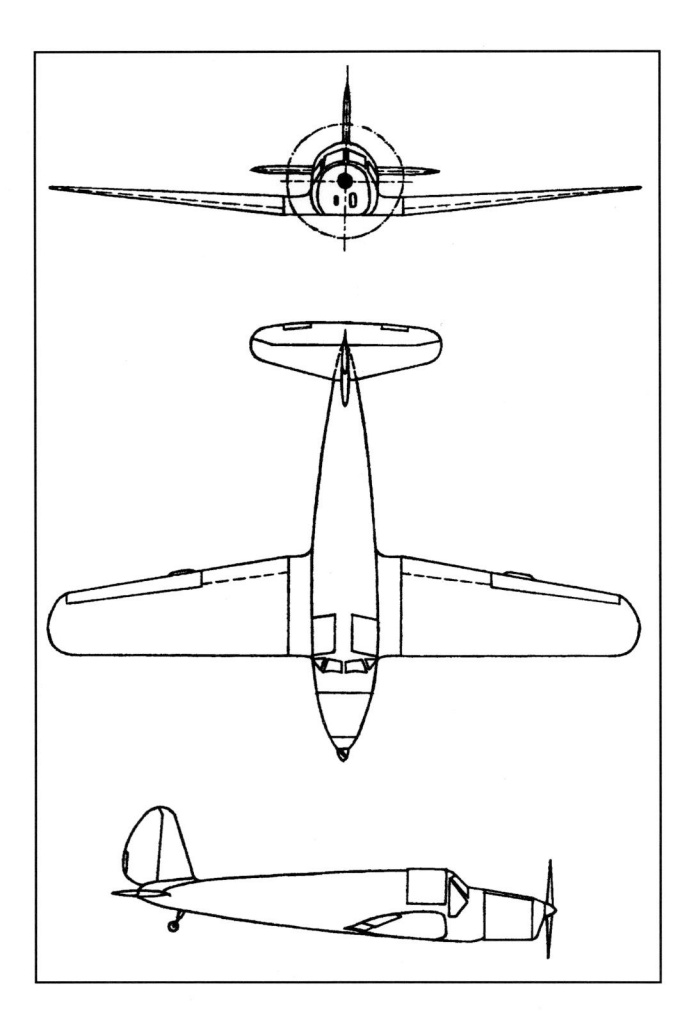

The Ar 79 sport and touring plane. Three-view (1937).

200 km/h cruising and 220 km/h maximum speeds were attributes which, even today, are barely attainable — given the low fuel consumption ... If the machine were flown 'properly' using trim tabs, it was possible to completely release the controls and the airplane would blindly fly straight ahead. If you wanted to upset the airfield safety personnel, you'd drop to about two meters height with your landing gear still retracted. Then, if you acted as though you were landing, the police would see 'red' and fire off a red flare. You'd then quickly pop the gear down, which had shock absorbers, and before you knew it, the crate was on the ground. If you ever really had to make an emergency landing, you'd sideslip in with fully extended flaps and you'd be halfway there — your descent rate would pick up rapidly, though, and those who could maintain control of the situation could quickly set the plane down at 60 km/h.[83]

The Arado 79 obeyed the pilot to the letter. I was myself a test pilot during the testing period, and everything had been thought of ... The Ar 79 gave the pilot a sense of unlimited security, which often unfortunately led to some foolhardy flight demonstrations. Such a thing happened to me one time, when I was flying from Villacoublay to Paris with the director of the repair workshop which Junkers had set up during the war for its Ju 88 bomber. We circled the Eiffel Tower at a height parallel to the first restaurant, and

I asked my passenger: "Are you safely buckled in?" Then we went for it. Pushing from the cruising speed of 200 to 250 km/h, then, whoosh!, upside down, three times, always passing by the restaurant, one loop after the other without ever losing altitude.[84]

With a view to Göring's motto that the Germans should be a nation of flyers, Arado sought out a gap in the market in the area of 'air tourism' and, in the short period of economic boom before the war, launched an intensive advertising campaign to draw attention to the new alternative to automobile and rail travel. In comparison with the refined automobile class the airplane was able to hold its own economically with its better performance. Nor did it need to shrink from comparison with competing prototypes or post-war developments in view of its relation of engine power to performance.[85]

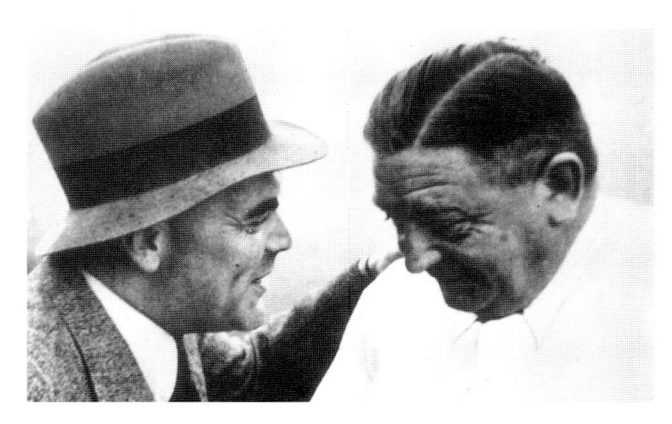

W. Blume (left) with the record-setting pilot Seelbach.

Ar 79 A, D-EKCX. Holder of the world speed record over 1,000 kilometers (1938).

Performance data for common German sport-, touring- and training aircraft

Model	hp	Load(kg)	kg/hp	Vmax
Ar 79	105	300	7.23	230
Ar 66	240	425	5.6	210
Ar 76	240	350	4.5	267
Fl 99	160	255	5.47	236
Kl 35B	105	290	7.15	210
Bü 180	60	245	8.4	175
Bf 108	240	545	5.63	291
Fw 44	160	335	5.62	185

Touring with the Ar 79:

Why the concept of a private touring airplane? If you were to ask this of a long-time aircraft owner, you would sense from his words the love of the flexibility which surrounds air tourism.

Flying according to your own will is wonderful, to be sure, but it isn't an altogether inexpensive hobby. However, if you must often and quickly make business trips, the Ar 79 ceases to become a luxury item any longer, even though the aircraft is constructed down to the finest detail with loving care. For the purchase price matches that of a good touring car, and maintenance costs are low as a result of selecting the best materials and having a fuel consumption of just 11 liters per 100 km. Travel costs in the Ar 79 are further reduced by considering that its route — the air route — is shorter and more direct than the trip by land. In a headwind the Ar 79, with its high speed, has a distinct advantage over a slower airplane: for example, with a 50 km/h headwind an aircraft with 100 km/h cruising speed only covers 50 km of ground, but an aircraft with 200 km/h cruising speed covers 150 km — three times as much, even though its only twice as fast ... And please take this into account: say your destination is 500 km away. A regional train travels an average speed of 80 km/h. Your vehicle maybe does the same. But the Ar 79 does over 200. By ground you need seven hours, but flying in the Ar 79 only two and a half. There and back is five hours instead of fourteen!

Do you know what that means? You save time and money. You're relaxed. You're not fixed to an itinerary. If you want to return home the same day, now you can! —You don't need to pack a suitcase, travel overnight by train or spend the night in a hotel. Instead, you can visit several relatively distant locales on the same day, if needed. And you have the added enjoyment of the wonderful experience of flying.[87]

The airplane, which initially was produced as prototypes D-EKCX and D-EHCR and later followed by three variants with airframe improvements, drew attention through several record-breaking flights. After participating in the Deutschlandflug D-EKCX set a world record on 15 July 1938 with an average speed of 229.040 km/h over a 1,000 km/h course.[88] Pilot Lüber flew twenty circuits of the fifty km route, measured out near Brandenburg, from 4:06 to 8:28 in the morning, flying at an altitude of between 50

Ar 79 A, D-EHCR. World speed record over 2,000 kilometers.

and 100 meters. In doing so, he broke the record which had previously been set by a Czech airplane. The Berliner press reported on 8 July 1938: "German Lightplanes in the Lead!" On 29 July pilot Seelbach in Ar 79 D-EHCR averaged 227.029 km/h over a 2,000 km course in eight hours and 48 minutes with a full load, thereby setting a second world record for Arado.

The record-breaking flight of 29 July 1938:

From Thornau — near Stendal -, where a white signal cloth had been laid out, the aircraft raced full throttle to the northern turning point, the tower of a country pub on the northern point of the Tegeler See in Berlin. Ten times, back and forth between Thornau and Berlin-Tegel, the plane covered the 100 km. Like a lightning bolt the machine shot over the ground, sometimes as low as 5-10 meters above the earth.

The record airplane reached the turning marker at almost precisely the same second as calculated beforehand, and company colleagues seemed clearly pleased after receiving the telephone report from record officials.

Ar 79 with droppable fuel tanks for long-range flying.

Ar 79, D-EHCR, With Rudolf Jenett (right) and Horst Pulkowski at the controls.

Pilots R. Jenett (outside right) and H. Pulkowski (center) saying their goodbyes to W. Blume prior to setting off for India and Australia on 17 December 1938.

After the fifth circuit it began to rain; the cloud base sank lower and lower, but the pilot never thought of giving up his attempt on the record — just the opposite, hoping the 'circuit wouldn't become tedious'. Thus, he flew a precise course over the 100 km back and forth, so that eventually the villagers and farmers, along with their 'cart horses', gradually became 'agitated'. One even tried to pelt the low-flying record airplane with stones. The pilot later jokingly reported that he would really liked to have used his thermos bottle as a missile.[89]

On 31 July NSFK-Sturmführer Kuhn took first place in race A at the International Air Races in Frankfurt am Main, winning the 'Ehrenpreis des Herrn Generalfeldmarschall Göring', and Oberstleutnant Junck secured himself second place in race B, taking the 'Ehrenpreis des Staatsekretärs der Luftfahrt und Generalinspekteurs der Luftwaffe, Generaloberst Milch'.

D-EHCR made history on a long-distance flight with Oberleutnant Pulkowski and Leutnant Jenett at the controls; the route was to cover the distance from Berlin to Australia and back. Prior to the flight, Rudolf Jenett took advice from Wolfgang Gronau, who had previously flown long-range Atlantic crossings. The tense political situation required that the flight over Dutch territory was strictly contingent upon avoiding restricted military areas. Acquiring the necessary documents, visas and overflight permission could therefore only be obtained with the help of the RLM and Shell Oil Company.[90] Jenett desperately sought for navigation aids in a variety of shops, but was only able to come up with a map of Australia in 1:6 million scale.

Takeoff occurred at 10:56 am on 17 December 1938 in -15 degrees Celsius weather, after the pilots (surrounded by media reporters) were given a sendoff by Walter Blume. The first stages were via Munich, Bolzano and Brindisi. They crossed the Mediterranean Sea at extremely low altitude in the worst weather conditions imaginable with the destination of Benghazi as their goal. In order to avoid the longer stretches over water and the worst of the forecasted bad weather, it was determined to fly to Australia via India. The 6,400 km segment from Benghazi to Gaya in India was to be covered in a single non-stop flight. The previous international distance record was 4,175 km. For this new record attempt the standard 60 liter tanks were replaced by a single 500 liter tank, supplemented with a 100 liter drop tank attached below the fuselage. The wing tanks were removed and their space used for storing luggage. If the crew wanted to access this storage area while on their trip, they had to lie on their backs below the wings — much to the amusement of spectators. Additional equipment and tools were carried in special metal boxes located in the narrow cockpit below the pilots' knees. All in all the airplane was overloaded by one-third, with the weight of the extra fuel alone roughly corresponding to the normal all-up rated weight of the standard airplane. At the request of Walter Blume, Ernst Udet had to personally intervene on two occasions in order to effect special permission for taking off at a higher weight than allowable. Since the aircraft had no radio equipment and the pilots could only orient themselves by compass and map, it was agreed that they would fire off flares when passing over certain points. If these were not seen from the ground a detailed search and rescue operation would be initiated. After nearly forty hours of flying, during which time the pilots were not even able to change seats (thanks to the plane's center control column), Gaya was reached and a new world record established.

On New Year's Eve 1938 Germany received the telegram message of the landing, which was immediately passed on to Staatsekretär Milch and General Udet. The propaganda echo in Germany was enormous. Milch telegraphed a personal message: "My best regards to the Ar 79 crew of Oberleutnant Pulkowski and Leutnant Jenett on their successful completion of the long-distance flight from Benghazi to Gaya!" Göring cabled: "I am proud that it was you in particular who have succeeded in ending the past year so successfully", and in doing so, indirectly expressed his satisfaction that it was two Luftwaffe members who had set the new record.

Ar 79. Press reports on the world flight records (1938/39).

R. Jenett (left) and H. Pulkowski during a stopover on the flight to India, which later continued on to Australia.

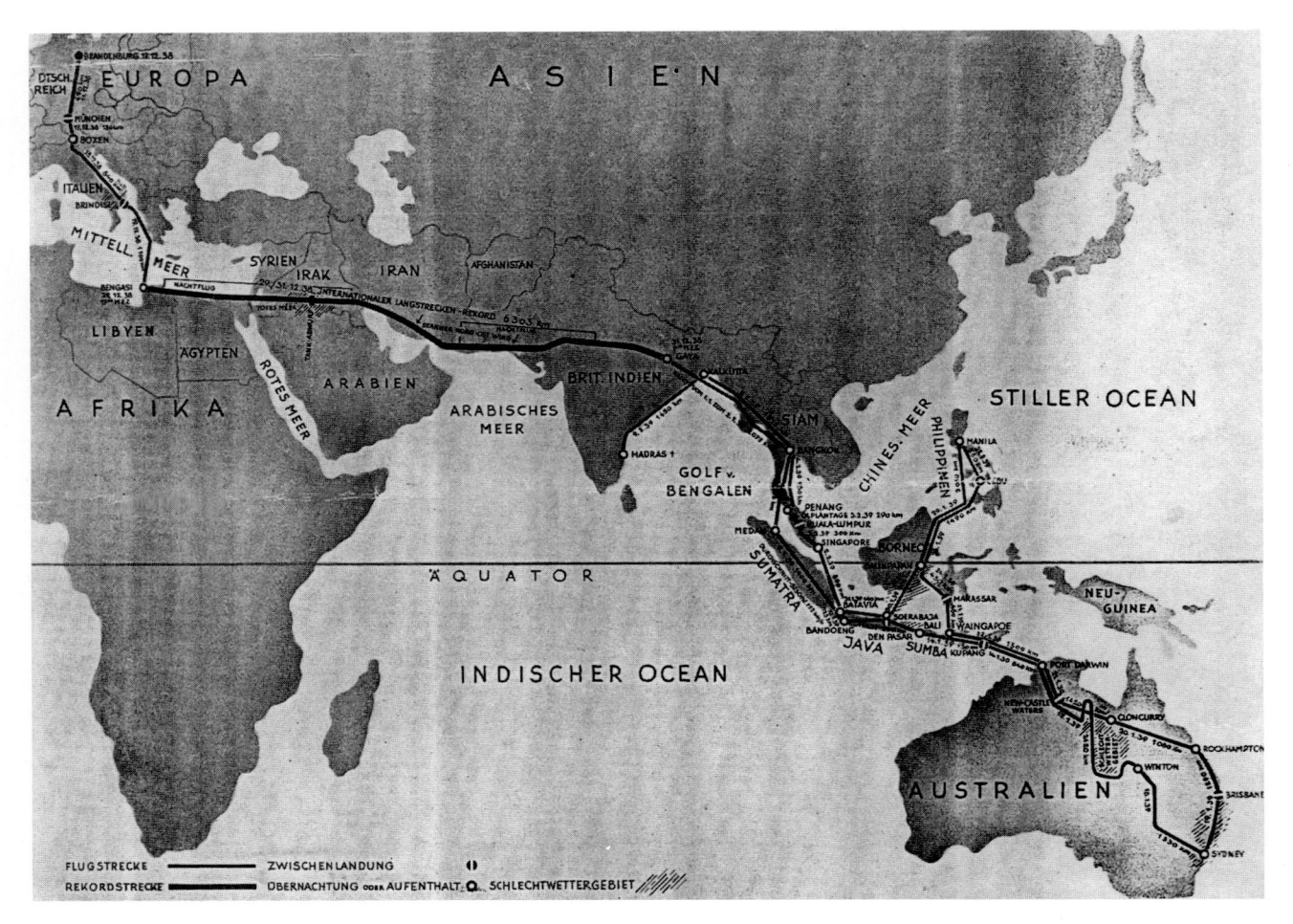

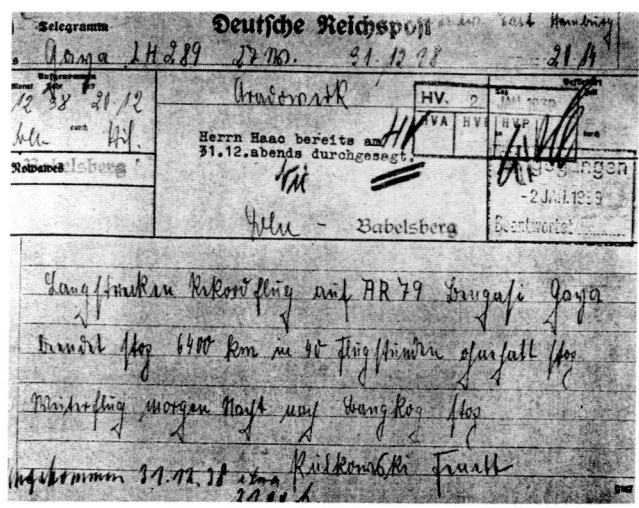

Ar 79. Flight route from 17 December 1938 to 5 February 1939 (above).
Ar 79. Telegraph report after the record flight to Gaya, India (31 December 1938 — right).

After a series of receptions, interviews and a short rest period, Pulkowski and Jenett continued on via Bangkok and Sumatra to Java. From Bali it was a 2,000 km non-stop flight over the Timor Sea to Darwin in northern Australia, where a congratulatory telegram was waiting for them from Elly Beinhorn, who had previously flown to Australia in a Bf 108. The final stretch was 3,500 km long through Australia's uninhabited interior to their end destination of Sydney. In case of emergency landing the airplane carried alum for filtering drinking water, weapons and a tent weighing just 1,200 grams — all stowed in the wing. The return journey passed via the Philippines and Singapore to Madras, where the airplane landed after covering some 37,000 km.

Rudolf Jenett took off from Madras the following morning to carry out a flight demonstration. With a maharajah as a passenger he began by carrying out low level aerobatics just above the ground, making cross-control banks in order to demonstrate the maneuverability and the type's ease-of-handling. Following this, he made two circuits of the field with members of the local aero club as passengers. The British press accused him of carelessness because of his low-level flying, calling him a 'bloody criminal'. After being replaced at the controls by Horst Pulkowski, a fateful collision with a large vulture occurred while making an airfield circuit at low altitude. The impact caused the aircraft to immediately crash. Investigation by British and Indian authorities revealed that the creature struck the propeller and the imbalance caused by the shattered propeller led to a break in the center spar of the left wing. The airplane made a half roll (possibly a 1 1/2 roll) before impacting the ground in an inverted state. Horst Pulkowski was killed instantly, his skull crushed. His Indian passenger never regained consciousness and died on the way to the hospital. Jenett, who scoured the airfield for bits of wreckage, came across innumerable propeller fragments the size of matches, located a short distance from the crash site. Previous tests in Rechlin had shown that a propeller breaks apart in just such a manner when a solid body comes in contact with the propeller arc. Rudolf Jenett was permitted by the senior-ranking local British authority to conduct a moving funeral service for his unfortunate partner. Upon his return he personally gave a detailed account of his experiences to both Udet and Milch.

The accident in no way tarnished the airplane's good reputation. It was exhibited at the time both at the Brussels Aero-Salon as well as at the 'ILIS' show in Stockholm and was utilized by leading Arado businessmen as a liaison airplane. Its owners included such prominent figures as Ernst Udet, Hanna Reitsch, Heinz Rühmann, the industrialist Krupp von Bohlen und Halbach as well as the general director of the Hungarian iron, steel and heavy machine company, Stephan von Horthy. As late as 1955 an Ar 79 was still flying under the registration D-EGUV, and even now an example of an Ar 79 B is numbered among one of the two remaining Arado planes left in Germany.

Restored Ar 79 B (Wk. Nr. 41), the next-to-last example in the series, in Berneck bei Göppingen (1980). —Above right: rudder. Center right: side view. Above: cockpit with additional equipment.

Funeral for H. Pulkowski, who lost his life in the crash in India.

Ar 79 with pilot Hanna Reitsch at the controls in Bremen (1942).

Chapter 14
The National Socialist Model Operation

The RLM used its influence upon the Reich-owned company to push contracts through which would otherwise have found little popularity. In doing so, it also demonstrated to privately owned firms what was meant by planned economic fulfillment of duty, favorably priced production, social care and ideological indoctrination of personnel.

With the exception of the large scale production facility in Neuendorf, by the war's outbreak most of Arado's branch sites had already been established. Wittenberg and Rathenow had been operating since 1938; Anklam was beginning production by the end of that year. Corresponding to the increase in production, the yearly turnover rose in 1938 from 23 to 76 million Reichsmark, of which 95 percent was tied in with the RLM. To round off the already ongoing construction efforts and to accommodate the new contracts brought on by the outbreak of the war, in 1939 new construction plans were made totalling 32.5 million Reichsmark; these included a repair and steel press works in Brandenburg.

The cast-iron control exerted by the RLM on senior management required that it provide the RLM's designated representative, the Fliegeroberstingenieur Gottfried Reidenbach, monthly conference reports with employment figures, construction plans, developmental activities and income, finance and production progress. Beginning with annual accounts for 1937 the Deutsche Revisions- und Treuhandaktiengesellschaft assumed responsibility for the fiscal reports. Profit margins were established by state pricing controls. The company's liquidity was exclusively dependent upon the 'Luftfahrtkontor GmbH'[91], contracted to the RLM. This establishment, which developed into an independent banking institution following an infusion of capital in 1938, made sole decisions (based on political necessities) in matters regarding interim investment credit, capital dividends and so-called state written guarantees which were designed to avoid losses in the event of a dropoff in armament production. Its subsidiary, the Luftfahrtanlagen GmbH, was from October 1938 responsible for the approval of all construction of facilities and determined which of these would be practical in a wartime economy.

As a result of the planned economic program rigorously carried out upon the Arado Flugzeugwerke the senior management functioned as the RLM's 'fulfillment' assis-

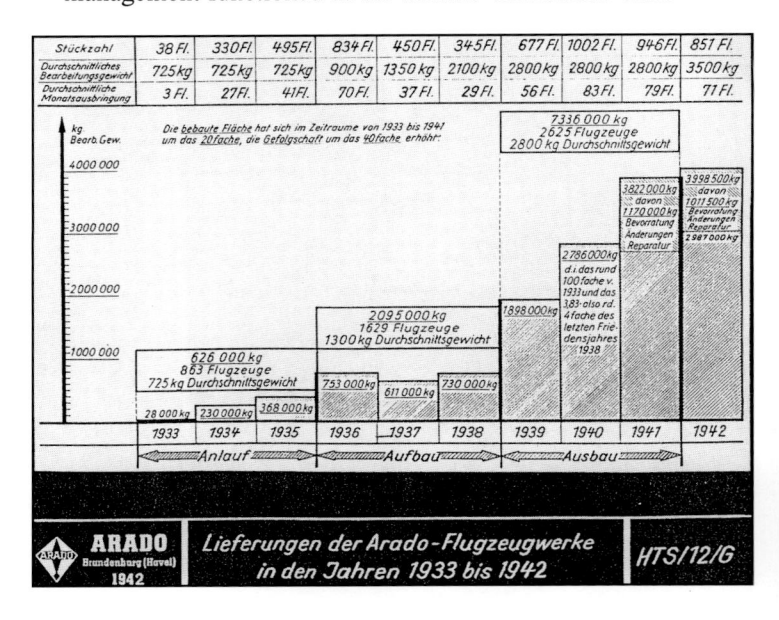

Productivity increases of Arado Flugzeugwerke 1933-1942 (right).

Balance of the Arado Flugzeugwerke (1939 — below).

tant, tailored toward preventing conflicts within the firm. Personnel transfers and questions of competence within the Technisches Amt, plus irritation with the establishment of the acquisition programs led to time-consuming recalculations and changeover of equipment on the part of the company, which in turn were felt through missed deadlines, impact on profits and loss of materials. The Ministerium, on the other hand, continually and categorically called for a drop in wage payouts, a reduction in the materials needed and an increase in profits. Applications for approval of large scale facilities expansion were often refused on the grounds that the high investment debts of the company did not permit such ventures.[92]

Although license production was consistently growing, the firm's developmental programs had been suffering for a long time. Ernst Udet's decision on 13 December 1938 to reduce the number of types in production had a serious impact on production of the Arado Flugzeugwerke's own designs. In fiscal year 1939 (up until the beginning of the war) Arado built its indigenous Ar 79, Ar 95 and Ar 197 as well as the Ar 96 and Ar 196. With production of the Ar 66 trainer ceasing after 1937, only the Ar 96 and the Ar 196 seaplane were still on the Amt's priority list.

With the Brandenburg facility primarily focusing on the production of He 111s from 1937 through the expansion phase, by 1938 the company was also license-building the Bf 109 fighter, along with the He 59 and the W 34 (the latter two ending their production runs). Wing production and final assembly of the Ju 88 bomber began. Wing construction for the Ju 88 alone made up approximately 50 percent of the total production output for the company in 1940.

Shortly before the beginning of the war the production in Warnemünde was directed toward the Bf 109 fighter, which began with the D-1 variant — manufacture of which ceased in 1940. This was followed by the E variants, of which nine E-6/N models were produced in Warnemünde by January 1941, followed by 46 E-7/Ns beginning in March of that year. From December 1940 until October 1941 Arado had also delivered 358 airframes for the Bf 109 F-2.

In addition to the production of the Ju 88, He 111 H (terminated) and the Bf 109, Arado also manufactured the Ar 196 and Ar 96. New types in the program included the He 177 bomber and the Fw 190 fighter. By the year's end 32 Fw 190 A-2 variants had been produced[94] and by the end of 1944 total production for this aircraft type had climbed to 3,944. According to information supplied by the Focke-Wulf-Werke on 8 December 1944, Arado was involved in the manufacture of larger components for the Fw 190 F-8/R1, F-9/R1 and the F-15/R1.

While in 1941 the construction of the Ju 88 bomber and Bf 109 F fighter determined the production profile of the company, the firm's involvement with the He 177 gradually increased. By the time 1940 turned into 1941 35 of the pre-production A-0 series had been produced in Warnemünde. There followed 130 examples of the He 177 A-1 series. By the beginning of 1942 well over 50 percent of the firm's production resources were being devoted to this bomber. From October 1942 Arado also became involved in the production of the He 177 A-3 series. The nearly 565 airplanes of the He 177 A-5 series were built simultaneously by Arado and Heinkel from October 1943 on.

The comprehensive license manufacturing program of this airplane, which never fully reached operational capability, proved to be a waste of production facilities urgently needed for other projects.

The prototype construction department began a period of stagnation after it had been given its own department within the so-called Junkershalle in Warnemünde. A shortage of space led to the activation of the first prototype construction hall in Brandenburg at the end of 1935, followed by another expansion of personnel and space with the building of Halle T and Halle S in 1936 and 1937, respectively. The increasing load brought on by the company's license production, however, precluded any further expansion of the prototype construction department from 1938 on — despite a massive expansion in production capacity. Even the design departments were initially forced to put a brake on planned expansion, a measure dictated by a shortage of both space and trained personnel. After a short burst of energy following the move to Brandenburg, company growth virtually ceased from 1937 onward. From 1 September 1939, the firm's technical office was even forced by the RLM to give up its engineers for other important wartime assignments, and the prototype construction department was assigned the responsibility of assisting in monitoring the

Production output breakdown for total of 250 Ju 88s, April 1940:

Junkers:	40 units
Dornier/Wismar and Heinkel:	60 units
ATG and Siebel:	50 units
Dornier/Oberpfaffenhofen:	30 units
Arado/Brandenburg and Henschel:	70 units

Additional license production (fuselages) from 1938 to 1940:

	1938	1939	1940
He 111	67	265	117
Bf 109	145	252	346
He 59	47	10	-
other:	85	60	130
total:	346	625	690

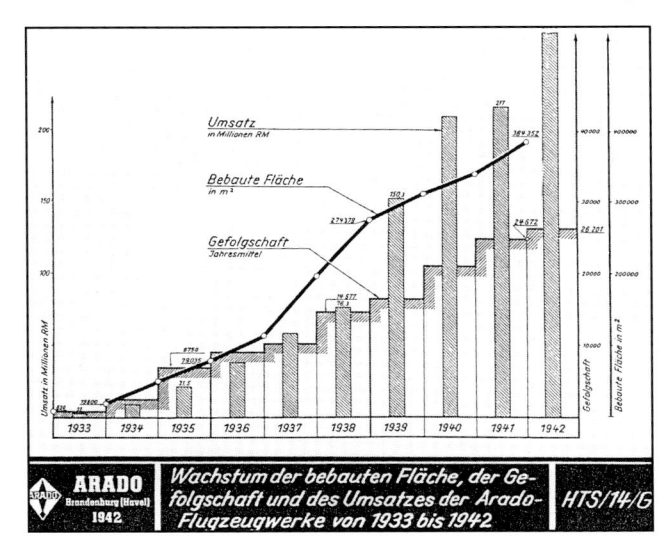

The economic development of the Arado Flugzeugwerke from 1933 to 1942 (sales, buildings, employees).

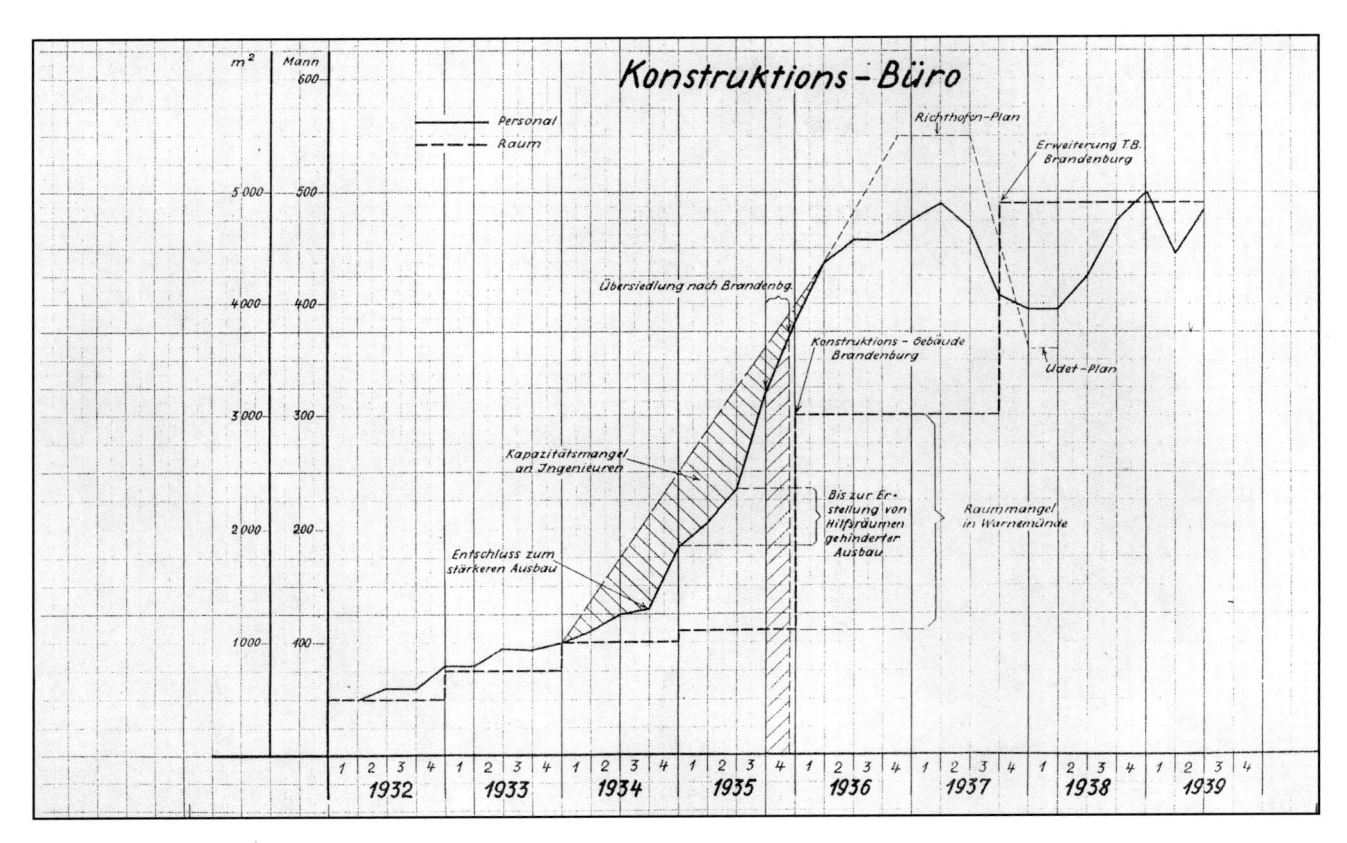

Development of the design bureau 1932-1939.

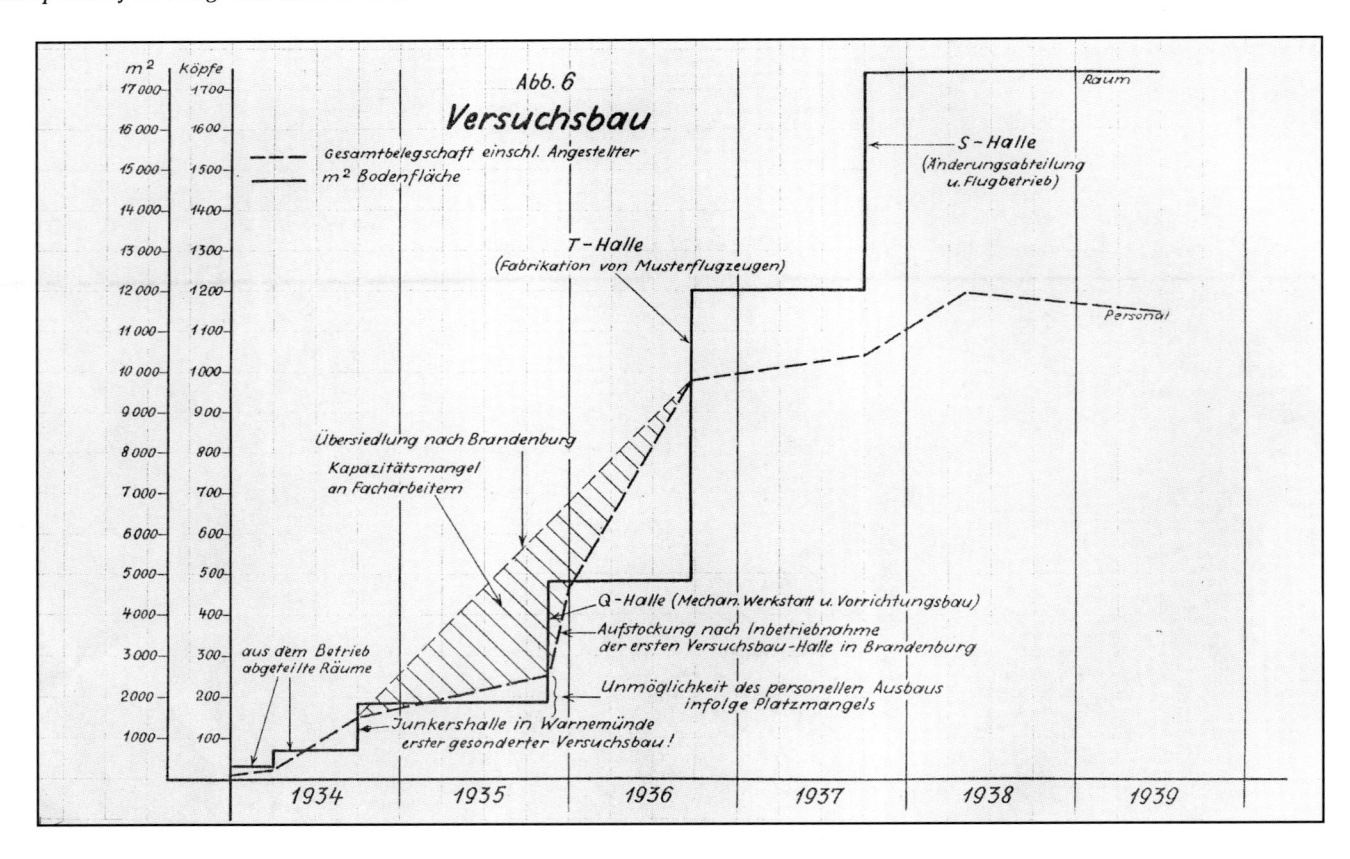

Development of the testing facilities 1934-1939.

overtaxed production department and watching over the aircraft repairs department. It was only as a result of a later reduction of the six departments into the categories of 'development', 'main operations administration' and 'production control' that the design bureau — classed under 'development' — was freed from supervising series production.

The expansion of the firm's facilities impacted the technical administration through its reorganization. A Betriebsgruppe Nord (Operations Group North, consisting of Warnemünde and Anklam) and a Betriebsgruppe Süd (Operations Group South, comprising Babelsberg, Brandenburg, Wittenberg, Rathenow) were created. The new category of 'central operations administration' took in all central tasking, including liaison with the RLM.[95] In November of 1940 the technical administration offices in Babelsberg moved in with the design bureau at Brandenburg.

Although the RLM's restriction hardly permitted Arado to make its mark from a technological standpoint, ideologically it became a role model when compared with privately operated firms. Alois Cejka, a member of the board of directors and Ministerialdirektor of the RLM responsible for contracts, assignments and finances, swore the senior managers to act in an exemplary manner and in a board meeting on 15 December 1941, criticized an "out-of-date drive for profit" which portrayed an "impermissible private economic

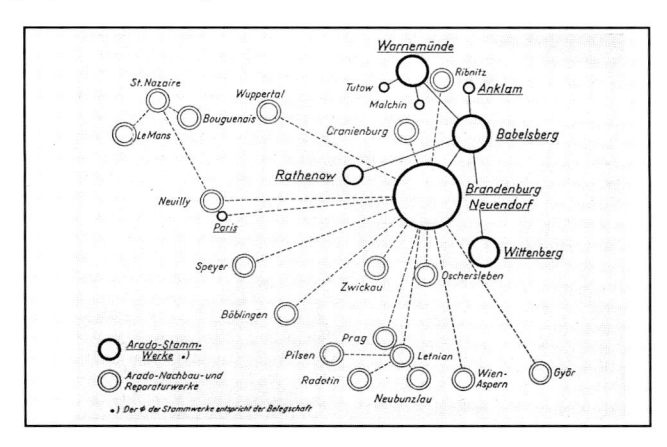

Home-, supplemental- and repair sites of the Arado Flugzeugwerke (1942).

W. Blume at the sailplane camp of the NSFK-Sturm 4/25 in Milow (1938).

Former Arado company housing in Warnemünde (1994 photo).

Performance certificate for the Warnemünde plant (1 May 1938).

thinking", saying that "all efforts should be geared toward series production." With the current wartime situation, it was much more important to conserve material and workers. High fixed prices were "no indication of good management."[96] In general, profits (with the exception of those used for social funding and savings) should primarily be utilized to reduce debt. According to official declarations Arado had fulfilled all its assigned tasks "in the true spirit of National Socialism." The employees' requisite job, social and ideological instruction had been provided for and investments were made which would have realized little profit in the private sector. There was a comprehensive job education program for employees and programs offering social and health needs as well as physical fitness. A branch of the National Socialist Fliegerkorps (NSFK) was established within the company, as were labor groups, women's labor groups, music and acting troupes and company sports teams. Particular importance was placed on the political and ideological training of employees. Participation in the Reichsparteitag, in courses and instruction of the Party and its organization and in DAF study programs was highly encouraged.

Brandenburg was awarded the "Gaudiplom (district diploma) for outstanding performance" in 1938. Babelsberg, Warnemünde and Rathenow followed. Rathenow and Warnemünde were recognized for exemplary job education, for healthy living and workers' communities and for their efforts in promoting "strength through joy." On 1 May 1940 Wittenberg was declared a "National Socialist Model Operation." In 1941 Warnemünde and Rathenow were also recognized as such. In 1942 the entire company was presented the certificate for "esteemed and exemplary service" for wartime production. By 1944 several branches had been awarded the title of "wartime model operation."

In official publications the senior management forbade any mention of the company's private economic character up to 1936, instead promoting the advantages of the National Socialist company operations. In 1940 they expressed their unrestrained recognition of Felix Wagenführ and eulogized those who had been "killed in tragic accidents", as well as those colleagues who were the first ones to have "died a hero's death for Führer and Fatherland." On the other hand, Lübbe's death just shortly beforehand received not the slightest mention.[97] Nor was there any mention made in company historical notes of the fact that Wagenführ, as before, remained a private stockholder within the company: "Herr Wagenführ, one of the old tried-and-true pioneers of German aviation, has been the senior partner of our company since its founding. The survival of our company in the difficult years before the collapse and the expansion of our new works from 1933 onward are closely tied to his name; Herr Wagenführ has served as the senior operations manager in the last four years, during which we — thanks to the exemplary behavior and performance of our employees — were able to complete all assigned tasks.[98]"

Former senior partner Heinrich Lübbe was present at modest gatherings due to his private patent activities and had hoped in vain for an adequate compensation to be made

Above: H. Lübbe's grave in the Berliner Südwestfriedhof in Stahnsdorf 91992). E. Rumpler and A. Rohrbach have also been laid to rest here.

H. Lübbe during treatment at the health resort in Bad Wildungen (circa 1937).

him. On the occasion of a confirmation on 10 March 1940 he had told friends he would be arriving at his hunting lodge near Ferchesar. The guests learned a short time later of his death when a gift arrived without Lübbe. On 7 March he had returned to Berlin from a business trip to Mannheim. His lungs had given him problems for many years, and pneumonia, which he had caught while traveling in an unheated train car, led to his death on the morning of 14 March 1940 at the age of 56. Lübbe was buried in the Südwestfriedhof in Berlin-Stahnsdorf.[99]

Due to the pressure of the times the leading aviation historians of the Third Reich, such as Peter Supf[100] and Heinz Bongartz,[101] were prevented from specifically naming Lübbe as the former senior partner of Arado. They glossed over this fact with vague references that Lübbe was "senior partner of one of the large aircraft manufacturing companies in Berlin" or that Arado "came under new ownership" in the '20s. The author Walter Zuerl even went so far as to completely omit Lübbe from a developmental history of the Arado Flugzeugwerke written during the time.[102] An anonymous historical overview of the Arado Werke's development, probably done at the behest of the Allies following the war, attempted to dismiss Lübbe's disappropriation as follows: "During the course of 1933 the owner of the Arado Werke, Herr Lübbe, ran into differences with the RLM and was forced to leave the company."

Because of this manipulation of history recent German aviation literature has given little indication of the extent of Lübbe's involvement in establishing and expanding the Arado Werke. It was left to an American aviation historian to appropriately characterize the nationalization of the Arado Werke as a "deterrent instigated by the Nazis as a warning to other aviation companies."[103]

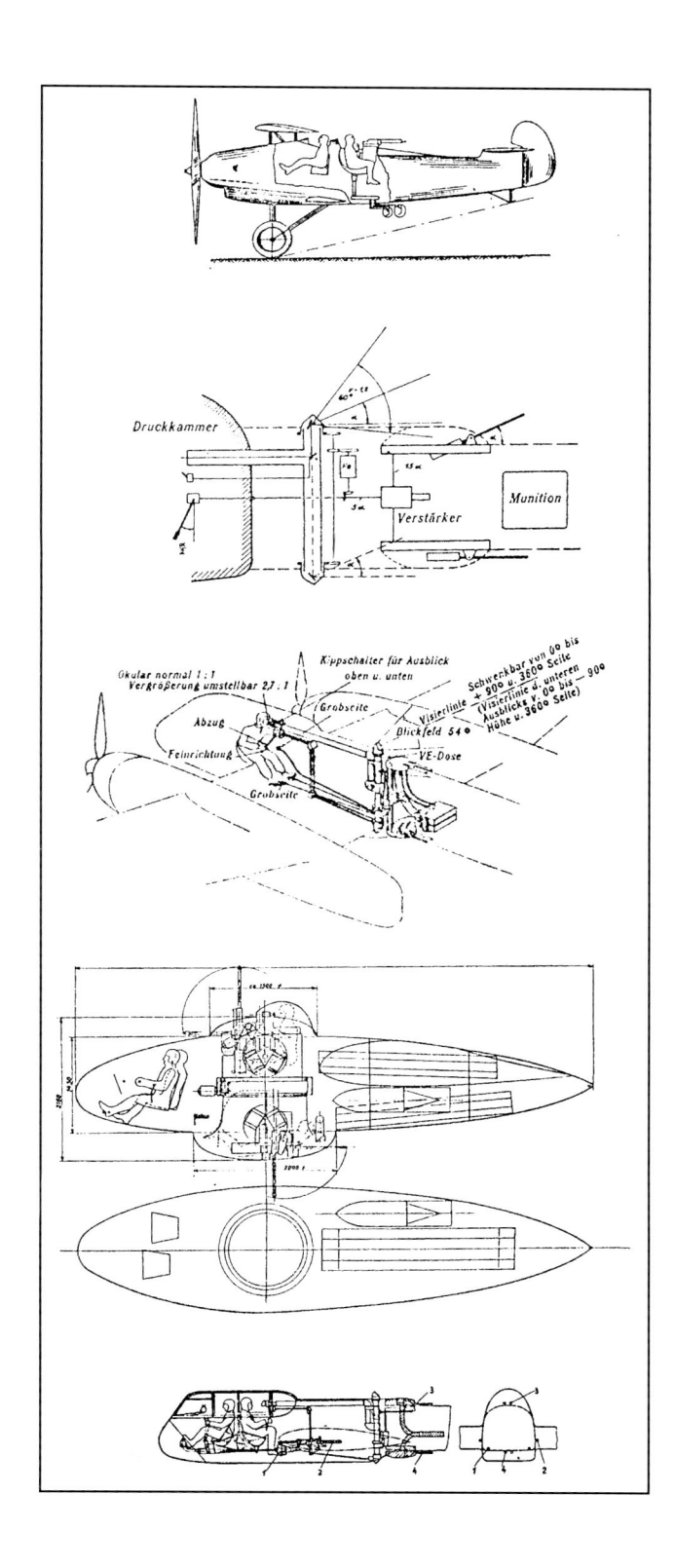

Above to below: W. Blume's design for a saddle mount turret driven by control vanes in a two-seat fighter (1930). Design of Kurt Bornemann, an Arado weapons technician, for a remote-controlled rear-firing weapon with electro-powered amplifier and sight outside the pressure chamber. W. Blume's design for installation of a remote-controlled rear-firing weapons system. W. Blume's design for a tub with 2 cm. Rh. Lb. 202 cannons. Design of W. Blume for a rear-firing weapon with periscope sight and remote controller.

Chapter 15
The Dream of a "High-Speed Two-Seater": The Ar 240/440 Attack Airplane

From early on, Walter Blume was keenly interested in developing a "high-speed two-seater" in the shape of a high performance Zerstörer, or attack plane, with the intent of rectifying the Luftwaffe's acknowledged numerical inferiority. In doing so, he hoped that the envisaged traversable armament (i.e. barbettes) would make a similar breakthrough as did the synchronized control forward firing fixed guns on single seat fighters in World War One, which had been developed with the assistance of Heinrich Lübbe.

According to Blume, around 1930 he had already taken the first step toward the realization of his plans with the fitting of a WWI LMG 08/1 in a two-seat fighter. Since manual traversing became virtually impossible at speeds approaching 400 km/h due to the air pressure in an open gun position, air resistance was to initially have been reduced by an auxiliary drive using an aerial rudder. This method, however, was not shown to be very effective during mockup testing.

In 1932, by which time Heinrich Lübbe had already developed a new type of 2 cm aircraft cannon, Blume was given a contract for developing an auxiliary rudder drive for a 2 cm Oerlikon cannon. However, calculations for a more versatile, mechanical auxiliary power drive using compressed air or hydraulic pressure, such as those necessary for large caliber weapons, showed that the required power was not attainable with existing materials. Blume's concept of an enclosed, traversable turret-mounted gun system providing acceptable angles of fire in minimal space therefore found few supporters at the time and remained an elusive dream.

From the beginning, Blume's gun turrets were designed to be aerodynamically integral with the aircraft fuselage and therefore part of the airplane's shape. In searching for the "combat aircraft's ideal shape" he first came up with a design for a flying wing with two hemispherical turrets in the rear. Once it was learned that the construction and size of such a design was utopian at the time, he concentrated on a smaller aircraft type with separate controls, giving an optimal field of fire for two gun turrets located above and below and carrying two 2 cm Ikaria cannons.

With the assistance of a weapons technician by the name of Jürgensmann, by the mid-1930s Blume began working on plans for the Zerstörer-Projekt E 500, which saw a 2 cm Rh. Lb. 202 cannon installed in a twin fuselage airplane having separate control surfaces. Work came to a halt after a turret mockup had been created in cooperation with Rheinmetall-Borsig AG, since the Technisches Amt gave priority to the high-speed, dive-bombing attack plane (which, incidentally, had no rear-firing armament). Only in 1938, when doubts began cropping up as to whether an attack plane could ever match the flight performance of a fighter, was Blume given renewed support for his high-speed two-seater project having heavy defensive armament.

Accordingly, Blume envisioned pressurized, remotely operated rear barbettes with twin periscopic sights for one-man operations. In cooperation with Siemens Apparate GmbH, the Askania Werke, the Optische Anstalt C.P. Goerz

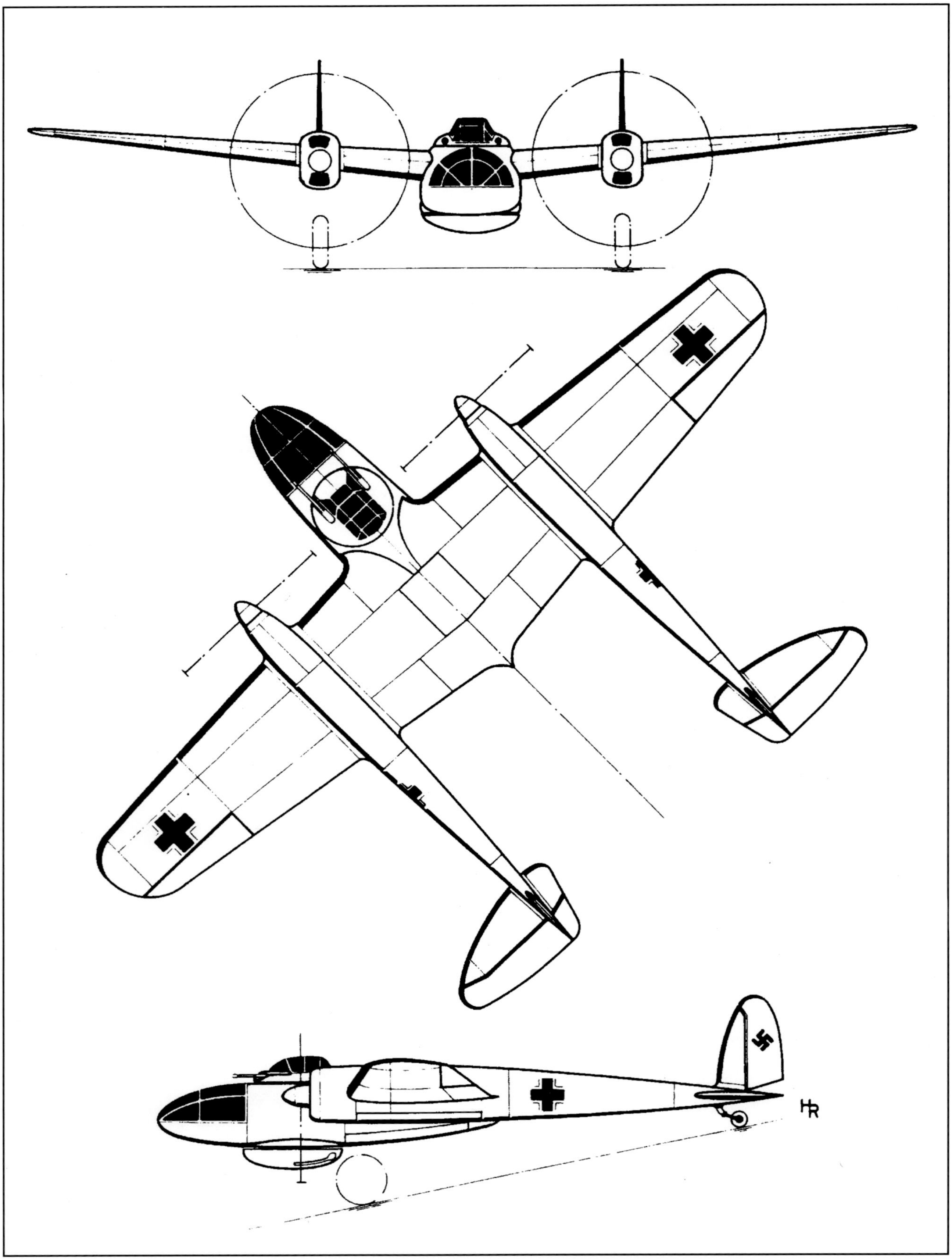
HR

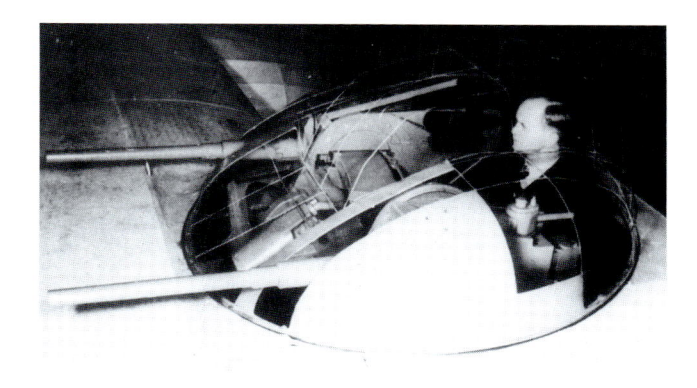

Arado E 500. Mockup of the gun turret.

Arado E 500 attack fighter project (1937 — left).

GmbH and the Deutsche Versuchsanstalt für Luftfahrt, Arado drew up plans in 1941 for the E 651 attack plane and the E 340 high-speed bomber; these were competing with designs from Junkers, Focke-Wulf and Dornier. Coordination of work took place at Arado under the watchful eye of weapons technician Kurt Bornemann.[104] Only the viewfinder and control mechanism of the gun positions were located inside the pressurized cabin; the gunsight and vision amplifier remained outside.

The E 340 bomber of 1936 bore some resemblance to the Zerstörer-Projekt E 500 in that it had two fuselage booms tapering back from the engines and terminating in the control surfaces. With the horizontal stabilizers protruding outward, this gave a clear field of fire to the rear. This particularly heavy attack plane, weighing 17,000 kg, was to have had five remotely operated gun positions providing overlapping kill zones. Suitable hydraulically operated gun turrets were undergoing evaluation at the time, but results still proved somewhat less than satisfactory. The airplane was to have achieved a top speed of 700 km/h at an altitude of 7,000 meters and have had a range of 4,000 km with the fitting of either the Jumo 222 or the DB 604 engine then in development. Again, however, only a mockup was completed before the project was suspended by the RLM in early 1941.

The E 651 heavy attack plane also never saw a completed model. This was laid out as a cantilever, low-wing design with two high-altitude engines carried at the fuselage/wing junction driving the airscrews via a miter wheel gearbox. If one engine cut out the remaining one would have driven both propellers, thereby countering the particularly dangerous situation during takeoff brought on by an asymmetrical engine failure or the loss in performance of a feathered propeller during flight.

This engine arrangement, which provided minimal air resistance, combined with a remotely controlled rear gun was to have been used on the follow-on Ar 240 Zerstörer. This project, accepted as the E 625, ended in failure, the details of its developmental history remaining sketchy even today. This was, on the one hand, due to the fact that the firm's unusually high technical goals could only be attained through great expenditure and on the other hand that the Technisches Amt never showed the desire to make the necessary means available or set clear directives. The Amt initially did not realize the full significance of the highly refined attack plane and for too long placed its hopes exclusively in Messerschmitt's more conventional competing design. Arado was pressured into keeping the project alive for multi-role tasks and, ever more strongly, to restrict its use to that of a reconnaissance platform. Indecisiveness on the part of the Amt continuously led to irritation and delays in the development of the project, so that — despite a large number of relatively successful prototype models — full-scale production was not attained before the new era of jet aircraft made all considerations regarding piston-powered airplanes moot.

The Technisches Amt, even before the war started, had initially approved the development of a pressurized cabin and remotely operated defensive armament. At the same time, however, it restricted the design (because of the short-

Arado E 340 attack fighter project (1939).

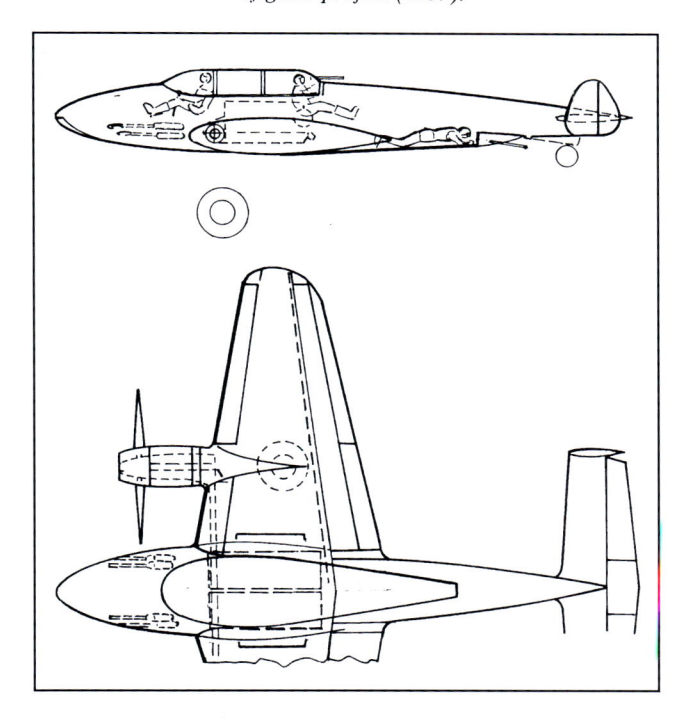

Arado E 651 attack fighter project (1937/38).

ness of the development time) to having separate engines located ahead of the wing and demanded that the airframe be kept small and the crew be reduced to two men. The original design became so watered down and complicated that the dive bombing requirement was lifted.

Designed by Wilhelm van Nes, the twin-engine midwing aircraft's engine nacelles were attached to a rectangular center wing section. They also housed the double-wheeled landing gear, which retracted to the rear without rotating. The tailplane was attached to the upper rear fuselage and was capped off with a two-piece tailfin on each end.

Wing area was kept to a minimum in order to achieve as high a speed as possible. This in turn resulted in the introduction of a series of new features. The high wing loading resulting from the limited wing area, coupled with a sharp increase in weight due to the pressurized cabin and dive brake, necessitated the use of high lift flaps in order to provide acceptably low landing speeds.

After factory testing with the Fowler flaps on the Ar 80 the company turned to the development of a patented "Arado landing flap" with a special "Arado travelling aileron."

The improvements achieved by this method were mainly centered on eliminating the unfavorable distribution of lift between the region of the landing flap and the aileron by developing a landing system which permitted the simultaneous extension of the aileron. In this context Arado had evaluated a so-called "fan aileron" on a trial basis. With the landing flap extended, the horizontally split aileron made use of its upper section to act as a fan-like bridge between the main wing and the extended aileron. This led to the development of the patented "Arado traveling flap." This was a section of the wing profile where the fixed, forward portion of the wing terminated at a point somewhat ahead of the trailing edge. The remainder of the wing section slid out from beneath the fixed part of the wing, was hinged and could be and extended to the rear. With this type of flap attachment no control surfaces were exposed outside the retracted wing profile (Arado patent by H. Rebeski for landing flap attachment, No. 674 937 from 26 January 1938 and 682 851 for an aileron system from 12 July 1938).

However, the diverse methods for reducing the landing speeds brought on a series of weight increasing supplemental systems, so that a critical wing loading of up to 330 kg/m² couldn't be avoided.

A "precision control system", whereby the ratio between control column, pedals and rudders could be adjusted by a handwheel to compensate for air pressure(speed), was

Ar 240 V 1, DD+QL (Wk. Nr. 240 001) with canopy over the center wing (May 1940)

utilized in order to better maintain mastery over the control forces. The company of Patin supplied a special pilot static airspeed indicator for this purpose. Ailerons and vertical and horizontal stabilizers were all counterbalanced. The tailplane had a fin which could be trimmed in flight. Wing and control surface deicing was accomplished by air heated in blower heaters.

To reduce air resistance the design called for annular radiators surrounding the engine gearbox coupled with a cooling system rated at 130 degrees Celsius.

The firm of Conti supplied bulletproof self-sealing fuel tanks. These had walls approximately 20 mm thick, consisting of three layers made of rubber and plastic. When a machine gun bullet penetrated, a small amount of kerosene oozed into the hole. This caused the middle layer to swell and seal the hole up. As these thick-walled tanks were not collapsible, the wing skin needed to be removable. Accordingly, a special type of buckle resistant skin covering was developed. To this end, the outer sheet of this covering was reinforced throughout with 25 mm thick crisscrossing strips. In order to save weight and not have to unnecessarily rivet the strip junctures all skin sections were sandwiched into a "waffle plate" by twice drawing them through a three-story high sheet press. Afterwards, the inner plate areas between the strips were cut out and the waffle plate was then electrically machine spot welded to the outer skin. Like many features of the Ar 240, this method was also relatively time consuming, but it was not — contrary to some claims — particularly costly due to a narrow spacing of the rivets.

Other unique features of the design included a dive brake, necessary for the airplane's supplementary role as a dive bomber. Since the special type of skin covering precluded any type of large holes being cut for such a brake, use was made of a simple expanding parachute brake at the rear tip of the fuselage.

Following publication of technical guidelines on 15 October 1938 Arado turned in the drawings for this highly developed attack airplane to the RLM at the end of the year. On 16 May 1939 the RLM approved construction of six prototype Zerstörer after having inspected a mockup of the design earlier, on 31 March 1939. However, even before the prototype's first flight the contract was raised to ten prototypes. Outbreak of the war caused a suspension of all future projects, but these restrictions were eventually lifted and the prototypes began testing around the end of 1939.

Ar 240 V 3. DB 601 E engine.

The ultimate version of the first two prototype Ar 240 attack planes could not be built as planned, since there were initially no counter-rotating engines available for the project. In the early stages of development, these were considered necessary to counter the roll momentum (movement in flight around the roll axis caused by the massive amount of engines' restoring moment in comparison with the propellers). It was feared that the long, narrow ailerons would not be adequate given the large airfoil trailing edge angle. According to former senior engineer Hans Rebeski the flight characteristics subsequently proved to be so good that the decision was made to dispense with the counter-rotating engines. These were passed on to Messerschmitt in an attempt to improve the handling characteristics of their Me 210 Zerstörer.

Ar 240 V 3, KK+CD (Wk. Nr. 240 003) with rear-firing gun and Arado's unique 'traveling' ailerons.

In order to provide as little air resistance as possible for the DB 601 inline engine radiators, these would have to be arranged around the airscrew reduction gearing. However, this design constraint negatively influenced the center of gravity and affected stability along the yaw and pitch axes. Stability along the axis of roll was affected inasmuch as the wing cross-section had a 40 percent thickness taper, whereby the ailerons were too short and narrow to be effective. It was for these reasons that the V 1 prototype demonstrated itself to be relatively instable along all axes during its first trials. As revealed in the diary entries of Flugbaumeister Walter Kröger, these were carried out on 25 June 1940 and not on 10 May as sometimes reported. Also, according to Kröger's notes, modifications may have been undertaken before the airplane began airframe, landing gear and engine testing on 18 April 1941. That same day, however, the aircraft was written off in an accident.

Built in conjunction with the first prototype, the Ar 240 V 2 was fitted with a new aileron. Numerous factory flights between 6 April 1941 and 11 December 1942 were carried out primarily to test the dive capabilities and the auxiliary 'leg coolers' on the landing gear, designed to overcome overheating during runup and at low speeds.

In February 1941, following a meeting with Generalstabsingenieur Lucht, Walter Blume called for an A-0 series of six aircraft for the purpose of further testing, to be delivered in the period from September 1941 to the end of April 1942. As a prerequisite for maintaining the deadlines Blume specifically named the inclusion in the "highest prioritization category", something which had been repeatedly denied him.

Ar 240 V 3.

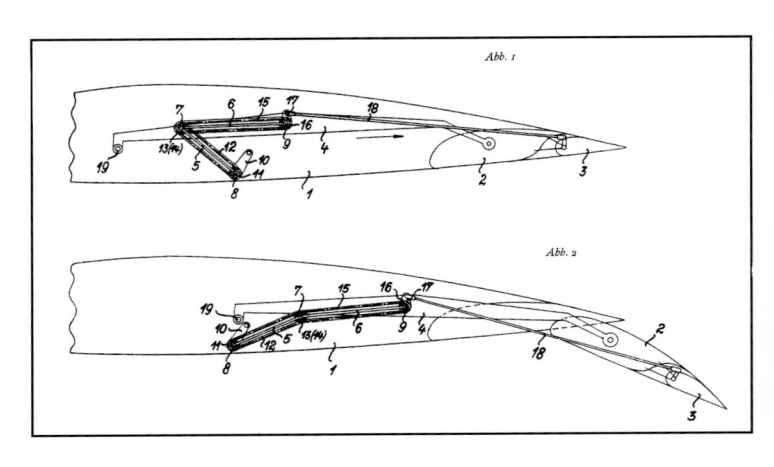

Ar 240 prototypes V 3 to V 6 were built in preparation for the A-0 pre-production series. The V 3 prototype, laid down as a Zerstörer, saw numerous changes during its test flight program which lasted from 9 May to 6 November 1941 (with occasional testing carried out until 18 April 1944). It is doubtful whether the wingspan was increased from 12.0 to 14.26 meters, as claimed, as this would have meant the first two prototypes would have had the smaller, probably unflyable wings with wing loading well over 300 kg/m². Changes made to ailerons and wing sections, plus the fitting of supplemental fins, were done in the interest of improving flight stability. The slats and dive brake were dropped. The latter was replaced with a new short cone. The simple control column was replaced with the previously mentioned handwheel control. The two-place crew compartment was redesigned with a pressurized cockpit and fitted with a jettisonable sliding canopy made of double-layered plexiglas with heating between the layers. The canopy was blended into the aerodynamic lines of the fuselage without having to make use of airflow-disrupting reinforcements. The glass was supplied by the firm of Kopperschmidt in Hamburg. It was an Arado design, however, and care had to be taken at the factory that the attachment points to the fuselage had to be able to take the additional forces stemming from the pressurized cabin. At the same time, the cockpit was moved forward — not for reasons of flight stability as often claimed — but for better visibility, particularly in its dive bombing role. This necessitated moving the engines a bit forward as well as, for center of gravity reasons, lengthening the fuselage — measures which only added more to the weight.

The V 4 prototype was designed as a dive bomber within the framework of preparing for the A-0 pre-production series. A first factory flight is noted as having taken place on 19 June 1941. After front-line testing the aircraft was presumably lost in an accident on 7 August 1941.

The generally similar Ar 240 V 5 and V 6 prototypes were the last two prior to the introduction of the A-0 pre-production run. Built in the latter half of 1940, they com-

Ar 240. Side view of the Arado landing flap (patent 682 851) with pivoting Arado 'traveling' aileron in retracted (picture 1) and extended (picture 2) positions. 1 = main wing, 2 = flap, 3 = aileron, 4 = flap extension arm.

pleted their maiden flights on 11 September 1941 and 18 January 1942, respectively.

In view of its intended role as an attack platform, it was to have been fitted with both forward firing as well as rear firing armament. Forward firing weapons included from two to six MG 17s or MG 151s, each which could be fitted in the nose, in the wing root and in the lower fuselage. The newly developed rear firing armament comprised a rotatable barbette with MG 81 Z, MG 131 and MG 151 guns in both the upper and lower fuselage. These were power driven remotely via a periscope sight. Excepting small shadow points caused by the control surfaces the entire rear hemisphere could thereby be covered. But this solution to the remotely controlled defensive armament system had only been achieved after nearly three years of work on the part of several companies. Tests in Göttingen's ice chamber revealed serious initial deficiencies in the periscopic sighting system. In dives, the icing became so severe that the entire apparatus froze and the optics clouded over. After the problem was solved by using super pressurized demoisturized air, it was discovered that the periscope — despite its 1.6x power — didn't give the gunner adequate target acquisition and was totally useless at night.

The FA 4 remote control system developed by Rheinmetall-Borsig was written out of the program, and the hydraulic powered FA 9 system, developed jointly by DVL and Arado, was fitted on the Ar 240 V 3. This system made use of the MG 81 Z on a Drehringlafette 77 Wa 3. After continuous improvements, this system was eventually installed in the Ar 240 v 5 and V 6 as the FA 13 with two barbettes housing two MG 131 each. Difficulties with the development of the rear firing barbettes meant that the first Ar 240 prototype entered flight testing minus its armament. The second prototype was only fitted with the standard forward firing weapons. The third prototype was employed as a high-speed reconnaissance aircraft over England following the removal of its weapons. Prototypes V 5 and V 6, despite original intentions, were also utilized as reconnaissance platforms and in March of 1942 were delivered to the Versuchsstelle für Höhenflüge (Test Facility for High Altitude Flights) in Oranienburg. The V 6 eventually made its way to the troops on the Eastern Front during the winter of 1942/43.

Oberstleutnant Theodor Rowehl (left).

Oberstleutnant Siegried Knemeyer, Chief of Development GL/C-3 at the RLM from 1943 (right).

On 7 June 1941 Blume provided the RLM with an overview of the projected delivery schedule and the state of testing, into which was included the planned development of the pressurized cockpit being undertaken at the Versuchsstelle für Höhenflüge. He took this opportunity to specifically point out that initial deficiencies had "generally been resolved." Flight control, particularly during take-off and landing, was so straightforward that "no special experience was needed in controlling the aircraft." When in a stall the airplane behaved in a completely harmless manner both with and without slats. On 3 August 1941 Ar 240 V 3 was put through its paces in Rechlin by Siegfried Knemeyer, the event being attended by Oberstleutnant Theodor Rowehl from the Versuchsstelle für Höhenflüge in Oranienburg. Flight handling characteristics along the vertical axis were said to be "consistently in order" and instrument flying "was quite possible without any difficulties." Only a reduction in aileron force and canopy glazing free of ribbing were recommended as desirable improvements. Rowehl promised to report the relatively successful results of the evaluation to Udet immediately. A foreboding of the design's future categorization can be derived from Rowehl's view that it was a "definite high-speed reconnaissance aircraft" as opposed to both the Ju 86P and Hs 130 high-altitude reconnaissance planes as well as the Me 210, which had "finally been rejected as a reconnaissance platform." The upshot of this was that there was no longer any question of the Ar 240 being used as an attack plane and that, even then, it apparently would only be a temporary solution prior to the introduction of faster "jet-powered reconnaissance versions."[105] The option of a multi-role combat aircraft was kept open with a view to efforts in cutting back the plethora of aircraft types in the Luftwaffe's inventory. However, its simultaneous use as a heavy fighter, attack aircraft, long-range reconnaissance platform and high-speed bomber was not in keeping with the previously agreed upon specialized requirements such as high altitude and dive bombing capabilities, meaning that the possibility of the plane's accelerated introduction into production was remote.

Rowehl's chief demands were that the reconnaissance version have a high rate of speed plus include heavy rearward firing armament. He inquired whether delivery would be possible by the autumn of 1941 if the specification for a pressurized cockpit were temporarily dropped. As revealed in an evaluation report following the conclusion of Ar 240 trials in Rechlin on 17 October 1941, Blume at this time was anxiously awaiting the award of a production contract for the "highest performing attack plane in the world." In the interim, takeoffs and landings were being carried out without any notable problems. The report went on to say that the aircraft was superior to all comparable designs due to its extremely small airframe dimensions, absolute full pressure height, higher speed, remote weapons operation with periscopic sighting system and its pressurized cockpit. It specifically praised the fact that the rear field of fire wasn't restricted by the empennage and that air resistance was particularly low since the upper barbette lay in an area protected by the cockpit from the airflow. When the V 5 prototype was evaluated by the E-Stelle in September of 1942 certain technical problems became apparent with single engine operations, engine operating temperature, carbon dioxide buildup and the temperature of the pressurized air, aileron effectiveness, maintenance and the weapons system. However, on the 25th of that month Arado provided reliable assurance that the remaining problems were being eliminated.[106] Nevertheless, the Amt continued to

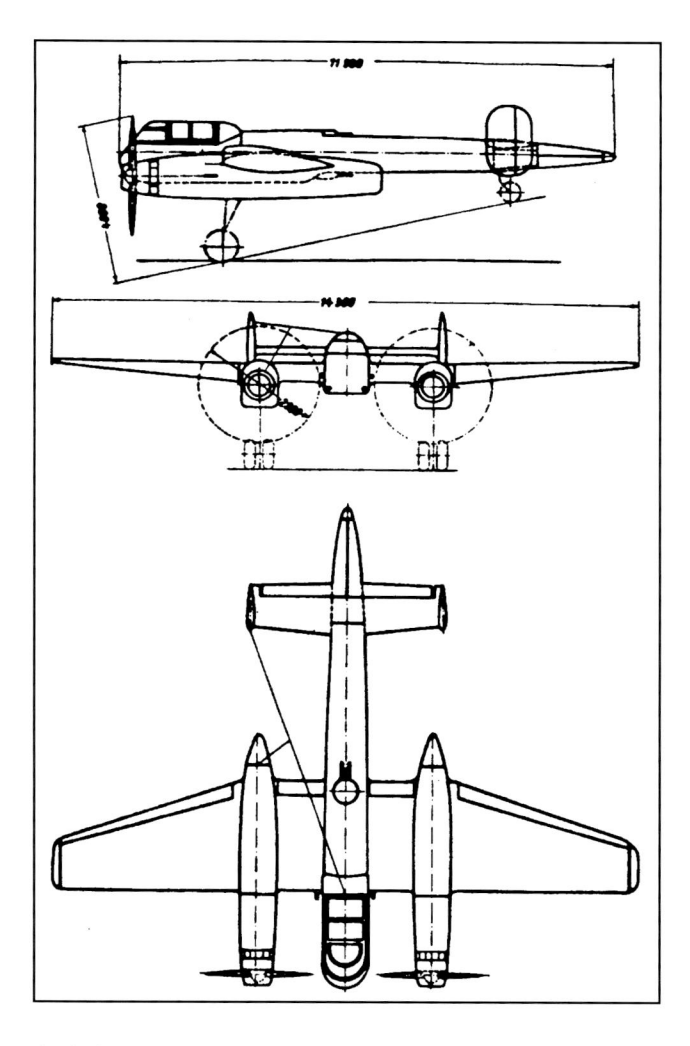

Ar 240 A. Three-view from 1 January 1942.

Ar 240 A-O (1942).

avoid issuing a definitive production contract, nor did it make a clear decision on the aircraft's future role.

The RLM classified the manufacture of a pre-production Ar 240 A-0 series into prioritization category 'SS' on 3 April 1941. These aircraft were envisaged as reconnaissance platforms, not equipped with the forward firing guns, and were built by Ago Flugzeugwerke in Oschersleben. It is not fully known whether four or five of these aircraft were built, nor which type of armament was used.

Also, the assumption that the Ar 240 A-01 and A-02 were identical with the Ar 240 V 5 and V 6 prototypes may be a false one.

The Ar 240 A-01 carried out its first flight on 5 June 1942. Additional test flights were conducted up to 31 August 1942 with pilot Walter Kröger at the controls. On 15 August a flight was recorded in Rechlin for evaluating the aircraft's handling characteristics. On 22 September Arado reported the airplane as flight ready and named its delivery date as 25 September 1942. Subsequent to the acceptance flight in Rechlin, weapons testing was conducted in Tarnewitz and a crew from the Versuchsstelle für Höhenflüge was briefed. Starting on 20 October 1942 a reconnaissance group on the Eastern Front began operating

W. Blume's notes from a speech given by Göring on 13 September 1942.

this particular aircraft near Kharkov, it eventually being lost on 16 March 1943. The Arado 240 A-02 was returned back to the company on 24 January 1944 following a crash landing. Arado 240 A-03 was written off following a landing accident in Italy and the Ar 240 A-04 was sent to Italy as its replacement in the autumn of 1943. This plane is said to have been seriously damaged as a result of engine damage and flown back to the company works after emergency repairs had been made. The Ar 240 A-05, probably the last pre-production model, is believed to have operated in Russia as an unarmed reconnaissance platform.

There was a confusing difference of opinion which reigned at the time of the Ar 240's conversion over to the higher performing DB 603 engine. In spite of claims to the contrary, it is doubtful whether this occurred with the Ar 240 V 3 to V 6 prototypes, since this engine wasn't operationally ready at the time. Notes and individual series listings contained within a status report on the Ar 240 V 5 issued by Arado in September 1942 showed that all pre-production Ar 240 A-0, including the Ar 240 V 4 through V 6, were to have been powered by the DB 601 engine. However, with regard to the Ar 240 A-03 and A-04 prototypes, there are indications given by the then-director of the design bureau and, more recently from British sources, which reveal that the higher performing DB 603 powerplant was actually the engine test fitted in these aircraft after their conversion to Ar 240 A-03/U1 and A-04/U2 standards in anticipation of the Ar 240 C production run. On the other hand, it can safely be ruled out that the BMW 801 TJ planned for installation into this latter series was ever actually fitted, despite contrary opinion in other publications. An increase in the dimensions of the wing's center section from 14.3 m to 16.6 m, larger control surfaces and a larger 3.4 m propeller appear to have been added changes brought on by the installation of these new and heavier engines on the conversion airplane. Earlier increases in the wing dimensions hadn't been needed, since even the first prototypes had adequate area for the Arado traveling flaps, sufficient to ensure the lift of the extended landing flaps couldn't be reduced by excessive tip vortices.

The planned construction of an A-series of the Ar 240 with DB 601 engines never came to fruition. Experience gained was derived solely from a B-0 reconnaissance version fitted with the DB 605/A1 engines. The two prototypes built by AGO for this purpose, Ar 240 V 7 and V 8, were delivered for evaluation in October and December 1942, respectively. The V 7 was to be used for engine tests, the V 8 for both engine and rear armament evaluation. Although company documents indicate that 20 aircraft in this series were to have been delivered in conjunction with RLM Plan No. 22, only two prototypes of the Ar 240 B-0 were ever actually built.

Once the V 3 through V 6 prototypes had been used in reconnaissance roles and not, as the company had originally intended, as Zerstörers, all subsequent models, i.e. the Ar 240 A-0 pre-production versions and the two V 7 and V 8 prototypes, also followed suit.

A key factor in the Amt's failure to provide specific planning guidelines rested with the technical overburdening of Ernst Udet in his capacity as Generalluftzeugmeister. His suicide in November of 1941 not only left behind a constrictive competence vacuum within the air staff, it also restricted Walter Blume's influence with the RLM even further. Looking for scapegoats, proceedings were carried out against leading colleagues within the Technisches Amt, which included Reidenbach and Tschersich, which were also both members of Arado's board of directors. The accusations, primarily coming from Siegfried Knemeyer (from 1943 Entwicklungschef — Chief of Development — GL/C3 in the Technisches Amt) not only included lack of planning and technical errors, but in the case of Tschersich also charges of "defeatism" and "extortion." There were shakeups within the Amt, but no formal accusations were ever made. Göring shifted the blame onto Reidenbach for dragging his feet on the development of refined attack planes. He further criticized the neglect regarding remote-controlled gun turrets and talked of a system of deception that would have to be eliminated by radical means.

H. Göring on the lack of development of a high-speed two-place combat aircraft:

I've got to say, what did these people have going through their minds? They were aware of the enemy's tail guns and they never considered building a tail gun for us. Actually, Reidenbach should be taken out this very night and without further ado shot dead ... When in eight days it's announced that the former Chief of Development, the former Chief of Planning and the former Chief of Staff of the Generalluftzeugmeister had been shot, you'd soon see that suddenly things would get cracking with this whole mess.[107]

A year later Göring leveled indiscriminate accusations at Milch — who had been favoring tried and tested aircraft types for a long time — for not having copied the high-speed British Mosquito bomber, and added word-for-word: "I have stated, and I would be quite blatant about it — I would copy anything of the enemy's that's good without having second thoughts for a moment."[108]

In a conference with industry representatives on 13 September 1942 Göring demanded that they "once and for all give up their individual company interests" and complained that promises which they'd made regarding bombers had not been kept.

In addition to Messerschmitt, Heinkel and Junkers were also heavily involved in the manufacture of high-speed high-altitude aircraft during the war. But their designs never reached production maturity, leaving the fitting of high-altitude superchargers to current types such as the He 111 R and the Ju 88 S as the alternative. However, performance figures which would have approached those of the Ar 240 could not be attained by such methods.

Göring stated that could easily be "consumed with rage", for everything to do with a high-speed bomber had "been used to fill up trousers" and that the high-altitude bombers were "piles of antiquated junk." He concluded his withering criticism of the Messerschmitt Zerstörer program with these words: "The Me 210 is an airplane which made me order that my epitaph include the words: He would have lived longer if the Me 210 hadn't been built."

Göring called for a "decisive design" for a high-speed bomber, one which would have to be drawn up within three months and be faster than enemy fighters. As before, however, he refused to acquiesce to the need for a specialized aircraft and instead insisted that the high-speed bomber, attack plane, night fighter and reconnaissance aircraft be developed from the same basic type. Furthermore, he stated that speed takes priority over protection, meaning that if necessary armament wouldn't be carried. A Zerstörer would have to have a penetrating radius of 1,000 km, a speed of 700 km/h and a bomb load of 1,000 kg. Walter Blume concluded from Göring's remarks that the Ar 240 fulfilled all prerequisites, both for the high-speed unarmed reconnaissance platform as well as for the heavily armed high-speed attack aircraft. However, Göring was neither willing nor able to guarantee Arado an immediate priority in the realm of Zerstörers.

It is noteworthy in this context that the Technisches Amt repeatedly criticized Arado for its "high developmental and design expenditures." As early as the end of 1940 W. Blume had expressed concern on the shortage of space and personnel within the design bureau. He complained of the absence of "an enclosed pre-development department with low pressure cold chamber, firing tunnel, engine test stand, weapons test stand, test stand for prototypes, mockup building facility, durability lab, materials research" as well as a wind tunnel. Günther Tschersich had refused necessary funding with the excuse "that only those construction projects would be approved which were geared toward increasing production."[109] Alois Cejka criticized an increase in expenses, which he attributed in part to unnecessary hiring of additional designers and an expansion of the design bureau. Reidenbach, a colleague in the Amt who was responsible for the ongoing supervision of the company, attempted to defuse the situation by stating that "development must be undertaken with long-term goals in mind" and that "there was a lot of catching up to do ... particularly in the area of research." Even the justification on the part of Arado's senior business partner, Heinemann, that the increase in expenses was primarily dictated by the war fell onto Cejka's deaf ears. He deftly ignored Walter Blume's carefully presented criticism that "outside developmental work has done nothing for us", that they'd "fulfilled their tasking well, despite many difficulties, restrictions and limitations" and that Arado couldn't be blamed if it didn't "receive the obvious recognition" it should have. In this context Blume specifically referred to the fact that "the Ar 231 and Ar 199, which "were fully developed and had been given good marks" could not be put into production "because the demand wasn't critical enough" and that "no prioritization grade had been assigned" for the development of the Ar 240.

One year later Cejka criticized an overstock of material, which Walter Blume — not without justification — attributed to "constant changes in programs." Blume complained that Arado was regularly faced with "completely contradictory tasking" and that the development department constantly had to deal with "changing conditions." In 1942 and 1943 Arado had designed several types "which received the full recognition of the RLM, but whose acquisition was restricted in deference to the Defense of the Reich program." For this reason deliveries continued of reliable types such as the Ar 196, while the fate of new types remained in doubt and "even the Ar 240, untouchable performance-wise" never achieved full-scale production.

By mid-1942 it was recognized that the Ar 240 Zerstörer would be classed as nothing more than a substitute for the competing Me 210, even though the front lines desperately needed a reliable aircraft of this type. Gerhard Weyert, a leader of an evaluation squadron equipped with the Me 210 Zerstörer, circumvented the Amt and in the summer of 1942, personally approached Walter Blume. He requested that, based on bad experience with the Messerschmitt attack plane, the Ar 240 be delivered as quickly as possible.

Ar 240 C, probably T9+GL, with increased-area stabilizers (Oranienburg, March 1944).

Ar 240 V 11, mockup for the attack bomber version (1942).

Criticism of Messerschmitt:

The following was a tragedy: the machine wasn't there at all, Messerschmitt then began producing it in series without an evaluation flight ever having taken place. When over 500 aircraft had been completed, trials showed the type to be a general failure. Then the many changes which you must certainly be aware of were eventually implemented.

The new formation of the unit was a disaster from the start, since the Me 210 still hadn't been delivered and the Me 110 was in such short supply that it couldn't even keep two attack wings plus a night fighter group and two attack groups outfitted sufficiently for combat operations. In recognition of this fact, this past spring I came across your model, sparked an interest for it with the gentlemen in the RLM — unfortunately without success. In Russia I then met up with a former test pilot for your firm who provided me with more detailed information on your Ar 240.

At the present time I am once again in Germany with my group, in the process of converting over to the Me 210. I'm curious to see whether the bird will make the grade this time; I still think that problems will still crop up in the future. Unfortunately, I can't get away since I'm standing in for my wing commander. Therefore, tomorrow I'm sending one of my squadron commanders off with instructions to check up on the state of affairs with Messerschmitt, with the Me 210 evaluation squadron, with Heinkel and with you, my dear Mr. Blume.

Oberleutnant Thierfelder is an old attack pilot, holder of the Knight's Cross and well versed in aircraft technological matters. Since there's a search for an attack plane going on throughout Germany, I've got your company in particular in mind. The Me 110 has reached the limit of its capabilities with the F-series, the Bf 210 (sic) is apparently only to be introduced without follow-on production, the Heinkel attack plane is just now being drawn up; the result of all this is a stop for our attack planes within a very short period of time. If possible and technically feasible, I would like to bring your Ar 240 into this hole; not as a gap-filler, but as recognition for your work which has hitherto been at the bottom of the stack, but should prove itself in a remarkable fashion as a reconnaissance plane.[110]

Things developed differently that hoped for by experienced test pilots and the front. On 16 March 1942 the RLM initially awarded a contract for construction of prototypes V 9 through V 12 and for material acquisition for 36 production aircraft. Arado wanted to keep the four prototypes for conversion to the C-0 series, which would have the DB 603 A engines — possibly using methanol/water injection. There were also plans for using the higher performing BMW 801 engine, possibly in conjunction with outer wings lengthened to 19.0 meters.

On 27 June the contract for the C-series was rescinded and the developmental contract for the V-series prototypes changed to "Kampfzerstörer" (loosely translated, a heavy fighter bomber). This made superfluous the planned movement aft of the pilot's seat, dispensing with the nose glazing for the high-altitude fighter version and efforts made to strengthening the offensive armament by dropping the defensive barbettes. It also invalidated considerations for external bomb racks in the case of the planned high-speed bomber. For use as a Kampfzerstörer the Ar 240 V 9 and V 10 had to be converted over for pre-evaluation testing of handling characteristics and engines, while the V 11 and V 12 had to be fitted out with their full complement of equipment prior to testing.

Blume pressed Erhard Milch for a clarification of the situation, who as late as 10 July 1942 had specifically mentioned the advantages of the "British long-range wooden airplane, the D.H. Mosquito" with regard to the matter of the high altitude bomber. Milch nevertheless let it be known that there could be no talk of a German high-altitude fighter at the present time and that in the area of "Kampfzerstörer" the successor to the Me 110 had yet "to be determined."

Rescinding the production contract had a negative impact on material deliveries, for some subcontractors thought that the Amt's decision also applied to the V-series. Additionally, once this had been straightened out their interest in quick deliveries had dropped since it was now just a matter of four instead of forty aircraft.

On 21 September 1942 Arado turned to the Amt with the urgent request that it revise its decision and approve the construction of an Ar 240 C-series fitted with the DB 603 engines.

Arado Flugzeugwerke's promotion of the Ar 240 C series:

Our recommendation is to therefore revitalize the earlier preliminary decision for 36 0-series aircraft, particularly in view of the good performance, the solid ruggedness and the modern heavy armament of the aircraft. Testing of the Ar 240 A-0/U1 (conversion aircraft with DB 603 engines) up to this point has shown that the Ar 240 with DB 603 engines have significant gains with regard to performance and qualities over the model with the DB 601 E engine. In addition, since the greater portion of ordered materials is available without any type of supply bottleneck, there is the possibility that these 36 aircraft can be built at AGO in conjunction with the B-0 series — if the decision is reinstated as soon as possible and there are immediate efforts made to deliver the necessary bottleneck components. If this were the case, there is also the possibility of producing a number of aircraft with the more powerful engines, of which a portion could be fitted with the BMW 801 J engines.[111]

Among experts it was hitherto generally supposed that there was an independent follow-on type to the Ar 240 in the form of an Ar 440. Latest speculations from the English side reinforce the suspicion that the ostensibly new Ar 440 was nothing more than an Ar 240 C with increased wingspan and DB 603 G turbo supercharged engines. According to company documents all Ar 240 A-0 and B-0, including the V-series, were carried under the designation Ar 240. Arado's selection of the Ar 440 designation for a follow-on development was probably an effort to underscore the improvements made. Messerschmitt had also taken a similar approach by designating the follow-on development of the Me 210 Zerstörer as the Me 410.

Blume's handwritten notes regarding "further developmental work", dated 6 November 1942, reinforce this thinking, since he noted the Ar 440 as a "current type" in this internal memorandum.

Ar 240/440. W. Blume's notes from 6 November 1942:

"Current types"

Ar 440. Assumed: Recon still wanted. Number yet unknown, probably 36 units. Manufacture: E-MMO. E. starting with entire aircraft, then no more than assembly.

TEW and T.: Shift to clean recon role with BMW 801 J.

How far can the airframe go to its maximum dimensions (fuselage plugs, outer wings) for this purpose. Control surfaces?

Particularly interested in obtaining a Ju 88, so as to analyze its performance dimensions."

"Ar 240. Use of available types:

V 3, A-04 TAE testbed. Tailor test program to fundamental or future tasking from the TAE. Test program to HE A-03 to Rechlin

Rest to Oberst R. What can be made from wood here?

B-0: Replacement parts possible for O.R.?

V 6: Repair by E"

These notes give the additional impression that the Ar 240 V 3 and A-04 were provided to the TAE (Technische Abteilung Aerodynamik, or Technical Department, Aerodynamics) and the HE (Hauptabteilung Entwicklung, or Main Department, Development) and the Ar 240 A-03 to Rechlin in conjunction with further development not mentioned in further detail.

It is questionable whether the Ar 240 V 3 prototype mentioned by Blume led immediately to the so-called Ar 440 V 1, as sometimes claimed. Assuming this isn't a mistake, this aircraft was in any case utilized in September 1944 for testing the pressurized cockpit of the Ar 234 jet airplane. While the A-03 and A-04, after modifications, had a significant part in the development of the Ar 240 C series, the remainder of the A-series may have played a role in evaluating a less-refined version using wood construction. The two Ar 240 B-0 prototypes may possibly have been chopped up for replacement parts.

Although nearly all manufacturing jigs and equipment were available for the series production of the Ar 240 C/440, W. Blume had little hope for it at the time. On 1 December 1942 he noted under short term goals: "temporary improvements made to current equipment, no new designs, e.g. Ar 440 — engines — fuel — smoothing. What other means? Ar 440 initially promoted as example for construction methods; classification considerations come later."

Unfortunately, there are no known detailed photos of the Ar 240 C/440 model. It was probably the T9+GL, of which there exists a photo dated March 1944 when it was operating with 3/Erp. Gr. Ob. d. L. in Oranienburg. This aircraft may possibly have been the Ar 240 V 12 or an earlier Ar 240 A-04/U2 model which might have already had the relevant and recognizable modifications such as enlarging the vertical stabilizers and tailplane done for evaluation purposes. Changes to the horizontal stabilizer stemmed from

Sketch of Ar 440 with rear-firing guns.

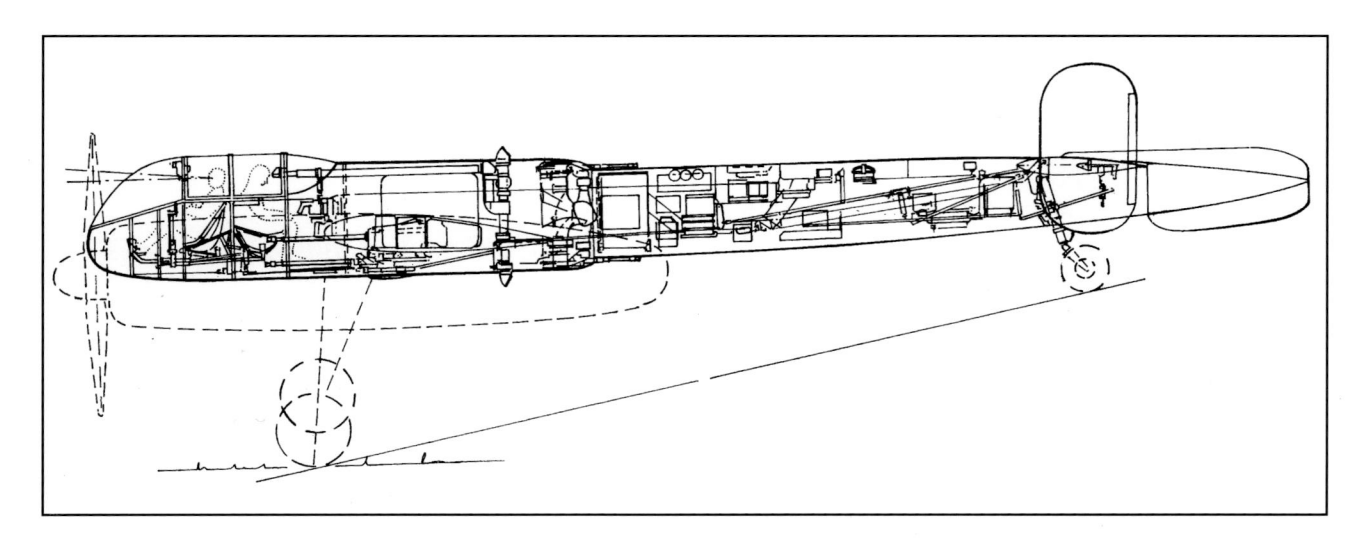

Ar 240 C, probably T9+GL, with DB 603 G engines.

Erhard Milch, Generalinspekteur der Luftwaffe.

the tailplane's trim tabs no longer extending to the fuselage. The photo comes from former pilot Horst Götz, who recently provided recollections of an "Ar 240 C with DB 603 G engine", with which he carried out over 40 overflights of England and Italy in early 1944. A later Ar 234 jet aircraft having the same registration code of T9+GL in April 1945 can be explained by the fact that this Ar 240 C was destroyed in the autumn of 1944 in Poland.

By the end of 1942, the gods were no longer favoring further development of the Ar 240/440. Hans Rebeski, former director of the design bureau, remembers when Erhard Milch toured the company hangars on 13 September 1942 during a visit to Brandenburg. Walter Blume attempted to bring to his attention an "abandoned" Ar 240 prototype "just standing there." Milch is reputed to have said: "Don't stir up this stupid nonsense with the Ar 240 any more!" and then left the hangar.

On 6 November 1942, when the course of the war was changing in Stalingrad, Milch called a development meeting at which Göring ordered the complete cancellation of the Ar 240 project. Milch immediately telegraphed Arado with the instructions to cease all work related to the project. Blume quickly arranged meeting with Milch on 26 November 1942, ostensibly for the purpose of discussing the damaged relations with the Technisches Amt. He subsequently recorded: "discussion with Gfm Milch: forming a circle of trust — projections for development, to be able to direct all sub-assemblies — guidelines for the firm." Yet Milch stood by his earlier refusal and, in a letter to Walter Blume a few weeks later, assured him that it had been "particularly difficult" for him, "since I was fully aware of the high state of technical development and the performance capabilities of your model."

At the end of 1942 Blume, despite the rejections of the Technisches Amt, still remained convinced that the Ar 440 would have been the ideal interim solution — both as a Zerstörer as well as a high speed bomber — prior to the advent of jet-powered aircraft. He came to the conclusion that there were two irreconcilable roles facing an attack plane: features found on a "heavy fighter" used to attack bombers would have to be dropped in order to focus on providing the craft with superior flight characteristics — since escort protection nearly always forced it to attack from an unfavorable position. The most critical requirements were a superior climb rate over enemy fighters, at the very least equality of speed and maneuverability, adequate armor protection and good high-altitude handling. The single-seat, twin engine, heavy fighter provided more reliability, better weapons effectiveness and longer range over that of single-engine fighters. A "Zerstörer in the more narrow sense" was tasked with intercepting enemy bomber formations and providing wide-ranging fighter cover. These necessitated high speeds, devastating weapons effectiveness, armor protection and an endurance of circa four hours. This Zerstörer would be ill-suited for escort protection. The manufacturer must be given a free hand in improving shape, visibility and armor protection for the engine, be able to take measures to increase speed, optimize weapons configurations and introduce counter-rotating propellers.

Regarding the "high-speed bomber", he made the assumption that the optimum solution for approaching speeds found on fighters would be to eliminate the fuselage as a drag-producing component and move the crew compartment to one of the engine nacelles. However, he was adamant in his opinion that marginally slower, existing types such as the Ar 240 C/440 with proven pressurized cockpit and remote-controlled rear guns could be made operational immediately, without delays from additional developmental work. In a comparison with the Ar E 530 twin-fuselage design, he felt that the Ar 440 had the following advantages: no interference of vision caused by a front engine

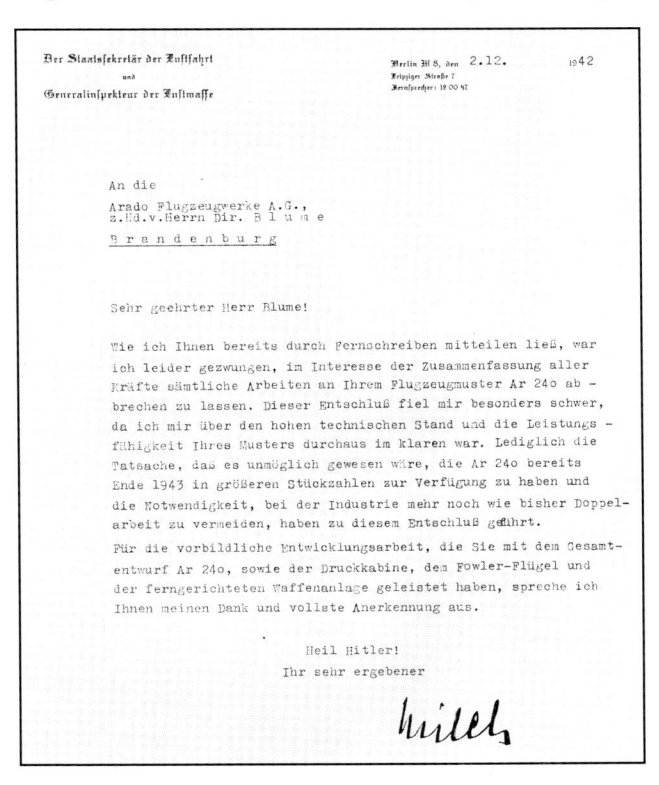

Ar 240. Message from E. Milch regarding cessation of work (2 December 1942).

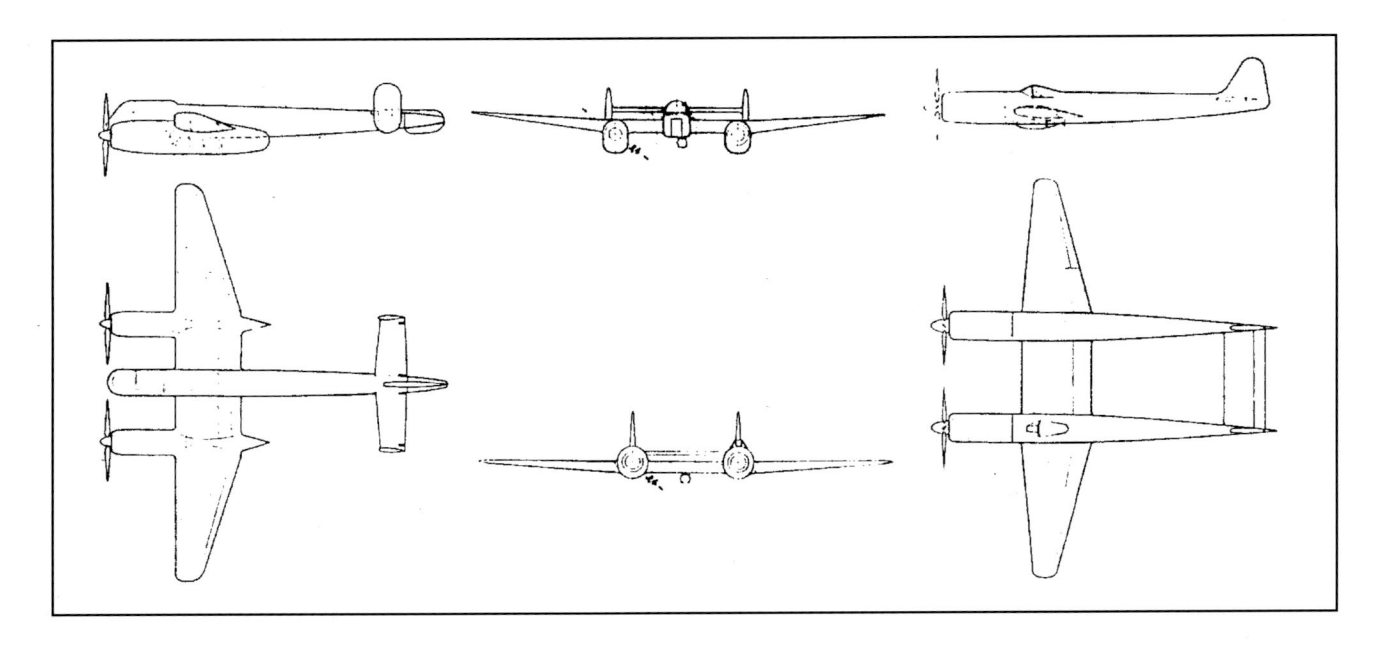

Right Arado E 530. Left: Ar 440.

when acquiring targets. Conditions for installing a gunsight were better, inasmuch as there were less approach restrictions and fewer steep dive angles to be concerned with. Although not yet developed, propeller brakes for reducing the interception altitude were only to have been standard equipment on the Ar 440.

Performance	E 530	Ar 440 (with armament)
takeoff power:	2 x 1,900 hp	2 x 1,900 hp
takeoff weight:	10,200 kg	11,980 kg (12,427 kg)
wing loading:	250 kg/m²	296 kg/m² (311 kg/m²)
climb speed:	11.5 m/s	8.4 m/s (7.9 m/s)
cruise speed:	648 km/h	615 km/h (603 km/h)
emergency boost:	780 km/h	750 km/h (740 km/h)
range:	1,850 km	2,100 km (2,070 km)

A report from a hastily organized "high-speed bomber flyoff" on 19 January 1943 in Rechlin revealed the superiority of the Ar 440 in comparison with the competing Me 410, Ju 88 S and He 219. It showed a speed advantage of 47 km/h and superior combat performance of the Ar 440 Zerstörer.

On 26 November 1942 Milch requested that Blume give his impressions on the state of future aircraft development. Blume accordingly obliged with a study presented on 14 January 1943 which was aimed at providing the manufacturers with a precisely defined field of work. Without specifically referring to the competition between Arado and Messerschmitt, he called it wrong to have a project running concurrently "with two firms locked in competition for it." The Amt should pass feasible solution alternatives from the various design proposals on to the firm ultimately contracted with the manufacture, respecting individual copyright. He recommended that "outsider developments", such as those from Alexander Lippisch, be given more consideration and that greater efforts be taken to solicit reports from experienced front-line officers.

Referring to the relevant experience of the Arado Werke in the area of high-speed bombers, attack aircraft, night fighters, all-weather fighters and converted recon aircraft, he made an attempt to persuade the Amt of the value of the Ar 440 Zerstörer. Blume specifically mentioned the difficulties with the Heinkel He 219 night fighter and stressed that, with regard to dive bombing capability, pressurized cockpit and remote-controlled weapon systems, Arado had long been testing these.

By this time the Luftwaffe was increasingly feeling the pinch of having inadequate means to counter the enemy bomber attacks. At a conference with leading aviation industrialists at Karinhall on 18 March 1943, Göring complained that the British Mosquito had an untouchable speed, while he stood before them with empty hands. The brain of German designers had "dried up", he said. They revelled in their initial successes with "childlike glee", but never considered any new ideas. And these had led to unimaginable oversights. The "view to a future" was missing, replaced by "petty quibbling." One change followed another, and altogether gave the impression of "complete stagnation." He posed a rhetorical question, asking where the industrialist spirit and individual initiative had gone which they'd counted on. Promoting old types was nothing profound. His own office had stopped functioning in earlier years. A military tribunal had been established, its initial purpose to gain an overview, but there would be no hesitation in meting out sentences in the future.

Regarding the sentiments of Göring, who conceded that state-owned companies had given a relatively good accounting of themselves, Blume noted at the conference that Messerschmitt trumpeted "on-going superiority", that he wended his way around "like an eel" and touted exaggerated performance figures "with an impudent air." Göring kept up his criticism of the Me 210 Zerstörer with the words: "A wonder plane was promised and, trusting in that, other potential models were stopped. Became the greatest of disappointments, cost much of our best blood."

Göring's appraisal of the Me 410 Zerstörer led Blume to note: "It's possible that this will bring relief. I don't believe it yet. Discussion. Milch: Messerschmitt to have no other tasking than to develop the 410 and fighters against England this year. 410 production must be assured."

Blume claimed that Göring specifically called for the "night-capable high-speed combat aircraft", the "high-altitude and high-speed bomber", the long-range attack fighter" and the "high-speed reconnaissance airplane", on which Arado had been carrying out preliminary work for years. He wrote down Göring's feelings as follows: "High-altitude bomber: requested even before the war; have always said that. Talked about projects even before war started; but nothing has been done. The Ju 86, that ancient pile of junk, was used as the solution! High-speed bomber: same situation as with high-altitude bomber. Nothing done here, either; easy road was taken: fighters equipped with bombs. Fw 190 is now the longest-ranging fighter-bomber! Now I am to tip the scales in our favor against England."

As the theme for a subsequent meeting with his senior engineers, Blume noted that the competition had "made wide-ranging promises with thousands of loopholes (when's and if's)" in order to "get the business." This could no longer be the course of action. The Reichsminister already given instructions accordingly and with the next occurrence will "even grab industry representatives and now have them sentenced." A bone of contention was the fact that decisions were often made at upper levels without first consulting him. As an example, financial approval for the Ar 440 had been red-lined two days prior to the meeting with Göring, despite prior positive indications. He didn't want to become a victim due to the "carelessness of a department or technical expert." With regard to Göring's call for "complete, operationally safe and easily maintained aircraft" he criticized the "pig-headedness existing even among ourselves." He regretted his "incessant preaching to crank out airplanes." The latest accidents in connection with the Fowler flaps and a broken hydraulic reservoir on an oleo strut could not happen in the future.

Without waiting for further developments, on 13 February 1943 Milch informed Kontrolingenieur Hennig that his earlier decision to reject the Ar 240/440 was final, this despite an endorsement from Göring for the go-ahead.

In early 1943 Blume wrote: "An operational Ar 440 as Kampfzerstörer or night fighter is no longer a possibility. Operation as a recon aircraft still uncertain ... assuming recon still an option. Number yet unknown, probably 36 units. Shifting over to clear-cut recon role with BMW 801J."

As late as the summer of 1944 Blume continued to send reminders, disregarding the Amt's promotion of the Me 410, which stressed the urgency of Ar 240 C/440 full-scale production as a stop-gap solution until the arrival of jet aircraft. On 15 September 1943 he requested an opportunity to discuss the matter with Milch, referring to his proposals from 14 January, and added: "In the interim I've thoroughly researched the area of 'high-speed two-seaters' with my design department, focusing on high-speed bombers, attack fighters, night and all-weather fighters and recon aircraft using both internal reciprocating combustion and turbine engines. Results show that it would be possible, given the developmental stage we have before us, to realize heavily-armed two-seaters which could carry a 2,000 kg bomb load, to break the 900-km barrier and approach the speed barrier of fighters." With regard to the Ar 240/440, this discussion had just as little impact as did the submission on 18 July of a similarly worded study to Oberstleutnant Siegfried Knemeyer.

Apparently, Milch rested his hopes for a "medium combat aircraft" with the jet airplanes then in development and, with a nod to the current war situation, felt that the Do 335 would bridge the gap. This highly refined aircraft, which had a piston engine in both the fore and aft fuselage, first flew in October 1943. However, it did not reach operational status before the cessation of hostilities.

Developmental planning in switching from piston-engine to jet-powered aircraft:

Pasewald: We now find ourselves in a critical situation wherein we are at the technical limits with the medium combat aircraft, specifically with the range as dictated by the required speed.

GenFeldm. Milch: In the area of engines with propellers! However, I believe there's a bright, new future beginning with the jet engine system.

Pasewald: We're starting here with a relatively disappointing range.

GenFeldm. Milch: Yes, that's true. Up to now the matter of the jet engine hasn't left the evaluation divisions of the companies. We've displayed a tremendous amount of courage on the fighter side, because something had to happen in this area. We're running with so many other fighters that we could stand it if we were to suffer a setback. But we're convinced that we've got the matter in hand. We want to run the same risk on the bomber side, but that will depend on time. The GL does not intend to put out poor quality material. It wants only to deliver the best whenever at all possible. It must, however, be clearly understood what can be built and what can't ... It's my opinion that we need the medium bomber in its best possible design within the next three years. We foresee an improvement only when the Dornier's new system arrives, with its two counter-rotating propellers fore and aft. Then we can move forward with speed. Even then the jump isn't as great as he projects. I think that the next leap in this arena will be possible only with the jet engine, and if Dornier actually does appear at the front with the new machines around the end of 1945, then I would say: by the end of 1948 we will perhaps have a sensible jet engine bomber.[112]

The final decision to stop all work on the Ar 240 was a bitter pill for Arado to swallow in view of its extensive investment and numerous prototypes built. Without the weight of defensive armament and with the aid of performance-boosting engines with fuel injection systems or three-stage turbo-superchargers the Ar 240 C/440 was the fastest German piston-engine aircraft of the day, effortlessly able to escape any attackers. The maximum speed with the DB 603 A was 660 km/h according to company data from 29 September 1942, so that in January 1943 W. Blume could justifiably say that the Ar 440 fitted with the DB 603 G "with 2960 hp engine performance, is currently the fastest two-seater with 680 km/h at 8 km altitude."

On the other hand, the initial stability problems had never been fully rectified. Horst Götz remembers associated remaining problems during the year 1944: "The aircraft, probably Ar 240/440 with DB 603 G engines, began to oscillate unpleasantly above 7,000 m, something which couldn't be eliminated even by enlarging the tailfins." In view of the fact that this highly developed and specialized aircraft pushed the extreme edge of the envelope, it's entirely possible that these remaining quirks could have been tolerated.

Developmental state of the Ar 240. Company report from 30 June 1944:

After lengthening the fuselage by 1 meter (and enlarging the wings), tumbling (coupled movement around the vertical and longitudinal axes) was improved, only became acceptable after the rudder assembly was built up (increased) and the engine nacelles were tapered to the rear. (Resulting speed increase around 40-50 km/h). This improved conditions to the point where tumbling disappeared altogether at low altitudes, as at over 8 km with fixed rudder. However, with free rudder was still annoying (constant to lightly oscillating). This state was not significantly influenced by any further increase of the wings or by lengthening the fuselage. It was considered acceptable, since the tumbling only occurred by deliberate interference or taking the feet completely off the pedals.

Despite these minor problems with flight stability, experienced Zerstörer pilots such as Oberleutnant Thierfelder gave excellent assessments of the Ar 240 A-04 based on evaluation of the type in Rechlin on 18 December 1943. Even the Versuchsstelle für Höhenflüge, in a report from 13 May 1943, stated that "the two Ar 240s have, in general, proven themselves well in the winter campaign in the East." The spiritual father of the airplane, Wilhelm van Nes, appeared indignant when it came to blanket criticisms: "Whoever judges the airplane to be a poor design has either never flown or can't fly."

Milch's attachment to the Messerschmitt attack planes was a painful to Blume inasmuch as this competing design had been built with the assistance of Walter Rethel (earlier dismissed from Arado), plus the fact that the Bf 110 had already proven to be a failure. Spin accidents repeatedly led to evaluations of the aircraft's stall and pitch behavior. It became apparent during the Battle of Britain that the aircraft's lack of maneuverability and inadequate defensive armament made it unsuitable for escort duties. And the Me 210 follow-on development proved to be even less of a mature design. Teething problems with regard to flight stability and landing qualities cropped up during the early testing stages. Numerous accidents during flight trials were caused by collapsing landing gear, which in turn was traced to the risky business of saving material and weight in exchange for which Messerschmitt was able to gain a speed advantage. In 1941, when the Me 210 Zerstörer was unable to be put into production due to numerous technical problems, production reverted back at considerable expense to its predecessor, the Bf 110. In March 1942 the project was stopped once and for all and the failed design was remedied somewhat with the follow-on Me 410.

Comparison of the Ar 240 with the Me 210:

With regard to the Ar 240, this aircraft was given high marks following its initial test flights with minimal adjustments. Even the Rechlin test center gave quite a good assessment of the aircraft. Unfortunately, Blume didn't understand how to effectively oppose Messerschmitt. Flight handling was so good that we didn't need the counter-rotating engines. We later had to turn these over to Messerschmitt; since the Me 210 had such poor handling characteristics they wanted to improve the characteristics somewhat by utilizing the counter-rotating engines.[113]

Performance comparison

	Ar 240C	D.H. Mosquito	Me 210A-1
takeoff power:	3,500 hp	3,070 hp	2,380 hp
wing surface:	31.3 m^2	41.80 m^2	36.20 m^2
empty weight:	5,500 kg	7,240 kg	7,070 kg
takeoff weight:	10,000 kg	11,400 kg	9,460 kg
wing loading:	320 kg/m^2	272 kg/m^2	261.3 kg/m^2
power loading:	2.86 kg/hp	3.7 kg/hp	3.97 kg/hp
Vmax:	700 km/h	486 km/h	573 km/h

As early as 1940, Udet had congenially informed Messerschmitt about inadequacies with the Bf 110 Zerstörer and missed deadlines with the program. On 27 June 1941, he imploringly expressed his concern with the casual attitude with which Messerschmitt produced the Me 210 Zerstörer before it had reached developmental maturity. He stressed that it was his "favored position as a designer", the "unlimited trust" which had been placed in him and Messerschmitt's important awards which gave occasion to take a more critical view of him and his work. Udet concluded with the advice: "I ask you to take all measures needed ... with the Me 210 to eliminate any setbacks of this kind."

Unconcerned, Messerschmitt countered by pointing out to Udet that a comparison of expenditures and success between the individual companies — without specifically naming Arado — clearly showed his work center to be the better.

Udet eventually gave up as did Milch, who accused Messerschmitt of thinking himself a "genius" when in fact it was his fault that the Me 210 was currently non-existent and no replacement for it was available. For his part, in 1943 Messerschmitt labeled Milch in front of Hitler as incapable and advised that Dornier's and Arado's competing designs be scrapped. This despite the fact that Göring had to drop the Me 210 from the program, since the aircraft could not be made suitable for front-line service with regard to its operational readiness and maintenance.

Over the years, as the developmental role of the Ar 240 changed, the last prototypes (Ar 240 V 9 through V 12, company designations Ar 240 C or Ar 440 C-01 through C-04) may have been projected exclusively for reconnaissance purposes. It is unknown whether they collectively were ever flown. There are flight log entries for the Ar 240 V 10 for test flights in Brandenburg on 22 and 23 October and 2 December 1943. According to the C-Amt's program for prototype models of the Arado Flugzeugwerke dated 24 April 1944, only the Ar 240 V 10 was still at the company's facilities as of that date.

It isn't fully clear whether a data collection flight with the Ar 240 V 3 for measuring heat exchange in the Ar 234's pressurized cockpit actually took place on 4 September 1944, as notated in company records.

Witnesses of the time, such as Hans Rebeski, remember that a few of the older prototypes were rounded up from Arado's

manufacturing hangars shortly before the end of the war, since "the Ju 88 could no longer successfully fulfill the reconnaissance role."

Model Ar 240.
Wk.Nr., registration code, engine, wingspan (date of manufacture):

V 1: 0001, DD+QL, DB 601 V26/V 52, 14.26 m (8/39). Attack fighter.
V 2: 0002, unk., DB 601 A/E, 14.26 m (8/39). Attack fighter.
V 3: 0003, KK+CD, DB 601 E, 14.26 m (5/40). Attack fighter. Prototype for A-0 pre-production series. Used as reconnaissance aircraft.
V 4: 0004, unk. DB 601 E, 14.26 m (5/40). Dive bomber. Prototype for A-0 pre-production series. Used as reconnaissance aircraft.
V 5: 0005, T5+MH, DB 601 E, 14.26 m (7/40). Attack fighter. Prototype for A-0 pre-production series. Used as long-range reconnaissance aircraft.
V 6: 0006, T5+KH, DB 601 E, 14.26 m (9/40). Attack fighter. Prototype for A-0 pre-production series. Used as long-range reconnaissance aircraft.
A-01: 0011, GL+QA, DB 601 E, 14.26 m (6/41).
A-02: 0012, GL+QB, DB 601 E, 14.26 m (7/41).
A-03: 0013, DI+CY, DB 601 E, 14.26 m (8/41).
A-04: 0014, DI+CZ, DB 601 E, 14.26 m (9/41).
A-05: 0015, unk. DB 601 E, 14.26 m (12/42) manufacture unknown.
A-03/U1: 01 0013, DI+CY, DB 603 A/0, 16.6 m (est. 26 Aug 42).
A-04/U2: 01 0014, DI+CZ, DB 603 A/0, 16.6 m (7/42) Use of entire series as reconnaissance aircraft.
V 7: 0015, DH+ZU, DB 605 A/1, 14.26 m (12/41). High-altitude recon. Forerunner of B-series. Two forward-firing MG-17 and lower turret with MG 151. Two 500 kg bombs.
V 8: 0016, unk., DB 605 A/1, 14.26 m (1/42). High-altitude recon. Forerunner of B-series.
V 9: 0017, BO+RC, DB 603 A/1, 16.6 m (5/42). Attack fighter. Prototype for C-series. Used as reconnaissance aircraft.
V 10: 0018, unk., DB 603 A/1, 16.6 m (6/42). Night fighter. Prototype for C-series. Used as reconnaissance aircraft.
V 11: 0019, unk., DB 603 G, 19.0 m (7/42). Attack fighter. Prototype for C-series. Planned conversion to reconnaissance aircraft.
V 12: 0020, unk., DB 603 G, 19.0 m (8/42). Attack fighter. Prototype for C-series. Planned conversion to reconnaissance aircraft.
V 13: Planned multi-role aircraft for D-series. Db 614/603[114] with three-stage turbo-supercharger.
V 14: Planned, enlarged bomber project for E-series, also as Ar 240 F Kampfzerstörer with supplemental Jumo-004 jet engine.
V 15: Planned photoreconnaissance aircraft with increased firepower and radar equipment.

Ar 240 A-0 data (26 Sept. 1942):

wxingspan:	14.3 m
length:	12.8 m
height:	3.7 m
wing surface area:	31.0 m²
engine:	DB 601 E
takeoff performance(2700 rpm, 1.42 ata):	2 x 1350 hp
combat performance at max altitude(2500 rpm):	2 x 1200 hp
max altitude(1.30 ata):	4900 m
VDM propeller, diameter:	2.96 m
empty weight:	6795 kg
load:	1895 kg
takeoff weight:	8690 kg
fuel:	1480 kg
weight at target:	7860
wing loading at target:	254 kg/m²
power loading at target:	3.28 kg/hp

Performance at target weight:
max speed at altitude of: emergency boost/military power

0 km	500/480 km/h
2 km	540/532 km/h
4 km	563/540 km/h
6 km	605/580 km/h
8 km	569/538 km/h
cruising/max cruising speed:	515/525 km/h
endurance:	3.6 hrs
range:	1870 km
fuel consumption:	218 g/hp/hr

time-to-climb to

1 km:	1.7 min
2 km:	3.2 min
4 km:	6.6 min
6 km:	10.5 min
service ceiling:	9300 m
landing weight:	7270 kg
landing speed:	148 km/h

Ar 240 B data (28 Sept. 1942)

wingspan:	14.3 m
length:	12.4 m
height:	3.75 m
wing surface area:	31.0 m²
engine:	DB 605 A
takeoff performance(2800 rpm, 1.42 ata):	2 x 1475 hp
combat performance at max altitude(2600 rpm):	2 x 1250 hp
max altitude(1.30 ata)	5800 m
VDM propeller, diameter:	2.96 m
empty weight:	7160 kg
load:	1925 kg
takeoff weight:	9085 kg
fuel:	1480 kg
weight at target:	8240 kg
wing loading at target:	266 kg/m²
power loading at target:	3.30 kg/hp

Performance at target weight:
max speed at altitude of: emergency boost/military power

0 km	523/503 km/h
2 km	570/550 km/h
4 km	595/578 km/h
6 km	614/600 km/h
7 km	630/622 km/h
8 km	600/590 km/h
cruising/max cruising speed:	540/550 km/h
endurance:	3.3 hrs
range:	1800 km
fuel consumption:	220 g/hp/hr

time-to-climb to
- 1 km: 1.5 min
- 2 km: 3.0 min
- 4 km: 6.4 min
- 6 km: 10.5 min

service ceiling: 10200 m
landing weight: 7620 kg
landing speed: 149 km/h

Ar 240 C data (26 Sept. 1942)

wingspan:	16.60 m
length:	13.35 m
height:	3.96 m
wing surface area:	35.0 m²
engine:	DB 603 A
takeoff performance(2700 rpm, 1.40 ata):	2 x 1750 hp
combat performance at max altitude(2500 rpm):	2 x 1510 hp
max altitude(1.30 ata):	5700 m
VDM propeller, diameter:	3.40 m
empty weight:	8885 kg
load:	2650 kg
takeoff weight:	11535 kg
fuel:	2065 kg
weight at target:	10345 kg
wing loading at target:	296 kg/m²
power loading at target:	3.43 kg/hp

Performance at target weight:
max speed at altitude of: emergency boost/military power
- 0 km 550/535 km/h
- 2 km 595/575 km/h
- 4 km 626/609 km/h
- 6 km 650/634 km/h
- 7.1 km 660/650 km/h
- 8 km 634/627 km/h

cruising/max cruising speed: 590/600 km/h
endurance: 3.4 hrs
range: 2020 km
fuel consumption: 230 g/hp/hr
time-to-climb to
- 1km: 1.4 min
- 2km: 2.8 min
- 4km: 5.8 min
- 6km: 9.2 min

service ceiling: 10500 m
landing weight: 9470 kg
landing speed: 153 km/h

Chapter 16
Victim of the Red Pencil: The Ar 232 Combat Transport

Production of the first combat transport in the world with the capability to operate from rough airfields fell victim to the reduction in types which took place during the course of the war. The Ar 232 was a worthy replacement for the obsolete Ju 52/3, having a speed roughly 70 km/h faster than the Junkers aircraft with twice the carrying capacity.[115]

Van Nes settled upon a cantilever mid-wing smooth skinned monocoque design with a spacious cargo area low to the ground. Behind the pilot's cabin was a bay 6.60 m long, a free width of 2.30 m and a height of 2.00 m. The aircraft was, from its inception, a thoroughly convincing design. Drawn up by Wilhelm van Nes, it was to have been robust and capable of operating from rough fields, be able to carry heavy and cumbersome loads far into the front lines,

Ar 232 B components (below).

Nr.	Rüstsätze	Gewicht kg
1.	A-Stand: 1 MG 81 Z beweglich mit 1000 Schuß	29 / 28
2.	B-Stand: 1 MG 81 Z beweglich mit 1600 Schuß	78 / 45
3.	C-Stand: 1 MG 81 Z beweglich mit 2000 Schuß	46 / 56
4.	Gr. FT-Rahmen (FuG X, Peil G6, FuBl.2)	115
5.	Kl. FT-Rahmen (FuG 16)	30
6.	Kurssteuerung (Rudermaschine i.Heck)	20
7.	Winter- oder Tropen-Ausrüstung	185
8.	Werkzeugtasche, Zurrseile, Bodenanker, Bezüge f. Kabine, Motor usw.	85
9.	Laufschiene und Laufkatze	79
10.	Klappsitze (6 Stück im Laderaum)	30
11.	Ausrüstung für Truppentransport (8 Sitzbänke)	193
12.	Führerpanzersitz (Differenzgew.)	60
13.	Schlauchboot	48
14.	Schlauchbootpanzerung	49
15.	Absprunganlage f. Fallschirmjäger	20
16.	Geschirr für Lastensegler	24

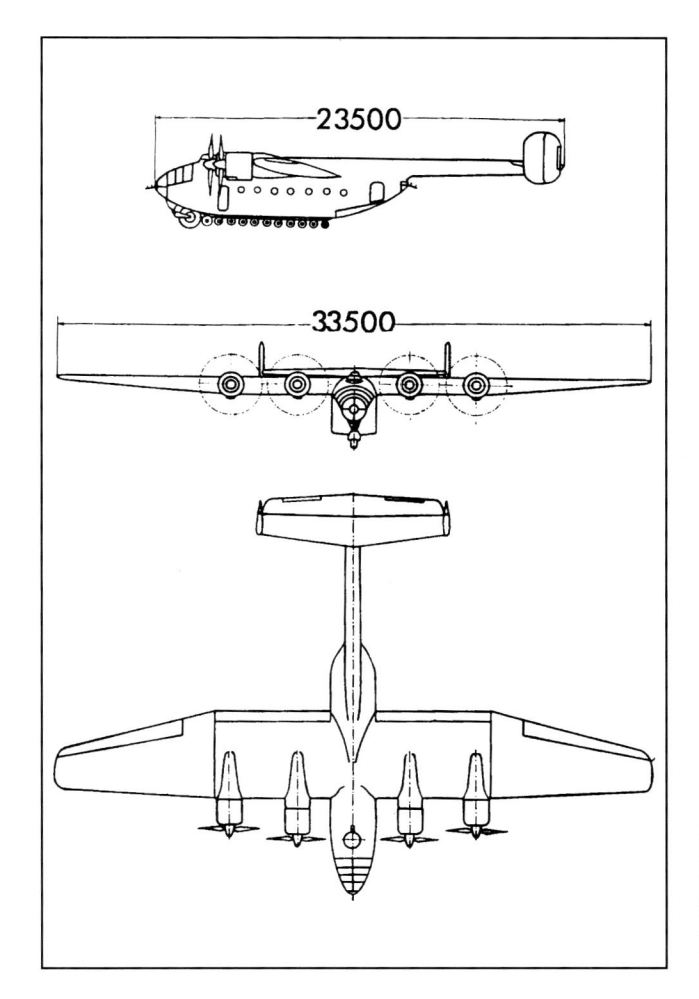

The Ar 232 B transport (three-view, 1942)

Ar 232 A, V 1, GH+GN.

The most significant innovation was the design of the landing gear, sometimes nicknamed the "Grendel" or "millipede." For operations from prepared airstrips the airplane was equipped with a standard tricycle landing gear produced by the company of Kronprinz in Solingen. During landing, the impact was absorbed by the forward extending nose gear, which used a hydraulic shock absorber to cancel out the landing energy. For this purpose it could be extended further than the level of a secondary main gear, consisting of 22 pneumatic tires in a caterpillar arrangement. This caterpillar gear enabled the aircraft to takeoff and land on extremely rough terrain, including over tree trunks up to 15 cm thick and ditches 1.5 meters deep. This type of landing, however, reduced the available cargo capacity.

On its first landing, the tricycle gear gave out and the aircraft dropped onto the caterpillar gear. Preflight testing of the landing gear extension carried out from a crane hook in the hangar showed that it functioned flawlessly. That it did happen on the rollout during flight trials, which took place on a specially designed obstacle-ridden field, was probably because additional forces came into play as the aircraft was moving forward. It was discovered that the

have rapid on- and off-loading times and have short takeoff and landing capabilities. An overhead loading crane was located inside the cargo bay. The rear part of the fuselage flooring could be hydraulically lowered as a loading ramp or for making cargo/parachutist drops during flight. The slender control surface boom, attached to the rear bulkhead of the fuselage and rear wing spar, was located at such a height that it did not interfere with loading. The cantilever tailplane rested on the boom, which ended in an attachment point for towing gliders.

The split rudder was located on either tip of the tailfin. The three-piece twin spar wing consisted of an all-through rectangular centerpiece to which were attached the two trapezoidal outer wings, each containing self-sealing fuel tanks and the main landing gear.

In order to achieve an acceptable landing speed the wings were fitted with the electrically activated "Arado traveling flaps" along their entire span, linked to their traveling ailerons. These landing aids, which Arado had been developing since 1938 and had also been fitted to the Ar 240 Zerstörer, increased wing area by 25 percent. Braking parachutes or rockets could be utilized for shortening the rollout length. If required, takeoff runs could be shortened through the use of rocket assisted takeoff packs. Another lift-boosting measure was the introduction of a boundary layer blower system in lieu of Fowler flaps.[116]

lower oleo strut, whose extended length was too short, became jammed in the upper one.

The engineer responsible for the project, Hans Rebeski, had a ring inserted which had the effect of restricting the lower oleo from extending as far.

The transport, designed for a four-man crew, was fitted with armor seats for the pilot and gun positions in the nose, on the upper fuselage and in the rear. In addition, machine gun ports could be integrated into the cargo pod for lateral defense. Auxiliary packages included winter or tropical kits, a radio set, a rubber liferaft, an oil burning heater, an emergency power unit and sundry tools.

At the beginning of 1941 the first two prototypes of the Ar 232, V 1 (GH+GN) and V 2 (VD+YA) began trials as prototypes for the A-series, each having two BMW 801 A engines. Despite popular opinion that there were only two prototypes built, it is safe to assume that there were actually ten pre-production Ar 232 A-0 aircraft manufactured (Wk.Nr. 100 003 to 100 012).

As indicated by Walter Blume's notes from a Göring speech on 13 September 1942, the transport was originally planned for operations in North Africa and the Arctic. Then it was decided to use both of the first two A-series transports, still undergoing flight testing, to airlift wounded personnel from the 6th Armee, surrounded near Stalingrad. It was the view of Hans Rebeski, design supervisor, that air-

Ar 232 A being test-flown over the Malge and the Brandenburg-Kirchmöser railway line.

Ar 232 A-010, TC+EG (Wk. Nr. 100 012) of Westa 5 on 7 August 1943 on Bear Island, Norway, with its landing gear sunk down into the soil.

craft in the testing phase shouldn't be used for front-line operations. It was therefore agreed with Walter Blume and the Luftwaffenkommando that Rebeski would accompany the aircraft to the front in order to provide training and guidance to the troops.

However, after final instructions regarding minor details and the loading of special tools had been given, the idea was scrapped when Rebeski was injured in an automobile accident, which prevented him from flying immediately. As a result, the first pre-production A-01 took off without him, loaded with the special equipment; he would follow later in the second airplane. During the afternoon the crew lost their sense of direction due to snow flurries over Poland. Instead of making a 180-degree turn, the inexperienced pilot made the mistake of going into a circular descending glide to acquire the ground. The airplane unexpectedly struck the ground in forested terrain and crashed. The entire crew was killed and the urgently needed supplies were lost.

Its sister plane, on the other hand, gave an excellent accounting of itself delivering supplies to the beleaguered city in January 1943. Once, when the transport attempted a landing at Zhitomir, roughly 20 enemy fighters were no-

Ar 232 A-010 in Banak (July 1943).

ticed circling the airfield. The crew decided to land in a field blanketed with 60 cm of snow, a feat which would have been impossible without the specialized landing gear. Since the aircraft was equipped with an internal starter, the engines were able to be cranked up the following morning without outside help. The Arado transport, which was also used in the evacuation of Sevastopol, eventually became the last airplane which was able to both fly into and out of Stalingrad unhindered.

On 17 July 1943 Oblt. Rudolf Schütze took off in Brandenburg with the twin-engine Ar 232 A-010, TC+EG (Wk.Nr. 100 012) to the northernmost airfield in Europe, the in northern Norwegian airfield at Banak. Schütze was to have carried out landings at Westa 5 in Spitzbergen and on Bear Island in deep snows and drop off automatic weather apparati. Necessary range for such flights was provided by the installation of auxiliary fuel tanks with a capacity of 5,000 liters.

On 24 July 1943, when landing on the south cape of Spitzbergen, the right main gear buckled in, so that the aircraft rolled onto its multi-wheeled gear and the plane tipped over onto the right wingtip. The crew eventually succeeded in righting the aircraft themselves, making good use of the height adjusting features of the landing gear.

On 7 August the same airplane sank into soft ground up to its wheel axles while landing on Bear Island. Recovery operations lasted all day and the crew was supplied by air with the necessary equipment.

On 26 August 1943 the transport was to have been flown back to Brandenburg for an overhaul and be replaced by a four-engine version. Radio contact was lost shortly after takeoff. Investigation of the crash, which cost the life of Rudolf Schütze, the rest of the crew, two company specialists and at least a dozen personnel on leave due to resulting fire, showed that the right engine failed shortly after takeoff at a point where the aircraft was still in the clouds. In order to find an emergency landing site, the pilot was forced by the terrain to bank right — into the dead engine. This maneuver, difficult as it was, was exacerbated by the fact that the twin engine Ar 232 A was difficult to keep in the air on a single engine because of little power reserve. The machine had therefore lost more altitude than expected. As it broke through the clouds, it was already flying lower than the surrounding mountains, roughly 150 meters high. In attempting to clear a mountain summit, it stalled out and struck just below its peak.

Ar 232 B. Rear view showing the Arado landing flaps.

In anticipation of a higher performing version of the transport the RLM called for the expeditious construction of a four-engine B-series. Four BMW 323 R2 radial engines, each with 1,000 hp output, were to have been utilized since the engines being used in the A-series were urgently needed for fighter production. Doubling the number of engines gave a better load/performance ratio (4.38 kg/hp vice 5.13 kg/hp) and consequently shortened the takeoff run, gave the plane somewhat of a higher top speed and reduced the time to climb.

Aside from lengthening the wing center section, installation of the two additional engines was accomplished with no other changes to the design. A pre-production batch of 20 aircraft, including the two V 3 and V 4 prototypes, was built of the Ar 232 B-0. The first four-engine version to take to the skies was the Ar 232 V 3, in May of 1942. Available data only exists for aircraft up to the Ar 232 B-017 (Wk.Nr. 110 029). Evaluation reports ceased in June of 1944. Assuming that the last of the ten A-series pre-production aircraft was assigned the Werknummer 100 012, the Ar 232 V 3 (B-01) and V 4 (B 02) would have been given Werknummern 110 013 and 110 014, respectively. This is further borne out by the fact that Werknummern 11023 was for the Ar 232 b-011, 110 029 for Ar 232 B-017 and 110032 for the last example of this type, the Ar 232 B-020.

The company often utilized the Ar 232 for transporting high priority aircraft parts. Six B-series aircraft were assigned to the Ergänzungs-Transport-Gruppe of 14 Staffel of Transportgeschwader 4. Five transports eventually found their way to KG 200, a special unit for secret and sabotage activities — activities in which the airplane was involved during two spectacular missions near the war's end.

Ar 232 B-017 (Wk. Nr. 110 029), G6+YY in Farnborough after its capture by the British (above).

Ar 232 B flight characteristics (22 July 1943 — below).

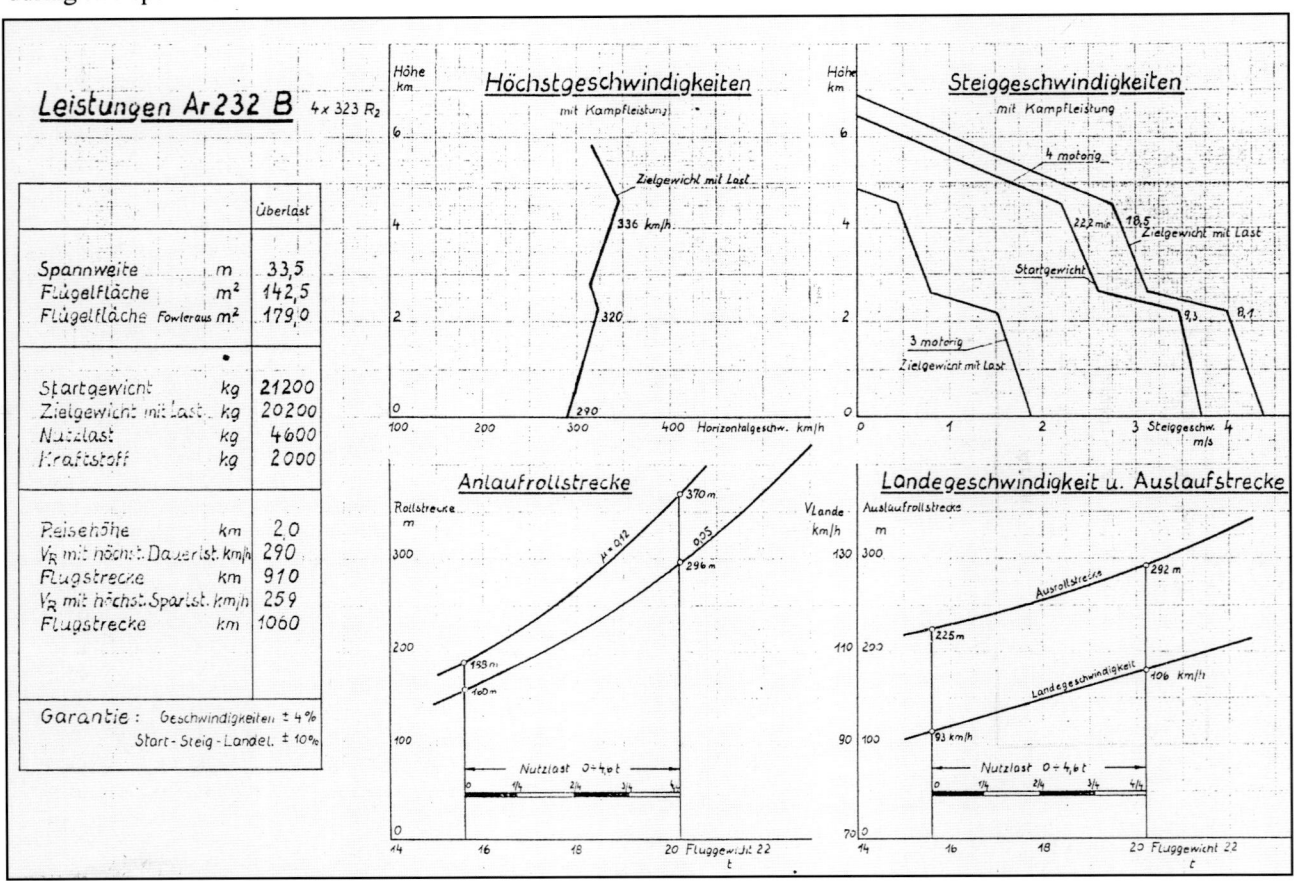

In 1944 senior ranking German officials developed a plan to murder Stalin under the codename Operation Zeppelin.[117] After a previous assassination attempt had failed, it was planned to kill Stalin on the 27th anniversary of the October Revolution using a remotely detonated bomb hidden inside a briefcase. Execution of this operation was entrusted to a former Soviet officer by the name of Polikov, who was given papers showing him to be the vice commander of a military security unit of the 39th Soviet Army. He was accompanied by Lidya Adamicheva-Shilova, who had been trained as a radio operator and was passing herself off as a second lieutenant in the medical corps. After completing his training Polikov was provided with special hand grenades, pistols, a rocket-like firing device, false identification papers and documents, stamped, blank forms and a Soviet M-72 motorcycle with sidecar.

An initial attempt at the operation using an A-series plane was broken off due to poor lighting conditions in the target area. The landing gear mechanism failed on the return trip to Minsk, the right oleo strut collapsed and the machine slid across the runway on its right wing. During the flight to the Geschwader's repair facility in Finsterwalde the right engine gave out and the aircraft only made it back to its original starting point after an emergency landing was made in a wheat field near Zareby, Poland and subsequent repairs had been completed.

In preparation of a second flight using a B-series aircraft three agents were parachuted into the woods near Smolensk to reconnoiter suitable former German airstrips. Apparently, however, the Soviets had been informed of their plans. According to them the radioman changed allegiance and told the enemy where the landing site was, so that the Soviet anti-aircraft defense was able to set up firing positions throughout the area and keep searchlights at the ready. In case the German flyers became suspicious trenches were dug across the field to prevent the plane from taking off again.

Ar 232 B-05, which took off with the agents on board on 6 September 1944, came under heavy anti-aircraft fire near Smolensk even before reaching the target area. Since in addition the weather was poor the pilot decided to change course and landed at an auxiliary airstrip near the village of Kuklovo, 150 northeast of the original destination. The airplane landed around 3 am, but as a recently rediscovered photo shows, one of its wings struck a tree on landing. The outer engine tore off, making takeoff impossible. After a Ju 88 was unable to locate the landing site, five German crew members who had hidden in a wood were captured and became prisoners of war; a sixth resisted and was shot.

The inserted agents had little chance of fulfilling their assignment once the landing had been discovered. On the morning of 7 September they were stopped by a patrol on the way to Moscow. Although their papers initially seemed to be in order, Polikov was arrested when it was noticed that he was wearing his decorations in the wrong place, unaware that regulations had changed.

Another special mission in which the Arado transport took part was Operation Scherhorn.[118] After Heeresgruppe Mitte had collapsed in the summer of 1944, a unit caught behind Soviet lines under the command of Oberstleutnant Scherhorn attempted a breakthrough to the West. Original plans called for six Ar 232s to be diverted from Fliegerkorps XIV to KG 200 for supplying the troops and airlifting out the wounded. In actual fact, there were only two machines[119] available when operations began on 8 December 1944. By February of 1945 it had only been possible to carry out occasional resupply flights, due to poor visibility, technical problems and enemy defenses. Despite untiring activity on the part of the Germans, the operation eventually proved fruitless because of an enemy deception tactic, for Scherhorn had already been captured and was being forced to fool the Germans with continuous radio communications.

Ar 232 B-017 (Wk.Nr. 110 029), which had been used as G6+YY in Operation Scherhorn in December of 1944, was confiscated by the British undamaged in Eggebeck at the end of the war. Captain Eric Brown of the RAF confirmed the excellent flying characteristics of the airplane, which as A3+RB was used on flights between England and Germany in 1945 and 1946.

A follow-on development which never saw production was the Ar 432 of composite construction with wooden outer wings and empennage. This design approach was originally to have been used for the Ar 232 B-0 and the Ar 232 C-0 series which never materialized. On 3 June 1944 there was a meeting in Landeshut regarding this approach, in which Siegfried Knemeyer as chief of GL/C-E, Walter Blume and nearly all the important department chairman from Arado were present. Although Walter Blume was critical of the fact that the general drawings weren't always available and sketches and diagrams couldn't be read without difficulty, he noted with satisfaction: "Chief GL/C-E quite happy with the type and method of our work. He was very pleased with tactical/technical approach."

According to the minutes of the meeting the Ar 232 B-04 prototype would be used for ongoing airframe tests with wooden control surfaces, while the Ar 232 V 1 was to be a testbed for alternate bearings, the Ar 232 B-02 for new weapons release systems, the Ar 232 B-011 for control and flight handling characteristics and the Ar 232 B-010 for testing paratroop operations. The Ar 432 A-01 prototype was

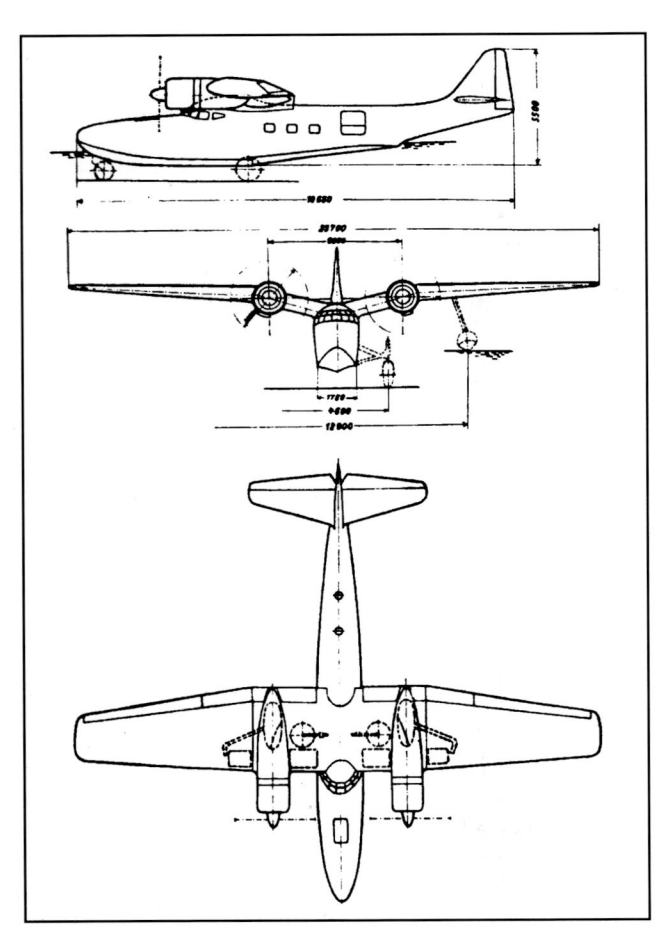

Three-view of the Ar 430 flying boat (1942).

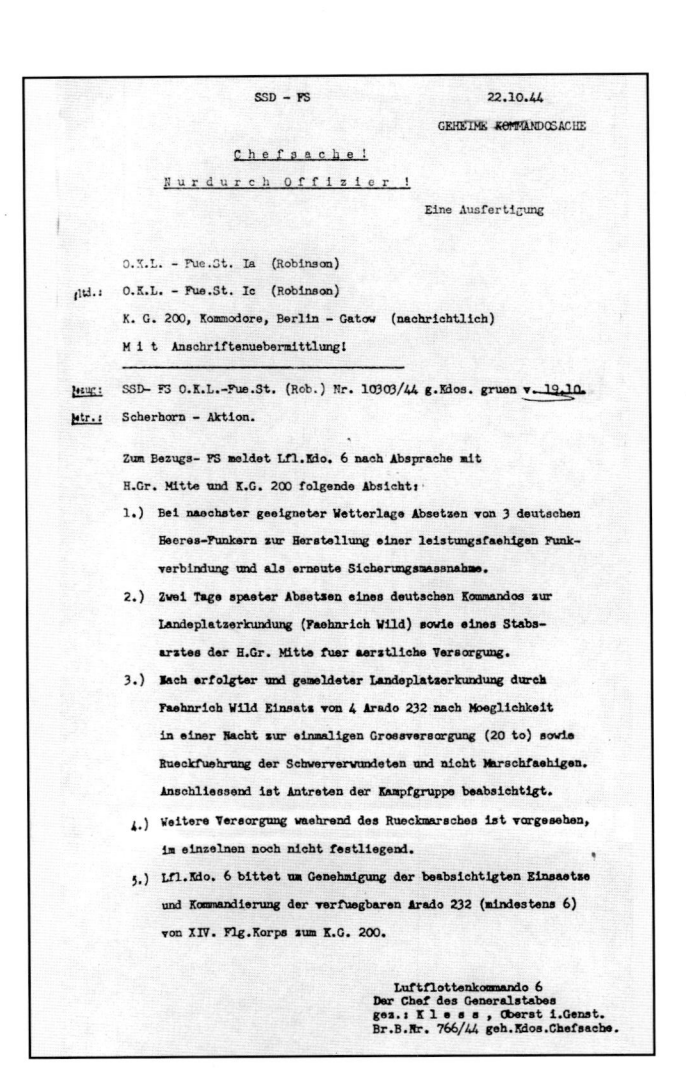

Ar 232. Readiness orders for Operation "Scherhorn" (22 October 1944).

to have been used for testing the final construction configuration of the design, while the Ar 432 A-02 would be used as the prototype for establishing the theoretical characteristic values of the series. A weekly report from Rechlin confirms that Ar 232 B-011 (Wk.Nr. 110 023) was employed in June 1944 at Arado for factory testing of the Ar 432 concept.

According to company files from 6 June 1944 Walter Blume, in accordance with the work program agreed upon with Siegfried Knemeyer on 3 June, called for a rapid realization of the Ar 432 and announced: "TV and TB, together with HN, are to visit the manufacturing works as soon as possible for the purpose of ascertaining operations layout and equipment capacities ..." Within this context Blume expressly pointed out that the GL/St. "Holz" (Wood) committee had been established on 2 June 1944, "since significantly more wood would have to be utilized."

On 10 June 1944 it was determined that the Ar 432 series was to begin production in October of 1945. It is unknown whether even the first two prototypes were ever completed. At least some individual sub-assemblies had been finished in Eger before the war ended. An Ar 432 was officially listed (File RL 36/41 Bundesarchiv) on the program of the last large-scale aviation exhibition in Lärz on 12/13 June 1944. This, however, could have been the Ar 232 B-020 (Wk.Nr. 110 032), which was possibly given an interim designation of Ar 232 C-01 or Ar 432 V 1. Ar 232 B-020 crashed on 14 June 1944 in the area of Rechlin. The projected deadline mentioned above may have meant that this aircraft would not have been able to have been flown in Rechlin beforehand. According to a report from the Arado company group EFoF (Entwicklung, Forschung, Flugerprobung, or Development, Research, Flight Testing) from 22 June 1944, on 13 June 1944 Ar 232 B-010 was demonstrated in Lärz instead. This aircraft, previously assigned as a testbed for paratroop drops, had been assigned to Rechlin for this purpose in June of 1944.

As a company report from 17 June shows, the terrain comprised four trenches up to 1.50 meters deep with an embankment on either side consisting of loose sand approximately 80 cm high; small bomb craters were scattered between the trenches. Takeoffs and landings were carried out over these obstacles. At one point the airplane was set down directly on a trench. The company report ended with the comment: "made a big impression."

It is doubtful whether, as sometimes claimed, an airplane from the B-series was ever fitted with four French Gnôme Rhône 14M twin radial engines; even four of these 700 hp engines would have had an output significantly less than just two of the previously employed BMW 801 engines. It is also unknown whether an aircraft planned for Arctic operations was fitted with a shock-absorbed ski in place of the multi-wheeled landing gear beneath the fuselage. At the very least, the method doesn't seem to have been practical.

There were plans for larger versions of the cargo plane, designated as Ar 532 and 632 and a Projekt Ar E 441, having a wingspan of 60 meters, six engines and a multi-wheel landing gear with 30 wheels.

Another project which was never implemented was the twin-engine Ar 430 amphibian transport, stemming from 1940/41. The mid-wing all-metal design, carrying a crew of two and up to eight passengers, had a two-step boat hull, a retractable tricycle landing gear, a three-part gull wing and side floats. In view of its intended service in Africa and the Mediterranean coastal areas it was equipped with air conditioning and had heated wing leading edges for de-icing. The finished drawings were handed over to the French company of Dewoitine in 1943. Despite building a mockup and water spray testing in the Paris waterways, the course of the war prevented any further developments being made after 1944.

Ar 232 A design characteristics (30 Aug. 1941)

wingspan:	32.0 m
length:	23.5 m
height over main gear (extended):	6.6 m
wing surface area:	135.0 m
VDM variable-pitch propeller, diameter:	4.3 m
normal weight/overloaded	
empty weight:	11235/11235 kg
load:	4765/7265 kg
takeoff weight:	16000/18500 kg
fuel:	2000/2000 kg
wing loading at takeoff:	118/137 kg/m²
power loading at takeoff:	5.13/5.92 kg/hp
takeoff roll:	200/355 m
takeoff distance to 20 m altitude:	445/720 m
Average cruising speed	
to target at 4 km altitude:	233/195 km/h
return at 4 km altitude:	252/252 km/h
endurance:	6.2/6.2 hrs
range:	1500/1380 km
fuel consumption:	215/215 g/hp/hr

Performance at destination weight with emergency boost:
weight at destination:	15000/17500 kg
max speed at altitude of:	
0km:	282/278 km/h
2km:	287/278 km/h
4km:	305/296 km/h
6km:	296/277 km/h
time-to-climb to	
1km:	2.8/3.9 min
2km:	5.7/8.0 min
4km:	13.0/18.6 min
6km:	22.0/34.6 min
service ceiling:	7600/6400 m
landing speed:	91/98 km/h

Ar 232 B design characteristics (30 Aug. 1941)

wingspan:	35.5 m
length:	23.5 m
height over main gear (extended):	6.6 m
wing surface area:	142.5 m²
VDM variable-pitch propeller, diameter:	3.5 m
normal weight/overloaded	
empty weight:	12780/12780 kg
load:	4720/7220 kg
takeoff weight:	17500/20000 kg
fuel:	2000/2000 kg
wing loading at takeoff:	123/140 kg/m²
power loading at takeoff:	4.38/5.0 kg/hp
takeoff roll:	157/220 m
takeoff distance to 20 m altitude:	350/460 m
Average cruising speed	
to destination at 4 km altitude:	236/13 km/h
return at 4 km altitude:	255/255 km/h
endurance:	5.7/5.7 hrs
range:	1400/1335 km
fuel consumption:	208/208 g/hp/hr

Performance at destination weight with emergency boost:
weight at destination:	16500/19000 kg
max speed at altitude of:	
0km:	283/280 km/h
2km:	303/300 km/h
4km:	312/308 km/h
6km:	305/292 km/h
time-to-climb to	
1km:	2.8/3.5 min
2km:	5.4/7.0 min
4km:	11.5/15.8 min
6km:	20.0/27.5 min
service ceiling:	8000/6900 min
landing weight at destination with load:	16500/19000 kg
wing loading:	116/133 kg/m²
landing speed:	92/99 km/h

Part III — Bearers of Hope in the War's Last Phase

Chapter 17
Total Commitment and Decentralization

In May of 1944 preparations were being made for the attempted assassination of Hitler in the hopes of concluding the war before the total collapse of Germany. At the same time, on 20 May 1944, the Kommando der Erpobungsstellen (Evaluation Center Command) directed an appeal — one which in earlier days would have been unimaginable — toward the Luftwaffe's leadership structure. The intent of the appeal was to stop the looming military defeat through a last-minute reorganization in planning and acquisition. Apparently it was recognized that the policy of forestalling the industry's private economic interests by a top-level central authority, a policy which initially had been pursued with such vigor, could not be maintained later on. The "self-administration of the industry" had also proved to be nothing more than an "illusion."

Criticism from Rechlin:
Rechlin, 20 May 1944.

If one were in a position to write a factual portrayal, an objective and true history of technology in the Luftwaffe since 1934, then a non-participant from today or, even better, a successor, would consider the whole thing to be someone's sick fantasy or a mocking satire. For no one would seriously believe that in reality there could be so much inadequacy, botched-up jobs, confusion, authority in the wrong place, failure to recognize the objective realities and overlooking sensible things all in one place ...
In summary, the following are recognized as critical:
1. Calm, calm, calm in the organization.
2. Rock-solid trust of the management in its representatives and all consequences; meaning
3. unwavering governing central authority within the RLM, which has been entrusted with providing for the general interest
4. No self-management of the industry which, instead of having the spiritual strength of their leading figures waste away in organizational work, should make use of them to increase production output.
5. Sensible personal policies free from historical traditions, particular emphasis on those things which cultivate a new crop of technical managers.

On 15 August 1944 the Rechlin engineers repeated their appeal in another memorandum. It is paradoxical, they said, that in a country such as America, where capital rules, there exists a "significantly more sensible order in the air force" than in Germany, where "the government has every legal means at hand to actually implement the requirements of the general interest." The reason for this chaos doesn't lie with the political system, but in personal political ambition. The most primitive rules of rational manufacturing have constantly been violated. This includes the indecisiveness with the development of the He 177 at Arado, whereby valuable production resources were wasted. Maintaining that high-altitude operations were pointless, even Udet stymied important planning at Arado, and the Ar 240 belongs to that group of aircraft which were rejected in favor of less capable types. Messerschmitt, more than anyone, has pushed beyond the realm of fighters and also undertaken Zerstörer projects which would have been better left to Arado or Dornier. In a "directed economy" each aircraft firm must be given its own specialized tasking. It was on the Führer's orders that "dissidents" be immediately removed from their offices and replaced by capable organizers such as Saur or proven experts like Reidenbach or Knemeyer.

Milch defended himself with the argument that he had drawn attention to Messerschmitt's unjustifiable special role in a timely manner, and called it "the most obscene thing conceivable when, now with the war going on, someone, for the sake of competition, produces something for later use."[120] He complained of the "idiocy of the designers", the abuse of so-called "Führer directives" and the demands of "unseasoned youth" who consider themselves "great popes" and "infallible." A truly clear policy on requirements never existed; instead, "lone men" find acceptance for their ideas "based on whim and fancy."

Nevertheless, he was to bear the main brunt of organizational restructuring which took place during the course of 1944. After a reduction in the positional authority of "Generalluftzeugmeister" in May, Milch retained only a portion of his earlier power, whereas Speer, from 1 August 1944 as Minister für Rüstung und Kriegsproduktion, assumed full responsibility for the air rearmament programs as well. With this change, the Luftwaffe's virtual independence of operations, brought about in 1933, was effectively annulled. Unlike the Rechlin group, Speer distrusted a dic-

Hermann Göring (left) accompanied by Walter Blume during a factory inspection (Arado-Bote 1944).

tatorial control in the area of technology and was therefore suspected of "once again introducing the parliamentary state among us."[121] Instead, he focused on acquiring a limited number of types and, in deference to the prioritization given to intercepting Allied bombing raids, gave special powers to Saur's "Jägerstab" (Fighter Staff), an organization that had been created by Speer himself.

The company's internal magazine, "Arado-Bote", remained loyal to the party line and from 1943 articles began appearing with the motto "Total Commitment in the Work Place." Despite Göring having previously been effectively stripped of power, on the occasion of a visit by the Reichsmarschall to the work site in 1944 the magazine announced in what was to be one of its last issues: "The Reichsmarschall can take back from his visit the certain knowledge that the Arado work community is today working with discipline and a full view toward fulfilling its tasks."[122]

The increasing material shortages, the effects of bomber attacks and the lack of a qualified work force nevertheless had a profound impact on the output capability of the Arado Werke. As early as 1942, there were nearly 4,000 foreign workers in comparison with 22,000 German employees working as a result of call-ups. By the end of that year the number of outside workers, mostly guest workers, prisoners of war and criminals, had risen to 17,600 while by this time there were only 9,300 German workers still remaining.

In view of the worsening production conditions and the recognizable change in the war, the Arado Werke's employees were sworn by Walter Blume to redouble their production efforts.

To the Employees of the Arado-Flugzeugwerke!

On 1 July 1943 I assumed the office of Chief of Operations. Arado has previously fulfilled its duty — often resting at the pinnacle — and stands arm-in-arm with the German People in its commitment to the war effort.

In view of the unprecedented struggles and endurance of our soldiers and the tough resolve of the unbending men and women in the West who, despite the hail of bombs, continue to produce, it is obvious that we must channel our efforts to perform even greater and better than before. Each one of us plays our part "in camaraderie and discipline, in learning and teaching."

In particular, I expect the management of our work centers to exercise exemplary behavior, calm and prudence in difficult situations as well as genuine care and help for every co-worker pressured by heavy commitment, worries and discontentment. You should pay particular attention to ensuring that you assign each worker to the right job and with his total commitment as quickly as possible.

We want to stick together when faced with setbacks and difficulties caused by the war, to avoid any type of unnecessary gossip and to enthusiastically buckle down to our work.

Title cover of the Arado-Bote employee's magazine (1942).

Senior manager F. Wagenführ during the opening of the traveling exhibit "Total Commitment in the Workplace" (1943).

Bomb damage suffered by the design bureau and assembly hangar (13) in Warnemünde following the air raid on 8/9 May 1942 (see plan).

We shall then surely achieve our targeted goals!

We shall do everything we can to help in bringing about the final victory in this, the struggle of our people for their existence or extermination. And if times become harder, then they shall find us ready.

Hail to our Führer! Blume, Chief of Operations.

Focused propaganda campaigns were geared toward the "mobilization of all reserves on the home front for gaining the final victory." Portraits of fallen employees hung in every work center. Arado workers serving on the front lines as soldiers described what "total commitment as soldiers" meant to them and what they expected in the way of support from the homeland. Felix Wagenführ opened a 'traveling exhibition' which showed 'Greater Germany as a European Power Order' and the fundamental premise of 'People in a Struggle for Existence'. Conservation efforts through standardization and rationing were propagated under the banners of "We're streamlining!" and "Get rid of everything that's unnecessary and superfluous!"[123] Within the guidelines of an 'Arado performance fitness program' an employee's exemplary behavior was recognized by the war service medal (Kriegsverdienstmedaille). The 'Dr. Fritz Todt Award' and a so-called 'DAF Performance Book', sponsored by Robert Ley, the Reich organization director of the NSDAP and director of the Deutsche Arbeitsfront were also coveted awards. Workers took part in the 'wartime job contest' (the KBWK, or Kriegsberufswettkampf). Several branches were declared as 'wartime model work centers'. The marching song "Arado voran!" (Arado Ahead!) stylized the worker as 'soldiers of the air' under the motto 'flying means victory'.[124]

Arado advertising campaign "We're streamlining" (1944).

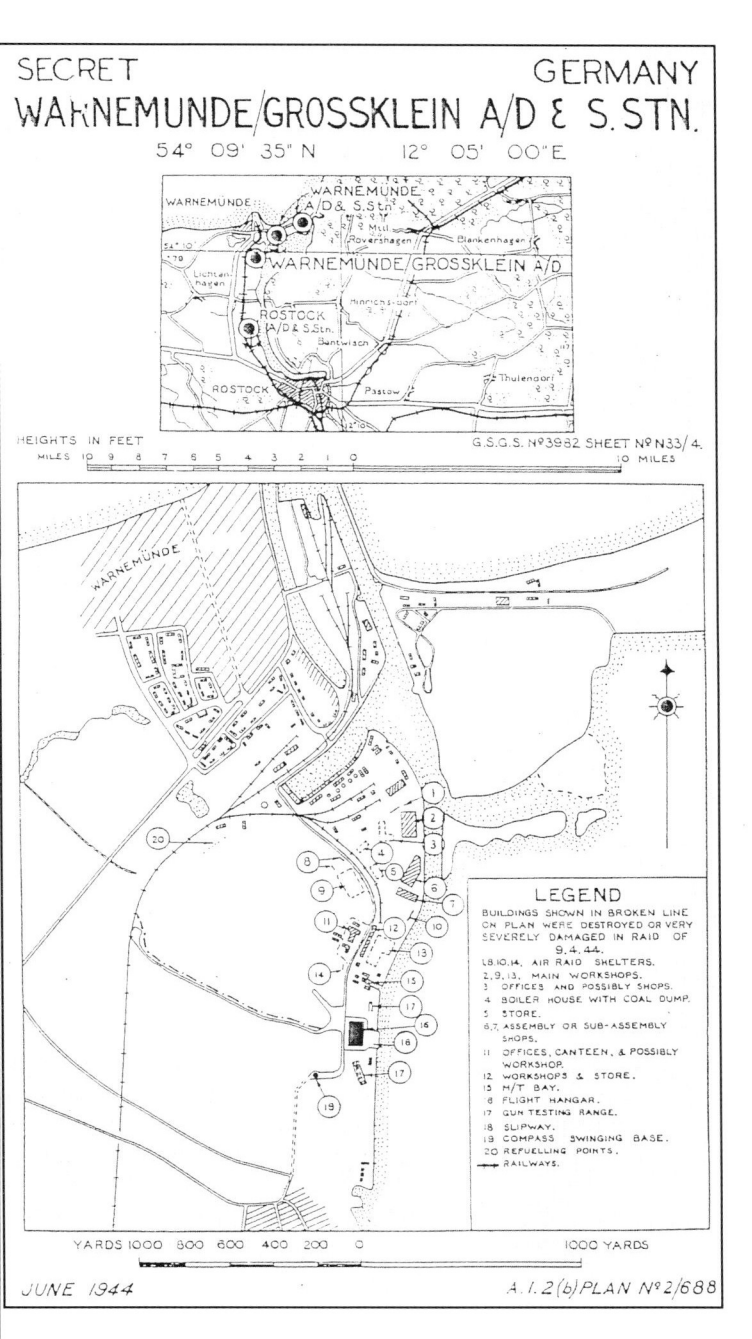

Damage inflicted on the Arado factory in Warnemünde after the bombing raid on 9 April 1944 (Allied aerial reconnaissance photo taken in June 1944). Damage (broken lines) was caused to the assembly hangars (13) and (9), the boiler house (4), warehouse (5) and other buildings.

As a result of the general tightening of the organizational structure, by the end of 1941 Arado's board of directors were no longer meeting to review the annual accounts, and even an audit by the Deutsche Treuhand AG was canceled. Min.-Dirig. Josef Mayer, a member of the board from the Reichsfinanzministerium, objected to this and declared that he would only give written approval of the business managers' report, which in his opinion was kept brief for security reasons, in view of the time constraints.

The increasing frequency of bombing raids on the Arado Werke necessitated the implementation of special measures for ensuring smooth production operations. Antiaircraft defenses were beefed up and barrage balloons were sent aloft all around Warnemünde. In an attempt to shut off production of the Fw 190 fighter, Allied bombers attacked Anklam and Warnemünde for the first time during the night of 8/9 November 1942. Passing overhead in multiple waves, nearly 60 twin- and four-engine bombers dropped approximately 100 impact and incendiary bombs over a two-and-a-half hour period. A secret damage assessment report shows that roughly 20 phosphorous incendiary canisters fell onto the southern edge of the factory grounds in the immediate vicinity of the firing range and hangar (16), while a large number of 50 kg bombs fell onto open areas. The assembly shops (6 and 2) located north of the Laak Channel went virtually untouched. Heavy caliber bombs caused damage to the airfield, however. The painting bay, the pre-assembly spraying area, administrative and office buildings, assembly hangars (13, 7 and 9), the power station on the Laak Channel and a few warehouses all suffered minor struc-

The production schematic of the decentralized Arado assembly sites (September 1943).

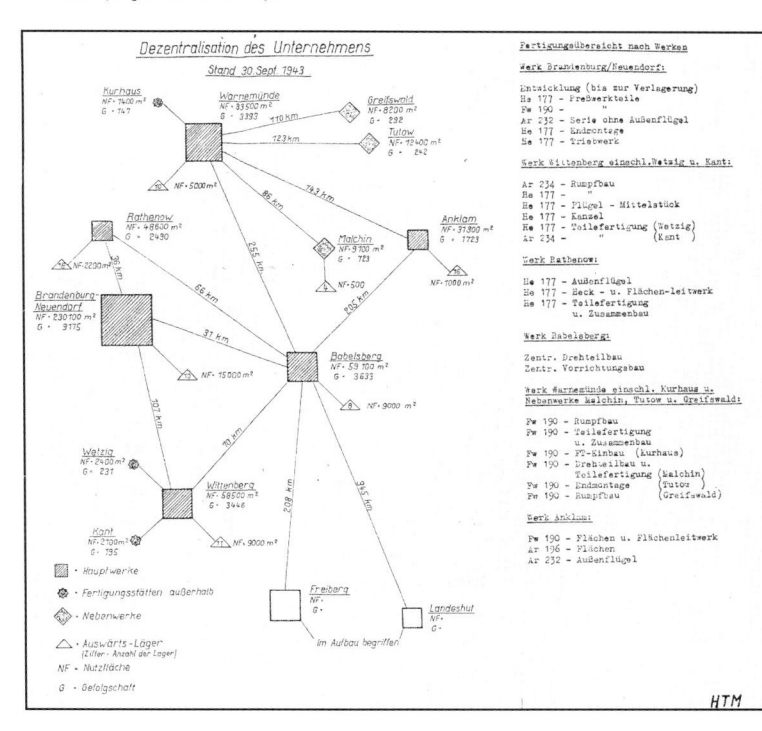

tural damage. Although none of the employees was injured, several members of the anti-aircraft teams were killed. Reputedly, 19 of the attacking bombers were either shot down or fell victim to the balloons. Renewed attacks on 29 July 1943 and 9 April 1944 left even greater damage in their wake. A study of the Allied reconnaissance flights regularly conducted over the area shows that the assembly shops (13 and 9), the boiler house and a few administration buildings were destroyed in the April raid. An attack on Anklam on 9 October 1943 by 150 B-17 bombers caused 40-percent damage to the Arado facilities there, destroyed parts of the city and hit the local sugar factory, leaving 400 dead in its wake. In spite of another attack on 4 August 1944 production in Anklam was not interrupted in any great way. As at Warnemünde, prisoners of war and foreign workers were continually carrying out makeshift repairs. In the Allies' view, the attack value eventually proved minimal.

Rathenow suffered serious bomb damage on 18 April 1944, primarily to the boiler house and to two of its three large assembly hangars. At the end of August 1944 large

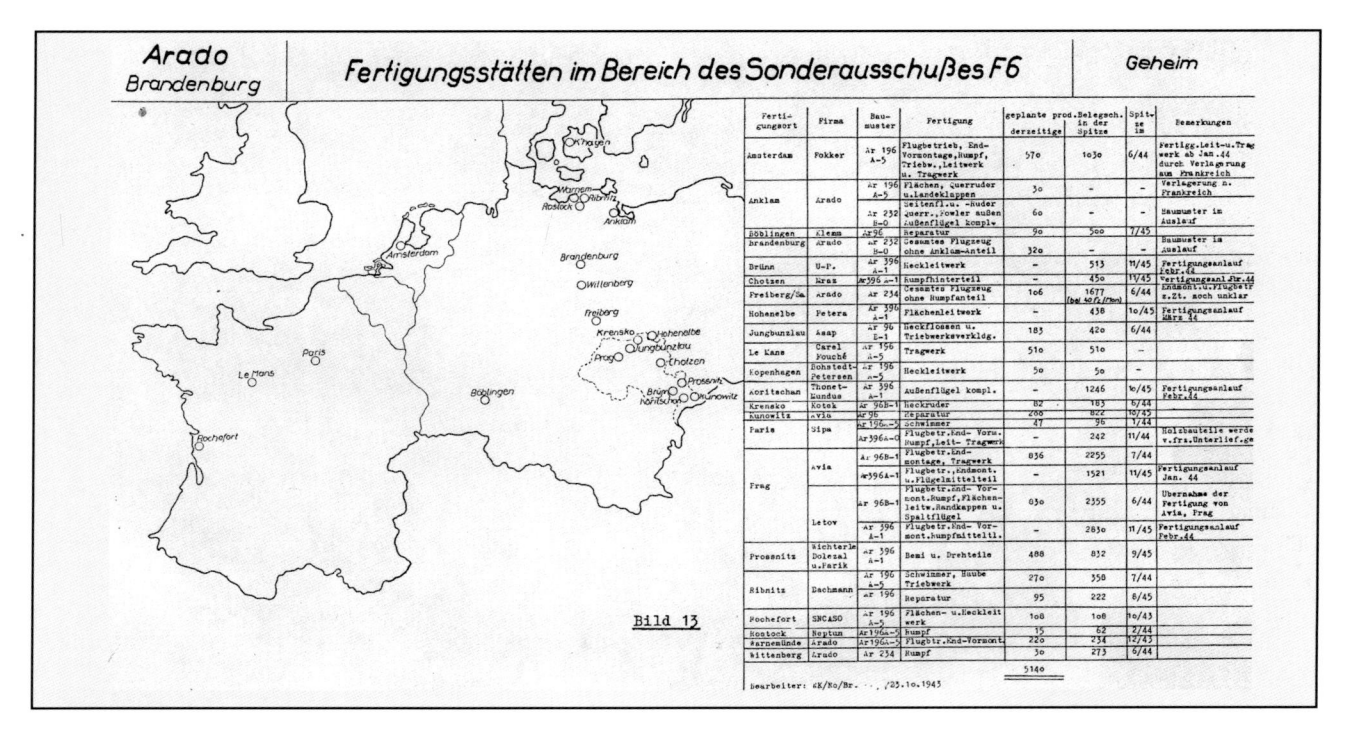

Assembly sites for Arado's indigenous development programs within the guidelines of the Sonderausschuss F6 (October 1943).

parts of Brandenburg were burned. On 14 April 1944 Babelsberg was 85-percent destroyed.

In anticipation of future bombing raids, an intensified decentralization of the company's production facilities took place from autumn 1943 onward, since it was determined that production in underground caves wasn't practical. By using dispersed, camouflaged manufacturing sites it was hoped that there would be fewer interruptions in production caused by air-raid alarms and that, in case of destruction, only a portion of the overall production would be affected. However, decentralization meant longer transportation time and led to short-term production outages during the conversion.

In addition to the main administration, the central turned-piece manufacturing facilities and the central equipment production facility remained in Babelsberg. At the end of 1943 the development and prototype construction departments, including the design bureau, relocated from Brandenburg to Landeshut near Hirschberg, Silesia under the guise of the local Weberei Max Kühl GmbH. In the absence of an airfield, flight testing took place at the village of Küpper near Sagan, sixty kilometers to the west.[125]

The six main work centers in Warnemünde, Anklam, Rathenow, Brandenburg, Babelsberg and Wittenberg, supplemented by numerous satellite facilities, were working at nearly full capacity at the end of 1943 with the final assembly, fuselage, wing and control surface construction of the Fw 190 fighter and the production of the He 177 bomber, which at this time was just beginning to taper off. The production of the Ar 232 transport in Brandenburg and Anklam was a comparative drop in the bucket. Some of the Ar 196 seaplanes and most Ar 96/396 trainers were built by satellite facilities such as Böblingen (Klemm), Hohenelbe (Petera) and Ribnitz. In addition, there were foreign manufacturers available for this purpose in Amsterdam (Fokker), Brünn (U-P.), Chotzen (Kraz), Jungbunzlau (Asap), Le Mans (Carel Fouché), Copenhagen (Rohstedt-Petersen), Korichan (THonet-Mundus), Krensko (Kotek), Paris (Sipa), Prague (Letov/Avia), Prossnitz (Wichterle Dolezal and Parik) and Rochefort (SNCASO). Production of the planned jet aircraft was to begin in Wittenberg as well as at the satellite work in Freiberg (Saxony) then under construction. The air support facility in Alt-Lönnewitz was also brought into the program in order to assist in final assembly.

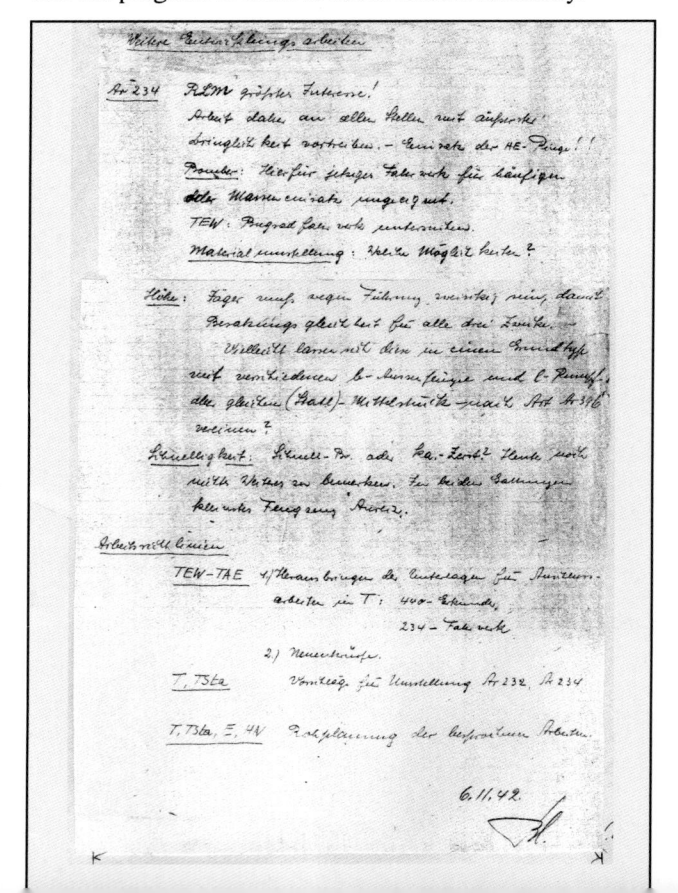

Chapter 18
The Leap To Jet Engine Power

Entering into the Technology of the Future: Projekt E 370

While the full-scale production of the highly-refined, propeller driven Ar 240/440 Zerstörer suffered continuing delays at the hands of the Technisches Amt, the jet-powered high speed aircraft developed parallel to the Ar 240 was given high priority from early on. After Arado's string of successes with fighter airplanes in the 'thirties, the many years of being forced to license produce and the elimination of selfish internal developments, in the last phase of the war Arado became a true bearer of hope with its jet-powered design.

Concept of the turbojet engine originated in 1935 from Hans von Ohain and Max Hahn in Göttingen and was further developed by Heinkel. On 27 August 1939 the Heinkel He 178 became the first aircraft to take off with this type of powerplant. When the Arado-designed Ar 234 A reconnaissance plane lifted off for a recce mission on 2 August 1944, it became — along with the Me 262 fighter — the first operational jet aircraft in the world.

Flight performance figures from Arado revealed from early on that the use of piston engines wouldn't lead to any further workable developments and that increased expenditure would not result in a corresponding improvement in performance. On the other hand, it was expected that turbojets would provide a jump in speed from 650 km/h to circa 885 km/h at 8,000 m and from 530 km/h to 790-840 km/h at lower altitudes.

By the time air superiority over England was lost in 1940, Oberstleutnant Theodor Rowehl was the officer responsible for reconnaissance operations. He succeeded in changing the Arado Werke's plans for a jet-powered bomber, instead having the RLM task the company to draw up plans for a high speed reconnaissance aircraft. This machine was to have a cruising speed of no less than 700 km/h and possess a range of 3,000 km. Preliminary work was carried out in the autumn of 1940 under the project number E 370. Since Arado was fully burdened with other projects at this time and Walter Blume showed little initial interest in jet engines, the development time dragged on for a relatively long period. It wasn't until September 1941 that a concrete proposal had been ironed out in the shape of the Projekt E 370/IV. When Theoodor Rowehl recommended an acceleration of the project one month later, conditions were still relatively unfavorable; the Technisches Amt under Ernst Udet proved to be barely able to act on its own and his successor, Erhard Milch, leaned toward the continued development of proven designs.

In February 1942 Milch, on the occasion of a visit to Brandenburg, issued a contract for a wooden mockup. In April the Amt gave its approval for the construction of six initial prototypes under the designation Ar 234. Since there were delays with the engines from Junkers and BMW, Arado planned to temporarily install propeller-driving engines.

W. Blume: notes on the developmental plans for the Ar 234 jet (6 November 1942 — left).

However, in spite of the shoulder-wing design, this approach was impractical due to the ground clearance being inadequate.

On 6 November 1942 Walter Blume noted under "Further Developmental Work — Criteria" that the war would reach a crescendo over the next two years. The design office (TWE) under Meyer, van Nes and Stelzer would need new work. The RLM is looking for a vastly superior model and has "the greatest interest" in the design of the Ar 234. Work was to therefore "proceed at all points with the utmost urgency." Drawings by the Arado engineer responsible for the project, Franz Meyer, dated 12 November 1942 and drawn up for a conference with the RLM, confirm that the Amt still had a certain "mistrust of turbine air engines" for the high-speed bomber. In Meyer's view, large contracts could not be expected prior to an evaluation of the Ar 234's performance. However, to achieve an "immediate solution" the "support of a reconnaissance aircraft for Rowehl" was conceivable. At this point in time the priorities which the Amt intended to establish regarding the Ar 240/440 and the Ar 234 future project could not be clearly determined. A combination high-speed bomber and high-altitude recon aircraft was nevertheless considered to be a "questionable undertaking" in the eyes of Meyer, and the fundamental basis for the program still required clarification. With regard to the "high-speed airplanes" he noted: "What can be done with the 234?"

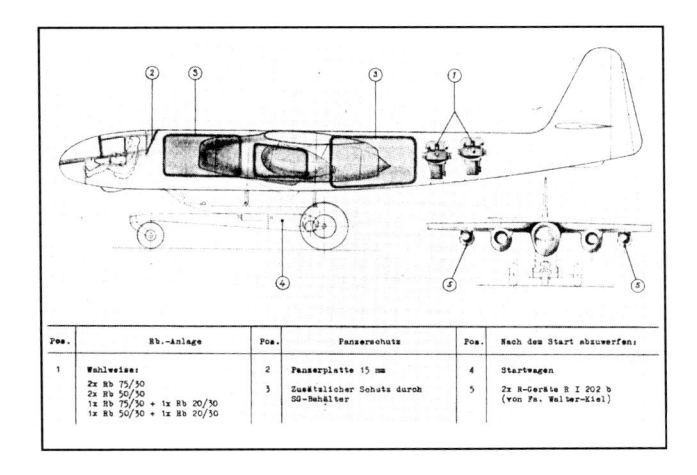

Ar 234 A. Drawing showing component features (13 July 1943).

It seems that smaller numbers were satisfactory for the jet reconnaissance aircraft, which Rowehl pressured Arado into aggressively pursuing. In December 1942 the Amt contracted for an additional 14 prototypes, even though the engines were still not available. Ar 234 prototypes V 1 through V 7, each having two Jumo 004 engines, were to have been finished by November 1943. Prototype V 8 was planned for evaluation of the BMW 003 and was due to be made available in January 1944. Finally, by July 1944 a further six aircraft would be fitted with two of these engines and the same number would have four.

According to design manager H. Rebeski, Arado developed the jet aircraft as a mid-wing design with two engines suspended beneath the wings in order to provide it with a low center of gravity during landings and also to keep the oleo compression struts short. Attachment points were found in the wings for Walter engines (R-Geräte, or

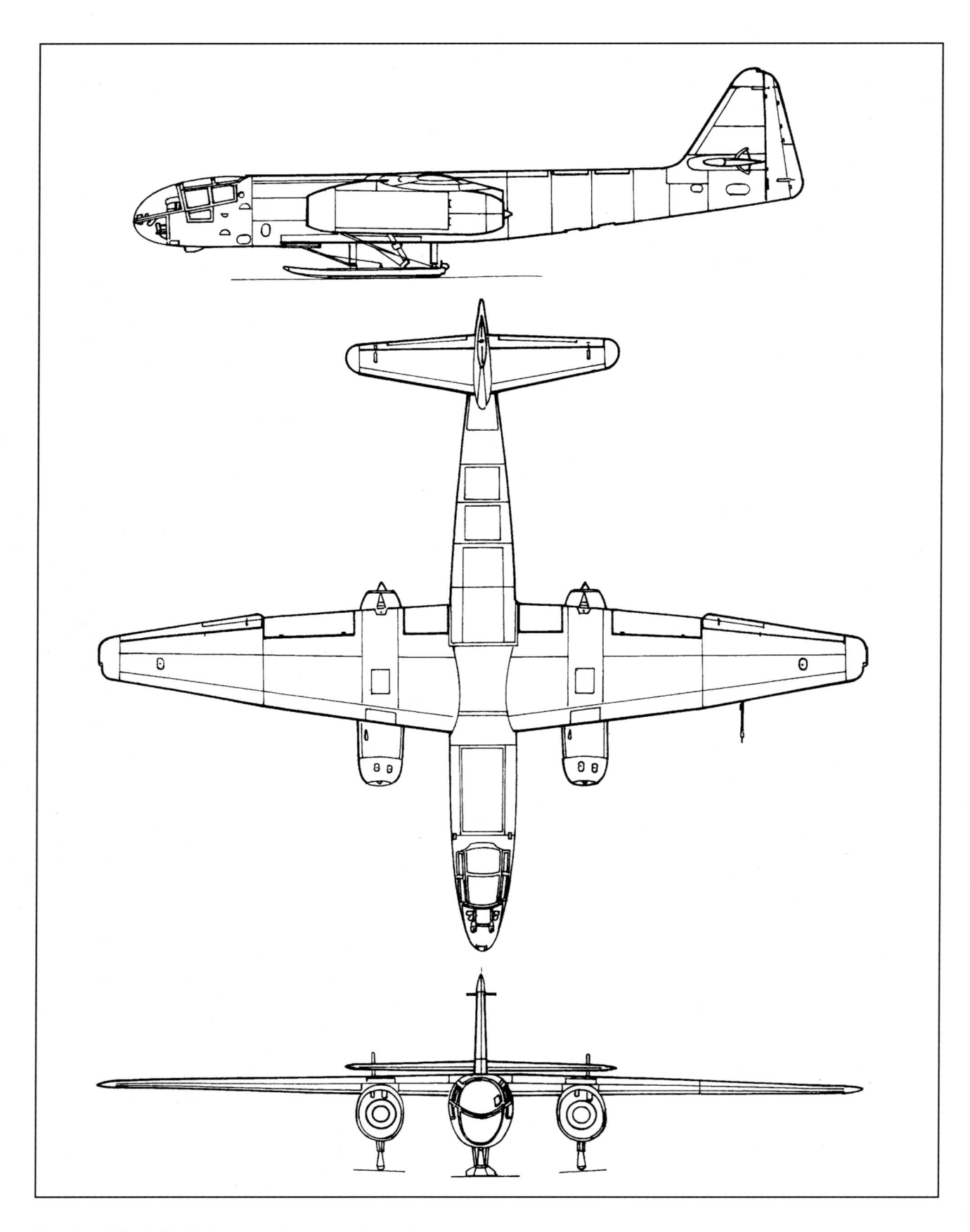

Drawing of the Ar 234 A jet reconnaissance airplane (1943).

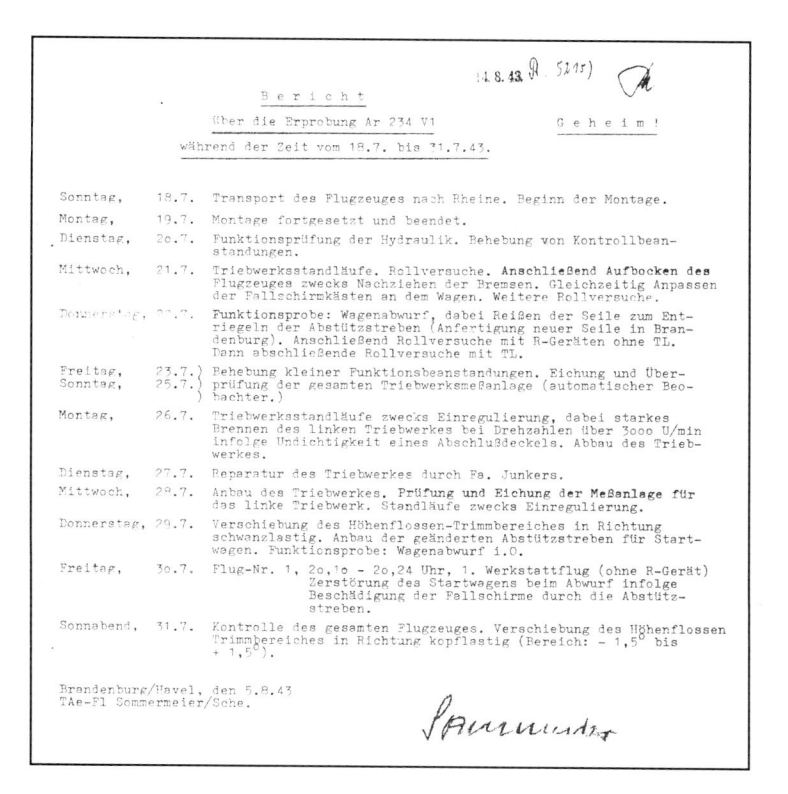

Ar 234 V 1, TG+KB (Wk. Nr. 130 001). Report on the initiation of testing (5 August 1943).

Ar 234 V 1 with trolley and landing skids after assembly in Brandenburg. Maiden flight on 30 July 1943.

RATO packs), which provided additional thrust for take-offs from shorter runways or when heavily loaded. These operated by means of a chemical reaction and created brief additional thrust. The pilot ignited the RATO packs electrically, which could then be dropped following takeoff and used again. The distinct full-view spherical plexiglas canopy was attached to the aircraft's nose and was accessed via a hatch on the upper side. The roof of the cabin, which was later modified to become the world's first fully pressurized production cockpit and had an oxygen system, could be jettisoned in the event of an emergency. The monocoque fuselage, made entirely of light metal with four main stringers, was broken down into several sub-parts for ease of manufacturing and quicker pass-through the heavy duty production machinery. The panels were overlapped in the direction of flight and, perpendicular to the direction of flight, were flush-joined to the underlying metal frame. Countersunk riveting was employed the areas exposed to the forces of airflow. In addition to the cockpit, the fuselage accommodated a self-sealing fuel tank, a retractable landing skid, an additional fuel tank, and space for either rearward-firing armament or two cameras or radios.

As it wasn't desirable to have the rear control surfaces exposed to the direct flow of the turbine exhaust, a feature commonly found on propeller-driven aircraft, the horizontal tailplane was accordingly set high and the tailfin was designed as a single unit. The tailplane was adjustable in order to balance out load changes without affecting the control surface profile. This was a necessary feature during attack runs made from a shallow glide profile. Rudder and tailplane were counterbalanced for offsetting the control forces. For trimming, the aircraft was designed with mechanically-driven autolock trim tabs on both the elevators and the rudder. The ailerons were fully balanced by means of iron weights in their leading edge. This type of balancing weight was selected to reduce the number of parts and gaps exposed to the airstream. Landing flaps were of a split trailing edge design and divided by the engines into inner and outer flap sections. They were actuated hydraulically, with a hydraulic jack driving the flap control mechanisms. This method ensured synchronous operation of all four sections. Oil pressure needed for the hydraulics was provided by toothed gear pumps, powered by the turbine engines. A hand pump was provided for emergency use in the event of engine pump failure or if the electrical system were to go out. The aileron extended simultaneously with the flaps in order to reduce the effects from the increase in lift. With the flaps extended and the ailerons lowered, the air gap created ahead of the aileron's leading edge had the effect of increasing drag at higher speeds. To counteract this negative feature a slat cover was used to bridge the gap. In order to automatically offset the anticipated changes in trim when the flaps were in the process of lowering, provisions were made for a hydraulic link between the flap and elevator trim tabs, meaning that the elevators moved independently of manual adjusting in two final positions and then became set.

The designers achieved minimal drag by choosing a cantilever, twin-spar wing with a very thin airfoil section. Independent main spars were not used for the wings due to the relatively small wingspan, so that they could be loaded and transported as a single piece. A refined finish to the skin was obtained by using a profile loft which permitted the skin covering to be rolled out over the wing framework, dispensing with having to cupellate the skin and reducing the danger of rippling.

Because of the thin wings it would only have been possible to retract an integral, conventional landing gear into the fuselage body, but the necessary widening of the airframe would have led to an increase in drag and weight. With the goal towards achieving a maximum speed superior to British fighters the idea of an integral landing gear was dropped on the reconnaissance variant; instead, the aircraft took off with a central skid extended below the fuselage and resting on a trolley which was released after takeoff. For landing, the aircraft landed on its central skid and two retractable side skids extending from the engine nacelles. Not only was the aircraft extremely light without its landing gear, it could also be immediately steered toward its target. In addition, the runway could be cleared for traffic immediately after the airplane took off.

137

With the delivery of the first Junkers engines in March 1943, preliminary evaluation began in the form of taxi runs and, on the evening of 30 July, the maiden flight of the Ar 234 V 1 (TG+KB) took place with factory test pilot Selle at the controls. The aircraft had previously been shipped unassembled in an Ar 232 to Rheine, since Brandenburg did not have a runway of adequate length. Flight handling was impeccable. Stability, rudder pressure, rudder effectiveness, and stall characteristics were so good that no changes to the control surfaces needed to be made. Indeed, the landing skids even operated perfectly — even the subsequent emergency landings in rough field conditions did not result in any damage to the aircraft. It was only the takeoff trolley which caused any initial problems. Hans Rebeski, the design manager, had recommended to Walter Blume from early on that the cart be left on the ground on takeoff. Nevertheless, Blume took up the suggestion of an airborne unit in Wittstock to have the aircraft break off its climb at 500 m altitude, make another approach and, at a speed of 250 km/h, drop the trolley from which two parachutes would deploy. The method was a failure. The takeoff cart dropped away after the pilot released the bomb shackle and then was caught in two support struts. Once these had reached a certain stretching point, the upper catches hooked onto the fuselage attachment points would release and at the same time the doors to the parachute housing would open. As the takeoff trolley fell away, the two hydraulic brake lines running to the wheel brakes were severed and sealed off with ball valves. However, the flow of air induced by the airplane flying immediately above the cart caused the parachutes to tangle up and become intertwined, and the trolley crashed to the earth.

Despite Rebeski's concerns Blume called for a second attempt using modified struts, which Rebeski ferried from Brandenburg to Rheine in an Ar 96 on 6 August. But another trolley was lost on the second takeoff of Ar 234 V 1 on 10 August at 1637 hrs. Once again, the parachutes didn't open smoothly, even though their timing had been delayed to a point where their deployment took place only after the struts had been released. The third takeoff on 29 August (and all subsequent takeoffs) proved ideal after the design underwent a complete overhaul, where the trolley was released immediately after takeoff at an approximate speed 150 km/h and slowed by a braking parachute.

These test flights demanded an unusually high flying capability from the pilot, for he was required to keep watch on a plethora of monitoring instruments and gauges without the support of a navigator. Since it was the engines which continually gave problems and often had to be changed out during the course of evaluation due to damage, it was important to monitor the exhaust temperature to avoid overheating the turbine fans and prevent cracks from appearing in the blades. The sensitive throttle levers required a fine touch both during takeoff and in flight so that the engines wouldn't lag in thrust or flame out. Particular care had to be taken with the throttle control above 4,000 m, since full combustion couldn't take place when there was a drop in injection pressure. At around 10,000 m throttling no longer became possible. Restarting a flamed-out engine could only be accomplished below 4,000 m and at speeds between 400 and 500 km/h, otherwise the rate of airflow was too great. Were the engines to suffer an outage, the ignition nozzle would have to be shut off immediately to prevent the engine from being flooded with fuel and catching fire.

On 10 August 1943 test pilot Selle had flawlessly carried out test flights for nearly an hour at speeds reaching 650 km/h, but on 29 August, as he was making his landing approach both engines flamed out at 300 m altitude because of heavy-handed throttling. The turbines couldn't be restarted and the aircraft didn't have enough altitude to make the runway. Although the plane itself was seriously damaged after crash landing in a paddock, Selle walked away uninjured.

Ar 234 V 1 in Rheine just after release of the trolley.

Ar 234 V 1 (below).

Ar 234 V 3, DP+AX. Prototype of the A-series with two Jumo 004 A-0 engines, taking off with the help of RATO packs. First flight took place on 29 September 1943.

The most spectacular crash as a result of an engine defect took place on 2 October 1943. After Selle had ferried the V 2 prototype to Alt-Lönnewitz in Saxony, he there conducted his sixth test flight, this time evaluating the climb performance of the airplane. At an altitude of 9,000 m he reported that the left engine was not responding. Vertical controls began vibrating as the aircraft descended to 4,500 m. A subsequent attempt to restart the engine failed. At the same time, Selle reported that all monitoring instruments were not registering. He had opened the cockpit canopy, but decided to save the plane — too late for bailing out. Shortly before reaching the airfield, the aircraft suddenly made a sharp roll to the left at low altitude and plummeted straight into a farmhouse, killing Selle.

Milch was given a detailed review of the crash at a GL meeting on 5 October. Based on radio communications with Selle, it was determined that the doomed pilot had not been aware of the impending catastrophe until the very last moment. It was known that one engine which had flamed out couldn't be restarted and that a fire had occurred; there was also the belief that a horizontal stabilizer had jammed. Since Junkers was operating on the false assumption that it was impossible for kerosene-fueled engines to catch fire, the aircraft had not been fitted with firewall between the engine and the wings. This lack of a firewall may have led to a ruptured duraluminum fuel line causing a fire to spread to the wings, burning through the skin and leading to an outage of all the instruments. Selle, therefore, would not have known of the increasing temperatures around the engine.

The circumstances surrounding the accident have often been erroneously described. A new, detailed portrayal of events was provided by Hans Rebeski, the engineer responsible for the investigation at the time, and clearly reveals that the immediate cause of the crash was due to the fact that the fire had reached control rod for the left outer landing flap had. Since the landing flap was fully extended, the rod was under a considerable amount of stress and broke. As a result, the left outer flap (between aileron and engine) suddenly retracted. This in turn caused a marked deflection of the aileron, since the right outer flap was still fully extended, and the unfortunate pilot wasn't able to compensate for this effect in time. Emergency measures were taken immediately following the accident to prevent similar incidences from happening: a firewall was fitted on the underside of the wing next to the engine and a catch plate installed which was designed to block leaking flammables from reaching the hot engine components. The control rods above the engine were no longer made of duraluminum, but of steel. All aircraft from Ar 234 V 3 onward were equipped with an automatic fire extinguishing system and an ejection seat.

Even during the ensuing trials conducted by Ubbo Janssen and Walter Kröger, the engines often suffered from breaks in their jet pipes or compression fans. Despite every conceivable safety measure being implemented, such a defect led to the fatal crash of pilot Walter Wendt in November of 1944. Walter Kröger gave a positive assessment of the quality found in the V 3 prototype in an interim report files on 30 December 1943 and commented: "The Ar 234 is an unusually lively aircraft with distinct fighter qualities. It is surprising how responsive and pleasant the aircraft is to fly, even at high speeds."

On 26 November 1943 the V 3 (Wk.Nr. 130 003) was demonstrated in front of Hitler in Insterburg. Hitler was quite enthusiastic and immediately called for the production of at least 200 machines by the end of 1944, to be manufactured as high-speed bombers.

Oberleutnant Horst Götz, flying the V 5, reached a maximum speed of 900 km/h in a shallow glide from 8,000 m. The aircraft, which virtually couldn't be flown to its limits, was in this case completely without rudder control. Even before reaching a speed of 840 km/h the control surfaces began shuddering, followed by pressure waves building up on the wings; these resulted from regions of accelerated airflow, which was in part due to the narrow gap between fuselage and engines.

First Combat Missions: The Ar 234 A and B-1 Reconnaissance Planes

Even before deliveries of the second production series had begun, by mid-1944 the Ar 234 A was already being used to fly its first combat mission; their primary goal was to monitor the Allies' invasion of France. This role could no longer be effectively fulfilled by the then-current reconnaissance types such as the Ju 86 R. In May of 1944 a decision was reached by Dipl.-Ing. Oskar Liebing, director of the technical evaluation department at Arado Flugzeugwerke, Oberstleutnant Siegfried Knemeyer from the Technisches Amt and Oberst Edgar Petersen of the Luftwaffe's evaluation centers to fit the V 5 and V 7 prototypes with two Rb 50/30 cameras and deploy them with the Versuchsverband des Oberkommandos der Luftwaffe (VersVerb OKL, or Evaluation Unit of the Luftwaffe High Command) under the command of Oberleutnants Horst Götz and Erich Sommer. V 5, T9+LH (Wk.NR. 130 005) was delivered on 1 June 1944, but was temporarily put out of commission on 28 August when it was accidentally hit by German anti-aircraft fire over Oranienburg.

However, history was made with the reconnaissance mission flown by Oberleutnant Erich Sommer on 2 August 1944 with the V 7 prototype T9+MH (Wk.Nr. 130 007).

At the end of July Sommer flew the aircraft from the Oranienburg airbase to Juvincourt near Rheims. On 2 August he took off and set out in the direction of Cherbourg, where the Allies had landed two months previously. After diving from an altitude of 10,500 m he used his cameras to capture the military situation along various areas of the front. The spoils of his mission were greater than those of the Luftwaffe's entire recon operations over the last two months. It took two days before twelve experts had evaluated the material and for the first time recognized the full extent of the enemy's advance.

Before the end of August, when Juvincourt had to be abandoned in the face of the Allied push, Sommer and Götz carried out approximately 13 additional recce missions. As

Ar 234 V 5, GV+IV (Wk. Nr. 130 005) and V 7, GK+IX (Wk. Nr. 130 007). First flights on 22 December 1943 and 22 June 1944. Analysis report based on reconnaissance missions (11 September 1944).

Ar 234 V 9, PH+SQ (Wk. Nr. 130 009). Prototype for the B-series with two Jumo 004 B-1 engines and bomb pylons, but minus the periscope. Maiden flight on 12 March 1944.

Götz, flying the Ar 234 V 5, was attempting to divert to an airfield behind German lines the aircraft's hydraulic system was accidentally hit by flak over Mons — the consequence of a lack of coordination with the German defense. Since his destination point of Brandenburg was in flames following a bombing raid, Götz belly-landed the plane in at the airbase in Oranienburg. Stones broke the canopy glazing and Götz received eye injuries. Immediately after landing the aircraft was rammed by an Fw 190 and became a total write-off.

The application of the airplane as a high-speed bomber, a role favored by Hitler, meant that the takeoff and landing methods used by the reconnaissance versions were unsuitable; loading the aircraft onto the trolleys was too time consuming during large-scale operations and there was always the danger that during this phase losses might occur from enemy strikes. It took 20 minutes to prepare the aircraft for takeoff. The trolley and RATO packs were gathered up immediately after they were dropped and preparations were begun for landing. Block and tackle frames, jacks and trolley stood ready, towed out to the aircraft behind vehicles. The time it took to jack up the aircraft and set it on its trolley again amounted to circa 30 minutes. An hour had passed by the time the airplane was again in its hangar.

In order to achieve greater mobility on the ground, plans were drawn up in early 1943 — even before the Ar 234 A reconnaissance version had completed its first flight — for an Ar 234 B series with conventional landing gear. The project was designated E 371. Fuselage dimensions were increased to accommodate the landing gear. With relatively high landing speeds of 160 to 170 km/h, it was decided to use a free-rolling 630 mm diameter nose wheel and two 950 mm main wheels fitted with dual brakes in order to achieve stable control during rollout. Since the pilot sat directly above the nose wheel and a smooth cushioning effect was wanted, compressed-air landing struts with oil damping were used for the main gear. For the same reason, as well as for space constraints, the nose gear was fitted with a non-flexing compression drag strut instead of a single-leg oleo.

The V 9 prototype, PH+SQ (Wk.Nr. 130 009), was the first to be fitted with the retractable gear and became the prototype for the B-series. The first pre-production B-0 aircraft began its evaluation program on 8 August 1944, two months after the Allies had landed in Normandy. From September 1944 on, the initial recon missions which had been flown by the Ar 234 A-series successfully continued with the B-1 models operated by Einsatzkommando 'Sperling', based in Rheine. The approaching winter weather posed the biggest obstacle, increasingly affecting visibility. The unarmed reconnaissance plane could shrug off any attacks thanks to its superior flight performance. However, pilots were instructed to avoid getting into turning maneuvers with the enemy. Enemy fighters also posed a threat during take-offs and landings, necessitating adequate flak defense around the home airfield. There was also a certain risk during the climb to operating altitude, which took about 30 minutes at speeds from 340 to 420 km/h.

The Oberkommando der Luftwaffe placed the utmost significance on these reconnaissance flights and ensured the Kommando that it would receive favored support. Reconnaissance operations were improved by the use of a vehicle fitted with a radio, which met the pilots at their aircraft immediately following a mission and from whence they could relay critical information.

When it became necessary to expand reconnaissance operations to include the southern areas of the Western Front, the Kommando Hecht was also set up under the command of Oberleutnant Erich Sommer in Biblis near the city of Worms.

Arado jet recon aircraft also contributed to the support of the ground troops during the Ardennes offensive, also known as the Battle of the Bulge, and over the battlefields of upper Italy during the last months of the war. On 10 April 1945 a reconnaissance plane stationed in Stavanger, Norway, carried out the last flight over Great Britain.

Series Production: The Ar 234 B-2 High-Speed Bomber

In view of the aircraft industry's failure to produce a capable bomber aircraft, a contract was issued on 9 February 1943 for converting two Arado jets into high-speed bombers. On 24 October 1943, following a comparison with the Ju 388 conventional night fighter, high-speed bomber and attack fighter, Göring and Milch both came to the conclusion that a jet bomber would be the ideal instrument for striking against a potential Allied advance. Based on overoptimistic assessment of the war situation, it was expected that such a concept would reach production status around 1948/49.

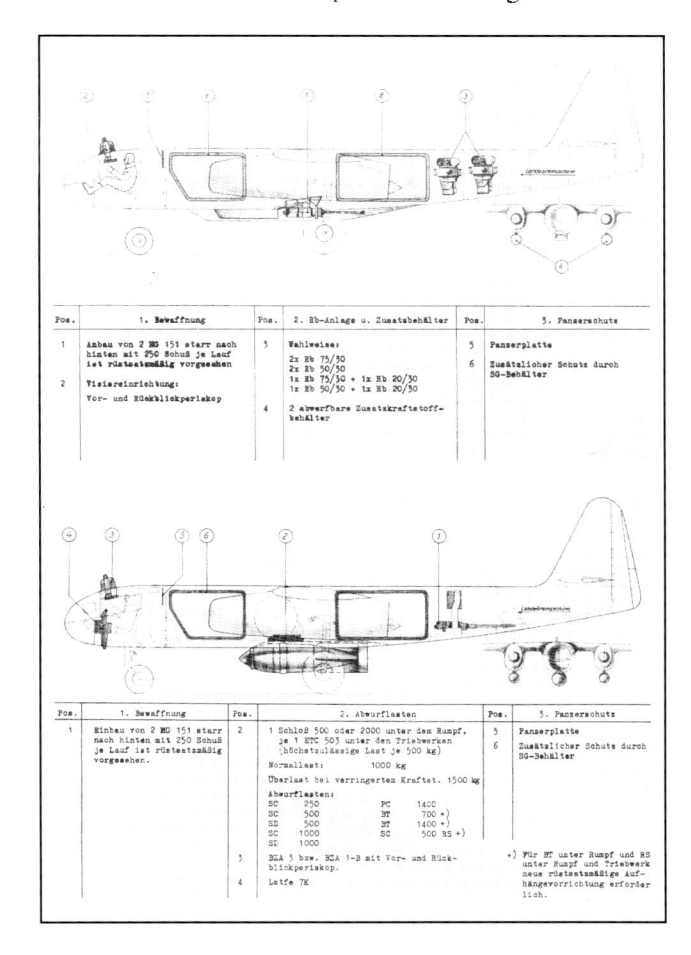

Ar 234 B drawings. —Above: Ar 234 B-1 reconnaissance plane (6 December 1944). Below: Ar 234 B-2 bomber (20 November 1944).

Meeting of Göring and Milch on 14 October 1943:

    Göring: What does the Ar 234 carry as a bomber?

    Knemeyer: Three 500-ers and normally a 3000 kg externally.

    Göring: How fast is it with external load?

    Knemeyer: Based on the V-models the company figures seem accurate; 680 with bombs.

    Göring: That's adequate. Then during the day they can fly strike missions.

    Milch: It is also an escort fighter over the ocean, since it has such good range — the real long-range fighter that we can actually do something with.

    Göring: But they're all single-seaters.

Milch: Provisions have also been made in the design or a second crewman. This is a system that we can simplify later, when we have larger engines. With the 803 (BMW 28 cylinder twin radial, maximum output 4100 hp/3015 kW. - Ed.) we can later build on the basis of the fundamental design. You can combine: a propeller in the front and turbojet in the rear, thereby giving you unheard of optional possibilities with the range.

On the afternoon of 5 November 1943 Göring and Milch were greeted by Walter Blumo on the occasion of their inspection of the Brandenburg construction facilities. At this point in time, five of the twenty jet-engine aircraft contracted for had been built as reconnaissance platforms. Walter Blume opened the half-hour meeting, which was attended by business director Heinemann, military experts Oberstleutnant Knemeyer, Oberst Petersen, and Oberstleutnant i.G. Diesing, with an introduction into the state of testing. In order to pique the interests of the Reichsmarschall with regard to new programs at Arado, Blume began detailing the advantages compared with jet-powered Me 262 being developed concurrently at Messerschmitt. However, Göring didn't permit Blume to continue on for long, saying he was pressed for time. He seemed indignant that, in view of a report from Oberstleutnant von Brauchitsch on an enemy air raid, a special telephone line had been set up for him as was usually the case. He also seemed displeased that, because of the ongoing dispersal of the development department and the expansion of production facilities, there were not sufficient technical documents made available to him. Göring's background knowledge of jet aircraft in general was limited and was mainly derived from Messerschmitt projects. He wanted to know if the Ar 234 had already flown, then made no reservations about expressing his interest in seeing the aircraft developed as a fighter-bomber and high-speed bomber. He was briefed on the reliability of the turbine engines, whether bombing equipment could temporarily be fitted, how converting the airframe from skids to standard landing gear was to be accomplished, how it was conceivable that a fighter-bomber, such as the British Mosquito, would actually be able to survive without defensive armament and how matters stood with bombing accuracy, increasing the range and overcoming Mach influences. He doubted Blume's figures regarding range and expressed an unfounded concern that, due to the turbojet engine's heat effect, it would even be possible to have ordnance pylons on the wings at all. Blume attempted to address specific manufacturing problems and mentioned that, in view of the company being fully involved in producing the Ar 96 trainer

From left: Walter Blume, Bruno Loerzer, Hermann Göring and Erhard Milch in Brandenburg on 5 November 1943.

and the extensive license building going on, there must be a willingness to provide additional credit, ensuring adequate supplies of steel and aluminum, authorization of new production facilities and reducing the number of skilled workers being inducted into the military. As he listened to this, Göring became cross. He abruptly interrupted Blume's requests with terse remarks about "people who still think in peacetime terms" and added meaningfully: "They should be beaten with the Moscow Declaration, and here applies the old Nuremburg saying: whoever's got the other one first hangs him, and you can't hang someone you don't have.

The people don't need to explain anything; if the Bolshevik comes in, we'll knock him dead in any case." There had already been enough talk regarding the matter of personnel induction. Göring said it is common knowledge that all developments in conjunction with turbine engines are to be given priority. If the Army makes it difficult in making buildings available, a telegram would suffice and "in the blink of an eye" their units would be cleared out. Ignoring the question as to whether it would be feasible to locate new work facilities underground, he made a blanket statement claiming that they would be set up in the tunnels of potash mines.

Following the meeting on November 5th 1943, a production contract for 100 Ar 234 B aircraft was issued, which was increased in December to 200 with delivery by the end of 1944.

On 10 March 1944 Walter Kröger flew the first prototype for the B-series, Ar 234 V 9 PH+SQ. Two days later Ubbo Janssen flew the airplane into Alt-Lönnewitz where further evaluation would be conducted.

There the aircraft was outfitted with additional equipment for its role, including bomb shackles, release system, two aft-firing MG 151/20 guns, an enlarged cockpit for accommodating the Lotfe bombsight, an autopilot system[126] and a periscope for improving visibility to the rear.[127] Fitting the pressurized cabin was accompanied by certain difficulties. Interior pressure was maintained by pressure release valves at a standard altitude pressure of 8,000 m. Accordingly, it was mandatory that the pilot was always wear his oxygen mask, for if the cockpit lost pressure at 14,000 m he would be killed instantly by the sudden decompression. With an oxygen mask, however, the pressure drop was only 6,000 m, and in this case it was easily possible for the pilot to put the plane into a steep glide and escape to safer altitudes.[128]

On 3 June 1944 in Landeshut, Oberstleutnant Siegfried Knemeyer discussed deadline goals with virtually all the managing directors of the Arado Flugzeugwerke. Regarding future areas of concentration in the program, Walter Blume subsequently noted: "Work is to be urgently accelerated. K.'s use of the term 'bomber' defines the direction in which he's thinking in order not to collide with Me. K. says: 'We've got a fast airplane ... The Ar 234, considered the superior craft, should reach its target as fast as possible with effective weaponry' ... Chief of GL/C-E quite happy with the methods of our work. Tactical-technical results pleased him greatly."

On 12 and 13 June 1944, as the first 20 aircraft in the Ar 234 B-series were finished, a demonstration of the latest German aircraft types took place at Rechlin in the presence of Milch, Speer and the fighter staff. Except for the pilots and the builders, all company employees were excluded. Arado pilot Walter Kröger subsequently felt that the competing Do 335, also planned as a high-speed bomber, blatantly stuck out and was said to be able to reach 740 km/h at an altitude of 8,000 m, but in comparison with the Ar 234 was a much more demanding aircraft.[129] The Me 262 was criticized for the poor design of its wings. On the other hand, Milch and Speer were particularly impressed with the Ar 234 V 10's performance, primarily its tight turning radius. Hauptmann Behrens, the pilot who flew the Me 262 at the show, confirmed that the Ar 234 had "all in all, made a considerably better impression than the Me 262."

Walter Kröger's report on a flyoff between the Ar 234 v 10 and Me 262 A-1a on 12 and 13 June 1944:

Arado 234 V 9 prior to application of markings.

The Ar 234 V 10 was very capably demonstrated by Eheim: a pass at extremely low altitude at 320 km/h, followed by a sharp climb to 2000 m, turn, again plunging to the airfield, pulling up again to 2000 m with a roll, then turbines cut back to idle, tight spirals to ground level in landing configuration. During the second demonstration on 13 June the program schedule was interrupted when both the Me 262s provided for the flyoff developed startup problems. The Ar 234, just having taken off, was contacted by radio and told to fill the gap by extending its display flight.

Eheim demonstrated the maneuverability of the Ar 234 to such an extent that Generalfeldmarschall Milch ordered a demonstration by the pilot and, supplemental to the normal program, a turning comparison between the Me 262 and Ar 234. The latter showed its clear superiority of the Ar 234 in a turning dogfight; Ar 234 V 10 had the Me 262 in its gunsights several times. On the other hand, the Me 262 was able to escape by virtue of its speed advantage. The overall impression of the Ar 234 was very favorable.

Additional equipment packages and the weight of the retractable landing gear meant that the Ar 234 B-series did not quite have the performance of the A-series. An acceptance flight in Lärz (Rechlin) on 12 July 1944 of the first series-produced aircraft, the S1, revealed a number of defects in manufacturing quality, many of which could be traced back to the loss of suitable skilled labor and poor-quality raw materials. The landing gear locking mechanism had easily bent, the skin had rippled in places, paint and sealing had come off and there was a draft in the cockpit. Application of power and takeoff trim proved to be unsatisfactory, and the instruments operated inaccurately or were difficult to read. The reduced rubber quality of the tires made it difficult to brake the aircraft in rainy weather.

The operational duration of the engines was generally limited. As a rule, engine overhaul took place after 25 hours' flight time. The life expectancy of an aircraft was established in April 1944 at 150 flight hours, corresponding to an operational life of 10 months.[130]

In Alt-Lönnewitz, near Falkenberg in Saxony, Arado technicians and the Rechlin evaluation team began training the pilot Hauptmann D. Lukesch from Kampfgeschwader 76.[131] On 26 August 1944 III/KG 76 received the first two production machines. Despite constant deliveries the first large-scale operation with the type was pushed back for months, due to a delay in the production readiness of the PDS 11 triaxial autopilot. This device was necessary for the aircraft's bombing role; it briefly assumed control of the airplane and, with the aid of the Lotfe 7K tachometric bombsight, permitted the bombs to be released at higher altitudes instead of from a dive. The aircraft was more easily able to escape attacks from enemy fighters when drop-

Ar 234 B-2, maintenance work at 8/KG 76 in Burg.

Ar 234 B-2, F1+BT, KG 76 in Münster-Handorf. Operations during the Ardennes Offensive in 1944/1945. Commander D. Lukesch is standing in the cockpit.

Captured Ar 234 B-2 in Farnborough, England (1945).

Ar 234 B-2, F1+GS (Wk. Nr. 140 312, of 8 Staffel/KG 76 (November 1944). Sole surviving example of the Ar 234, captured in Stavanger and restored in 1987. (National Air and Space Museum, Silver Hill, Maryland — above).

Ar 234 B-2, F1+GS, NASM. Cockpit and trim regulators, fuel feed and rpm gauge (left). To the right are switches for controlling the electrical systems, radio and engine. Behind the control columns (which can be folded away to the side) are the Lotfe bombsight and the RF2C sighting mechanism above the canopy (left).

ping ordnance from higher altitudes; this method was approved following satisfactory testing in Rechlin during October of 1944. However, unlike the dive bombing attack, high-altitude level bombing was only successful when visibility was good. The pilot of a single-seat aircraft had a heavy workload, piloting the aircraft, checking for fighters sneaking up behind him and executing the bomb run. Since visibility in the narrow one-man cabin had worsened with the installation of additional instruments, a periscope was fitted which could be adjusted for forward and rearward views.

Without incurring significant losses Kampfgeschwader 76 carried out numerous operations from its base in Münster-Handorf, supporting the Ardennes offensive and later operating during the battles along the Oder and in the final struggle for Berlin. This unit was equipped with between 100 and 120 of the high-speed Ar 234 B bomber. The most spectacular operations took place in March 1944 against the Ludendorff Bridge in Remagen, which could not be destroyed despite the multiple sorties flown by over 40 of Gefechtsverband Kowalewski's available aircraft. Oberstleutnant Robert Kowaleski commanded KG 76, the first commander of a Kampfgeschwader equipped with jet-powered aircraft. The planned establishment of additional Geschwader units was never implemented. The advance of the enemy forced the sole operational unit to continually pull back northward, with the last operations taking place on 3 May 1945. On 5 May nine remaining aircraft escaped to Stavanger in Norway. On 22 February the first Arado jet bomber fell into Allied hands. The British brought a few captured aircraft to Farnborough for testing, but scrapped the entire lot in 1948.[132] Four bombers which had been captured undamaged by the Americans were also lost, with the sole exception of an example now on display in the National Air and Space Museum.[133] A high-speed bomber which had fallen into Soviet hands found its way to the Rechlin test facility, which they'd rebuilt, for evaluation, but in view of significant damage to the engines was never sent back to the Soviet Union.

The First With Four: The Ar 234 C High-Speed Bomber

After the decision had been made to use the Jumo powerplants for the Messerschmitt Me 262 fighter, Arado was forced to switch over to BMW's engines, which were not as developed as the Jumo engines.[134]

Unlike the Jumo, the lighter BMW powerplant had an annular combustion chamber and hollow turbine blades, which were cooled by bleed-off compressor air. In view of the reduced thrust of the BMW engine, adequate power reserves were met with the fitting of four powerplants. So as not to unnecessarily delay the beginning of series production, a simple solution was first tried by attaching two BMW engines to the existing points for the Jumo engines and fitting two more onto the points for the now-superfluous rocket packs. This had the anticipated result of reducing yaw stability and at the same time increasing the roll moment during a sideslip, conditions which could lead to the aircraft tumbling dangerously at higher altitudes. Another solution which called for attaching both engines together using an intermediate member, then affixing the entire combination to the existing Jumo engine mounts, had the disadvantage of positioning the engines too close to the fuselage. After limited success during testing of the V 6 prototype, GK+IW (Wk.Nr. 130 006), which had been fitted with the four independent powerplants, the decision was made in favor of the paired-nacelle arrangement as fitted to prototype V 8, GK+IY (Wk.Nr. 130 008).

To eliminate isolated air acceleration, the engines were kept as far from the fuselage as possible. The V 8 prototype, whose first flight took place on 4 February 1944, made history as the first four-engine jet aircraft in the world.[135]

In March 1944 concrete plans were drawn up for the four-engine Ar 234 series, consisting of the C-1 reconnaissance variant and the C-2 bomber version. In September, however, the decision was made to include the C-3 bomber and C-4 reconnaissance variants, both of which had a fully

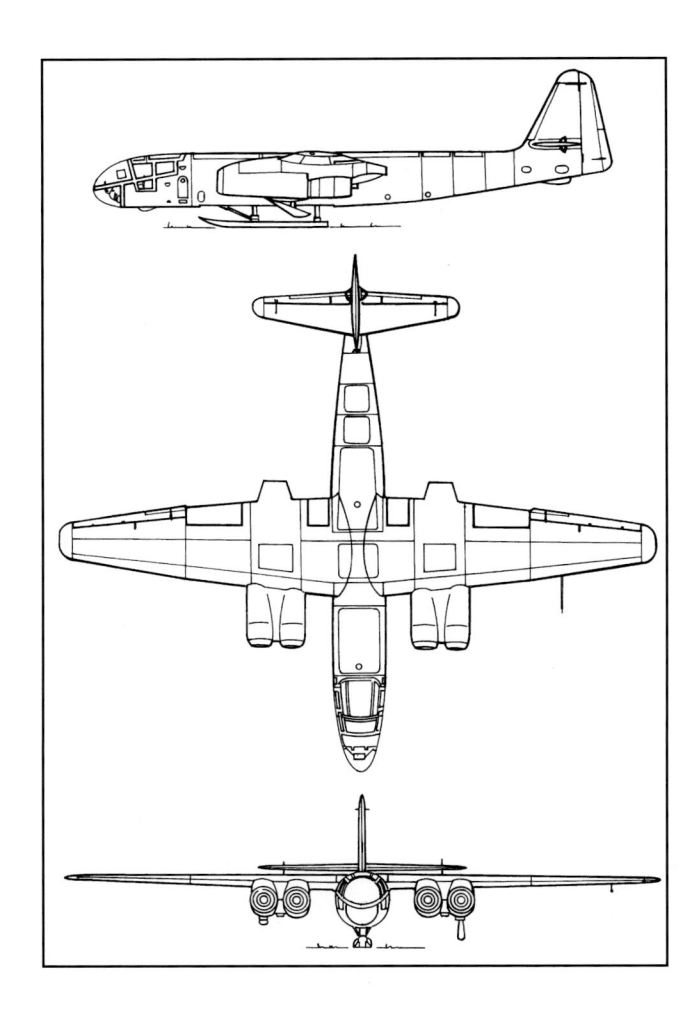

Drawing of Ar 234 V 8, GK+IY (Wk. Nr. 130 008) with two paired BMW 003 A engine pods. First flight took place on 4 February 1944.

Ar 234 V 8.

pressurized cockpit with a slight upward bulge to improve visibility to the rear. Variants C-5 and C-8 were planned as bombers, while versions C-6 and C-7 were to operate in the long-range recon and night fighter roles, respectively. Prototypes V 19 through V 30 were made available for evaluation purposes, and although all were built, none were ever able to be thoroughly put through their paces.

On 19 July 1944 Oberstleutnant Knemeyer and Walter Blume inspected a cockpit mockup for the Ar 234 C-3 high-speed bomber in Landeshut and established the details in the matter of the aircraft's armament. The first prototype

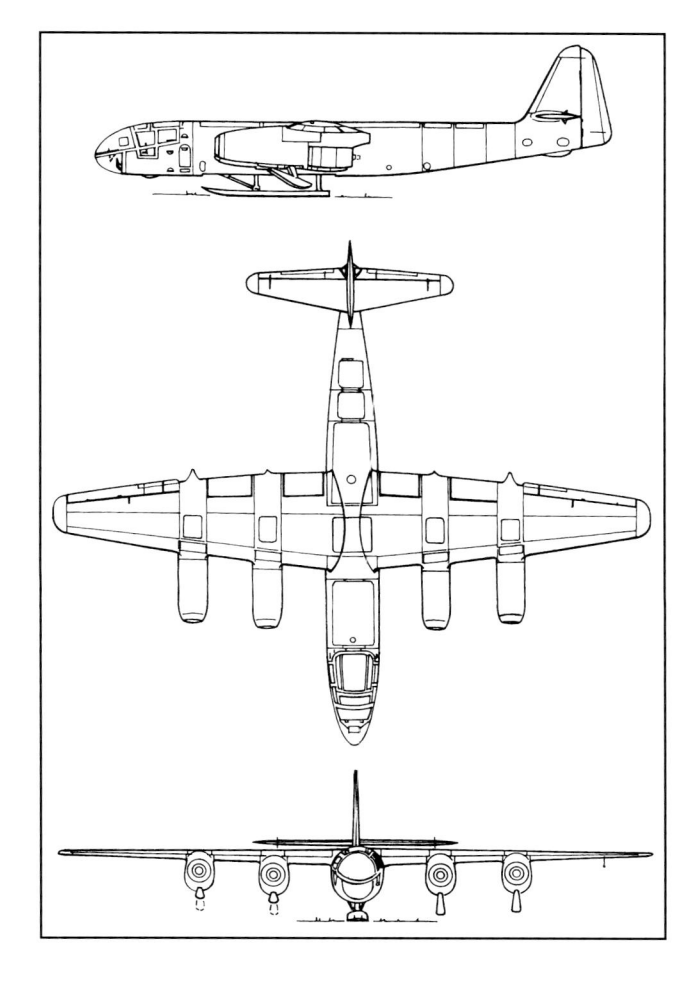

Drawing of Ar 234 V 6, GK+IW (Wk. Nr. 130 006) with four single BMW 003 A engines. First flight 25 April 1944.

Ar 234 V 6.

for the C-series was the V 19, PI+WX, which flew for the first time on 16 October 1944. Subsequent to the flight-technical evaluation of prototypes V 19, V 21 and V 22 between 5 November and 21 December 1944 in Sagan, results showed that nothing had fundamentally changed over the B-series. However, the engines proved to have certain problems.

Evaluation report from Sagan on V 19, V 21 and V 22, dated 4 January 1945:

At present, the BMW powerplants are affecting the test program the most; lately during nearly every flight and engine goes out. Around 30 percent of all flights have to be aborted during takeoff, because either an engine didn't kick in or problems with the internal combustion starter cropped up. The engine as such doesn't have a bad feel in flight; the BMW engine accelerates significantly better than the Jumo and matches the latter's performance through proper management of the permissible gas temperature. It's just that the engine still has 'teething troubles', and in my opinion, there isn't the prerequisite interest at BMW to eliminate these problems as fast as possible, to here and now see for themselves the problems we're having. We currently are carrying out more turbine and airframe testing.

Ar 234. Delivery schedule of the Ar 234 B-2 with 210 units projected to June 1945; 3660 of the C-3 and 230 units of C-4 models were to be built from February 1944 to March 1946, equating to a total production of 4100 aircraft (as of 28 July 1944 — below).

The Ar 234 C-3 bombers, with their extraordinarily high wing loading of 455 kg/m² and 12.3 ton takeoff weight (14.18 with RATO) were extremely capable aircraft and, in spite of occasional criticism, were highly regarded by the front-line troops. The airplane was capable of carrying a bomb load of 1,500 kg and had a range of 1,400 km — which could be increased to 1,900 km with auxiliary fuel tanks.

According to the delivery program from 28 July 1944, by April 1945 the production cycle of the Ar 234 B would have run out after 190 units had been delivered. In February of 1945 production of the Ar 234 C-3 bomber was to have begun and from December 1945 total monthly output would have reached 500 aircraft. From April 1945 on there would have followed the Ar 234 C-4 recon plane, at a rate of 20 per month, so that by March 1946 230 units would have been delivered. By this point in time the total number of Ar 234s produced would have been 4,100 aircraft.

J. Goebbels' journal entry from 22 March 1945:

The meeting with Oberst Baumbach boosted the Führer's spirits immensely. He now places the greatest hopes in the new jet airplanes. In this month 500 will have already been manufactured and in the next month 1000. The airfields for these numbers are being produced with the utmost effort. The Führer must arrange all this personally, since Göring hardly bothers with it anymore. The Führer is constantly musing, wondering whether these aircraft — if they really achieve the breakthrough — won't prove to be too late.[136]

Production, however, suffered from a lack of workers. Although Siegfried Knemeyer pulled experts away from Focke-Wulf (over the objections of Kurt Tank) only a few reconnaissance aircraft and approximately 19 bombers were ever built. Their operations with Kampfgeschwader 76 remained relatively ineffective due to fuel shortages, on-going destruction of the last airbase enclaves and constant attacks from Allied fighters.

In southern Germany the remaining machines deployed to airfields in Manching, Füstenfeldbruck and Neubiberg. Only a few aircraft were captured intact by the Americans, since the majority were blown up by their crews beforehand. The Soviets, however, acquired a large number of Ar 234 C-3s at Alt Lönnewitz.

After the loss of Alt-Lönnewitz the test center was first moved to Brandenburg-Briest and then to Wesendorf in the Lüneburger Heide. Several C-series prototypes were lost during heavy bombing of Wesendorf on 4 April 1945. Those facilities were abandoned in the face of advancing British forces, with aircraft moving to Warnemünde and later Kaltenkirchen in Schleswig-Holstein. The last flight of an Ar 234 C prototype took place on 1 May 1945 with company pilot Günther Eheim at the controls of V 25.

Emergency Measure: The Ar 234 "Nachtigall" Night Fighter

In 1942, with the Western Allies attacking with their higher-performing bombers and untouchable Mosquitos, the German stop-gap night fighters had reached their limits. Göring declared in the autumn of 1942 that the "loans" he was constantly having to make of his bombers and day fighters was the wrong road for the night battles. Nevertheless, as late as August 1943 in the spirit of Hitler in a GL meeting he called for all jet aircraft to initially be used as high-speed bombers, counter to the ideas which Milch had also been advancing. According to Speer's journal entry from 22 June 1944, at this late date even Hitler himself wanted to employ the Me 262 jet, not as a fighter, but as a high-speed bomber until the Ar 234 entered full-scale production.

Ar 234 V 21, PI+WZ (Wk. Nr. 130 061) with four BMW 003 As engines and modified cockpit. Final prototype for the C-3 series. First flight on 24 November 1944.

Ar 234 V 21.

148

Ar 234 V 13, PH+SU (Wk. Nr. 130 023) with four BMW 003 As engines and a B-series fuselage. Prototype for the Ar 234 C-3, the first four-engined production jet bomber in the world. First flight on 6 September 1944 (above).

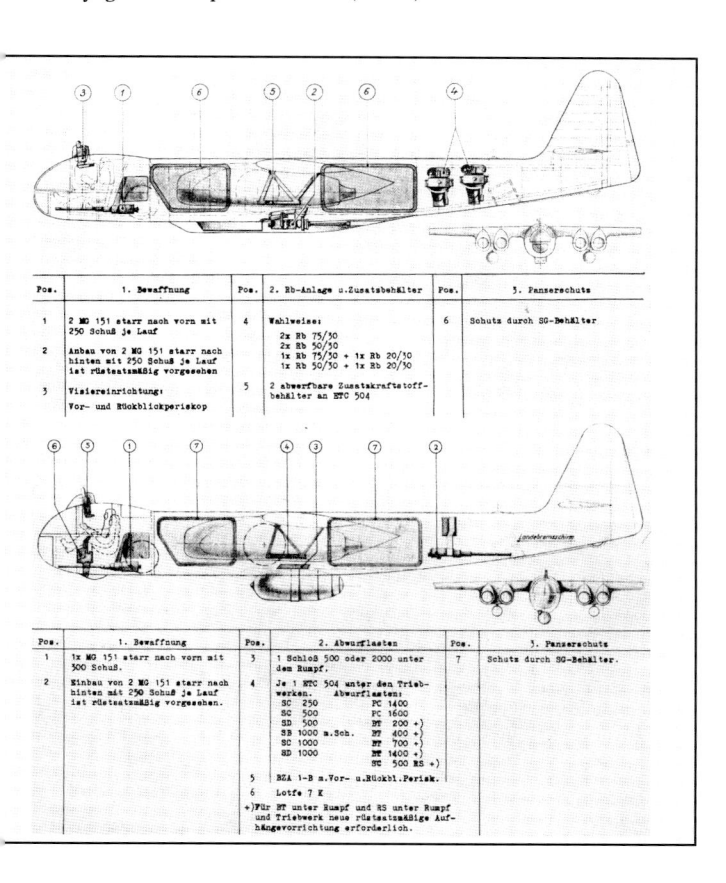

Above: drawing of the four-engined Ar 234 C-4 reconnaissance airplane (Sept. 1944). Below: drawing of the four-engined Ar 234 C-5 high-speed bomber with two-place cockpit (Dec. 1944).

GL meeting on 20 August 1943:

Von Lossberg: My view is that the next job we've got to tackle within the next six months is the bomber with turbojet powerplants, focusing on speed and not so much on altitude.

Milch: Arado is doing this.

von Lossberg: But only in very few numbers.

Milch: But it's not in production yet.

von Lossberg: And with performance figures that show a relatively modest range!

Milch: We'll hear more later on concerning the matter of turbojet bombers. This is starting up, only we can't give up on one so as to exclusively build the other, just the opposite in fact: in areas where we've wanted to be brave and courageous we've instead taken a blow to the head — with the jet fighter. During the meeting in question Messerschmitt probably put it in such a way as to suggest that he had concerns.

von Lossberg: I don't think that's true.

Diesing: I believe the jet bomber to be the decisive factor. Even the Führer has said that he envisions the potential of the jet engine more from the bomber perspective when dealing with large numbers.

Milch: I see it initially as the basis for fighters, and I can't expect that another person who only occasionally gets involved in such matters would assess it the same as a specialist. When you're on the defense, you've got to make your defensive forces as strong as possible.

149

When in mid-1944 it was finally realized that the jet-powered night fighter was the last possibility for defense against the bomber streams, the development program changed and — in addition to the Me 262 — the Ar 234 B-2 high-speed bomber was converted into the Ar 234 B-2/N night fighter. The codeword for the night fighter was "Nachtigall" (Nightingale).

Wilhelm van Nes, Arado's director of projects, had proposed a night fighter variant back in mid-1943. But it wasn't until July 1944, two months before the Messerschmitt Me 262 was considered for conversion to a makeshift night fighter, that concrete planning began in earnest. An emergency program implemented by Walter Blume and Siegfried Knemeyer on 12 September 1944 called for a "lightning-fast" conversion of 30 aircraft "in order to effect rapid operational deployment and, in so doing, bring about relief in the air situation." It was estimated that the first prototype would be finished on 25 October 1944 and would be built under the direction of Hans Rebeski in Sagan independent of the development department located there. Three additional test aircraft would serve as platforms for evaluating target search, radar warning and navigation equipment. 14 conversions would subsequently take place in Alt-Lönnewitz in November, with 15 following in December. Rebeski was informed that operations would be carried out from Burg bei Magdeburg.

Workshop conditions in Sagan seemed to Rebeski to be completely inadequate, so he had the conversion work moved to Werneuchen, northeast of Berlin; the radar evaluation center plus Lufthansa's and Siemens' workshops for radar installation had the necessary equipment and were all located in the immediate vicinity.

The conversion program, drawn up on such short notice, caused problems with getting suitable skilled workmen and acquiring the necessary components. To somewhat alleviate the former, Oberstleutnant Knemeyer temporarily provided 150 military technicians from Oranienburg.

Weights and center-of-gravity had to first be recalculated. In order to avoid wasting time with the development of a two-seat cockpit, space for the radar operator was found in the former camera compartment in the aft part of the airplane. After removing those components exclusive to the bomber role, the aircraft was to have been fitted with an

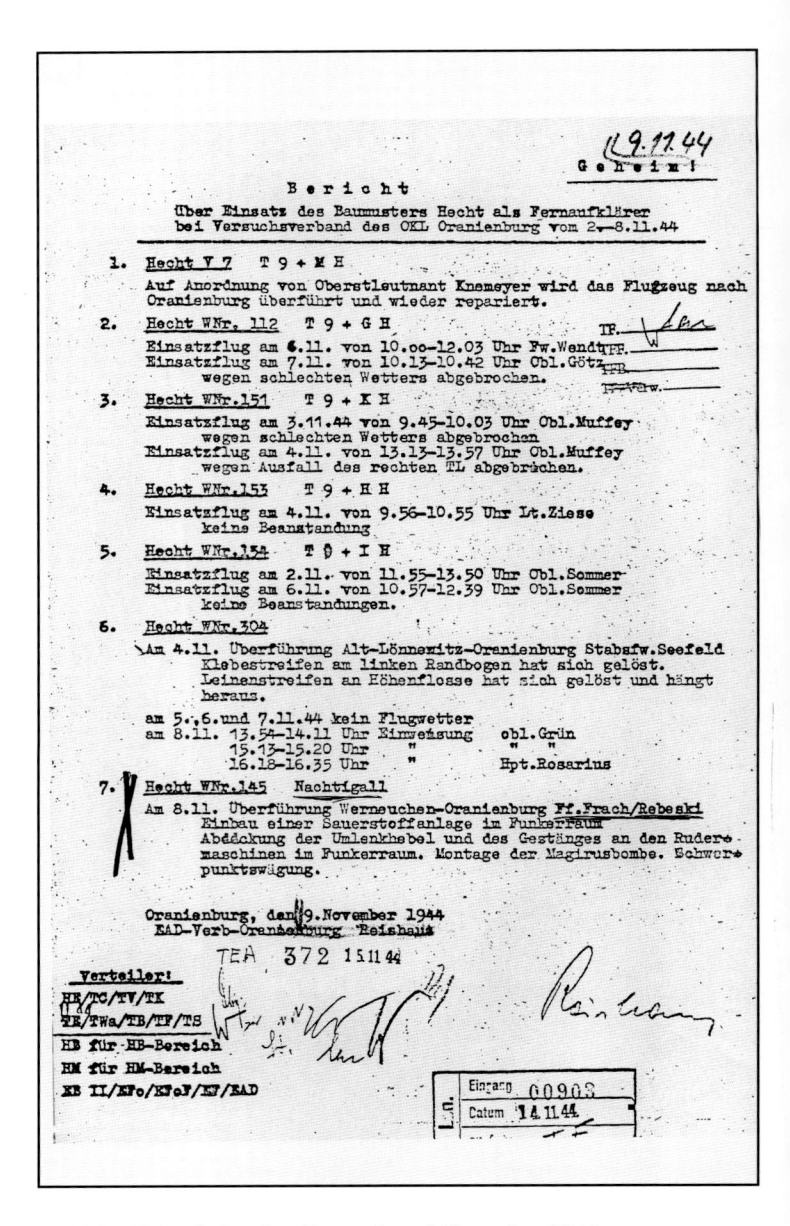

Ar 234 B-2N night bomber. Report from 9 November 1944 on the transfer to Werneuchen-Oranienburg (para. 7 — right).

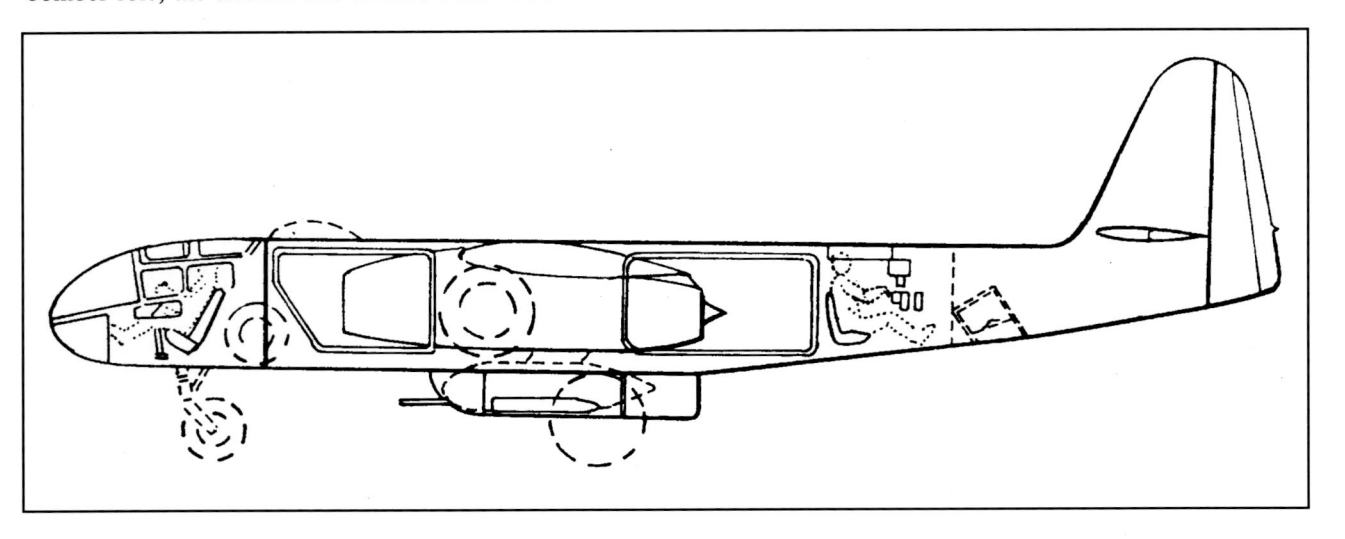

Ar 234 B-2N "Nachtigall" night fighter (Wk. Nr. 140 145).

antenna, two MG 151/20 guns for armament, a so-called "Magirusbombe" and the requisite radar systems such as the FUG 218 Neptun, FUG 120 Naxos, FUG 350 Berhardine and the FuBl 2 instrument landing system.

Developmental delays and supply shortages for these new components inevitably led to delays in the program and the implementation of temporary measures. Eventually, the final decision regarding the radar system was made in favor of Siemen's FuG 218 Neptun.

On 20 September 1944 the Ar 234 B-2 (Wk.Nr. 140 145) arrived at Werneuchen for the purpose of the first conversion. Minutes from a meeting in Brandenburg on 5 November indicate that by this time the conversion had been completed. According to information supplied by Fritz Reishaus, field liaison engineer for the Arado Flugzeugwerke, the first prototype was flown on 8 November by the Frach/Rebeski crew from Werneuchen to Oranienburg, where it received follow-on conversion work and was made available for flight testing.

On 13 October 1944 Walter Blume sent a reminder to Oberstleutnant Knemeyer, noting that the three additional Ar 234s which had been promised for prototype work had not yet been provided, although there was now a sufficient number of mechanics and component parts.

In mid-November it was learned that the RLM had suddenly red-lined further modification work, a measure which had been undertaken in order to ensure all Ar 234 high-speed bombers were available for the upcoming Ardennes offensive.

In December 1944 the Oberkommando der Luftwaffe anticipated the establishment of two night fighter Geschwader, each outfitted with the Ar 234 B-2/N and Me 262-1a/U1 provisional night fighters. According to the plan, the 3/Versuchsverband OKL under Hauptmann Josef Bisping would receive three additional Ar 234 B-2/N night fighters on a monthly basis.

Bisping carried out several combat sorties, but wasn't able to score any kills. On 13 February 1945 the aircraft he was flying crashed in Oranienburg, killing both him and his radar operator. The airfield illumination had accidentally been turned off while the plane was taking off and the pilot pulled the aircraft up too sharply.

On 1 March Hptm. Kurt Bonow accepted a second Ar 234 B-2/N (Wk.Nr. 140146) and carried out several evaluation flights. His radar operator had considerable difficulties getting used to the system, and even Kurt Bonow came to the conclusion that jet aircraft were ill-suited for operations against fast piston-engine aircraft.

At the beginning of April a third and final Ar 234 B-2/N (Wk.Nr. 140 608) night fighter was provided for pure evaluation testing. Operational capability of the night fighters came to a standstill following a bombing raid against Oranienburg on 12 April 1945.

With the exception of the Me 262 which, unlike the situation with the Ar 234, was initially planned as a fighter and only temporarily modified as a high-speed bomber, no German jet aircraft achieved full operational status during the Second World War. Junkers planned a large high-speed bomber with the Ju 287, which completed its maiden flight on 16 August 1944. Only two prototypes were completed, however. By the war's end, Heinkel had a high-speed bomber design, the He 343, in its program. This was about 1.5 times as large as the aircraft which served as its basis — the Ar 234. Of this design, only wind tunnel models, mockups and a few sub-assemblies for two planned prototypes were ever built.

Chapter 19
Unrealized Projects

While most of Arado's ambitious projects which appeared in the last months of the war hardly made it past the planning stages, subsequent designs of the Ar 234 C-series had taken concrete shape before the war's end.

According to the company records, the following basic types existed with four BMW 003 A turbine engines:

Ar 234 C-1: reconnaissance.
Ar 234 C-2: bomber.
Ar 234 C-3: bomber.
Ar 234 C-4: reconnaissance.
Ar 234 C-5: bomber. As C-3 but two-seat.
Ar 234 C-6: reconnaissance-project.
Ar 234 C-7: night fighter.

The Ar 234 C-8 bomber was to have been fitted with two Jumo 004 D engines.

Aside from the C-3 and C-4, the highest priority among this series of projects was given to the planning of the night fighter in its final form. This aircraft type, with its weapons tailored to the night fighting role and its complicated electronics suite, exemplified the most outstanding technological features extant at the war's end.

At the end of December 1944, prior to manufacturing the optimal night fighter based on the Ar 234 C-7, efforts were made to incorporate the C-3 variants into this role. A meeting was held in Brandenburg on 5 January 1945, during which the necessary work and deadlines were outlined. Since it would be realized more quickly, prototype conversion of the Ar 234 C-3 N night fighter was to begin in Sagan with the Ar 234 V 27 and be completed by 28 February. Other projects would take a back burner. Hans Rebeski was to inform the production department on 15 January regarding the extent of changes and provide Walter Blume with a brief description by the 11th of the month.

After justifiable criticism of the single-seat, fully-glazed cockpit Arado concentrated on a night fighter based on the Ar 234 C-3 which had a redesigned cockpit with a radio operator's seat next to the pilot, forward firing guns consisting of two MG 151/20 and two MK 108 and would be fitted with the FuG 244 Bremen night fighter radar. Various advanced weapons systems were occasionally tested, including the R4M Orkan rocket built by Curt Heber in Osterode, as well as cannons up to 50 mm.

The Ar 234 P night fighter series was to have been developed from the Ar 234 C-3. Working with Professor Tank via the Focke-Wulf offices in Berlin, the following versions were planned:

a) Ar 234 B1: two-man cockpit, 4x BMW 003 A1 (engine shifted aft to compensate for center-of-gravity), with armor.
b) Ar 234 B2: one-man cockpit, second crewman in rear fuselage, 4x BMW 003 A1 (standard location as with Ar 234 C-3), with armor.
c) Ar 234 P3: As P2 with 2x He S 011 A.
d) Ar 234 P4: As P2 with 2x Jumo 004 D.

The use of R4M rocket rounds in place of the 2x MK 108 weapons pack took high priority. The FuG 218 Neptun was planned for installation since the Bremen radar was not yet available. According to a memorandum from Hans

Rebeski dated 9 January 1945, the fitting of dummy equipment suites took place in Sagan.

On 24 January 1945 a special commission for the development of night fighters, under the direction of Kurt Tank, advocated the use of the Ar 234, Me 262 and Do 335 versions in this role. Despite the urgency in finding an immediate remedy, demands were made for fundamental changes to the Ar 234. Oberleutnant Kurt Welter, a member of the Me 262 evaluation team, criticized the extensive nose glazing of the Ar 234 since the attacking pilot could be hit by debris from enemy aircraft and, in addition, the reflective glass hindered visibility during takeoff and landing.

On 2 February 1945 Generalstabsingenieur Roluf Lucht, Oberstleutnant Siegfried Knemeyer and Kurt Tank were accordingly informed by Walter Blume that the Ar 234 P2 single-seat night fighter would be given priority by the Technisches Amt. In addition, a slightly modified Ar 234 P5 project would be laid down, with completion anticipated by the end of May. The fuselage was to be lengthened to the fore and the fighter would include an upward-firing gun, a three-man cockpit and two He S 011 A engines. With a takeoff weight of 11,400 kg it would have been the heaviest in the series.

On 26 February 1945 the first drafts for the new night fighter were drawn up in Focke-Wulf's Bad Eilsen facility. In addition to Focke-Wulf and Arado, developmental contracts were also issued to Blohm und Voss, Dornier, Heinkel, Messerschmitt and Gotha.

Ar 234 P5 night fighter. Projection for May 1945, dated 2 February 1945 (right).

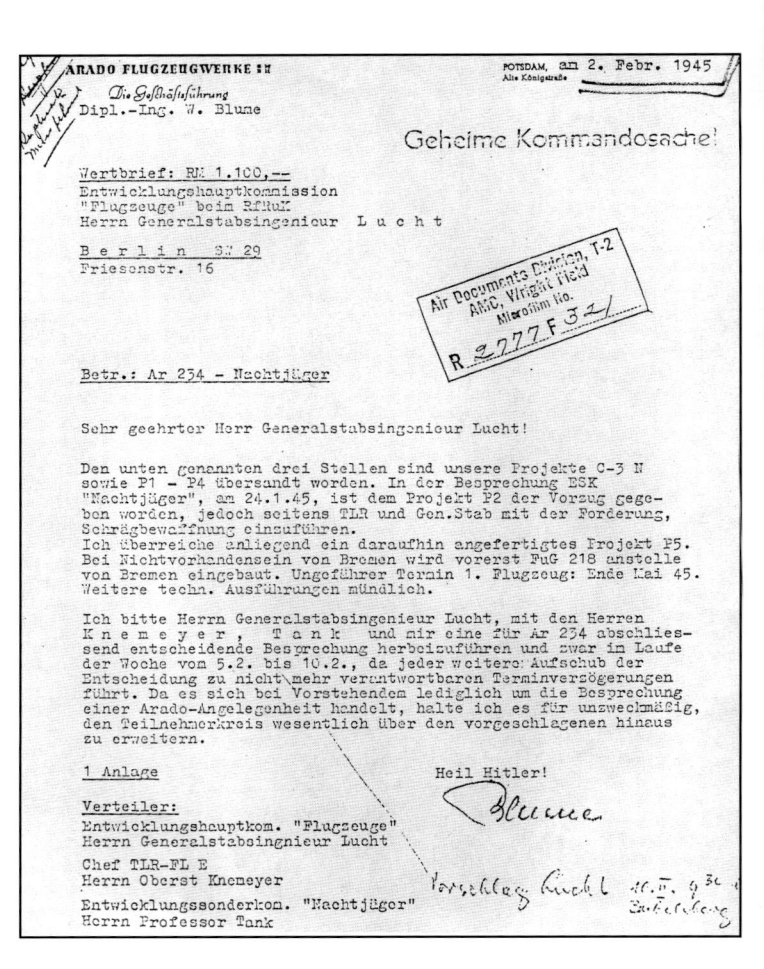

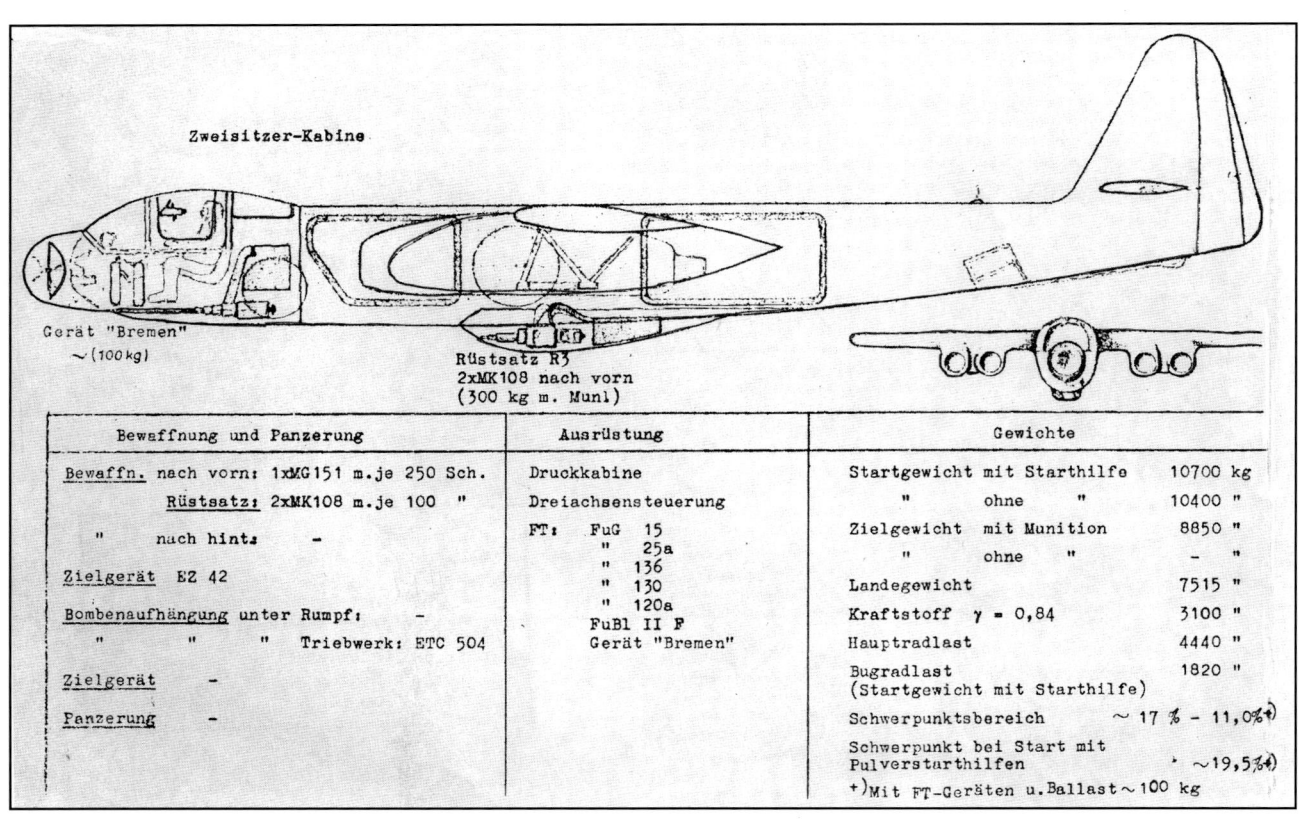

Ar 234 P1 night fighter. Draft with two-seat pressurized cockpit, Bremen radar set and weapons pack (below).

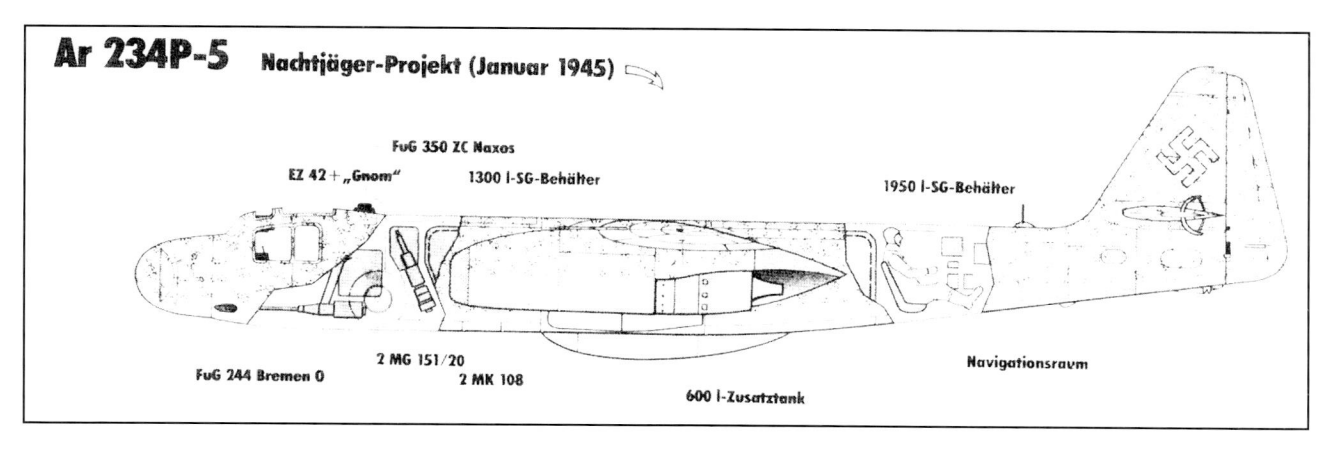

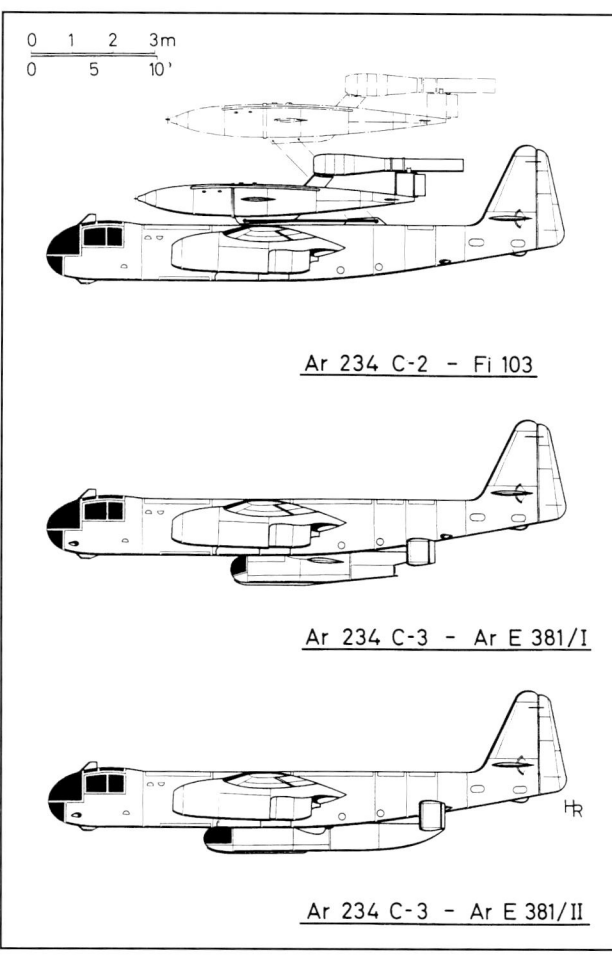

Ar 234P-5 Nachtjäger-Projekt (Januar 1945)

- FuG 350 ZC Naxos
- EZ 42 + „Gnom"
- 1300 l-SG-Behälter
- 1950 l-SG-Behälter
- FuG 244 Bremen O
- 2 MG 151/20
- 2 MK 108
- 600 l-Zusatztank
- Navigationsraum

Ar 234 P5 night fighter with two He S 011 A engines and upward-firing weapons. Draft. (above)

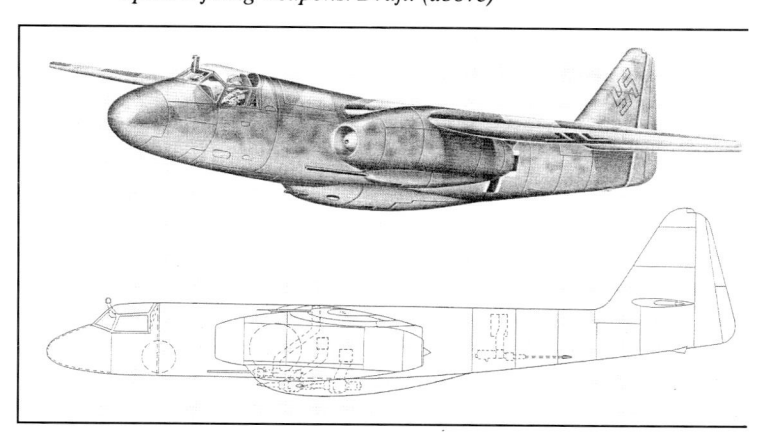

- Ar 234 C-2 – Fi 103
- Ar 234 C-3 – Ar E 381/I
- Ar 234 C-3 – Ar E 381/II

Above: Ar 234 C-2 project with Fi 103 (V1) in piggyback configuration. Center and below: E 381 project with Ar 234 C-3 as a carrier for a midget fighter.

Twin-engined jet fighter project based on the Ar 234 (1943) (Meyer/Schick).

Impossible demands on the part of the Luftwaffe regarding design modifications wasted valuable time when the firms were accordingly forced to rework their proposals. When these were returned to Oberstleutnant Knemeyer at the final conference on 20 and 21 March, only Arado and a handful of other firms were contracted to continue on with the project, but by this date the time had run out.

In retrospect, a development relating to the jet fighter had been broken off, one for which Arado's design office had repeatedly submitted proposals since the inception of the turbine engine. Although the RLM had only authorized Arado to build reconnaissance aircraft and bombers, the design bureau began working on the concept of a jet fighter as early as late December 1941. This resulted in the Projekt E 480, which was not only to have been fitted with the DB 614 piston engine, but also with a turbine engine. In May of 1943 Arado proposed a fighter project which resembled the Ar 234 recon version then under construction, but this was rejected in favor of the Me 262. In mid-1943 Arado introduced a twin-engine turbojet fighter, a pure rocket fighter and a fighter with a combination turbine and rocket engine (which the company favored) in conjunction with a study on high-speed two-seaters, but none of these was ever built. The 16/43-23 study from 3 June 1943 for a twin-jet fighter was a follow-on development of the Ar 234 having swept wings. Power was to have been provided by two He S 109-011 engines, giving it a speed of 920 to over 1000 km/h at an altitude of 10 kilometers. In November of 1944 the Projekt E 581, a single engine high-performance jet fighter, was undertaken and, after varied alterations came to be known as the Projekt E 555. Original plans called for the BMW 003 turbine engine in this aircraft. Later Arado conformed the development to the ongoing requirements by making use of the He S 011 engine. No data is to be had for this variant's flight performance. The long, dissipative intake and the large upper surfaces indicate that it would have had poor performance as it neared its maximum speed.

On the other hand, the low wing loading would have given the design superior maneuverability and good climbing and high-altitude performance. Provisions were made for two MK 108 guns in the wing roots. Work may have stopped once Arado began concentrating on the Ar I flying wing night fighter, which was in a relatively advanced state of development by the time the war ended. This was a low-wing design with a delta layout having two He S 011 turbine semi-buried within the rear fuselage. The aircraft was drawn up according to guidelines set down on 27 January 1945 and had an initial crew complement of two. A second version, drafted up in March and submitted to the Entwicklungshauptkommission in Berlin had its fuselage enlarged in order to carry a third crewman (pilot, radar observer and navigator on ejection seats in a pressurized cabin) and had an increased fuel capacity. Two MK 213 30 mm guns, two MK 108/20 upward-firing guns near the centerpoint and two MK 213s for defense in the aft fuselage were to have comprised the aircraft's armament suite. Maximum speed would have been 810 km/h at 9,000 meters. On 20 and 21 March experts voiced their criticism of the large, drag inducing wing surfaces and the unfavorable engine configuration. This led to a draft with a smaller, more sharply raked wing which the American manufacturer Chance-Vought utilized after the war in the design of one of its carrier planes — which incidentally reached a speed approaching 1100 km/h.

A more feasible alternative to the Ar I project was Arado's Ar II high-speed bomber and night fighter design from March 1945, with a standard layout and making use of swept wings. The aircraft was also to have been pow-

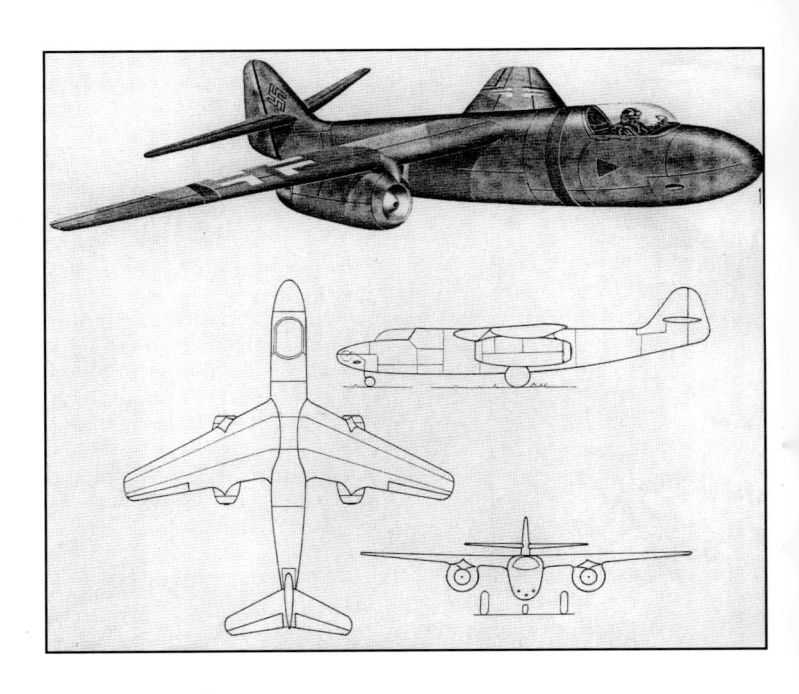

Project TEW 16/43-23 for a twin-engined fighter with swept wings, based on the Ar 234 (June 1943) (Meyer/Schick).

Ar E 583. Project for a twin-engined tail-less Ar I night fighter (1945). (Meyer/Schick).

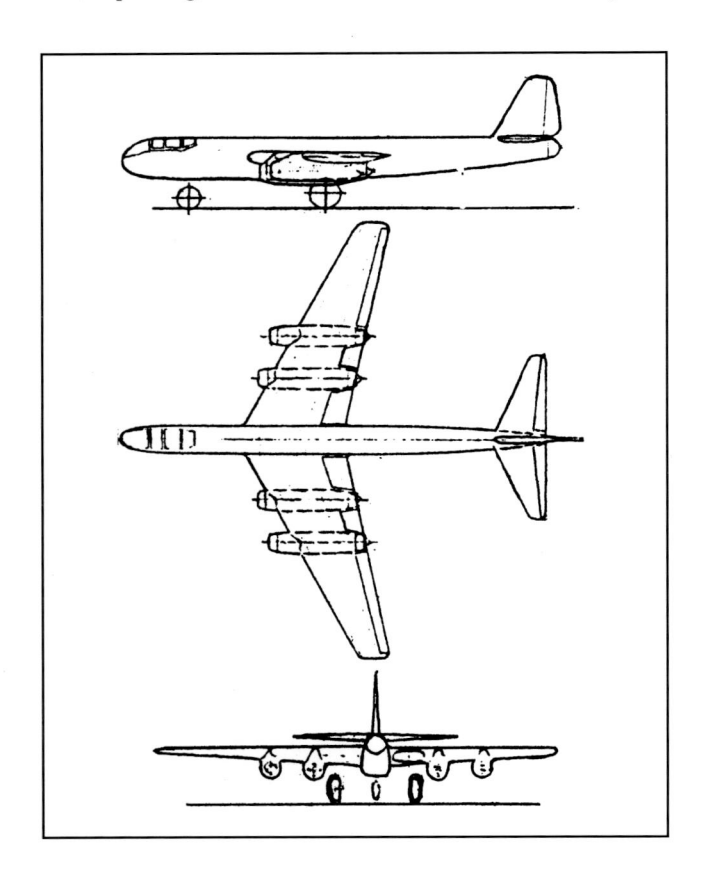

ered by two He S 011 engines and have similar armament. However, maximum speed was slower at just 775 km/h.

In 1944 Arado, Blohm und Voss, Fieseler, Focke-Wulf, Junkers, Siebel and Heinkel participated in the RLM-sponsored project for a "Volksjäger", or people's fighter, to which Messerschmitt was vehemently opposed. By the time the guidelines had been officially released on 10 September 1944, the Heinkel Werke already had achieved an irreversible developmental lead through its deliberate solicitation of preliminary information. Once the construction contract had been awarded to Heinkel on 30 September 1944, Arado, as with most of the remaining firms, chose not to pursue the project any further.

Ar E 560. Project design for a four-engined Ar II high-speed bomber with swept wings, based on the Ar 234.

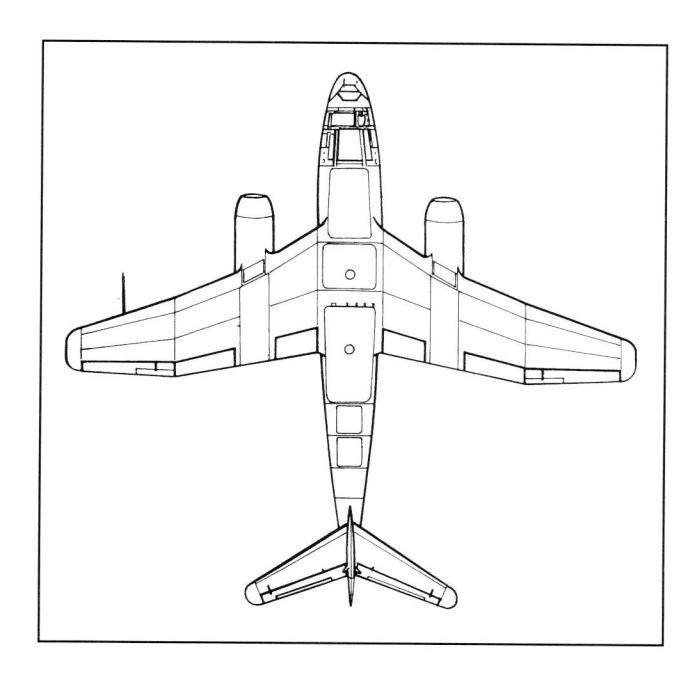

Ar 234 V 16, PH+SX (Wk. Nr. 130 026). Swept-wing design, unfinished at the war's end.

A series of other Arado projects were found in the planning stages at the end of the war, indicating that the company belonged to the leading group of the German aviation industry. In Landeshut on 5 November 1944 Oberstleutnant Knemeyer established the guidelines for future overall planning with Walter Blume and senior Arado engineers. This included a miniature fighter, operations with a piggy-back glide bomb, the Ar 234 as a carrier plane for the Fi 103 (V1), the matter of increasing jet aircraft range through towed fuel tanks, shape improvements for bombs and, above all, the use of "fast wings." After the original V1 flying bomb launch sites had to be given up, operations continued with heavy losses using the slow He 111 H-22s of KG 53. Circa 1,200 flying bombs took off with this unit, of which only 66 reached their target. The last mission took place at night, on 5 January 1945, against London. With the Ar 234 the flying bomb would be carried piggy-back or towed to the target area. According to a company memorandum from 13 January 1945, for this project Arado had provided the Deutsche Forschungsanstalt für Segelflug in Ainring with documents for the construction of an Ar 234 B (Series 8) model, with which tests were undertaken in the Darmstadt wind tunnel. Although the prototype entered flight testing, it was written off in a crash on 14 March 1945 after a series of test flights which proved less than satisfactory. According to company records from 8 August 1944, tests were

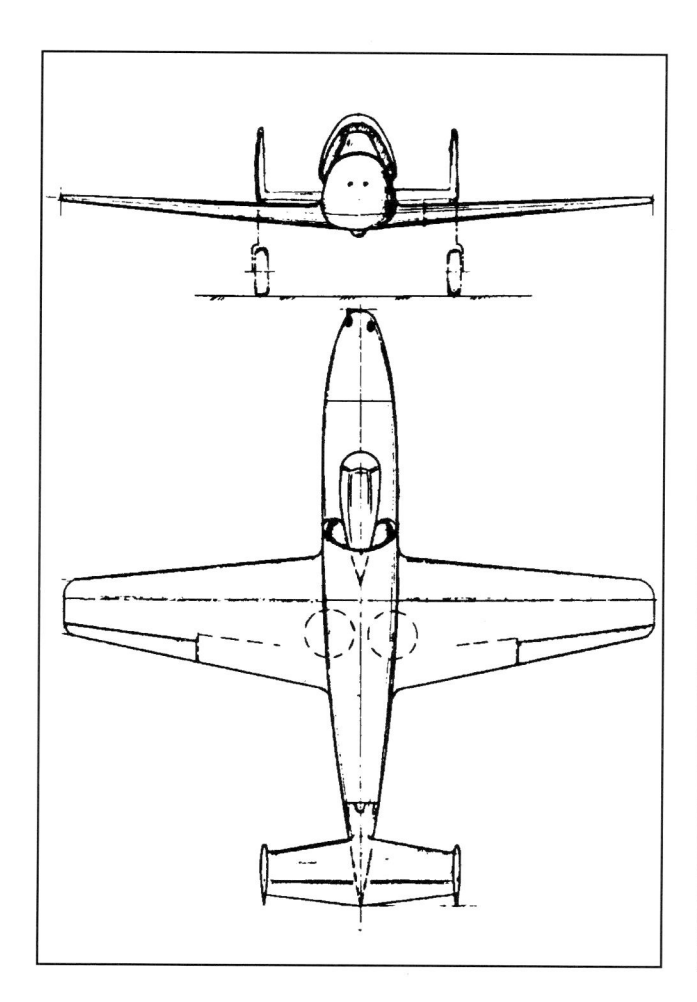

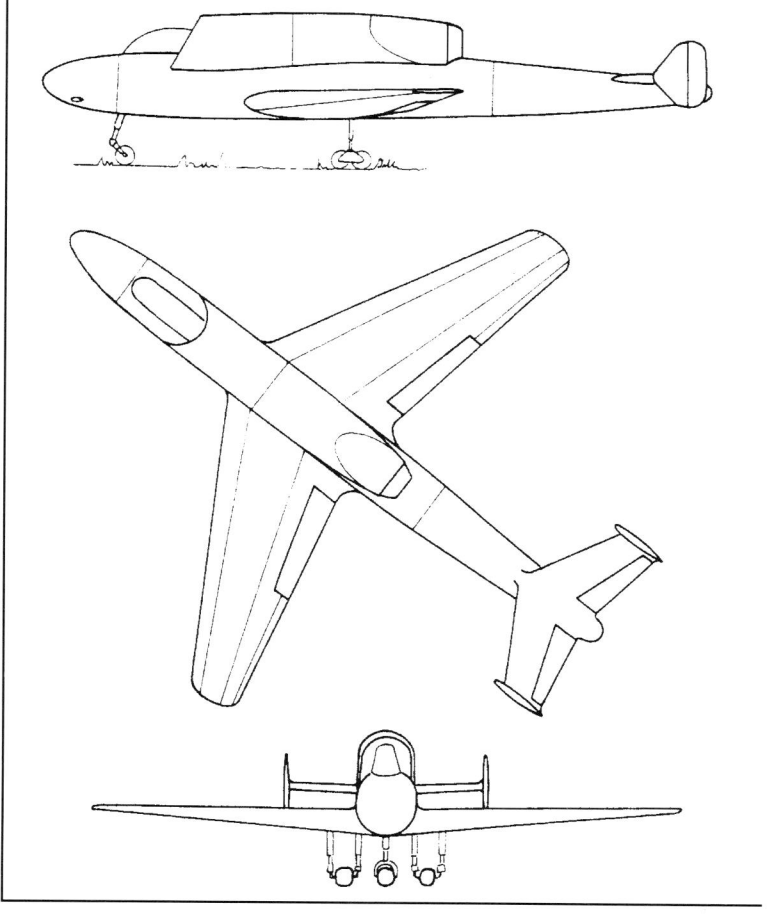

Ar E 580. Design sketch for a jet-powered "people's fighter" (12 September 1944).

Project TEW 16/43-15: "combination fighter" with both turbine and rocket engines and swept wing configuration (1943). (Meyer/Schick).

155

carried out under Projekt E 377 for evaluating the Hs 293 glide bomb underneath an Ar 234. This involved takeoff by means of a trolley, as on the initial variant, with the bomb resting on it below the fuselage. A combination using an Me 262 as command airplane was tried, as was a version using towed fuel tanks to give the plane a range of 2,000 km and more. Although the Projekt E 381 was never built, it involved a manned miniature fighter armed with a 30 mm cannon being carried aloft by an Ar 234 C for a one-time attack against nearby targets. The rocket fighter was to have landed on skids and, after being retrieved by a special team, could be turned around for another mission.

Another unrealized project was the Ar 234 F variant with swept, laminar-flow wings, the design of which would have delayed the onset of problems associated with approaching supersonic speeds.[137]

Other variants which were never built were the Ar 234 D reconnaissance aircraft with DB 021 turboprop engines, the E-series Zerstörer, a version of the Ar 234 R with rocket engines — which was to have been launched by an He 177 from high altitude, and a rocket-powered high-altitude reconnaissance platform. Other studies included a multi-engine jet bomber, the E 555 and a four-engine E 560 turbojet bomber with swept wings.

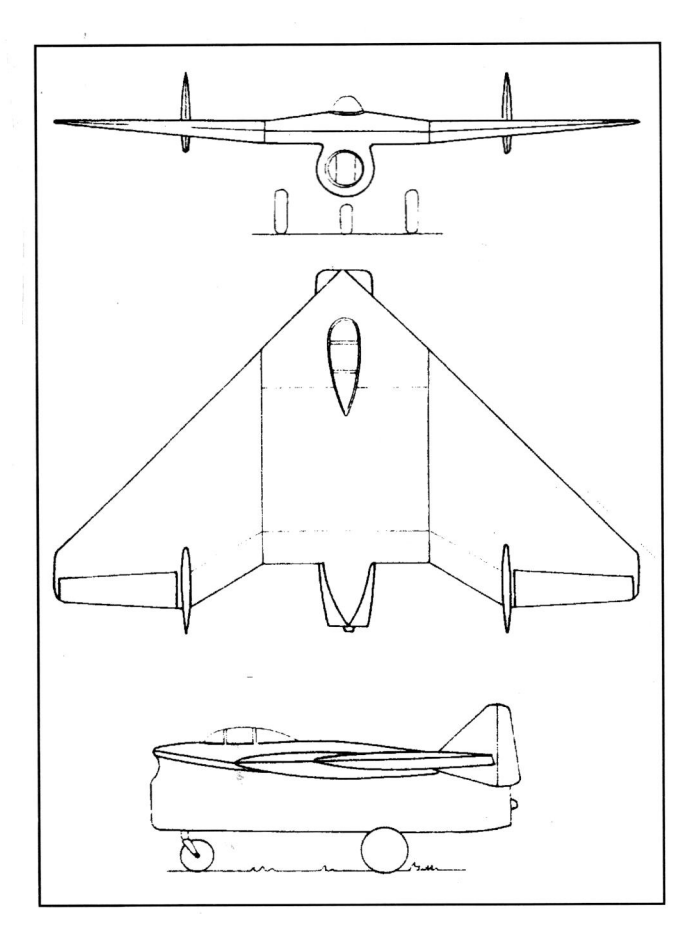

Ar E 581-5. Project design for a single-engined high-performance jet fighter (1944/45). (Meyer/Schick).

Chapter 20
Collapse And Liquidation

In early 1945, as development of turbine-powered night fighters and fighter bombers entered the decisive stages at Arado, the first indications of a breakup were already perceptible. Although there were broad-ranging projects still in the planning stages and the company had even been presented with a very favorable credit for over a million marks from the Bank Für Handel und Verkehr in Chemnitz as late as January 12th, 1945, the collapse of the economic infrastructure was beginning to have an ever-increasing crippling effect on Arado's development and production programs.

The British had learned from deserters that the Ar 234's production was still proceeding apace as late as the beginning of 1945, with ongoing work carried out in the assembly shops at Alt-Lönnewitz under the command of Oberst Modrow.[138] The facilities in the eastern regions were the first to be reinforced against a ground assault, followed in March by those in the west. Roughly 500 men under the command of an SS unit armed with 2,000 Panzerfaust weapons and a railway demolition team, responsible for laying mines, were put on readiness alert. A wide variety of over 200 aircraft were stationed in the surrounding woods for front-line operations in the Breslau sector. Hangar I held the Me 262s and Ar 234 Bs of III/KG 1; in Hangar II and III were a few He 111s of KG 53 and an Ar 234 A scheduled for breakdown. In Hangar IV the firm of Altan GmbH, a subsidiary of Arado, carried out the assembly of Gotha glider transports. Hangars V and VI could be entered only with a special pass; there Altan produced four to five Ar 234 B variants per week, parts for which were delivered regularly until February 1945. After approximately 200 had been built, production was switched over to the Ar 234 C. Material deliveries, however, became increasingly more sporadic. At the end of March there were six to eight finished Ar 234 Cs in Hangar V. Of an additional six aircraft, which received their final outfitting in Hangar VI, four had been factory test-flown by the end of March 1945.

On the instructions of Walter Blume, the design department and drawing office were moved west from Silesia from February to March in the face of the Soviet advance. It was only with the support of the RLM that Hans Rebeski was able to prevent his co-workers from being inducted into the Volkssturm as ordered by the gauleiter of Silesia. After temporarily locating in Brandenburg, Rebeski continued the drawing office's work with 200 personnel under extremely difficult conditions in a hangar of a Luftwaffe unit in Dedelstorf/Lüneburger Heide. The design office under Wilhelm van Nes was provisionally lodged in the conference room of a public house in nearby Hankelsbüttel, where the nearby airfield of Wesendorf was available for flight testing. However, even this area was overrun by the enemy at the beginning of May 1945. In Wesendorf the Allies captured the twin-engine Ar 234 V 12 prototype, the Ar 234 V 16 with its new crescent-shaped wings and the Ar 234 V 20 prototype. These aircraft had been severely damaged in a bombing raid on 4 April 1945. A fully operational Me 262 was also captured.

A hangar of the Arado Flugzeugwerke in Lönnewitz today, still preserved in its original condition.

On 16 May 1945 the American Captain Anthony F. Dernbach compiled a secret report for the US Army Air Force in which he reported the confiscation of photos, files and film on takeoff rockets, takeoff trollies, landing skids and twin-pod engines for the Ar 234, all of which were in need of urgent evaluation.

Goebbels was deeply shocked when he learned of the destruction of 100 Me 262s in an air attack on Easter Monday, but still held onto the hope that a change could be made through organizational reform: "One can imagine what effect this has on the worker who struggles night and day to do his part in sweeping the German skies clear of the enemy. The Luftwaffe isn't even capable of establishing the most basic of prerequisites. This can't be changed by an overhaul of the organization, but through a fundamental reform of the head and members."[139]

By that point in time there was already a clear manifestation of a breakup within the leadership structure of the Arado company. On 6 April Alois Cejka and Carl Hennig were still carrying out negotiations from the RLM's dispersed administration center in Dessau for the purpose of taking over old He 177 and Fw 190 components from warehouse stock. But Walter Blume, despite earlier slogans of holding out to the end, had already headed west. As chance would have it, Hans Rebeski met up with him a week after Easter while on a business trip from Dedelstorf to Brandenburg. Together with his wife, Blume had set out by car in the opposite direction with the destination of Wennigsen near Hannover, where the main development branch was ostensibly to have been set up.

At approximately the same time, Goebbels was writing in his journal: "It has been revealed in this critical situation that many old Party members who had succeeded in attaining the highest posts after the seizure of power, were nothing more than petty bourgeoisie, who abused their given authority in good times and showed themselves to be unworthy when confronted with the great test of their worth."[140]

In the war's closing days an Ar 96 carried out one final, rather remarkable mission. At the controls was Ritter von Greim, whom Hitler had appointed in Göring's place as the new Oberbefehlshaber der Luftwaffe. Accompanied by pilot Hanna Reitsch, Greim, under the most dramatic circumstances, succeeded in a final meeting with Hitler inside the besieged city of Berlin.

At the same time, the firm's management at the Brandenburg branch directed that all construction and design documents be burned in bomb craters as the Soviet troops drew closer. Although remnants of the hurriedly torched records were discovered, the Russians paid them scant attention. On the other hand, the aircraft and manufacturing equipment which they found there were soon dismantled and carted off. Once the final gutting of Brandenburg facilities by the firm of Ibag had taken place and the sales proceeds had been transferred over to the Soviets, only the design buildings, the press works and the heating chamber remained behind. Today the Zahnradfabrik ZF Brandenburg GmbH sprocket manufacturing plant is located on the company's former site. Severely damaged, the facilities in Rathenow and Neuendorf were occupied by the Soviets until 1991. Circa 45 buildings, including four large hangars, have survived. Warnemünde was completely torn down, so that there is little to remind one of the former owners on today's site of the Kvaerner-Warnow-Werft. For the most part, the Babelsberg buildings were destroyed by air raids in April of 1945.[141] Under the Soviet military administration's order no. 124 S the facilities were seized and placed in the care of the city, which signed leases with the Matras-Maschinen- und Transportgerätebaug GmbH and other companies. In Wittenberg the buildings were used to house those returning to their homeland and resettled persons and, from 1947 until they pulled out in 1992, as Soviet tank and infantry barracks. The administration building, community center, cafeteria and a few apartments have survived. The facilities in Anklam, also severely damaged in bombing raids, were ordered pulled down by the Russian district commander and used for rebuilding the local sugar factory. The work site at Alt-Lönnewitz, which for the most part escaped unscathed, was vacated by the Soviets as late as 1993 and handed over for other uses. The hangar in Dedelstorf which had formerly housed the design bureau is now used by an armored tank unit of the Bundeswehr.

On October 24th 1945, in the presence of a notary, one of the last shareholder's meetings took place in the conference room of the Bank der Deutschen Luftfahrt Aktiengesellschaft, during which Ernst Runge and Artur Müller acted on behalf of the bank and Felix Wagenführ participated as the sole remaining private stockholder. Included in the order of business was the recall of executive directors Rudolf Heinemann and Walter Blume, whose place of residence was specifically noted as being unknown. Martin Blancke, a long-time senior engineer with Arado, was confirmed as the interim executive director. He had been installed as the commissioned director by the Soviets on 7 May 1945 and appointed by a court decision on 13 August as the senior director. He planned on a resumption of operations, but a work council had called for his removal from office as early as 7 August. The Potsdam Oberbürgermeister bowed to this decision and permitted the business documents and accounts of the Arado Flugzeugwerke to be seized from the local Provinzialbank. Blancke rejected the decision of the council and, in an appeal to the Berlin Oberbürgermeister, initially continued his activities as a representative of the Luftfahrtbank. In accordance with a decree from the Brandenburg government on 9 September 1949, however, he was eventually replaced by two members of the work council, who were named as "responsible parties for the former Arado armament operation." A trust company was contracted for wrapping up financial matters and filed its report in 1948. According to the report, there were bank credits in the amount of 61 million RM with the Bank der Deutschen Luftfahrt in Berlin and a branch of the Dresdner Bank in Potsdam. These bank debts were part of a considerable group of claims against

Prof. W. Blume in Duisburg at the end of the war.

the RLM. The claims of the now-closed banks were transferred to the Landeskreditbank Brandenburg in Potsdam and the assets, amounting to four million marks, were siphoned off by the Soviets. The remaining business documentation was taken over by the Deutsche Zentralfinanzverwaltung.

The former works of the Arado Flugzeugwerke, located exclusively within the Soviet zone of occupation, were turned over into nationally-owned property.

Prof. Walter Blume became executive director of the Forschungsgesellschaft Blechverarbeitung in 1948, followed by that of the Aluminium-Zentrale in Düsseldorf. In 1953 he founded the Ingenieurbüro für Leichtbau und Strümungstechnik in Duisburg-Ruhrort, which spawned the Leichtbau- und Flugtechnik GmbH; under his management the production of airplanes would be reborn. On 21 April 1953 the Arado Flugzeugwerke was formally dissolved as a company. The Industriebeteiligungsgesellschaft m.b.H. in Bonn was named as its liquidator. On 22 June 1953 the business center was moved from Potsdam to Bonn following a new shareholder's agreement and there entered into the commerce registry. According to press reports, this measure was not taken in order to resume aircraft production, but so "that the legal prerequisites for dissolving the company might be established."

Nevertheless, in volume 6/1955 of the magazine 'Flugwelt' there was the impression that the tradition of the Arado Flugzeugwerke would continue on, for Professor W. Blume, as "chief designer and general director of Arado" ... currently maintained "an engineering office in the Tausendfensterhaus in Duisburg." In actual fact, at the time Blume was receiving support from former Arado engineers in the design of the Bl 500 sport and touring plane. Johannes Spross became responsible for project planning, Wilhelm van Nes for aerodynamics and design, Oskar Liebing for statistics. Hans Rebeski directed the actual construction program. The Bl 500 was an improved four-seat version of the 1938 Ar 79 sport plane, which was built in small numbers in Bremen by the successor company to the Focke-Wulf operations as the Bl 502 and 503 from 1955 to 1958. Blume was involved in the development of the Italian Piaggio P-149 and had business dealings with the Weser Flugzeugbau, Hamburger Flugzeugbau and the French Nord Aviation company in connection with the manufacture of the C 160 Transall. He was vice chairman of the Wissenschaftliche Gesellschaft für Luft- und Raumfahrt (WGLR) and director of the Technischer Ausschuss in the BDLI.

By the time of his death, on May 27th 1964, there was no further talk of resurrecting the Arado Flugzeugwerke, which had finally and irrevocably been liquidated in 1961.

Hans Rebeski, the former chief engineer of the Arado-Werke, in 1994. The site of the former Arado yards is in the background. Rebeski began working for Arado in 1928, became foreman in 1930, team leader in 1935 and was promoted to director of the design bureau in 1940. After the war, he was involved with MBB in the Hamburger Flugzeugbau with the design of the Transall C-160 and Airbus A-300.

Notes

Part I: The Creative Years

Chapter 1:
1. Business headquarters in Berlin, Potsdamerstrasse 103a

Chapter 2:
1. Wanner Zeitung, 28 May 1912.
2. Argentine Daily News, 7 January 1913
3. Berliner Vossische Zeitung, 15 Sep 1913
4. Berliner Lokalanzeiger, 18 Sep 1913
5. In spite of his own claims, Fokker was not heavily involved in the invention, nor was it exclusively derived from a patent by the engineer Franz Schneider. See J.A. Kranzhoff: Flugzeuge, die Geschichte machten. Fokker DR I. Stuttgart 1994
6. Even as late as 1925 Schneider unsuccessfully, although not without some justification, sued Fokker for 600,000 marks for patent violation. Lübbe was more attuned to Fokker's business practices and, according to Fokker's flight instructor Mario Scherff, the only one whom Fokker "couldn't beat down financially."
7. In May of 1924 Curt Heber, Lübbe's former assistant at Fokker, disguised himself as a merchant and acquired Napier Lion engines from the British company.
8. German-Russian cooperation was made possible by the Treaty of Rapallo, signed on 16 April 1922. In February 1923 Kurt Student was a member of the first negotiating commission.

Chapter 3:
1. In the time period from 1 April 1926 to the end of the year only 90 airplanes were produced by the 16 aircraft companies then in existence. (German aircraft statistics of 1926, published by the Reichsverkehrsministerium, Berlin 1928, pg.6 f).
2. S = Schulzwecken, training purposes
3. C = suitable for C-class pilot's license training.
4. The covername stood for "Heimat Tagjäger" (Homeland Dayfighter).
5. SD = Schulflugzeug in Doppeldeckerbauweise, biplane trainer
6. IFW 5/6, 1928, p. 134
7. Rechlin Letters, 3rd issue, Letter No. 24, p. 14.
8. S = See-Ausführung, naval version

Chapter 4:
1. Previously, the Reichspost had not approved mail flights to be made with a "grade" aircraft, but later authorized Euler to make the flight.
2. On 3 January 1928 Lindbergh was introduced to his future wife, the daughter of Ambassador Morrow, through Lübbe's brother-in-law Joseph Gadbury, a passionate flyer and staff member of the American embassy in Mexico.
3. Moedebeck/Taschenbuch für Flugtechniker und Luftschiffer. Berlin 1923, p.607.
4. Luft Hansa Nachrichten, Special Number 2, 10 Oct 1929, p.4.
5. Deutscher Flugbetrieb, in: Ikarus, volume 8, 1927, p.57.
6. This route was first conquered in several stages by Gustav Basser and a passenger in July 1914 in a Rumpler plane.
7. Luft Hansa Nachrichten 10 Oct 1929.
8. Eichentopf was himself killed in a later airplane crash.
9. E. Milch, Diary from 19 Dec 1947. In 1945 the future Generalfeldmarschall Milch was required to answer to the Allies at the Nuremberg Military Tribunal. Freiherr von Gablenz was killed on 21 August 1941 in an airplane crash over the Chiemsee.
10. Report from the DVS Braunschweig pilot Stutz, dated 4 August 1930, on the Arado L IIa D-1873.
11. Part of an advertisement in 'Luftwacht', Volume 1, January 1931. The normal price for a type L II was 18,500 marks.

Chapter 5:
1. Ottilie Lübbe, 14 December 1931.
2. Ottilie Lübbe, 14 December 1931.
3. From an American source: George M. Chinn: The Machine Gun. Washington 1955, Volume I, p. 548
4. One of the first 2 cm aircraft cannons from Becker was tested around 1917 in a Hansa Brandenburg seaplane built by Heinkel. Eventually, in 1934 the small-caliber fixed MG 17 developed by Rheinmetall was finally used; after being tested in Travemünde by Dipl.-Ing. Mix was declared ready for acquisition.
5. Chinn, Volume IV, p. 529
6. Raab's patent contracts with an American partner company, in which a member of the board of directors was the father-in-law of Lübbe's friend Charles Lindbergh, was annulled — after Raab's reputation had been undermined through German influence.
7. Report by Obersting. Mix and Cornelius. Rechlin letters, 4th issue, 1982, 5.4. The term "Lübke" is an error. Research into Lübbe's weapons patent was carried out in vain both by Rheinmetall and Ingenieur Heinz Simon, who from 1933 was responsible for weapons evaluation. According to unconfirmed sources Lübbe eventuall sold his patent to the Swiss firm of Oerlikon.

Chapter 6:
1. Dokumente und Dokumentarphotos zur Geschichte der deutschen Luftwaffe, published by Karl-Heinz Völker, Stuttgart 1968, pp. 60-61, 65.
2. According to Junkers documents dated 15 September 1934 the price of the first license-built machine was 87,000 RM and 57,000 RM beginning with the third aircraft.
3. D. Woodman: Hitlers Luftflotte startbereit, Paris 1935, pp.79-80. The first Jagdgeschwader (fighter wing) of the Luftwaffe was JG 132 'Richthofen', established on 1 April 1932 under Ritter von Greim.

Chapter 7:
1. With reference to a balance correction from 1 Jan 96 the Contocorrent debt of 349,921 RM was reduced by a 120,000 loan guaranteed by Lübbe. Because of apparent tax evasion a company tax was called for.
2. C.-A. v. Schoenebeck: Unpublished Memoirs. The claim that the Ar 65 fighter designed by W. Rethel was 'specially developed' by him is unfounded.
3. According to his own claims, Von Schoenebeck's monthly income at Arado was significantly higher than an officer's wages.
4. A 1 Nr. 769/63.
5. Heinkel was awarded 10,957,338 RM, Dornier 9,392,000 RM, BMW 7,744,3000 RM, Junkers 6,087,393 RM, Si

emens 6,042,500 RM. Lesser sums were distributed to Focke-Wulf, Argus, Klemm, BFW, Daimler and Hirth.
6. Two further contract alterations took place on 29 Mar 1933 and 21 Dec 1933.
7. Potsdam-Babelsberg, Kaiser-Wilhelm-Strasse 1-3.
8. 1936: 112,000 square meters. 1937: 196,000 square meters. 1942 250,000 square meters.

Chapter 8:
1. Repair work done by the Klemm-Flugzeugwerke in 1940 and 1941.
2. JG 134, 132 and 26.
3. Other well-known test pilots and instructors at the time were Eduard Neumann (approx. 80 flights with the Ar 66 at DVS Cottbus in 1934, between 1935 and 1938 tested the Ar 64, 65 and 68 at JG 2 Jüterbog, JG 26 Düsseldorf and at DVS Schleissheim) and Rudolf Stark (with the exception of the Ar 69 and 77, all other types in the period from 1933 to 1935).

Chapter 9:
1. Stressed-skin construction with longitudinal formers. Proposal of W. Rethel submitted to the Lilienthal-Gesellschaft für Luftfahrtforschung on 16 Sep 1937 in Rostock.
2. The V-2 was also retro-fitted with the Jumo engine.
3. R. Platz to A.R. Weyl on 20 March 1955. Platz left Fokker in the 1920s because he couldn't convince him to change from a composite construction method, and later went on to supervise design at Dornier and MIAG.
4. Heinkel wondered about the "fixed fascination with biplanes" which the Technisches Amt continued to have as late as 1934 and by this time considered the design to be "scrap metal" (Stürmisches Leben. Stuttgart 1953, pp.275 and 277)
5. Letter to the author dated 4 July 1993.
6. H.M. Mason: Die Luftwaffe, Vienna/Berlin 1976, p.188.

Part II — New Role as a Reich-Owned Company

Chapter 10:
1. Comparative figures for Arado/Warnemünde: 1,375. By 1 April 1938 the estimated number of employees available for mobilization purposes was 5,600 (Brandenburg) and 2,475 (Warnemünde).
2. Dorothy Woodman, loc. cit., pp.14-15.
3. Dokumente und dokumentarfotos zur Geschichte der deutschen Luftwaffe. Published by K. H. Völker, Stuttgart 1968, p.188
4. Henschel planned the takeover of the nationalized Junkers Werke, Fieseler took over the dissolved Raab-Katzensteinwerke, and Siebel assumed control of portions of the Klemm Werke.
5. The Lübbe family's position can be ascertained from an essay test taken by daughter Erika on 7 May 1935, in which she "rejected all communist, socialist and other campaign fronts who no longer heed God's word, but seek to further their aims using the meanest and lowest methods."
6. Margrit Lübbe, 5 July 1948.
7. Margrit Lübbe, 22 Sep 1986.

8. The Luftfahrtkontor, on behalf of the RLM, carried out fiduciary functions regarding administration of finances and shares.
9. Die Arado Flugzeugwerke. BA Freiburg, Lw 103.
10. Secret memorandum from Franz Velder, attorney-at-law, to the Finanzamt Teltow regarding Arado's financial state of affairs, dated 28 Sep 1939.
11. Tschersich was formerly a department manager with Junkers.
12. The paragraph regulated the decision authority of the advisory board.
13. According to the memorandum of association from 25 June 1936, paragraph 10, sub-paragraph 4, every 1,000 RM of the face value of a person's holdings guaranteed a vote.
14. Wagenführ's salary as managing director was 72,000 RM in 1941, Heinemann's was 84,000 RM, Blume's was 84,000 RM with an additional 57,991 RM for a one percent share of license contracts and a forty percent share of patent valuations from 1933 to 1943.

Chapter 11:
1. Report of the deutsche Revisions- und Treuhandgesellschaft from 1937, in which the yearly results for 1934 to 1936 were also approved after the fact.
2. Standard armament consisted of a fixed, forward-firing machine gun and a traversible rear-firing gun.
3. Stationed on the Tirpitz, Bismarck and Prinz Eugen, as well as on the auxiliary cruisers Orion, Thor, Komet, Kormoran, Michel, Stier and Pinguin.
4. This includes service with the 161st Coastal Patrol Wing of the Bulgarian air force and with the 101st and 102nd Coastal Patrol Wing of the Romanian air force.
5. Figures taken from Werner Baumbach's book: Zu spät. Aufstieg und Untergang der deutschen Luftwaffe. München 1949. Other sources estimate the total production to have been either 493 or 526 aircraft.
6. Mission of 1 Staffel/Küstenflieger 706 against the British submarine HMS Seal on 5 May 1940 (War correspondent Otto Paust, Sept. 1940).
7. LC Nr. 841/39 IVg.

Chapter 12:
1. Patent No. 674 564 Klasse 62b from 15 April 1939.
2. Report No. 12 of the Arado research group Weigmann TFo on the development of the new design Ar 96 tailplane (press sheet framework) from 12 April 1940.
3. Arado company study.
4. Contract amount including repair work for the Ar 66 was approximately two million RM for 1940.
5. Memorandum TB/20/III/44 from 20 March 1944 by Hans Rebeski.

Chapter 13:
1. Company brochure
2. Rudolf Jenett, 2 June 1993.
3. Richard Perlia, Aerokurier, No.3, 1992, p.58.
4. Flight performance, range and capacity corresponded to those of the significantly higher powered Siemens ATG sportplane of 1964.
5. VDI Issue No. 13 from 1 April 1939, p.375.
6. Company advertising. The Ar 79 costed around 18,000 RM with a rebate of 5,000 RM from the Reichsluftfahrtministerium, less than the 20,000 RM

Cabriolet DB-380 A driven by H. Lübbe from 1934 on.
7. Class C, Category 3.
8. Internal company report from 1938.
9. Later speculation that the flight had military spying undertones could not be suppressed.

Chapter 14:
1. From 1942 on known as Bank der Deutschen Luftfahrt.
2. W. Blume's motion at the advisory council board meeting on 22 June 1939.
3. Report from the Deutsche Revisions- und Treuhandgesellschaft for 1939, p.33
4. Report from the Deutsche Revisions- und Treuhandgesellschaft for 1940.
5. W. Blume was director of the 'Technische Entwicklung' (TE, or Technical Development), 'Hauptverwaltung Entwicklung'(HE, or Central Administration of Development) and 'Hauptverwaltung Betrieb' (HB, or Central Administration of Operations) departments.
6. The maximum allowable profit permitted by the RLM was nine percent of the sales cost.
7. Report for fiscal year 1939. Sixty workers had been killed in accidents, four died while in military service. In 1941 Oberregierungsrat Heinrich Wiegandt, a member of the advisory council, was also killed in combat.
8. Advisory board minutes from 9 December 1943.
9. Included among the prominent figures buried here are aviation pioneers E. Rumpler and A. Rohrbach.
10. Das Buch der deutschen Luftgeschichte, Berlin 1936, vol.2, p.58. Hanns Baudisch, public relations officer of the NSFK -Standarte 40, forced Supf to in 1941 to suppress other names for political reasons as well.
11. Luftmacht Deutschland, Essen 1939, p.164.
12. Zuerl called upon the Deutsches Museum to "completely" eradicate the name of "the Jew Edmund Rumpler."
13. Edward Homze to the author, 7 April 1993. See also: Arming the Luftwaffe, University of Nebraska Press, 1976, p.192.

Chapter 15:
1. See: K. Bornemann: Eine neuartige bewegliche Waffenanlage. Yearbook of the Deutsche Akademie für Luftfahrtforschung II. Berlin 1941/42.
2. Memorandum from Arado TAe (aerodynamic branch of the design office under the direction of Dipl.-Ing. Wilhelm Blass), dated 5 August 1941.
3. Letter from the Arado Flugzeugwerke to the Versuchsstelle für Höhenflüge in Oranienburg, dated 21 September 1942.
4. David Irving: Die Tragödie der Deutschen Luftwaffe, Frankfurt 1970, p.316.
5. Irving, p.315.
6. Advisory board meeting from 13 November 1940.
7. G. Weyert in written correspondence with W. Blume, 12 August 1942.
8. Deadline overview for the RLM prepared by Wilhelm Blass, 29 September 1942.
9. GL meeting on the matter of the high-speed bomber, 19 July 1943.
10. Hans Rebeski, director of the Arado Werke's design bureau.
11. The 2,020 hp DB 614 was never built.

Chapter 16:
1. The Allies weren't able to develop an equivalent transport type until after the war, designing the Fairchild C-82. This aircraft flew missions during the Berlin Airlift.
2. Extending and pivoting the flaps was a method patented by Arado under patent no. 738 636, from 21 March 1940. Although a boundary layer blower system had already been tested and was included in a design description of the Ar 232 A and B, a shortage of hydrogen peroxide prevented its use in place of the Fowler flaps.
3. See Günther W. Gellermann: Moskau ruft Heeresgruppe Mitte. Coblenz 1988, p.86 ff., Also: Der Spiegel, No.30 1967, p.42 ff.
4. Gellermann, p.112 ff.
5. Probably G6+YY and G6+XY.

Part III — Bearers of Hope in the War's Last Phase

Chapter 17:
1. Roluf Lucht, chief engineer of the Technisches Amt, took over from Theodor Croneiss as managing director of Messerschmitt near the end of the war.
2. Speer on 1 August 1944. In: Die technische Luftrüstung und Luftwaffenindustrie. BA Freiburg, Lw 103, No.25b, p.36.
3. Arado-Bote, Year 8, vol.1-2, 1944.
4. Production simplification included reducing the number of rivets in building a twin-engined aircraft, which could run to 100,000 in 23 variations and require 13 different types of rivet guns.
5. One of the first employee songs from 1940 was composed for ceremonious occasions, while the second — performed for the first time by an choir of apprentice workers in Brandenburg — was to instill "camaraderie and togetherness."
6. Codename 'Sagos'.

Chapter 18:
1. Autopilot system was a Patin LKS 7D-15, first installed on prototype Ar 234 V 11.
2. First used on prototype Ar 234 V 10.
3. A pressure accumulator, designed by the firm of Dräger, wasn't able to be evaluated before the war's end.
4. The aircraft had a conventional engine both fore and aft.
5. These values corresponded to that of the standard Bf 110 Zerstörer. (As a comparison, the He 11, Ar 196 and Ar 96 had values of 350, 700 and 900 hours, respectively.)
6. Conversion training later also took place in Prague and at the instrument flying school in Copenhagen.
7. An initial listing of Allied models was provided by "Flight" magazine on 10 May 1945.
8. There are no Arado jet-powered aircraft in German museums.
9. The engine control's tempermental nature could only be offset with the use of the Jumo regulator.
10. Prototype Ar 234 V 13, PH+SU (Wk.Nr. 130 023), became the third aircraft to be fitted with four BMW 003 A-0 powerplants in paired nacelles.
11. J. Goebbels: Tagebücher 1945. Hamburg 1977, p.345.

Chapter 19:
1. V 16, which was to have been the prototype for the Ar 234 F, was blown up in Wesendorf to prevent it from falling into the hands of the advancing Soviet forces.

Chapter 20:
1. Allied secret report A.T.I. (K) and U.S. Air Interrogation from 15 April 1945.
2. J. Goebbels: Tagebücher 1945. Die letzten Aufzeichnungen. Hamburg 1977, p.387.
3. W. von Oven: Finale Furioso. Mit Goebbels bis zum Ende. Tübingen 1974, p.623.
4. Those north of the Friedrich Engels Strasse (formerly Kaiser Wilhelm Strasse) and south of the Schlaatzweg.

Appendices

1. Technical Data
2. Arado Projects
3. Personnel of the Arado Werke
4. Table of Surviving Arado Aircraft
5. Bibliography
6. Photo Credits
7. The Author

Arado Aircraft from 1925 to 1945
Technical Data

Model (year)	Type	Engine/Performance	Length(m)	Height(m)	Wing-span(m)	Wing Area(m²)	Empty Weight(kg)	Takeoff Weight(kg)	Vmax(km/h)	Climb Rate(min/m)	Ceiling(m)	Range(km)
S I (1925)	Trainer	Bristol Lucifer/ 120 hp	7.44	2.85	11.50	16.5	615	915	140	8/1000	4000	-
SC I (1926)	Trainer	BMW IV/230 hp	8.70	3.10	12.82	29.4	1000	1500	183	4.5/1000-2000	5200	-
SC II (1927)	Trainer	BMW Va/360 hp	8.96	-	13.20	-	1275	1985	185	-	-	-
SC III (1928)	Trainer	Siemens Sh 12/96 hp	7.50	2.75	11.50	27.3	600	825	128	-	3700	-
SD I (1928)	Fighter	Bristol Jupiter/ 425 hp	6.75	3.20	8.40	16.7	850	1230	275	1.7/1000	8000	-
SD II (1929)	Fighter	Siemens Jupiter/ 530 hp	7.40	3.20	9.90	22.9	1445	1770	238	-	7000	-
SSD I (1929)	Fighter	BMW VI/650 hp	10.00	3.50	10.00	30.9	1627	2030	280	-	6800	-
W II (1929)	Trainer	2 Siemens Sh 12/2x96 hp	12.55	3.20	17.40	53.8	1680	2000	145	16/1000	2000	-
SD III (1929)	Fighter	Siemens Jupiter/ 490 hp	7.75	-	9.90	-	-	-	225	-	-	-
V I (1929)	Mail plane	P&W Hornet/ 500 hp	12.00	3.15	18.00	47.2	1350	2520	210	22.5/4000	4000	2000
L I (1929)	Sport plane	Salmson AD 9/40 hp	6.00	-	10.00	-	275	500	140	-	-	-
L II (1929)	Sport plane	Argus As 8a/ 95 hp	6.72	2.28	10.50	16.0	405	670	165	-	-	-
L II A (1930)	Sport plane	Argus As 8a/ 95 hp	6.72	2.28	11.00	17.0	460	780	168	7.8/1000	2000	700
64 B (1931)	Fighter	Siemens Jupiter/ 530 hp	-	-	-	-	-	-	250	-	-	-
65 F (1932)	Fighter	BMW VI U/ 750 hp	8.40	340	11.20	30	1490	1865	282	8.4/4000	7350	420
66 C (1933)	Trainer	Argus As 10c-2/240 hp	8.30	2.93	10.00	29.6	905	1330	210	4.1/1000	4500	716
67 A (1933)	Fighter	RR Kestrel VI/ 600 hp	7.90	3.10	9.68	25.1	1270	1660	340	-	9300	-
69 B (1934)	Trainer	Bramo Sh14 A/ 150 hp	7.22	2.75	9.00	20.7	540	840	184	-	5600	560
76 A1 (1934)	Trainer	Argus As 10C/ 240 hp	7.20	2.55	9.50	13.3	750	1070	267	-	6400	470
77 A (1935)	Trainer	2 Argus As 10C/ 2x240 hp	12.50	3.20	19.20	50.5	1930	2940	240	-	5000	720
68 E1 (1935)	Fighter	Jumo 210 Ea /690 hp	9.50	3.30	11.00	27.31	600	2200	335	10/6000	8100	500
80 V2 (1935)	Fighter	Jumo 210 C/ 610 hp	10.10	2.75	11.80	21.0	1645	2100	410	9.5/6000	10000	600
81 V3 (1935)	Dive Bomber	Jumo 210 C/ 648 hp	11.65	3.60	11.20	35.6	2070	3198	345	11/4000	7700	790
95 A-0 (1936)	Multi-role	BMW 132 Dc/ 880 hp	11.80	3.20	12.50	45.4	2540	3565	310	15.5/6000	7100	1100
197 V3 (1937)	Bomber	BMW 132 J/ 815 hp	9.20	3.60	11.00	27.8	1800	2425	370	-	9200	-
195 V3 (1937)	Multi-role	BMW 132 K/ 960 hp	10.50	3.60	12.50	46.0	2460	4130	290	-	6000	650
79 A (1937)	Sport plane	Hirth HM 504 A/105 hp	7.60	2.10	10.00	14.0	526	1120	230	-	4500	1025
198 V1 (1938)	Tac. Recon.	BMW 323 A/ 900 hp	11.80	4.60	14.90	35.2	2180	3114	317	-	7400	960
199 V3 (1939)	Trainer	Argus As 410C/ 450 hp	10.97	4.36	12.70	30.4	1676	2060	260	-	6500	740
96 B-2 (1940)	Trainer	Argus As 410A/ 460 hp	9.13	2.64	11.00	17.1	1295	1700	340	6.8/3000	7100	1100
231 V1 (1940)	Tac. Recon.	Hirth HM 501a/ 160 hp	7.82	3.12	10.18	15.2	833	1050	170	6/1000	3000	500
196 A-3 (1941)	Tac. Recon	BMW 132 K/ 960 hp	10.96	4.45	12.44	28.3	2335	3303	320	-	7000	800
232 A-0 (1941)	Transport	2 BMW 801 A-1/2x1560 hp	23.50	6.60	32.00	135.0	11235	18500	296	2.9/1000	7600	1500
232 B-0 (1942)	Tran-4 sport	BMW 323 P/ 4x1000 hp	23.50	6.60	33.50	142.5	12780	2000	308	2.9/1000	8000	1340
240 A-0 (1942)	Str. 2 Recon.	DB 601 E/ 2x1175 ph	12.81	3.95	14.33	31.3	6350	9980	668	-	10200	2200
440 A-0 (1942)	Str. 2 Recon.	DB 603 G/ 2x2000 hp	14.39	3.97	16.60	35.0	9370	12540	752	-	9600	2680
234 A (1943)	Str. Recon.	2 Jumo 004/ 2x860 kp	12.60	4.42	14.20	26.4	4800	7900	760	16/8000	1100	2000
234 B (1944)	High-spdBmr.	2 Jumo 004/ 2x860 kp	12.60	4.42	14.20	26.4	4650	9410	745	-	9500	1560
396 A-1 (1944)	Trainer	Argus As 411 T/ 600 hp	9.29	3.72	11.00	18.3	1440	2060	354	-	8000	790
234 C-3 (1945)	Str. Recon.	4 BMW 003A/ 4x800 kp	12.60	4.42	14.20	26.4	5850	11550	890	10/8000	12200	1440

Arado Projects[142]

233	flying boat (1940)
234	C with Fi 103 piggyback
234	C with Fi 103 towed
234	C with two Vf L 11 'Schneewitchen' glide torpedoes
234	V 16 with swept wings
234	V 26 with laminar-flow wings (standard configuration)
234	V 30 with laminar-flow wings (swept configuration)
234	radar platform
E 300	anti-submarine (1938)
E 310	multi-role carrier aircraft
334	follow-on development of 234
340	twin-engined bomber with 2x Jumo 222 or DB 604, from E 500
E 370	recon with multi-wheel landing gear, became 234 (1940)
E 371	Ar 234 with landing gear
E 375	high-speed bomber, 2x Jumo 012
E 377	glide bomb for Mistel project, carried beneath Ar 234 C (1944)
E 380	Ar 196 follow-on development with folding wings
E 381	rocket-powered miniature fighter, carried beneath 234 C-3 (1944)
E 385	high-speed bomber, 2x BMW P 3303 (Oct 1942)
E 390	commercial liner with pressurized cabin, 4x Jumo 208 (1940)
E 395	multi-role aircraft(bomber, recon), 2x He S 011 (Jan 1944)
E 396	trainer
E 401	float version of Ar 232
E 430	flying boat (1940)
432	follow-on development of 232
E 433	Ar 232 of composite construction
E 440	high-speed bomber (1942)
441	large-capacity transport, 4x BMW 801
E 470	large-capacity transport (1941)
E 480	piston-jet engine combination fighter. Was to become Ar 655 (Dec 1944)
E 490	combination fighter with DB 609
E 500	twin-boom attack fighter (1936)
E 530	twin fuselage high-speed bomber and long-range fighter
E 530	twin fuselage long-range fighter. 2x DB 603G
532	four-engined transport
E 555	long range bomber. 14 studies in both flying wing and standard layout. 2x He S 011, 2x BMW 018, 3x BMW 018, 4x Jumo 012
E 560	four-jet high-speed bomber with swept wings
E 561	heavy twin-engine attack fighter with extension shafts (1937/38)
E 580	people's fighter of composite materials, 1x BMW 003 (1944)
E 581	single-seat flying wing fighter, 1x He S 011 (1944/45)
E 583	night fighter, probable classification of Ar I and II
E 625	became Ar 240
632	four-engined transport aircraft
E 651	heavy attack fighter (1937/38)
	Ar I flying wing night fighter, 2x He S 011
	Ar II swept-wing high-speed bomber/night fighter fm. Ar 234
TEW	16/43-13 rocket fighter, swept low-wing design (1943)
TEW	16/43-15 combination fighter with turbine and rocket engines, swept-wing (1943)
TEW	16/43-19 high speed bomber, attack fighter, recon, night and all-weather fighter, twin-jet swept mid-wing design (1943)
TEW	16/43-23 twin-jet fighter, swept shoulder-wing design from Ar 234 (1943)[143]

Personnel of the Arado Werke

Affeldt, Otto. Engineer and pilot. Previously with Fokker. 1931-1932 director of the technical operations bureau in Warnemünde. Responsible for calculations, work planning and machine construction.

Batholomäus: Test pilot at the Erprobungsstelle Travemünde, occasionally worked at Warnemünde.

Beckmann, Heinrich. Dipl.-Ing.[144], director of development group.

Blancke, Martin. O.-Ing.

Blass, Wilhelm. Dipl.-Ing., TEA from 1932, later TAe-Fl, EFoF and director of operations in Sagos.

Blume, Walter. Dipl.-Ing., professor, defense economy manager, HT from 1932. HE 1935-1945. Business director 1938-1945.

Bornemann, Kurt. Dipl.-Ing., TWa from 1936.

Brumner, Paul. Dipl.-Ing. TEA.

Burger. E-BaL

Cejka, Alois. Ministerialdirektor im RLM, advisory board member from 1939 on.

Faehlmann. TE, transferred to Focke-Wulf in 1934.

Feld. TV

Förhing. Walter. Engineer, construction group components and controls in Warnemünde from 1932, director of TB 2 (design bureau) from 1935 on.

Frach Adolf. Pilot, EFof.

Friedewald, Hans. Drafting department. Transferred from Albatros.

Fröhlich, Josef. Dipl.-Ing., construction group flying surfaces from 1932.

Eheim, Günther. Pilot, EFof.

Göschl, Toni. O.-Ing, HTM-Bab (Materialverwaltung, or Materials Admin.)

Greiner. TP

Grunert. Engineer.

Haensel, Dr. Werner. Businessman, junior partner and business director 1925.

Heinemann, Rudolf. Dipl.-Ing., business director 1936-1945.

Hergesell, Dr. Wilhelm. Member of advisory board from 1936.

Höhnert, Helmuth. General director, advisory board member from 1936.

Hoffmann. Design group landing gear from 1932.

Hollmig. TS from 1938.

Hormel, Walter. Kpt.Lt.a.D., senior business partner 1925.

Hoyne, Egmont. TEA.

Hübner. TAe-Fl.

Janssen, Ubbo. Pilot, EFoF.

Jung, Dr. Senior civil servant with the RFM, advisory

Kunz. Pilot, EFoF.

Kürth. Aircraft builder, responsible for final assembly and test flights in Warnemünde up to circa 1933.

Lehmann, Walter. TEA

Libau: HBB

Liebing, Oskar. Dipl.-Ing. TAe-Fl, TV and KFo. From 1933 operations director and management ERoF in Sagos, EFoF management in Wesendorf from March 1945.

Liebscher. HBA

Lübbe, Heinrich. Engineer, senior business partner 1925-1936.

Lukert, Hans-Joachim. TEA.

Lutzweiler, Otto. TEA.

Mayer, Josef. Ministerialrat in RFM, advisory board member.

Meyer, Dr. Emil. Member of board of directors of the Dresdner Bank, advisory board member from 1936.

Meyer, Franz. Department manager for TE from 1932, from 1943 also with EFoF.

Oppermann. HBF-F

Prinz. TAF Landeshut.

Rebeski, Hans. O.-Ing., from 1929 foreman in Warnemünde, later with construction group components and controls, director of TB 1 (design bureau) from 1938, managing director of design bureau Dedelstorf from March 1945.

Reichel, Dr. Kurt. Dipl.-Ing., successor to F. Keidel as operations director in Warnemünde from 1932, later HB Babelsberg (production director, series production)

Reidenbach, Gottfried. Oberstingenieur RLM, advisory board member 1940-43.

Reinhardt, Walter. construction group fuselage, engine, control surfaces from 1932, director of TB 1 (design bureau) and TC (chief of construction) 1935-38.

Reishaus, Fritz. EAD (field liasion engineer)

Reitz. TEA.

Rethel, Walter. O.-Ing., company's first chief design engineer 1925-38, transferred to Messerschmitt.

Roehnert, Hellmuth. Chairman of Rheinmetall-Borsig A.G. in Berlin, vice-chairman of advisory board.

Rothstein. TAe-Fl, EFoF.

Rudorf, Fritz. Member of board of directors of the Bank der Deutschen Luftfahrt, advisory board member.

Rüter. First director of the technical bureau in Warnemünde.

Salchow. Jig/machinery construction.

Sartorius. TF

Scheu. TEA

Schrader. TTrie group director in Warnemünde

Selle. Pilot, TAe-F, EFoF.

Serno, Erich. Major a.D., authorized signatory, business director 1933-38.

Sieke. Director of Works in Warnemünde from 1926 to 1933, then employed by the Bachmann company in Ribnitz.

Sommermeier. TAe-Fl, EFoF.

Sperling, Hugo. TEA

Stange. Engineer.

Stelzer, Robert. Engineer, TE

Spross, Johannes. O.-Ing., HB (Planning and Production)

Steike. TC-As (assistant to chief of design)

Tops. O.-Ing. HB (Series Production)

Truschel, Julius. TEA

Tschersich, Günther. Gen.-Ing. with RLM, advisory board member 1936-43.

Uhlig. TTrie in TB 1.

van Nes, Wilhelm. Dipl.-Ing. Chief of design from 1937, EB, TE, TEA

Wagenführ, Felix. Oberst a.D., junior business partner 1926-1945. Business director 1926-43, advisory board member 1943-45.

Wagner. TEA.

Walland, Hans. TE

Walther, Dr. Senior civil servant with the RFM, advisory board member 1937-38.

Weigmann. TFo

Wenzel, Heinz. Dipl.-Ing., TS (Statics)

Wienstein, Dr. Gustav. Civil servant, advisory board member from 1936.

Wolter. TA group director

Zeunert, Fritz. TEA

Table of Surviving Arado Aircraft:

Type	Year/Code	Location
Ar 66 d	1936/-	Deutsches Museum, Germany
Ar 66 c	1937/-	Keski-Suomen Ilmailumuseo, Finland
Ar 66 c	-/-	Gardemoen Airfield, Norway
Ar 79 B	1941/D-ECUV	Deutsche Lufthansa Berlin-Endowment
Ar 96 B-1	-/PD+EJ	Museum f. hist. Wehrtechnik, Nuremburg
Ar 96 B	-/-	Vojenske Muzeum, Prague
Ar 196 A-3	1939/-	Bulgarian Museum of Aviation, Plovdiv
Ar 196 A-5	1944/GA+DX	NASM, Washington
Ar 196 A-5	1944/GA+DX	Naval Air Station, Willow Grove, USA
Ar 234 B-2	1944/F1+GS	NASM, Washington
Ar 396	-/F-WLKH	LA Ferté Alais, France
Bl 502	-/D-EGEM	Langenlonsheim, Germany

For those interested in model kits, the company of Revell produces a model of the Ar 196 A-3 and Faller (Dragon) offer several variants of the Ar 234.

Acronyms:

E-BaL = Abteilung Bauaufsicht Luftfahrt, or Quality Control Dept./Aviation Construction

EAD = Abteilung Aussendienst, or Foreign Service Dept.

EB = Entwurfsbüro, or Drafting Bureau

EFof = Entwicklung/Forschung/Flugbetrieb (from 1943), or Development/Research/Flight Operations

HB = Hauptverwaltung Betrieb, or Central Admin. Operations

HBA = Hauptverwaltung Betrieb und Auftragswesen, or Central Admin./Operations and Contracting

HBB = Hauptverwaltung Betrieb Brandenburg, or Cen-

tral Admin. Brandenburg Operations
  HBF-F = Hauptfertigungsabteilung, or Central Assembly Dept.
  HE = Hauptverwaltung Entwicklung, or Central Admin./Development
  HT = Hauptverwaltung Technik, or Central Admin./Technology
  KFo = Konstruktion/Forschung, or Construction/Research)
  RFM = Reichsfinanzministerium, or Ministry of Finance
  RLM = ReichsLuftministerium, or Ministry of Air
  TA = Technische Abteilung Ausrüstung, or Technical Dept./Armament
  TAe-Fl = Technische Abteilung Aerodynamik, Entwurf-Flugerprobung, or Technical Dept./Aerodynamics, Design-Flight Testing
  TC = Technisches Büro Chefkonstrukteur, or Technical Office/Chief of Design and Construction
  TE = Technische Abteilung Entwicklung, or Technical Dept./Development
  TEA = Technische Abteilung Entwurf und Ausrüstung, or Technical Dept./Design and Armament
  TF = Technische Abteilung Festigkeit, or Technical Dept./Durability
  TFa = Technische Abteilung Fahrwerk, or Technical Dept./Landing Gear
  TFo = Technische Abteilung Forschung, or Technical Dept./Research
  TP = Technische Abteilung Planung, or Technical Dept./Planning
  TTrie = Technische Abteilung Triebwerk, or Technical Dept./Engines
  TS = Technisches Büro für Serienfertigung, or Technical Bureau for Series Production
  TV = Technische Abteilung Versuche, or Technical Dept./Testing.
  TWa = Technische Abteilung Waffen, or Technical Dept./Weapons
Munich 1961.
  Killen, John: The Luftwaffe. London 1967.
  Kober, Franz: Die ersten Strahlbomber der Welt. Friedberg 1980.
  König, Friedrich: Die Gesichte der Luftwaffe. Rastatt 1980.
  Koos, Volker: Luftfahrt zwischen Ostsee und Breitling. Berlin 1990.
  Kosin, Rüdiger: Die Entwicklung der deutschen Jagdflugzeuge. Coblenz 1983.
  Kranzhoff, Jörg Armin: Die Geschichte um Heinrich Lübbe. Warum blieb ein Flugpionier unbekannt? Jägerblatt Vol. 1/1990.
  Kranzhoff, Jörg Armin: Arado Flugzeuge — Es begann in Warnemünde. In: Blätter zur Geschichte der deutschen Luft- und Raumfahrt VII, Bonn-Bad Godesberg 1995, pp. 51-102.
  Kranzhoff, Jörg Armin: Fokker DR I. Stuttgart 1994.
  Lang, Gerhard: Arado 240. Flugzeug Profile 1/1989.
  Mason, Herbert Molloy: Die Luftwaffe. Vienna/Berlin 1976.
  Munson, Kenneth: Die Weltkrieg II-Flugzeuge. Stuttgart 1973.
  Nowarra, Heinz J.: Die verbotenen Flugzeuge 1921-1935. Stuttgart 1980
  Nowarra, Heinz J.: Die deutsche Luftrüstung. Coblenz 1993.
  Nowarra, Heinz J.: Deutsche Jagdflugzeuge 1915-1945. Friedberg 1985.
  Nowarra, Heinz J.: Deutsche Nahaufklärer 1910-1945. Stuttgart 1981.
  Nowarra, Heinz J.: Vom Doppeldecker zum Turbinenbomber. Ein technisch-historisches Porträt der Arado Flugzeugwerke. Der Landser, Vol. 521. Rastatt 1981.
  Pawlas, Karl R.: Arado 234. Nuremberg 1976.
  Raab, Antonius: Raab fliegt. Hamburg 1984.
  Reitsch, Hanna: Fliegen — mein Leben. Stuttgart 1951.
  Rieckhoff, H.J.: Trumpf oder Bluff? 12 Jahre Deutsche Luftwaffe. Genevea 1945.
  Ries, Karl: Luftwaffenstory. Mainz 1974.
  Ries, Karl Luftwaffe, geheimer Aufbau. Mainz 1970.
  Roeder, Jean: Bombenflugzeuge und Aufklärer. Coblenz 1990.
  Schick, W./Meyer, I.: Geheimprojekte der Luftwaffe, Stuttgart 1994.
  Schliephake, Hanfried: Wie die Luftwaffe wirklich entstand. Stuttgart 1979.
  Seifert, Karl-Dieter: Geschäft mit dem Flugzeug. Berlin 1960.
  Schwertfeger, Werner/Selinger, Franz: Wetterflieger in der Arktis 1940-1944. Stuttgart 1982.
  Smith, Richard/Creek, Eddie: Arado 234 Blitz. Sturbridge 1992.
  Smith, Truman: Berlin Alert. Stanford 1984.
  Völker, Karl-Heinz: Die Entwicklung der militärischen Luftfahrt in Deutschland 1920-1933. Stuttgart 1962.
  Völker, Karl-Heinz: Dokumente und Dokumentarfotos zur Geschichte der deutschen Luftwaffe. Stuttgart 1968.
  Völker, Karl-Heinz: Die deutsche Luftwaffe 1933-1939. Stuttgart 1967.
  Wagner, Wolfgang: Die ersten Strahlflugzeuge der Welt. Coblenz 1989.
  Woodman, Dorothy: Hitlers Luftflotte startbereit. Paris 1935.
  Zuerl, Walter: Deutsche Flugzeugkonstrukteure. Munich 1938.
  Zuerl, Walter: Entwicklungsgeschichte der Arado Flugzeugwerke. Flieger Vol. 1/1942.

Photo Credits

Amt Falkenberg (1),
G. Aleman (2),
G. Beer (1)
F. Brekow (1),
Bundesarchiv Koblenz (2)
G. Chinn(1)
P. Couderchon (1),
E. Creek (20)
P.W. Cohausz (3),
Dasa Bremen (34)
Deutsches Museum Munich (2)
H.J. Ebert (16),
Fokker Archives Amsterdam (4)
M. Griehl (5)
R. Renett (6)
Meyer/Schick (6),
Monogram Aviation Publications (2)
Museum für Verkehr und Technik Berlin (1),
H. Rebeski (53),
A. Rethel (7),
Rhineland Westphalia Economic Archives Cologne (3),
H. Redemann (1),
H. Schliephake (26),
I. V. Schoenebeck (1),
F. Selinger (5),
G. Sengfelder (1),
P. Supf (6),
W. Zuerl (2).

Bibliography

Aleman, Gilberto: Vuelos Historicos en Tenerife. La Laguna 1993.
Arado Flugzeuge. Luftfahrtverlag W. Zuerl. Steinebach (no year given)
Blume, Walter: Festigkeitseigenschaften kombinierter Leichtbaustoffe. Cologne 1958.
Bewaffnung der Flugzeuge. Yearbook of the German Akademie der Luftfahrtforschung II, Berlin 1942.
Boak, G./Miller A.: The Arado Ar 240 and Ar 440. (unpublished manuscript)
Bongartz, Heinz: Luftmacht Deutschland. Essen 1943.
Cescotti, Roderich: Kampfflugzeuge und Aufklärer. Coblenz 1989.
Chinn, George M.: The Machine Gun. Washington 1955.
Cohausz, Peter W.: Deutsche Oldtimer. Planegg 1991.
Dabrowski, Hans-Peter/Koos, Volker: See-Mehrzweckflugzeug Arado Ar 196. Waffen-Arsenal, Vol. 126.
Dressel, J./Griehl, M.: Taktische Militärflugzeuge in Deutschland 1925 bis heute. Friedberg 1992.
Eichelbaum, Hans: Das Buch von der Luftwaffe. Berlin 1939.
Entwicklung der Arado-Flugzeuge. Arado Company Booklet 1943.
Feuchter, Georg W.: Geschichte des Luftkriegs. Bonn 1954.
Galland, A.: Die Ersten und die Letzten. Munich 1953.
Gellermann, Günther W.: Moskau ruft Heeresgruppe Mitte. Coblenz 1988.
Gersdorff, Kyrill von/Grasmann, Kurt: Flugmotoren und Strahltriebwerke. Coblenz 1981.
Green, William: Warplanes of the Third Reich. London 1970.
Gröhler, Olaf: Geschichte des Luftkriegs 1910 bis 1945. Berlin 1977.
Heinkel, Ernst: Stürmisches Leben. Stuttgart 1953.
Hentschel, Georg: Die geheimen Konferenzen des Generalluftzeugmeisters 1942-44. Coblenz 1989.
Hermann: The Rise and Fall of the Luftwaffe. London 1943.
Homze, Edward L.: Arming the Luftwaffe. University of Nebraska Press 1976.
Irving, David: Die Tragödie der Deutschen Luftwaffe. Frankfurt/Berlin/Vienna 1970.
Kens, Karlheinz: Die deutschen Flugzeuge 1933-45.

The Author

Jörg Armin Kranzhoff, born in 1937, comes from a Rhenish family of artists. After studying German, English, Geography, Linguistics and Art History at the Universities of Bonn and Cologne, he completed the state exams for the office of teaching at upper schools and was awarded a doctorate. He has contributed to scientific publications on German etymology and machine language applications. The author taught for many years as an upper school instructor, and is married to the granddaughter of aviation pioneer Heinrich Lübbe. He recently published a monograph on the Fokker DR 1 single-seat fighter, and a monograph on the Rumpler Taube is currently in the works.

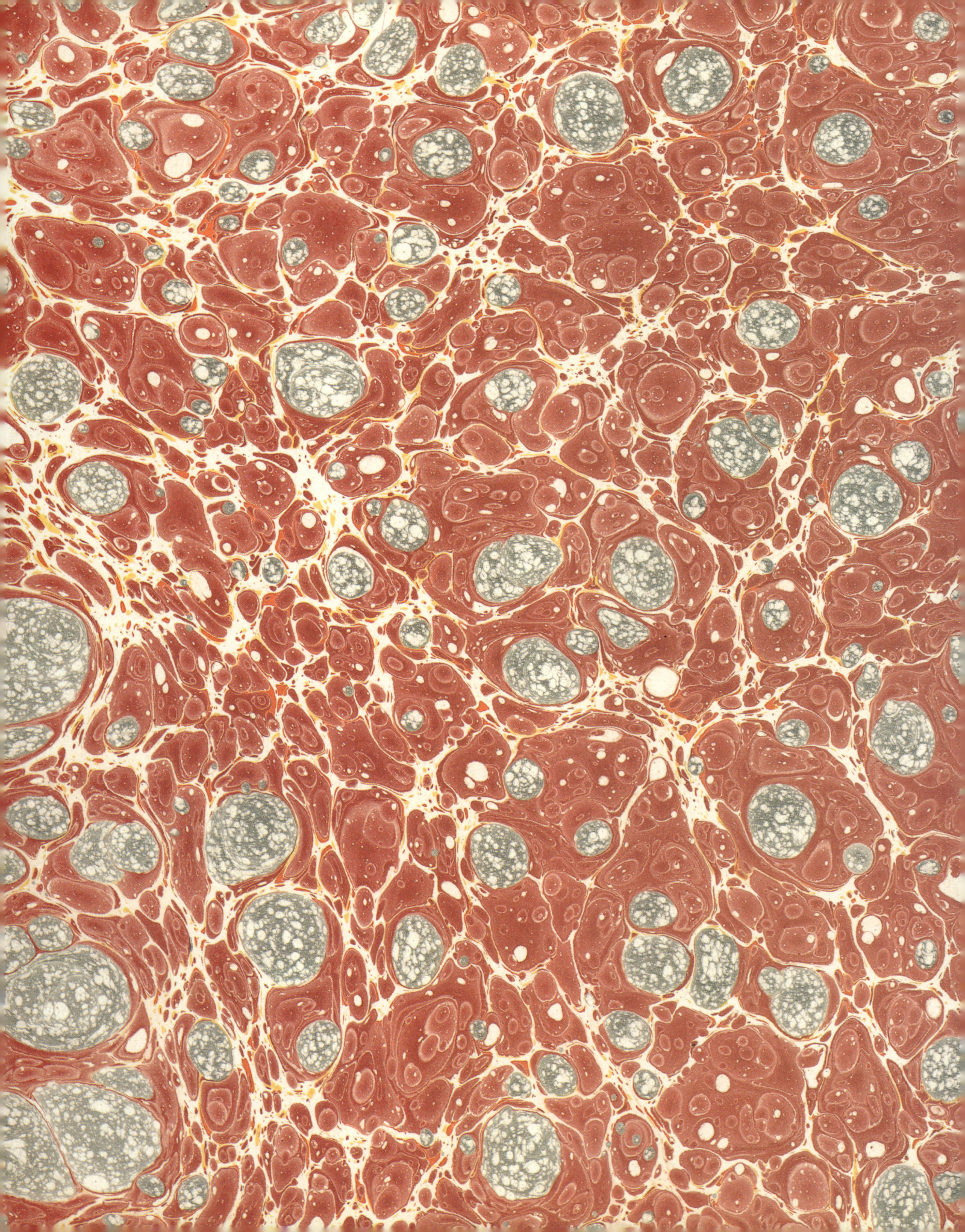